Capitalizing on Creativity at Work

Fostering the Implementation of Creative
Ideas in Organizations

Edited by

Miha Škerlavaj

Professor, BI Norwegian Business School, Norway

Matej Černe

*Assistant Professor, Faculty of Economics, University of
Ljubljana, Slovenia*

Anders Dysvik

Professor, BI Norwegian Business School, Norway

Arne Carlsen

Professor, BI Norwegian Business School, Norway

EE Edward **Elgar**
PUBLISHING

Cheltenham, UK • Northampton, MA, USA

Published by
Edward Elgar Publishing Limited
The Lypiatts
15 Lansdown Road
Cheltenham
Glos GL50 2JA
UK

Edward Elgar Publishing, Inc.
William Pratt House
9 Dewey Court
Northampton
Massachusetts 01060
USA

Paperback edition 2017

A catalogue record for this book
is available from the British Library

Library of Congress Control Number: 2015957867

This book is available electronically in the **Elgar**online
Business subject collection
DOI 10.4337/9781783476503

MIX
Paper from
responsible sources
FSC
www.fsc.org   FSC® C013604

ISBN 978 1 78347 649 7 (cased)
ISBN 978 1 78347 650 3 (eBook)
ISBN 978 1 78811 327 4 (paperback)

Typeset by Servis Filmsetting Ltd, Stockport, Cheshire
Printed and bound by CPI Group (UK) Ltd, Croydon, CR0 4YY

Contents

Figures

Tables

Contributors

Darija Aleksić, Teaching Assistant, Faculty of Economics, University of Ljubljana, Slovenia

Bernardo Balboni, Research Fellow, University of Trieste, University of Modena and Reggio Emilia, Italy

Saša Batistič, Research Fellow, University of Portsmouth, UK

Tim Bednall, Adjunct Lecturer, Swinburne University, Australia

Sabina Bogilović, Teaching Assistant, Faculty of Economics, University of Ljubljana, Slovenia

Guido Bortoluzzi, Assistant Professor, MIB School of Management, Italy

Benedicte Brøgger, Professor, BI Norwegian Business School, Norway

Robert Buch, Associate Professor, Norwegian School of Sport Sciences, Norway

Arne Carlsen, Professor, BI Norwegian Business School, Norway

Matej Černe, Assistant Professor, Faculty of Economics, University of Ljubljana, Slovenia

Anders Dysvik, Professor, BI Norwegian Business School, Norway

Naiara Escribá-Carda, Research Fellow, ESIC Business and Management School, Valencia, Spain

Alessandro Giudici, Assistant Professor, Cass Business School, UK

Spencer Harrison, Associate Professor, Boston College, USA

Tomislav Hernaus, Assistant Professor, Faculty of Economics and Business, University of Zagreb, Croatia

Thomas Hoholm, Associate Professor, BI Norwegian Business School, Norway

Janez Hudovernik, Independent consultant, Pro Acta, Slovenia

Peer Hull Kristensen, Professor, Copenhagen Business School, Denmark

Adeline Hvidsten, PhD Candidate, BI Norwegian Business School, Norway

Marko Jaklič, Professor, Faculty of Economics, University of Ljubljana, Slovenia

Robert Kaše, Associate Professor, Faculty of Economics, University of Ljubljana, Slovenia

Jana Krapež Trošt, Teaching Assistant, Faculty of Economics, University of Ljubljana, Slovenia

Bård Kuvaas, Professor, BI Norwegian Business School, Norway

Antonella La Rocca, Postdoctoral Fellow, Akershus University Hospital/ Norwegian Business School, Norway

Veronica (Cai-Hui) Lin, Post-Doctoral Research Fellow, Nottingham Trent University, UK

Maja Lotz, Associate Professor, Copenhagen Business School, Denmark

Bjørn Erik Mørk, Associate Fellow, IKON Research Unit, University of Oslo, Norway

Anja Svetina Nabergoj, Lecturer, Hasso Plattner Institute of Design, Stanford, USA

Christina G.L. Nerstad, Associate Professor, BI Norwegian Business School, Norway

Peter Parycek, Professor, Donau University, Austria

Aleš Pustovrh, Teaching Assistant, Faculty of Economics, University of Ljubljana, Slovenia

Ingo Rauth, PhD Candidate, Chalmers University, Sweden

Karin Sanders, Professor, Australian School of Business, Australia

Ralph Schoellhammer, PhD Candidate, University of Kentucky, USA

Judith Schossböck, Donau University, Austria

Helen Shipton, Professor, Nottingham Trent University, UK

Miha Škerlavaj, Professor, BI Norwegian Business School, Norway

John Sumanth, Assistant Professor, Wake Forest University, USA

Andrea Tracogna, MBA Director, MIB School of Management, Italy

Liisa Välikangas, Professor, Aalto University, Finland

Sut I Wong, Associate Professor, BI Norwegian Business School, Norway

Ivan Župič, Development Associate, PACINNO project, COBIK, Slovenia

1. Capitalizing on creativity: on enablers and barriers

Matej Černe, Arne Carlsen, Miha Škerlavaj and Anders Dysvik

WHY CAPITALIZING ON CREATIVITY?

What does it mean to capitalize on creativity in organizations? This is not a trivial question. Most research on creativity – whether at work, in the arts or in science – sees it as a combination of what is novel and useful (Amabile, 1996; Simonton, 2004; George, 2007). It is inherent in the very concept of creativity that for ideas to be creative they must be somehow taken up in the field and considered valuable by key stakeholders (Csikszentmihalyi, 1999); mere novelty is not enough. A creative idea is per definition one that is also useful, but does that mean one that has already been capitalized on? Well, not really. It is also true that most scholars or practitioners talking about creativity and innovation will associate the former closer to idea generation and the latter to implementation (Hennessey and Amabile, 2010; Anderson et al., 2014).

Our way out of these seemingly inconsistent definitions is to complicate the notion of usefulness. Useful to whom and to how many? To what degree? At what point in time? Ideas are rarely born novel or useful or not – they are made novel or useful in how they are expanded upon, molded, fattened, reiterated and connected to the ideas of others, when they are worked upon (Carlsen et al., 2012).

It is this working upon of ideas when moving towards and expanding upon realization that we take further issue with here. Capitalizing on creativity is not like traveling down a one-way street filled with a sequence of glorifying moments where ideas travel unaltered from their birth to their realization. The journeys (Van de Ven et al., 1999) are far messier because ideas seldom stay the same when people connect with them. A study of 'nexus work' by Nashville music producers shows how ambiguity of idea quality triggers repeated bouts of problem definition, integration and synthesis (Lingo and O'Mahony, 2010). A process analysis of US healthcare policy groups describes how evaluations are core activities in collective creativity (Harvey and Kou, 2013).

Transforming ideas into front-line practice may involve a range of activities for experimentation, local adoption and meaning-making (Reay et al., 2013). Managing the successful expansion of a retail chain of women's luxury accessories that grew from a handful of stores to over 300, first of all meant unleashing creative resources of store managers and employees, not replicating the concept (Sonenshein, 2013). When escaping from the dungeons of reification and simplified assumptions of laboratory studies, we see, quite paradoxically, that capitalizing on creativity may mean embracing the ambiguous, open-ended and unfinished to unleash more creativity.

With some unease, we will explore the capitalizing of creativity in part by using the word 'implementation'. The word implementation means 'fulfilling', or seeing something through to the end by 'carrying it out' or 'performing'. We use the word mostly in its performative sense, whether capitalizing on creative thought, ideas, or actions. Implementation is about the process, effort and tools required to install something into a functioning operation and the change(s) in state or quality of ideas when they are worked upon. Such an approach enables the exploration of 'the black box' of micro-individual-level innovation processes through the relationship of its beginning and end phases. In reality, the innovation process is complex, and idea generation and implementation do not necessarily proceed in a linear fashion, but can take place interchangeably (Anderson et al., 2004). Organizations need to generate and implement ideas throughout the innovation process in a constantly changing manner (Rosing et al., 2011).

It is possible to approach capitalizing on creativity with a narrower definition of implementation as carrying out something more or less preset (for example, Baer, 2012). For example, a recent study by three of the editors of this book (Škerlavaj et al., 2014) qualified the relationship between idea generation and idea implementation at the individual level as curvilinear, inverted u-shaped, where moderate levels of creativity (both in terms of the quantity and level of creativity of ideas) seem to be most beneficial for idea implementation.

Most chapters in this book will use a more process-oriented conception of both ideas and the work done to them. Implementation in a broad sense means working on ideas and mobilizing resources to move towards realization. This mobilizing may in itself call for and involve more creativity (that is, both more novelty and usefulness) along all stages of work, with recursive loops in between (Van de Ven and Sun, 2011), and engaging widening circles of audiences and users. In short, we start from the point that capitalizing on creativity means (1) expanding novelty and usefulness in quality, (2) expanding from the few to the many, and (3) expanding from realized creativity at certain points in time to more enduring consequences.

The present book is about capitalizing on the creativity of individuals, teams and organizations, and ultimately, as we shall see, also users. If organizations fail to generate, shape, adapt and implement highly creative ideas they fall short of contributing to organizational prosperity (Levitt, 2002). Therefore, the focus of the book is on conditions that foster individuals', teams', or firms' implementation activities and performance. The main premise is that if these can be properly identified and fostered, creative power can be better harnessed and systematically directed to generate profit, competitive advantage and human prosperity.

The book examines what can be done to capitalize on creativity by examining processes at five different levels of analysis: individual, team, leadership, organizational, and policy-making. Individual, team, organizational and country (policy-making) levels were chosen as a relatively standard and common set of levels in multilevel research (Klein and Kozlowski, 2000; Kozlowski and Klein, 2000; Černe et al., 2013). We added another level that characterizes leadership as a crucial contingency in work dynamics at individual and group levels, including micro-innovation activities (De Jong and Den Hartog, 2007; Rosing et al., 2011; Škerlavaj et al., 2014).

The book as a whole attempts to integrate macro-level innovation research with micro-level creativity work (Agars et al., 2008) and propagates multi-level approaches and theorizing. It also includes complex (bottom-up or top-down) research designs that account for the interdependence between creativity and innovation at different levels of research and analysis. Preclusion of those levels of analysis might also drive researchers' or practitioners' approaches to dealing with the idea generation–idea implementation relationship, be it separated or intertwined, linear or curvilinear, subsequent or concentric, making this research question another key issue of our book.

INDIVIDUAL LEVEL

In Chapter 2, Hernaus examines the role of job design in idea implementation–oriented work behavior. He first reviews and mutually compares job characteristics for creativity-oriented and implementation-oriented work behavior, followed by a presentation of personal and positional determinants of innovative work behavior. This serves as a starting point for other micro-level chapters of this book. He focuses on the explanation of their complex and intertwining relationship, and how understanding their interplay can provide the human resource (HR) managers with tools needed to develop job characteristics fit for individual employees instead of following 'one-size-fits-all' solutions. Finally, Hernaus suggests job crafting (Berg, 2014) as a useful tool for creative-idea implementation, and provides practical examples of its application.

In Chapter 3, Aleksić, Škerlavaj and Dysvik delve into the intra-psychic processes of transforming creative ideas into implemented innovations, building upon the flow theory (Csikszentmihalyi, 1975). They argue that flow experience, defined as 'a state in which people are so involved in an activity that nothing else seems to matter; the experience itself is so enjoyable that people will do it even at a great cost, for the sheer sake of doing it' (Csikszentmihalyi, 1991, p. 4), prompts a faster transition from the intention to carry out an activity to its actual implementation (Baumann and Scheffer, 2010). They enrich this theoretical perspective with empirical data from a specific setting: start-up companies, which are highly useful sources of information on how to foster idea implementation, because implementation of creative ideas is at the core of their functioning. The authors conduct analysis of interviews and other available secondary data of well-known start-up companies, identify common challenges related to creative-idea implementation and provide an explanation of how flow experience helps to overcome those challenges.

Chapter 4 is co-authored by Bogilović, Škerlavaj and Wong, and examines idea implementation in a culturally diverse environment. Specifically, it focuses on the role of cultural intelligence, that is, an individual's capability to function effectively in a culturally diverse environment and with people from a culturally diverse environment (Ang and Van Dyne, 2008), in the idea-implementation process. The authors address some of the potentially negative aspects of cultural diversity in a diverse work environment, and examine how cultural intelligence can mitigate negative consequences of a culturally diverse environment and in turn acts as a cornerstone of idea implementation. After briefly reviewing some of their research on cultural intelligence and idea generation, the authors provide practical examples of how individuals with high cultural intelligence implement creative ideas along with culturally diverse colleagues.

TEAM LEVEL

In Chapter 5, Černe, Kaše and Škerlavaj seek to increase our knowledge into the important, yet often overlooked process between idea generation and idea implementation: idea championing, or advocates of an implementation of particular product, for the success of technological innovation. Their chapter begins by describing the concept of idea championing and provides evidence of its importance, before moving on to how idea championing manifests itself in the context of teams and related consequences more generally, and team-level idea implementation outcomes specifically. Since innovation champions may assist innovation processes by overcoming organizational barriers and resistance, the process of championing is what the authors emphasize in their chapter. The authors show how the extant literature suffers from a lack of rigorous empirical investigation on idea champions at the micro-level. Fortunately, they provide increased insight into the underlying mechanisms of idea championing. In addition, they show how the micro-level process of idea championing is influenced by innovation processes in teams and provide specific advice to managers and organizations.

In Chapter 6, Krapež Trošt and Škerlavaj combine decision-making (Rusou et al., 2013) and team-innovation literatures to outline and test a multi-level model of team-level innovation antecedents by building upon the dual process theories (DPTs). Specifically, they build upon cognitive-experiential self-theory (CEST; Epstein, 1990), to examine two qualitatively different thinking modes – intuitive mode and deliberative/analytical/rational mode – as antecedents of team-level innovation. The authors conduct a multi-level study of R&D teams in four companies located in Germany and Slovenia, and find that team intuition more strongly relates to team idea generation, whereas individuals' perceptions of team-level need for cognition as a proxy for rationality more strongly relate to team idea implementation.

Is curiosity mainly a fuel for creativity, or can it be an outcome of it, one that aids the adoption and dispersion of creative products? That is a core question dealt with by Harrison (Chapter 7), who urges us to reconsider the linkages between curiosity and creativity. Harrison shows how curiosity can be fodder for discovery narratives that stir how people connect to, become fascinated by or identify with new creative products – and consequently adopt them. Capitalizing on creativity may thus mean embracing mystery, here understood as a controlled revealing of secrets, inviting customers to solve a puzzle. Curiosity then becomes a motivational backbone and a social resource that goes beyond the generation of an idea and strongly influences how others connect to, adopt and disperse a new creative product.

In Chapter 8, Nerstad discusses how mastery and performance motivational climates interplay to moderate the curvilinear relationship between frequent idea generation and implementation at work. By drawing on the theoretical lens of achievement goal theory (Nicholls, 1989; Ames, 1992a), she argues for how these environmental forces are important for the innovation process and presents empirical findings supporting the relevance of accounting for such interplay. Specifically, she argues that ideas are most frequently implemented in contexts characterized by both high-mastery and high-performance climates.

LEADERSHIP

Chapter 9 is co-authored by Černe, Škerlavaj and Dysvik. The authors explore a crucial boundary condition in the relationship between idea generation and implementation at the individual level – the extent to which employees feel supported by their group/team supervisors. The chapter significantly builds upon the authors' own previous experimental work on the role of perceived supervisor support in implementing creative ideas (Škerlavaj et al., 2014) by extending its theoretical underpinnings and demonstrating its practical value using illustrative case studies.

In Chapter 10, Buch and Kuvaas review and extend the existing literature regarding the association between leader–member exchange (LMX) and the implementation of creative ideas. Research has convincingly demonstrated that a high-quality LMX relationship constitutes an important driver of employee creativity (for example, Elkins and Keller, 2003). Nevertheless, while most scholars investigating LMX relationships have assumed that LMX falls on a continuum from low to high quality, LMX research on creativity would benefit from further enrichment of the LMX construct. Buch and Kuvaas add to the literature by introducing the role of economic LMX in the context of idea implementation. An economic leader–member exchange (ELMX) relationship is not the exact opposite of a social leader–member exchange (SLMX) relationship (cf., Blau, 1964; Shore et al., 2006). Kuvaas et al. (2012) addressed this gap in the literature and found ELMX to relate negatively to outcomes such as in-role and contextual performance. Building on this, Buch and Kuvaas propose that an SLMX relationship will be favorable, and an ELMX relationship will be unfavorable for the implementation of creative ideas.

Chapter 11 is co-authored by Černe, Sumanth and Škerlavaj and delves into authentic leadership as a predictor of not only idea generation, but also idea implementation at the individual level. Consistent with scholars' long operating under the implicit assumption that positive leadership behaviors yield perpetual benefits, without any downside or negative consequences, most previous studies exploring authentic leadership phenomena have neglected its potential pitfalls. The chapter reviews recent research on authentic leadership that acknowledges the fact that this construct may not always provide positive benefits, and explicitly focuses on how leaders that are deemed 'too authentic' may in fact contribute heavily to their followers' diminished or at least plateauing returns on innovation (in other words, individual-level idea implementation). They test the curvilinear relationship in a multi-method study (that is, field study and lab experiment), and conclude by presenting practical examples of overly authentic and consequently overly narcissistic leaders, and finally offering practical advice on overcoming the (mis-)perceptions of narcissism.

ORGANIZATIONAL LEVEL

Chapter 12 is co-authored by Carlsen and Välikangas who challenge implicit (or even explicit) assumptions in much of the literature on innovation and creativity with regard to ideas as discrete entities that stay more or less unaltered in points of time to then be implemented in processes subsequent and clearly separated from their generation. Carlsen and Välikangas differentiate between an orthodox view that implies a linear sequence to creative work where implementation is a matter of execution, and a process view where implementation is best understood as discovery. The key realization is that the implementation of creative ideas means that we recognize that ideas are more or less always in flux and being worked upon. This argument is supported by four cases from recent empirical research (Carlsen et al., 2012; Välikangas and Romme, 2013) and further illustrated with an example of a company that built an innovation program to develop more discovery capabilities in the organization.

Chapter 13, co-authored by Župič and Giudici, examines the concept of business model innovation in more depth by focusing on four main types of business models according to Zott and Amit (2010): novelty, lock-in, complementarities and efficiency based. The authors portray those types by presenting three short cases, illustrating (1) how a company innovated on its business model to gain competitive advantage, (2) how a disruptive innovative business model not only has firm- but also industry-wide impact, and (3) how it is difficult for established companies to engage in business model innovation, identifying the barriers to successful business model innovation implementation.

In Chapter 14, Batistič and Kaše narrow in on the social network perspective of idea implementation as the relational phenomenon and examine the structural position (namely, centrality, brokerage and clustering) of individuals within relational networks of idea implementation. Adopting the 'taking charge' perspective (Morrison and Phelps, 1999), the authors theorize and empirically examine sociometric data collected in a medium-sized knowledge-intensive IT firm. The results suggest that a formal structure plays an important role in the idea implementation network, especially when it is related to the control of such process, contributing to the literature on the social and interactionist perspective of the micro-innovation process.

In Chapter 15, Hudovernik, Škerlavaj and Černe examine the role of proactive employee behaviors for idea implementation in three companies based in Slovenia that are operating within the automotive industry. The chapter thus focuses on identifying predictors of innovation performance beyond position of company, level of autonomy and ownership types, and even individual-level innovation predictors that stem from employee personal characteristics. Specifically, the authors take an evidence-based theory-building approach on the foundations of multiple case studies to contribute to the literature on the drivers of employee proactive behavior as an antecedent of innovation performance. They suggest a guiding framework on proactive behavior that expands existing research on its individual-level drivers, namely top management support and philosophy, assigning key individuals for innovation, specific organizational-level innovation processes, which all in turn contribute to higher levels of idea implementation.

In Chapter 16, Rauth and Nabergoj combine perspectives from design thinking and sensemaking in a study of uptake of radical ideas at the Consumer Products Company. Three sets of workshops, all using design thinking in their format, are investigated. They identify six practices that foster sensemaking, idea development and capitalization on ideas across multiple organizational levels; namely: the engagement of functionally and hierarchically diverse individuals, the establishment of heterogeneous teams, the iterative involvement of individuals, and the exposure to, engagement in and acting upon conflicting views. At the core here is the intentional iterative sensemaking in groups subjected to contradicting views from various stakeholders. This process enables development of shared common sense of creative ideas as the major platform for their productive uptake.

In Chapter 17, Tracogna, Balboni and Bortoluzzi examine business models and the growth of high-tech and science-based new ventures in Italy. The central idea of their study is that the performance gap of innovative new ventures mostly refers to the inappropriateness of their business models (Zott and Amit, 2007, 2008). The authors analyze the business model evolution of three innovative new ventures, revealing that in all the three cases the initial business models have been significantly changed over time to adapt to new contingent factors and to assure a better match with the market demand and the entrepreneurial objectives. Contrary to the well-rooted idea that the market potential of innovative start-ups is reflected in its initial business model, it takes a lot of adaptation and fine-tuning to implement (that is, ensure the long-term survival) creative ideas (in their case, initial creative start-up business models).

Chapter 18 is co-authored by Shipton, Sanders, Bednall, Lin and Escribá-Carda. The authors focus on HR practices or combinations of practices that are important for idea implementation, why this might be so and what this means for managers seeking to implement human resource management (HRM) to employees on the receiving end. Following Collins and Smith (2006) the authors suggest that high-commitment HRM prompts innovation by supporting, guiding and facilitating the exchange and effective combination of knowledge. Furthermore, in building the social climate that gives rise to knowledge exchange and combination, HRM practices signal the importance of cooperation, offer opportunities for employees to develop share codes and language and manifest trust in one another (Collins and Smith, 2006). What matters, however, is not the existence of practices per se, but the way in which they are interpreted and enacted by employees. A strong HRM system is distinctive, consistent and consensual (Bowen and Ostroff, 2004). It 'stands out' to employees, clearly signaling what actions are required to achieve strategic goals. Through consistency, high-commitment HRM is internally aligned; through consensus, all key stakeholders convey the same message to employees.

Chapter 19 is co-authored by Lotz and Kristensen and narrows in on multinational firms and their potential to co-create and innovate in lateral collaborative communities through joint learning activities. They label them 'multi-polar learning communities' because they magnify the ability to accumulate knowledge and co-create new organizational innovations through knowledge-sharing and interactive learning across different domains and poles. Drawing on empirical evidence from a case study in a Danish multinational corporation experimenting with the development of multi-polar learning relationships across their production sites, the chapter examines the organizational architectures of multi-polar learning communities, their governance arrangements, and how they foster micro-practices of co-creation in global work arrangements.

The process of active adaptation during the implementation phase is further investigated in Chapter 20 by La Rocca, Hvidsten and Hoholm. The authors use a practice lens on creativity and present a case study of the practices of adopting a new IT system on electronic patient journals, a system that is at once standardized and caters to various user needs. La Rocca et al. identify three sets of creative coping responses to the new system: (1) *expanding* the system to involve more functions and better accommodate a broader range of stakeholder perspectives, (2) *reinterpreting* functions and negotiating authority relations in new service offerings, and (3) *orchestrating* an assemblage of artifacts and activities to better exchange information and coordinate service activities. Together the three practices highlight how successful implementation of creative ideas is enabled by ongoing creative efforts of users.

In Chapter 21, Mørk and Hoholm also use a practice-based approach to an in-depth comparison of two longitudinal cases of innovation originating in the medical R&D department of Oslo University Hospital. At issue is both the role of the R&D department, the bridging of disciplines and change versus reproduction of practices. The authors identify four sets of practices that were key to implementing breakthrough innovations in this setting: (1) enactment of expertise in well-established fields, (2) exploring advanced procedures in new fields, (3) improving procedures in new fields, and (4) relating novel practices to wider networks of practice. These four practices speak to several important tensions in capitalizing on creativity, such as mastering existing practices while exploring new and aligning practices locally as well as translocally.

POLICY-MAKING

Chapter 22 is co-authored by Jaklič and Pustovrh, and analyzes different national innovation policy mixes (that is, sets of 'narrow' and 'broad' governmental policies aimed at fostering innovation) that countries that are successful in implementing innovations across various domains apply. Using a quantitative comparative method (QCA), the authors analyze different configurations of innovation policies leading to successful innovation outcomes. They obtain a number of different solution paths leading to national innovation success, revealing that no individual policy tested is either necessary or sufficient for innovation success. Finally, they offer cases of successful and less successful national innovation policy programs applied in representative countries.

In Chapter 23, Parycek, Schoellhammer and Schossböck deal with governmental ideation systems supported by information and communication technologies. They first legitimize the idea of an innovative governance and present modes of innovation within governance, including the structures that support participation and collaboration in collective action. After an overview about concepts like open government, open innovation and open government data (OGD) and the collective structures that support participation and collaboration (in particular, crowds, communities, networks and hierarchies), the authors describe a case of governmental ideation and collaboration by describing the success factors for implementation of OGD within the City of Vienna from both an internal and external perspective.

In Chapter 24, Brøgger further broadens the take on innovation in her chapter on the development of a small social media venture, a company founded by a person diagnosed as autistic. Brøgger shows that the growth of this firm can be regarded as what she calls a triple-embedding process whereby the company has been positioned within the different demands and opportunities in the market, the local community and the public sector. The author further argues that administration, in the sense of doing things in tried and tested ways, has been key to this embedding process.

The book concludes with a discussion (Chapter 25, Škerlavaj, Dysvik, Černe, and Carlsen) on key findings and topics identified within the book as well as suggests avenues for future research and practice of capitalizing on ideas.

REFERENCES

Agars, M.D., J.C. Kaufman and T.R. Locke (2008), 'Social influence and creativity in organizations: A multilevel lens for theory, research, and practice', in M.D. Mumford, S.T. Hunter and K.E. Bedell-Avers (eds), *Multi-level Issues in Organizational Innovation*, Amsterdam: JAI Press, pp. 3–61.

Amabile, T.M. (1996), *Creativity in Context*, Boulder, CO: Westview Press.

Anderson, N., C. De Dreu and B. Nijstad (2004), 'The routinization of innovation research: A constructively critical review of the state of the science', *Journal of Organizational Behavior*, **25**(2), 147–73.

Anderson, N., K. Potočnik and J. Zhou (2014), 'Innovation and creativity in organizations: A state-of-the-science review, prospective commentary, and guiding framework', *Journal of Management*, **40**(5), 1297–333.

Ang, S. and L. Van Dyne (2008), 'Conceptualization of cultural intelligence: Definition, distinctiveness, and nomological network', in S. Ang and L. Van Dyne (ed.), *Handbook of Cultural Intelligence: Theory, Measurement, and Applications*, New York: M.E. Sharpe, pp. 3–15.

Baer, M. (2012), 'Putting creativity to work: The implementation of creative ideas in organizations', *Academy of Management Journal*, **55**(5), 1102–19.

Baumann, N. and D. Scheffer (2010), 'Seeking flow in the achievement domain: The achievement flow motive behind flow experience', *Motivation and Emotion*, **35**(3), 1–18.

Berg, J.M. (2014), 'The primal mark: How the beginning shapes the end in the development of creative ideas', *Organizational Behavior and Human Decision Processes*, **125**(1), 1–17.

Blau, P.M. (1964), *Exchange and Power in Social Life*, New York: John Wiley.

Bowen, D.E. and C. Ostroff, (2004), 'Understanding HRM–firm performance linkages: The role of "strength" of the HRM system', *Academy of Management Review*, **29**(2), 203–21.

Carlsen, A., S. Clegg and E. Gjersvik (eds) (2012), *Idea Work. Lessons of the Extraordinary in Everyday Creativity*, Oslo: Cappelen Damm.

Černe, M., M. Jaklič and M. Škerlavaj (2013), 'Authentic leadership, creativity, and innovation: A multilevel perspective', *Leadership*, **9**(1), 63–85.

Collins, C. and K. Smith (2006), 'Knowledge exchange and combination: The role of human resource practices in the performance of high-technology firms', *Academy of Management Journal*, **49**(3), 544–60.

Csikszentmihalyi, M. (1975), *Beyond Boredom and Anxiety: The Experience of Play in Work and Games*, San Francisco, CA: Jossey-Bass.

Csikszentmihalyi, M. (1991), *Flow: The Psychology of Optimal Experience: Steps Toward Enhancing the Quality of Life*, New York: HarperCollins.

Csikszentmihalyi, M. (1999), 'Implications of a systems perspective for the study of creativity', in R.J. Sternberg (ed.), *Handbook of Creativity*, Cambridge, UK: Cambridge University Press.

De Jong, J. and D. den Hartog (2007), 'How leaders influence employees' innovative behavior', *European Journal of Innovation Management*, **10**(1), 41–64.

Elkins, T. and R.K. Keller (2003), 'Leadership in research and development organizations: A literature review and conceptual framework', *The Leadership Quarterly*, **14**(4), 587–606.

Epstein, S. (1990), 'Cognitive-experiential self-theory', in L. Pervin (ed.), *Handbook of Personality Theory and Research*, New York: Guilford Press.

George, J.M. (2007), 'Creativity in organizations', *The Academy of Management Annals*, **1**(1), 439–77.

Harvey, S. and C.Y. Kou (2013), 'Collective engagement in creative tasks: The role of evaluation in the creative process in groups', *Administrative Science Quarterly*, **58**(3), 346–86.

Hennessey, B.A. and T.M. Amabile (2010), 'Creativity' [review], *Annual Review of Psychology*, **61**(1), 569–98.

Klein, K.J. and S.W.J. Kozlowski (2000), 'From micro to meso: Critical steps in conceptualizing and conducting multilevel research', *Organizational Research Methods*, **3**(3), 211–36.

Kozlowski, S.W.J. and K.J. Klein (2000), 'A multilevel approach to theory and research in organizations: Contextual, temporal, and emergent processes', in K.J. Klein and S.W.J. Kozlowski (eds), *Multilevel Theory, Research, and Methods in Organizations: Foundations, Extensions, and New Directions*, San Francisco, CA: Jossey-Bass, pp. 3–90.

Kuvaas, B., R. Buch, A. Dysvik and T. Haerem (2012), 'Economic and social leader–member exchange relationships and follower performance', *The Leadership Quarterly*, **23**(5), 756–65.

Levitt, T. (2002), 'Creativity is not enough', *Harvard Business Review*, **80**(7), 137–44.

Lingo, E.L. and S. O'Mahony (2010), 'Nexus work: Brokerage on creative projects', *Administrative Science Quarterly*, **55**(1), 47–81.

Morrison, E.W. and C.C. Phelps (1999), 'Taking charge at work: Extrarole efforts to initiate workplace change', *The Academy of Management Journal*, **42**(4), 403–19.

Nicholls, J.G. (1989), *The Competitive Ethos and Democratic Education*, Cambridge, MA: Harvard University Press.

Reay, T., S. Chreim, K. Golden-Biddle, E. Goodrick, B. Williams and A. Casebeer et al. (2013), 'Transforming new ideas into practice: An activity based perspective on the institutionalization of practices', *Journal of Management Studies*, **50**(6), 963–90.

Rosing, K., M. Frese and A. Bausch (2011), 'Explaining the heterogeneity of the leadership–innovation relationship: Ambidextrous leadership', *The Leadership Quarterly*, **22**(5), 956–74.

Rusou, Z., D. Zakay and M. Usher (2013), 'Pitting intuitive and analytical thinking against each other: The case of transitivity', *Psychonomic Bulletin & Review*, **20**(3), 608–14.

Shore, L.M., L.E. Tetrick, P. Lynch and K. Barksdale (2006), 'Social and economic exchange: Construct development and validation', *Journal of Applied Social Psychology*, **36**(4), 837–67.

Simonton, D.K. (2004), *Creativity in Science: Chance, Logic, Genius, and Zeitgeist*, Cambridge, UK: Cambridge University Press.

Škerlavaj, M., M. Černe and A. Dysvik (2014), 'I get by with a little help from my supervisor: Creative-idea generation, idea implementation, and perceived supervisor support', *The Leadership Quarterly*, **25**(5), 987–1000.

Sonenshein, S. (2013), 'How organizations foster the creative use of resources', *Academy of Management Journal*, **57**(3), 814–48.

Välikangas, L. and A.G.L. Romme (2013), 'How to design for strategic resilience', *Journal of Organization Design*, **2**(2), 44–53.

Van de Ven, A.H. and K. Sun (2011), 'Breakdowns in implementing models of organization change', *Academy of Management Perspectives*, **25**(3), 58–74.

Van de Ven, A.H., D.E. Polley, R. Garud and S. Venkataraman (1999), *The Innovation Journey*, New York: Oxford University Press.

Zott C. and R. Amit (2007), 'Business model design and the performance of entrepreneurial firms', *Organization Science*, **18**(2), 181–99.

Zott C. and R. Amit (2008), 'The fit between product market strategy and business model: Implications for firm performance', *Strategic Management Journal*, **29**(1), 1–26.

Zott, C. and R. Amit (2010), 'Business model design: An activity system perspective', *Long Range Planning*, **43**(2), 216–26.

PART I

What can we do about it as individual employees?

2. Job design at the crossroads: from 'creative' jobs to 'innovative' jobs

Tomislav Hernaus

Organizations rely on their employees to introduce new products/services, improve business processes, and develop new working methods. Therefore, managers and human resource management (HRM) professionals need to boost employee creativity and workforce innovativeness. High-involvement human resource practices in general, and job design specifically, can create a supportive and stimulating work environment that enhances innovative work behavior (IWB).

Job design represents a useful HRM tool that can significantly change daily working practices. It describes the content and organization of one's work tasks, activities, relationships, and responsibilities (Parker, 2014). It not only shows how jobs, tasks, and roles are structured, enacted, and modified, but also explains what the impact of these structures, enactments, and modifications is on individual, group, and organizational outcomes (Grant and Parker, 2009). In particular, job design directly modifies the motivating potential of jobs (for example, Hackman and Oldham, 1976), and has either a direct or an indirect effect on various work behaviors (for example, Parker and Ohly, 2008).

Job or work characteristics – objective, relatively stable and measurable job design attributes (for example, Morgeson and Campion, 2003) – are regarded as relevant individual-level factors for stimulating IWB. They represent individual determinants of organizational innovation that are important for both the generation and the implementation phases of the innovation process (Patterson et al., 2009). Farr (1990) goes even further, stressing that employee creativity and innovative behavior can be seen as outcomes of various job design interventions.

Meta-analytic research has confirmed that job design and related job characteristics are crucial predictors of individual innovation (Hammond et al., 2011). It seems that employees respond more innovatively to intrinsic-driven motivators such as job resources and challenges than extrinsic-driven ones (for example, compensation and incentive systems). Therefore, the aim of the chapter is to explore the relationship between job design and individual innovation, hence to analyze relevant individual-level, job-related aspects of innovation with a particular emphasis on implementation-oriented work behavior. After a short overview of the job design concept, job characteristics for creativity-oriented and implementation-oriented work behavior are revealed and mutually compared. A comparative review analysis of 'creative' and 'innovative' jobs is followed by addressing personal and positional determinants of IWB and explaining their complex relationship. Finally, job crafting is offered as a useful tool for enhancing individual innovation, and its practical example is showcased.

JOB DESIGN FOR CREATIVE IDEA IMPLEMENTATION

Although previous findings emphasize that the implementation of creative ideas is an organizational issue more strongly predicted by group and organizational characteristics than by individual (personal and job) characteristics (for example, Axtell et al., 2000; Baer, 2012), the latter should not be underestimated. Studies suggest that individuals who are willing and able to innovate often extend their contribution beyond the scope of their job requirements and at the same time realize a continuous flow of innovations (Parker et al., 2006).

Job design and related job characteristics can be understood as contextual antecedents and a driving force for IWB (for example, Oldham and Cummings, 1996; Axtell et al., 2000; Shalley et al., 2004). Their influence on creativity (idea experimentation and generation) has already been recognized in the literature. For instance, Oldham and Cummings (1996) examined the influence of task characteristics (that is, job autonomy, skill variety, task identity, job feedback, and task significance) on creativity and found that a composite index of these job characteristics was an effective predictor of creative work behavior. Greenberg (1992) indicated that particular job characteristics (in other words, job autonomy and task identity) contribute to the creativity of artistic workers, while Harrison et al. (2006) more broadly indicated the relevance of various job characteristics for predicting creativity at work (Ohly and Fritz, 2010). Finally, Hammond et al. (2011) concluded that jobs could be eventually designed to promote creativity. Such 'creative' jobs usually consist of non-routine tasks; they are challenging and very complex in their nature, and have a broader span of task activities. Additionally, they are characterized by high levels of autonomy and job control, provide skill variety and feedback, and require problem-solving. According to Cummings and Oldham (1997), the main purpose of 'creative job design' is to provide employees with the information and freedom to recognize divergent needs and pursue novel ideas in useful ways.

However, until recently, studying the nature of job design for creative idea implementation has been largely neglected (for example, West, 2002). Although it seems to be a question of execution, implementation-oriented work behavior is critical, especially for very creative ideas that are more difficult to implement due to their 'out-of-the box' nature, increased risk, and higher uncertainty (Janssen et al., 2004). Such a view is in line with Bledow et al. (2009) who assume that the problem of conflicting task demands is more pronounced for radical innovation than for incremental innovation. They also recognized different task demands of idea generation and implementation, which leads to the conclusion that different phases of an innovation process call for various individual behaviors (for example, Scott and Bruce, 1994; De Jong and Den Hartog, 2010), and therefore require different job settings.

Previous studies did not differentiate job design requirements along the creativity-implementation behavior continuum. IWB was conceptualized as a single construct (for example, Yuan and Woodman, 2010) predicted by a common level of job characteristics. For instance, Oldham and Cummings (1996) and Shalley et al. (2004) found that jobs designed to be complex and demanding (that is, jobs with high levels of autonomy, task challenge, feedback, significance, identity, task and skill variety) are positively associated with creativity and innovation. Scott and Bruce (1994) revealed that employees with routine jobs (more structured, repetitive, and granting less autonomy) show less innovative behavior than employees whose jobs are non-routine. Furthermore, Amabile et al. (1996) found that excessive workload hinders innovation while job challenge enhances it. Finally, Bunce and West (1995) reported that high job demands are positively associated with individual innovation.

Of course, this does not mean that some job characteristics do not have a similar effect on various stages of IWB. Quite the contrary, job autonomy has been found to relate positively to both creative and innovative behaviors (Axtell et al., 2000; Shalley et al., 2000). Jobs with little discretion in how, when, or where work is accomplished may stifle an employee's ability to be innovative. Alternatively, providing employees with freedom and independence to determine which procedures should be used to carry out a task may increase the likelihood that they will be willing to implement them within their job. In addition, empirical findings suggest that jobs may be also redesigned to facilitate creativity and innovation at work by increasing complexity (Hammond et al., 2011). Interaction with others is another social job characteristic vital not only for idea generation but also for the implementation of new ideas (Hülsheger et al., 2009). When implementing new solutions, employees need to listen to the voice of customers and be prepared to modify their 'playing toy' (that is, innovation) to enhance its ability to achieve market success.

While enriched jobs in general should promote both kinds of employee innovative behavior, differences are still present in certain job characteristics. For instance, according to Ohly et al. (2006), routinization enhances idea implementation more than creativity. Job complexity might also be more important for implementing ideas than for having them because employees in more complex jobs tend to see it as their task to improve working procedures (Frese et al., 1999), which does not necessarily lead to more ideas. However, when an employee in a complex job has an idea, she or he sees it as her or his job to implement it themselves (Oldham and Cummings, 1996; Frese et al., 1999; Ohly et al., 2006). Job resources in general (for example, job autonomy, social support, performance feedback, skill variety, task significance) are also more important for creative idea implementation than for idea generation. Finally, it should be mentioned that job design can also impose some negative structural barriers on idea implementation. For instance, job demands (for example, work pressures, role ambiguity, and emotional demands) seem to be associated through an inverted-U relationship with innovation implementation. Either very low or very high levels of job demands (West, 2002) and time pressure (Ohly et al., 2006) might lead to low levels of implementation success.

This comparative review analysis has clearly revealed similarities and differences in job characteristics related to different stages of IWB, as shown in Table 2.1.

PERSONAL AND POSITIONAL DETERMINANTS OF INNOVATIVE WORK BEHAVIOR

Innovative behavior should be expected from the entire workforce. Innovativeness is something that everybody can aspire to, and that can be additionally supported by a challenging and differentiated approach to job design. While, traditionally, some people and jobs are viewed as much more innovative (for example, researchers, brand managers, engineers) than others (for example, administrative staff, maintenance workers, salespersons), psychologists have confirmed that IWB depends on personal traits (for example, risk-taking aptitude, personal initiative, need for cognition, role breadth self-efficacy, personal values), as well as individual competencies or skills (for example, networking ability, cognitive ability, teamwork ability). Additionally, an employee's proactive behavior (for example,

Table 2.1   *Job characteristics for enhancing innovative work behavior*

	Task characteristics	Knowledge characteristics	Social characteristics
'Creative' Jobs	High job autonomy	High job complexity	Low to medium task interdependence
	High task variety	High skill variety	Medium interaction with others
	High task identity	High problem-solving	Low to medium social support
	Medium time pressure	High information processing	
'Innovative' Jobs	High job autonomy	High job complexity	High task interdependence
	Medium task variety	Medium skill variety	High interaction with others
	Medium task identity	Medium to high problem-solving	High social support
	Medium to high time pressure	Medium information processing	

Hudovernik et al., Chapter 15 this volume) seems to be particularly important in the idea-implementation phase of the innovation process as it involves overcoming social barriers and assures persistence (Patterson et al., 2009). Individuals can significantly improve their odds of implementing creative ideas when they are highly motivated to move their ideas forward to realization and/or when they are skilled networkers (Baer, 2012).

Personal determinants of innovativeness can make a difference as they represent an individual's innovative potential. However, without providing creative employees with appropriate job design features, their innovative potential will never be realized. In addition, even though personal traits are relatively stable psychological attributes, they can be modified to a certain extent by redesigning jobs. Specht et al. (2011) found that personality changes throughout the life span, but with more pronounced changes in the young and older individual, and that this change is partly attributable to social demands and experiences. Eventually, an HRM goal is to strive towards person–job fit, which means to appropriately align employees' personality and individual needs with work criteria and job design requirements (for example, Edwards, 1991; Hogan and Holland, 2003).

Beyond the personal, more adjustable positional or job determinants of employee innovativeness should be acknowledged as well. Although innovation is usually not a formal part of employees' standard job description,

Kanter (1988) already suggested that the obligations of one's position could serve as an initial impetus that activates employee innovation. Yuan and Woodman (2010) reported that employees who perceive innovativeness as a part of their job requirements seem to feel it is more appropriate to engage in innovative behavior, as implementing innovative ideas will eventually benefit their work.

Expected innovative performance outcomes of employees could be also related to their hierarchical status, job tenure, and the nature of work; it has been found that middle and higher occupational levels allow more opportunity for individual innovation (Scott and Bruce, 1994). Managers in particular feel more responsibility to change and innovate because of the expectations tied to their roles and positions (Kanter, 1988; Fuller et al., 2006). They generally have better opportunities to identify and implement creative ideas as their jobs offer greater autonomy, wider access to resources, and better social ties due to the interdependent nature of managerial work. On the other hand, employees working in positions in which innovativeness is not explicitly required (for example, non-R&D-related jobs, shop-floor workers) may be less motivated to apply new ideas as they do not consider new ideas or processes as helpful to their work (Yuan and Woodman, 2010). Finally, job tenure seems to be negatively related to IWB as, according to Dorenbosch et al. (2005), the longer employees remain in the same function, the less they will engage in innovative activities. However, these positional aspects of the work environment can be easily manipulated in order to provide intrinsic incentives necessary for individual innovation.

Personal and positional determinants of IWB are not standalone, but rather intertwined concepts. Research has shown that the job context in which employees are embedded has a substantial influence on their creative and innovative behavior either directly or via interaction with individual difference variables (Anderson et al., 2014). They appeared to interact and substitute for each other, which is aligned with the interactionist perspective of human behavior (for example, Woodman et al., 1993; Shalley et al., 2009). For instance, a study conducted by Wu et al. (2014) suggests that job context can substitute for an individual's need for cognition when it comes to individual innovation. Individuals' disposition to enjoy thinking can compensate for their non-innovative job context, as creative and proactive individuals will try to make the best of their non-challenging job requirements. On the other hand, complex, flexible, and demanding jobs supplemented with adequate job resources and challenges would additionally enhance the employee's potential to innovate. This means that job characteristics moderate the effect of personal traits on IWB. While poor job characteristics can provide behavioral constraints on highly motivated and creative individuals, enriched job design will have a positive influence on both proactive and reactive employees. Obviously, besides managers and HRM professionals, employees themselves can also accelerate this 'holy trinity', particularly by practicing job crafting.

JOB CRAFTING AS A TOOL FOR ENHANCING IDEA IMPLEMENTATION

Job crafting represents one of the most valued tools for reshaping the work environment. It is a bottom-up, employee-driven job redesign technique that captures the ways in which individuals actively change the behavioral, relational, and cognitive boundaries of their jobs to alter personal experiences and identities at work (Wrzesniewski and Dutton, 2001). Job crafting could also be understood as a type of proactive work behavior through which employees customize their jobs to their individual needs and preferences (Berg et al., 2008), instead of reactively performing the job that the organization created (Tims and Bakker, 2010).

Through job crafting an individual can: (1) actively intervene and personally increase a motivating potential of his or her job, (2) take charge and strengthen his or her social status and position (for example, Batistic and Kaše, Chapter 14 this volume), and (3) keep or make job activities meaningful and challenging. Recent studies suggest that employees do craft their job characteristics (for example, Berg et al., 2010; Petrou et al., 2012; Tims et al., 2013). Besides job satisfaction, work commitment, and individual well-being, practices relating to job crafting can also foster innovation, particularly when it comes to creative idea implementation (for example, Parker and Collins, 2010; Wu et al., 2014). For instance, employees can exhibit 'task crafting' and induce horizontal job expansion by adding extra and diverse work activities to their job portfolio, changing ways of completing existing tasks or by taking more autonomy and responsibility for self-implementation of ideas. 'Cognitive crafting' may change the perception of the job by vertically expanding the existing job scope. Intellectually demanding and problem-solving tasks can increase the level of work engagement, and motivate employees to complete implementation projects on the run. Finally, 'social' or 'relational crafting' is related to changing the interactions with others and gaining or providing the social support. By recreating personal social networks (changing the content, strength, and density of social interactions), employees can significantly improve the adoption and the success rate of their creative idea implementation initiatives. In the end, implementing creative ideas is a 'human' or social-political process (for example, Van de Ven, 1986) that

---

BOX 2.1   ACADEMIC JOB CRAFTING AS A DRIVER OF CREATIVE IDEA IMPLEMENTATION

University professors are knowledgeable individuals who handle multidextrous jobs with a diverse set of teaching-, research- and service-related tasks. In order to be acknowledged and respected, they need to practice innovative work behavior by continuously switching their job characteristics from the creativity to the implementation mode. Having autonomous jobs and being mostly self-driven, scholars cope with the emerging academic competition by introducing job-crafting strategies. This is a particularly useful job design intervention within the current high-stakes research environment. For instance, an individual can practice a task-crafting strategy by initiating a new research process that starts with generating a creative idea. Usually, he or she invests a lot of his or her time, uses certain job resources, puts in a significant cognitive effort, and engages in a certain level of interaction with colleagues needed to develop a future research plan. As an ambitious principal investigator who is trying to collect funds for planned research, he or she has a 'creative' job and tries to shape and sell the idea to the research council committee. It is a work-intensive and creative process characterized by considerable information processing and problem-solving thinking, which provides a high task variety and requires a broad skill variety. However, things change upon receiving the research grant. The accepted creative idea needs to be implemented within the proposed timeframe, thus increasing the work time pressure and introducing cognitive crafting. A research team is formed, tasks are divided and coordinated among team members (meaning that a principal investigator can now focus on particular assignments, that is, his or her task variety, skill variety, and task identity somewhat decrease), and higher levels of social interaction and social support are also expected (relational crafting). Thus, by embracing various aspects of job crafting, the principal investigator 'moves' into an 'innovative' job that more strongly supports a creative idea implementation.

---

necessarily involves communication and collaboration, as well as influencing others. Therefore, 'innovative job design' and job crafters need to develop and promote both teamwork and negotiation skills relevant for implementing innovative solutions. An example of job crafting experience widely present across academia is described in Box 2.1.

FINAL THOUGHTS

We have addressed an important and emerging issue of designing jobs that enable creativity and innovation. In particular, while HRM professionals have mainly investigated job requirements for creativity-oriented work behavior, this chapter provided a useful impetus for demystifying the road less taken – how job design could boost innovative performance.

By thoroughly examining job similarities and differences related to different stages of IWB, we concluded that 'innovative' jobs are more socially-enriched (that is, higher social interaction, task interdependence, and social support are required) and less task-enriched (in other words, lower task variety and task identity) than 'creative' jobs. Nevertheless, the level of knowledge job characteristics remains a constant throughout the innovation process.

The roles of personal and positional determinants of IWB have been additionally explained. Particularly thought-provoking is the idea that personal traits, together with individual competencies and skills can substitute for the lack of innovative job context. Proactive employees with high self-efficacy, developed risk-taking aptitude, and a high need for cognition can make their jobs more challenging and innovation-oriented. Therefore, we have proposed three job design interventions (task, relational, and cognitive crafting) as promising individual techniques for creating an innovative work environment. By crafting their everyday task activities, work relationships, job resources, demands and challenges, employees can directly influence their job context, create flow experiences (see Chapter 3) and eventually build up their innovativeness and performance outcomes. Ultimately, their reactions to a particular innovation will actually determine the ultimate success of implementation efforts (Choi and Price, 2005), which will eventually lead to sustainable organizational success.

REFERENCES

Amabile, T.M., R. Conti, H. Coon, J. Lazenby and M. Herron (1996), 'Assessing the work environment for creativity', *Academy of Management Journal*, **39**(5), 1154–84.

Anderson, N., K. Potočnik and J. Zhou (2014), 'Innovation and creativity in organizations: A state-of-the-science review, prospective commentary, and guiding framework', *Journal of Management*, **40**(5), 1297–333.

Axtell, C.M., D.J. Holman, K.L. Unsworth, T.D. Wall, P.E. Waterson and E. Harrington (2000), 'Shopfloor innovation: Facilitating the suggestion and implementation of ideas', *Journal of Occupational and Organizational Psychology*, **73**(3), 265–85.

Baer, M. (2012), 'Putting creativity to work: The implementation of creative ideas in organizations', *Academy of Management Journal*, **55**(5), 1102–19.

Batistic, S. and R. Kaše (2016), 'Idea implementation as a relational phenomenon: A social network perspective', *Capitalizing on Creativity at Work: Fostering the Implementation of Creative Ideas in Organizations*, Cheltenham, UK and Northampton, MA, USA: Edward Elgar Publishing.

Berg, J.M., J.E. Dutton and A. Wrzesniewski (2008), 'What is job crafting and why does it matter?' *Theory-to-Practice Briefing*, Ann Arbor, MI: University of Michigan.

Berg, J.M., A. Wrzesniewski and J.E. Dutton (2010), 'Perceiving and responding to challenges in job crafting at different ranks: When proactivity requires adaptivity', *Journal of Organizational Behavior*, **31**(2–3), 158–86.

Bledow, R., M. Frese, N. Anderson, M. Erez and J. Farr (2009), 'A dialectic perspective on innovation: Conflicting demands, multiple pathways, and ambidexterity', *Industrial and Organizational Psychology*, **2**(3), 305–37.

Bunce, D. and M.A. West (1995), 'Personality and perceptions of group climate factors as predictors of individual innovation at work', *Applied Psychology: An International Review*, **44**(3), 199–215.

Choi, J.N. and R.H. Price (2005), 'The effects of person–innovation fit on individual responses to innovation', *Journal of Occupational and Organizational Psychology*, **78**(1), 83–96.

Cummings, A. and G.R. Oldham (1997), 'Enhancing creativity: Managing work contexts for the high potential employee', *California Management Review*, **40**(1), 22–38.

De Jong, J.P.J. and D. Den Hartog (2010), 'Measuring innovative work behaviour', *Creativity and Innovation Management*, **19**(1), 23–36.

Dorenbosch, L., M.L. van Engen and M. Verhagen (2005), 'On-the-job innovation: The impact of job design and human resource management through production ownership', *Creativity and Innovation Management*, **14**(2), 129–41.

Edwards, J. (1991), 'Person–job fit: A conceptual integration, literature review, and methodological critique', in C.L. Cooper and I.T. Robertson (eds), *International Review of Industrial Organizational Psychology*, Vol. 6, Chichester, UK: Wiley, pp. 283–357.

Farr, J.L. (1990), 'Facilitating individual role innovation', in M.A. West and J.L. Farr (eds), *Innovation and Creativity at Work: Psychological and Organizational Strategies*, Chichester, UK: Wiley, pp. 207–30.

Frese, M., E. Teng and C.J.D. Wijnen (1999), 'Helping to improve suggestion systems: Predictors of making suggestions in companies', *Journal of Organizational Behavior*, **20**(7), 1139–55.

Fuller, J.B., L.E. Marler and K. Hester (2006), 'Promoting felt responsibility for constructive change and proactive behavior: Exploring aspects of an elaborated model of work design', *Journal of Organizational Behavior*, **27**(8), 1089–120.

Grant, A.M. and S.K. Parker (2009), 'Redesigning work design theories: The rise of relational and proactive perspectives', *The Academy of Management Annals*, **3**(1), 317–75.

Greenberg, E. (1992), 'Creativity, autonomy, and evaluation of creative work: Artistic workers in organisations', *Journal of Creative Behavior*, **26**(2), 75–80.

Hackman, J.R. and G.R. Oldham (1976), 'Motivation through the design of work: Test of a theory', *Organizational Behavior and Human Performance*, **16**(2), 250–79.

Hammond, M.M., N.L. Neff, J.L. Farr, A.R. Schwall and X. Zhao (2011), 'Predictors of individual-level innovation at work: A meta-analysis', *Psychology of Aesthetics, Creativity, and the Arts*, **5**(1), 90–105.

Harrison, D.A., D.A. Newman and P.L. Roth (2006), 'How important are job attitudes? Meta-analytic comparisons of integrative behavioral outcomes and time sequences', *Academy of Management Journal*, **49**(2), 305–25.

Hogan, J. and B. Holland (2003), 'Using theory to evaluate personality and job-performance relations: A socioanalytic perspective', *Journal of Applied Psychology*, **88**(1), 100–112.

Hudovernik, J., M. Škerlavaj and M. Černe (2016), 'Proactive employee behaviors and idea implementation: Three automotive industry cases', *Capitalizing on Creativity at Work: Fostering the Implementation of Creative Ideas in Organizations*, Cheltenham, UK and Northampton, MA, USA: Edward Elgar Publishing.

Hülsheger, U.R., N. Anderson and J.F. Salgado (2009), 'Team-level predictors of innovation at work: A comprehensive meta-analysis spanning three decades of research', *Journal of Applied Psychology*, **94**(5), 1128–45.

Janssen, O., E. van de Vliert and M. West (2004), 'The bright and dark sides of individual and group innovation: A special issue introduction', *Journal of Organizational Behavior*, **25**(2), 129–45.

Kanter, R.M. (1988), 'When a thousand flowers bloom: Structural, collective and social conditions for innovation in organization', in B.M. Staw (ed.), *Research in Organizational Behavior*, Vol. 10, Greenwich, CT: JAI Press, pp. 169–211.

Morgeson, F.P. and M.A. Campion (2003), 'Work design', in W.C. Borman, D.R. Ilgen and R.J. Klimoski (eds), *Handbook of Psychology: Industrial and Organizational Psychology*, Vol. 12, Hoboken, NJ: Wiley, pp. 423–52.

Ohly, S. and C. Fritz (2010), 'Work characteristics, challenge appraisal, creativity, and proactive behavior: A multi-level study', *Journal of Organizational Behavior*, **31**(4), 543–65.

Ohly, S., S. Sonnentag and F. Pluntke (2006), 'Routinization, work characteristics and their relationships with creative and proactive behaviors', *Journal of Organizational Behavior*, **27**(3), 257–79.

Oldham, G.R. and A. Cummings (1996), 'Employee creativity: Personal and contextual factors at work', *Academy of Management Journal*, **39**(3), 607–34.

Parker, S.K. (2014), 'Beyond motivation: Job and work design for development, health, ambidexterity, and more', *Annual Review of Psychology*, **65**(1), 661–91.

Parker, S.K. and C.G. Collins (2010), 'Taking stock: Integrating and differentiating multiple proactive behaviors', *Journal of Management*, **36**(3), 633–62.

Parker, S.K. and S. Ohly (2008), 'Designing motivating work', in R. Kanfer, G. Chen and R.D. Pritchard (eds), *Work Motivation: Past, Present, and Future*, New York: Routledge, pp. 233–84.

Parker, S.K., H.M. Williams and N. Turner (2006), 'Modeling the antecedents of proactive behavior at work', *Journal of Applied Psychology*, **91**(3), 636–52.

Patterson, F., M. Kerrin and G. Gatto-Roissard (2009), *Characteristics and Behaviours of Innovative People in Organisations*, London: NESTA Policy and Research Unit.

Petrou, P., E. Demerouti, M. Peeters, W. Schaufeli and J. Hetland (2012), 'Crafting a job on a daily basis: Contextual correlates and the link to work engagement', *Journal of Organizational Behavior*, **33**(8), 1120–41.

Scott, S.G. and R.A. Bruce (1994), 'Determinants of innovative behavior: A path model of individual innovation in the workplace', *Academy of Management Journal*, **37**(3), 580–607.

Shalley, C.E., L.L. Gilson and T.C. Blum (2000), 'Matching creativity requirements and the work environment: Effects on satisfaction and intent to turnover', *Academy of Management Journal*, **43**(2), 215–24.

Shalley, C.E., L.L. Gilson and T.C. Blum (2009), 'Interactive effects of growth need strength, work context, and job complexity on self-reported creative performance', *Academy of Management Journal*, **52**(3), 489–505.

Shalley, C.E., J. Zhou and G.R. Oldman (2004), 'The effects of personal and contextual characteristics on creativity: Where should we go from here?' *Journal of Management*, **30**(6), 933–58.

Specht, J., B. Egloff and S. Schmukle (2011), 'Stability and change of personality across the life course: The impact of age and major life events on mean-level and rank-order stability of the big five', *Journal of Personality and Social Psychology*, **101**(4), 862–82.

Tims, M. and A.B. Bakker (2010), 'Job crafting: Towards a new model of individual job redesign', *South African Journal of Industrial Psychology*, **36**(2), 1–9.

Tims, M., A.B. Bakker and D. Derks (2013), 'Daily job crafting and the self-efficacy–performance relationship', *Journal of Managerial Psychology*, **29**(5), 490–507.

Van de Ven, A. (1986), 'Central problems in the management of innovation', *Management Science*, **32**(5), 590–607.

West, M.A. (2002), 'Sparkling fountains or stagnant ponds: An integrative model of creativity and innovation implementation in work groups', *Applied Psychology: An International Review*, **51**(3), 355–87.

Woodman, R.W., J.E. Sawyer and R.W. Griffin (1993), 'Toward a theory of organizational creativity', *Academy of Management Review*, **18**(2), 293–321.

Wrzesniewski, A. and J.E. Dutton (2001), 'Crafting a job: Revisioning employees as active crafters of their work', *Academy of Management Review*, **26**(2), 179–201.

Wu, C.-H., S.K. Parker and J.P.J. de Jong (2014), 'Need for cognition as an antecedent of individual innovation behavior', *Journal of Management*, **40**(6), 1511–34.

Yuan, F. and R.W. Woodman (2010), 'Innovative behavior in the workplace: The role of performance and image outcome expectations', *Academy of Management Journal*, **53**(2), 323–42.

3. The flow of creativity for idea implementation

Darija Aleksić, Miha Škerlavaj and Anders Dysvik

More than 60 years ago Levitt found that being creative is not enough and that 'ideas are useless unless used' (Levitt, 1963, p. 79). Despite increasing recognition of the importance of innovation at work, studies of how to foster innovation are still relatively rare (Baer, 2012). Furthermore, little progress has been made in understanding how psychological factors affect idea implementation (Anderson et al., 2014).

Thus, the aim of this chapter is to provide insight into the role of psychological factors in transforming individuals' *intentions* to implement an idea into actual idea implementation. Building on flow theory (Csikszentmihalyi, 1997b), we offer a new theoretical perspective on how to foster idea implementation at work. Adding to our current knowledge, we propose that individuals who have flow experiences will be more inclined to implement creative ideas (Baumann and Scheffer, 2011). Flow is defined as 'a state in which people are so involved in an activity that nothing else seems to matter; the experience itself is so enjoyable that people will do it even at a great cost, for the sheer sake of doing it' (Csikszentmihalyi, 1991, p. 4). Thus, we propose that flow experience may be an important factor that stimulates implementation of creative ideas. For example, if we think of some well-known individuals such as Mark Zuckerberg, the late Steve Jobs or Bill Gates who managed to successfully implement their ideas, we can see that they have at least one thing in common – they all enjoyed and loved what they did, or do. Consequently, since individuals who are often in flow enjoy their work, feel happier, and can work actively for a longer period of time (Csikszentmihalyi et al., 2004), we propose that the more individuals experience flow, the more likely it is that individuals' intention to implement an idea will result in actual implementation.

We begin this chapter by establishing arguments and theoretical evidence for how flow experience at work might mediate the relationship between individuals' intention for idea implementation and actual idea implementation. We enrich theoretical perspective by analyzing interviews, books, and other available secondary data of well-known start-up companies. We test our hypothesis using a three-step procedure for testing the mediation effect (Baron and Kenny, 1986). Next, we identify some challenges of idea implementation and provide explanation of how flow experiences help to overcome these challenges. We build this part of the chapter from the perspective of start-up companies since their success and sustained survival is highly dependent upon both idea generation and implementation. Initially, the creative idea is more or less everything that start-up companies have. Their inner desire encourages start-up companies to devote their time, money, and energy to idea implementation. Successful start-up companies are thus companies that managed to implement the creative idea. However, for start-ups, the journey from the creative idea to its successful implementation is uncertain and challenging. Flow experience may play an important role in dealing with these challenges. Thus, we tested the influence of flow experience on idea implementation by interviewing the chief executive officer (CEO) and chief technical officer (CTO) of a Slovenian start-up company that is developing an easy-to-use application for reducing the cost of hotel services.

GO WITH THE FLOW – FLOW EXPERIENCE FOSTERS IDEA IMPLEMENTATION

Every idea implementation starts with the generation of a good idea. Thus, creativity serves as a building block for innovation (Amabile, 1988). However, this does not apply to all ideas. We can roughly divide ideas into two groups: ideas with great potential for implementation and ideas that do not have much potential for implementation. For example, if we researchers in the field of management come up with an idea of how to improve the functioning of spaceships so that space travel will become cheaper, this idea has a very little potential for implementation. This is because we do not have enough domain-relevant knowledge and skills, which are important factors that promote idea implementation (Baer, 2012). Since we choose to work in the field of management, we are likely not very interested in spaceships and they do not give us a sense of joy. In other words, individuals choose 'behaviors that make them feel fully alive, competent, and creative' (Seligman and Csikszentmihalyi, 2000, p. 9). Thus, we are probably not motivated enough to invest our energy in developing this idea to the extent that it could be implemented.

The starting point of idea implementation is forming an intention ('I intend to implement the idea'), which reflects the amount of effort individuals are willing to invest in its implementation (Bird, 1988). In effect, once we have ideas with great potential for implementation, intention is needed in order for them to become manifest (ibid.). According to Ajzen (1991), individuals with intention to start a business (to implement their idea) are highly likely to carry it out. However, the process from intention to implementation is complicated.

Once we have the intention to implement an idea, it is more likely that we will actually implement it when an idea comes from an activity that we often perform, enjoy doing, and that arouses our curiosity (Grant, 2008). Only individuals who continue to follow their sense of enjoyment in chosen activities can develop their talent and creativity (Shernoff et al., 2003). One of the first principles of innovation followed by Steve Jobs is 'do what you love' (Gallo, 2011). As Jobs said: 'Have the courage to follow your heart and intuition' (ibid.). To be creative, people must learn to enjoy the fact that they are curious (Csikszentmihalyi, 1997b), as is the case with artists, musicians, and dancers, who are among the most creative professionals. Thus, enjoyment, an important component of flow experience (Bakker, 2008), may stimulate in individuals the intention to actually implement the idea.

Furthermore, as already stated, flow is 'a state in which people are so involved in an activity that nothing else seems to matter; the experience itself is so enjoyable that people will do it even at a great cost, for the sheer sake of doing it' (Csikszentmihalyi, 1991, p. 4). Individuals who experience a high level of flow are completely absorbed in their work and thereby forget what is happening around them (Csikszentmihalyi and LeFevre, 1989; Bakker, 2005). As Nikola Tesla (who loved and was fascinated by electricity, resulting in many inventions that changed the world) said: 'I do not think there is any thrill that can go through the human heart like that felt by the inventor as he sees some creation of the brain unfolding to success. . . Such emotions make a man forget food, sleep, friends, love, everything'.

Flow experience is an important component that affects the work of highly creative artists and scientists (Csikszentmihalyi, 1997a). Individuals who often experience flow see more opportunities to be fully involved in the implementation of complex tasks (Baumann and Scheffer, 2011). Flow experience is also connected with exploratory behavior (Ghani and Deshpande, 1994), defined as curiosity, increased interest in learning, and exploratory thinking (Hoffman and Novak, 1996). Curiosity plays a very important role in idea implementation.

John T. Meyer, the cofounder of Lemonly (a design agency, specializing in visual marketing and interactive infographics) said that, 'As a start-up leader, you can never stop asking the question, "Why?" Curiosity should

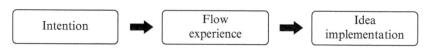

Figure 3.1   A conceptual model – intention, flow experience and idea implementation

run through your veins, as you believe there is always a better way to do something. We get into this business to create change, but don't ever stop being curious' (Young Entrepreneur Council, 2013). Therefore, we should promote flow experience, and thereby curiosity, if we want to promote idea implementation. Individuals who often experience flow will be able to constantly seek challenges, be flexible, curious, and open to new possibilities, as well as enjoy experimenting with new ideas (Csikszentmihalyi, 1991; Ceja and Navarro, 2011). For example, we can say that Drew Houston, a software engineer and cofounder of Dropbox, was constantly seeking challenges and enjoyed experimenting with new things as he had created six start-ups before Dropbox. The implementation of his seventh idea brought him billions. Thus, since the flow experience prompts a faster transition from the intention to carry out an activity to its actual implementation (Baumann and Scheffer, 2011), flow experience should have a positive impact on actual implementation of ideas (Figure 3.1).

RESEARCH METHOD AND SUMMARY OF RESULTS

In order to investigate the empirical relationship among the individuals' intention, flow experience, and idea implementation (=Figure 3.1), we collected data from two innovative Slovenian companies. The final sample consisted of 75 responses. 'Intentions' were measured using a seven-point scale over seven items developed by Douglas and Fitzsimmons (2013), measuring intentions to engage in a range of entrepreneurial behavior. 'Flow at work' was assessed with a 13-item work-related flow scale (WOLF) developed by Bakker (2008). Further, 'idea implementation' was measured using two items from a scale developed by Zhou and George (2001) that concerned idea implementation (Montag, 2012). We controlled for gender, age, type of employment, and work experience.

We wanted to test whether flow mediates the relationship between intention and idea implementation. We used a three-step procedure for testing this mediation effect, as recommended by Baron and Kenny (1986) and others (Kenny et al., 1998; Krull and MacKinnon, 2001). The first step was to establish that intention (the independent variable) is related to idea implementation (the dependent variable). The result showed that intention is significantly related to idea implementation ($\beta = -0.22$, $p < 0.05$). The second step was to establish that intention is related to flow experience, and this step was also supported. Finally, it must be demonstrated that flow experience (the mediator) is related to idea implementation, controlling for intentions. Since the relationships between intention, idea implementation, and flow experience were no longer significant, the results indicated full mediation (Baron and Kenny, 1986).

FLOW EXPERIENCE HELPS TO OVERCOME THE CHALLENGES OF IDEA IMPLEMENTATION: A START-UP PERSPECTIVE

Once individuals decide to implement a creative idea, the process towards fulfilling it begins. When we start with the implementation of something new, we cannot accurately define the essentials for successfully implementing a new idea. Start-ups often do not go as planned and thus entrepreneurs must be resourceful in overcoming the challenges they face (Holland and Herrmann, 2013). Alex Ljung, a founder and CEO of SoundCloud (the audio platform that enables anybody to upload, record, promote and share their sounds on the web) said that when they started with the implementation of their idea, they did not have a clue about the things they needed to do but, as he said, they learned things while doing it and this is what made the process of idea implementation so interesting (YouTube, 2012).

According to flow theory, experienced balance between challenges and skills is crucial for experiencing flow (Csikszentmihalyi, 1991). If individuals experience flow while implementing their new idea, autotelic experience, as one dimension of flow, will invoke pleasant feelings so that individuals will be willing to do almost anything to experience it again (ibid.). Jason Meinzer, senior sales consultant and the cofounder of Zagster (a company that designs, builds, and operates bike-sharing solutions), said that it is the most wonderful thing to wake up every morning with the thought that all day you will be doing something you enjoy doing, and that this is such a pleasant feeling that it is very hard to describe it with words (YouTube, 2013).

In order to experience flow continuously, individuals have to constantly seek greater challenges and further develop their skills (Csikszentmihalyi, 1997a) since one cannot continuously experience flow by dealing with the same challenge. Thus, while we might enjoy the process of idea implementation, problems with developing and testing products or services, and financial, marketing and any other problems common for start-up companies will be perceived as a challenge that an individual has to over-come in order to re-experience flow. The Slovenian start-up CEO agrees:

> I've always wanted to have a business of my own. Before this start-up I had a lot of ideas but when I started to work on these ideas I somehow gave up on them very quickly. I cannot explain why. The current idea is different. Despite all the challenges we are facing, I still believe in this idea and I enjoy this challenging process of its implementation. And this enjoyment encourages me to keep going forward.

Furthermore, a challenge that also defines whether you make it (idea implementation) or break it is how to find an investor. Start-up compa-nies usually have to deal with this problem, since in order to earn money with the implementation of their idea they first have to invest money to develop the idea into a product or service. If they do not have enough of their own money they need to find an investor who will believe in their idea and financially support its implementation – a very big challenge. Timothy Ericson, CEO and cofounder of Zagster said that fund-raising was one of the hardest and the most stressful things he has ever done, since he had to deal with rejections every single day, meet hundreds and hundreds of investors, in order to find investors who would invest in his idea. However, he says, if you experience flow while implementing your own idea, you will cope more easily with this challenge (YouTube, 2013). Namely, those engaged in flow activities may experience higher well-being (Collins et al., 2009) and those with strong psychological well-being tend to have a greater positive attitude, which empowers them to solve problems and to handle crises smoothly (Fredrickson et al., 2003; Zhang et al., 2015).

Furthermore, when in flow, individuals become fully concentrated on the implementation of their goals, which encourages involvement in the imple-mentation of activities and focus on relevant stimuli (Csikszentmihalyi, 1991). An individual who wants to implement his or her idea has a very specific goal in mind: to find funding for idea implementation. This spe-cific goal promotes flow experience because flow is likely to occur when an individual is faced with a task that has specific goals that require specific responses (Csikszentmihalyi, 1997a). In addition, while experiencing flow, focus is narrowed to the activity itself, everything else is forgotten, and all distractions are excluded from consciousness (Csikszentmihalyi, 1991; Chu and Lan, 2010) as an individual seeks novelty and opportunities for action (Ceja and Navarro, 2011). Thus, when in flow, individuals may per-ceive the negative feelings caused by rejections of potential investors as a distraction and the negative feelings may soon be forgotten.

Flow, stimulated by this specific goal of finding investors, will influ-ence individuals' task performance by focusing attention on the specified objective, stimulate task-related effort (Barsky, 2008), and will promote generation and implementation of new ways of attracting investors. As the CTO from the Slovenian start-up says:

> Currently I am faced with many problems that I have to solve. Some are bureaucratic in nature and I really don't like dealing with them because they are boring. However, I like dealing with technical issues. On these issues I can work for hours because they are interesting, and I can easily focus my attention to them. Sometimes I even forgot that I am working on solving problems – I see it more as playing a fun game.

DISCUSSION

Since ideas are of little or no value unless implemented (Levitt, 1963) we should strive for idea implementation. This challenging journey begins with the formation of the intention to implement. Intention is a state of mind that directs individuals' focus to achieve a goal (Bird, 1988). When an individual's goal is idea implementation, the stronger is the intention to implement the idea, and the greater is the likelihood that he or she will engage in actual idea implementation. Strong intention to implement an idea is a good starting point for idea implementation; however, intention is not sufficient to lead to actual idea implementation.

In this chapter we set out to deepen our understanding of how psychological factors affect idea implementation. Specifically, we theoretically proposed and empirically illustrated that flow experience seems to play an important role in converting ideas into actual idea implementation. Thereby we contribute to the flow theory by empirically examining the role of flow experience in idea implementation. This chapter is, to the best of our knowledge, the first to introduce the flow theory into the field of innovation more broadly and idea implementation in particular. We believe our chapter also makes an important contribution to the field of entrepreneurship research by providing evidence that flow mediates the relationship between entrepreneurial intentions and actual idea implementation. In line with our observations, it seems that in order to successfully proceed through the process from intention to actual idea implementation, individuals should experience flow – that is, they should become deeply involved and sense the enjoyment when performing their chosen activity. Furthermore, idea implementation is often accompanied by a number of challenges. If individuals experience flow when implementing the idea, they can cope with these challenges more easily. This is because flow is a functional state that motivates activity. When in flow, individuals need to constantly seek challenges. Thus, they should be flexible, curious, open to new possibilities, and enjoy experimenting with new ideas (Csikszentmihalyi, 1991; Ceja and Navarro, 2011).

We also contribute to idea implementation theory by providing evidence that psychological factors may have an important role in idea implementation. Specifically, we found that flow experience should enhance idea implementation at the individual level, since flow prompts a faster transition from the intention to carry out an activity to its actual implementation (Baumann and Scheffer, 2011). The higher the level of flow experience, the greater the chance of successful implementation of the idea. Thus, individuals who want to be innovative should look for potential ideas for implementation within their activities that allow them to experience flow.

REFERENCES

Ajzen, I. (1991), 'The theory of planned behavior', *Organizational Behavior and Human Decision Processes*, **50**(2), 179–211.

Amabile, T.M. (1988), 'A model of creativity and innovation in organizations', in B.M. Staw and L.L. Cummings (eds), *Research in Organizational Behavior*, Vol. 10, Greenwich, CT: JAI Press, pp. 123–67.

Anderson, N., K. Potočnik and J. Zhou (2014), 'Innovation and creativity in organizations: A state-of-the-science review, prospective commentary, and guiding framework', *Journal of Management*, **40**(5), 1297–333.

Baer, M. (2012), 'Putting creativity to work: The implementation of creative ideas in organizations', *Academy of Management Journal*, **55**(5), 1102–19.

Bakker, A.B. (2005), 'Flow among music teachers and their students: The crossover of peak experiences', *Journal of Vocational Behavior*, **66**(1), 26–44.

Bakker, A.B. (2008), 'The work-related flow inventory: Construction and initial validation of the WOLF', *Journal of Vocational Behavior*, **72**(3), 400–414.

Baron, R.M. and D.A. Kenny (1986), 'The moderator–mediator variable distinction in social psychological research: Conceptual, strategic, and statistical considerations', *Journal of Personality and Social Psychology*, **51**(6), 1173–82.

Barsky, A. (2008), 'Understanding the ethical cost of organizational goal-setting: A review and theory development', *Journal of Business Ethics*, **81**(1), 63–81.

Baumann, N. and D. Scheffer (2011), 'Seeking flow in the achievement domain: The achievement flow motive behind flow experience', *Motivation and Emotion*, **35**(3), 267–84.

Bird, B. (1988), 'Implementing entrepreneurial ideas: The case for intention', *Academy of Management Review*, **13**(3), 442–53.

Ceja, L. and J. Navarro (2011), 'Dynamic patterns of flow in the workplace: Characterizing within-individual variability using a complexity science approach', *Journal of Organizational Behavior*, **32**(4), 627–51.

Chu, L.-C. and C.-H. Lan (2010), 'Relationship between job characteristics and flow experience of R&D personnel: Case study of a high technology company in Taiwan', *Journal of Global Business Management*, **6**(1), 1–10.

Collins, A.L., N. Sarkisian and E. Winner (2009), 'Flow and happiness in later life:

An investigation into the role of daily and weekly flow experiences', *Journal of Happiness Studies*, **10**(6), 703–19.

Csikszentmihalyi, M. (1991), *Flow: The Psychology of Optimal Experience: Steps Toward Enhancing the Quality of Life*, Philadelphia, PA: HarperCollins Publishers.

Csikszentmihalyi, M. (1997a), *Creativity: Flow and the Psychology of Discovery and Invention*, Philadelphia, PA: HarperCollins Publishers.

Csikszentmihalyi, M. (1997b), *Finding Flow: The Psychology of Engagement with Everyday Life*, Philadelphia, PA: HarperCollins Publishers.

Csikszentmihalyi, M. and J. LeFevre (1989), 'Optimal experience in work and leisure', *Journal of Personality and Social Psychology*, **56**(5), 815–22.

Csikszentmihalyi, M., C. Kolo and T. Baur (2004), 'Flow: The psychology of optimal experience', *Australian Occupational Therapy Journal*, **51**(1), 3–12.

Douglas, E.J. and J.R. Fitzsimmons (2013), 'Intrapreneurial intentions versus entrepreneurial intentions: Distinct constructs with different antecedents', *Small Business Economics*, **41**(1), 115–32.

Fredrickson, B.L., M.M. Tugade, C.E. Waugh and G.R. Larkin (2003), 'What good are positive emotions in crisis? A prospective study of resilience and emotions following the terrorist attacks on the United States on September 11th, 2001', *Journal of Personality and Social Psychology*, **84**(2), 365–76.

Gallo, C. (2011), *The Innovation Secrets of Steve Jobs: Insanely Different: Principles for Breakthrough Success*, New York: McGraw-Hill.

Ghani, J.A. and S.P. Deshpande (1994), 'Task characteristics and the experience of optimal flow in human–computer interaction', *The Journal of Psychology*, **128**(4), 381–91.

Grant, A.M. (2008), 'Does intrinsic motivation fuel the prosocial fire? Motivational synergy in predicting persistence, performance, and productivity', *Journal of Applied Psychology*, **93**(1), 48–58.

Hoffman, D.L. and T.P. Novak (1996), 'Marketing in hypermedia computer-mediated environments: Conceptual foundations', *The Journal of Marketing*, **60**(3), 50–68.

Holland, D.V. and D. Herrmann (2013), 'Dog eat dog world: Challenges of an entrepreneurial start-up', *Journal of the International Academy for Case Studies*, **19**(5), 9–23.

Kenny, D.A., D.A. Kashy and N. Bolger (1998), 'Data analysis in social psychology', in D. Gilbert, S. Fiske and G. Lindzey (eds), *The Handbook of Social Psychology*, 4th edition, Cambridge, MA: Harvard University, pp. 233–65.

Krull, J.L. and D.P. MacKinnon (2001), 'Multilevel modeling of individual and group level mediated effects', *Multivariate Behavioral Research*, **36**(2), 249–77.

Levitt, T. (1963), 'Creativity is not enough', *Harvard Business Review*, **41**(3), 72–83.

Montag, T., C.P. Maertz and M. Baer (2012), 'A critical analysis of the workplace creativity criterion space', *Journal of Management*, **38**(4), 1362–86.

Seligman, M.E.P. and M. Csikszentmihalyi (2000), 'Positive psychology: An introduction', *American Psychologist*, **55**(1), 5–14.

Shernoff, D.J., M. Csikszentmihalyi, B. Schneider and E.S. Shernoff (2003), 'Student engagement in high school classrooms from the perspective of flow theory', *School Psychology Quarterly*, **18**(2), 158–76.

Young Entrepreneur Council (2013), 'Which qualities do successful startup leaders share?' *Upstart*, 23 October, accessed 2 December 2015 at http://upstart.

bizjournals.com/resources/advice/2013/10/23/qualities-of-successful-startup-leaders.html?page=all.

YouTube (2012), 'SoundCloud co-founder, Alex Ljung, my startup story' [video], *YouTube*, accessed 2 December 2015 at https://www.youtube.com/watch?v=e-9byqSonKY.

YouTube (2013), 'Startup stories: Zagster' [video], *YouTube*, accessed 2 December 2015 at https://www.youtube.com/watch?v=RDVmM4HuIKw.

Zhang, P., D.D. Wang and C.L. Owen (2015), 'A study of entrepreneurial intention of university students', *Entrepreneurship Research Journal*, **5**(1), 61–82.

Zhou, J. and J.M. George (2001), 'When job dissatisfaction leads to creativity: Encouraging the expression of voice', *Academy of Management Journal*, **44**(4), 682–96.

4. Idea implementation and cultural intelligence

Sabina Bogilović, Miha Škerlavaj and Sut I Wong

Managers and employees frequently set their goals according to simple mathematical equations, where the path to success is pretty straightforward, and almost everybody knows that $1 + 1 = 2$. Thus, Livermore's (2011) equations state that diverse teams + low cultural intelligence = frustration and low participation. And that on the other hand, diverse teams + high cultural intelligence = innovation. These equations are simple to understand, and therefore cultural intelligence, defined as an individual's capability to function effectively in a culturally diverse environment and with people from a culturally diverse environment (Ang and Van Dyne, 2008), should be part of every culturally diverse innovative company. However, is this really the case?

Diversity, including cultural diversity, is an everyday fact in the workplace (Homan et al., 2008), and for several decades researchers have believed, based on value in argument, that cross-cultural interactions in workplaces may stimulate individuals' new ideas, different problem-solving styles, knowledge, perspectives and skills (Cox and Blake, 1991; Williams and O'Reilly, 1998; Pelled et al., 1999). On the other hand, empirical evidence shows that cultural diversity may also provoke the emergence of social categorization processes (Tajfel and Turner, 1986) that hinder the use of available information (Van Knippenberg et al., 2004), reduce group cohesion, the individual idea implementation capabilities (Anderson and King, 1991) and innovations in organizations (Hülsheger et al., 2009). During the social categorization process individuals start to categorize colleagues as in-group/out-group members based on cultural similarities and differences. However, recent research shows that individuals' high cultural intelligence is a relevant predictor in intercultural creative collaborations, while it engenders greater idea sharing between culturally diverse colleagues (Chua et al., 2012; Crotty and Brett, 2012).

Yet, cultural intelligence as a more novel construct is more or less unknown to managers and employees. Individual cultural intelligence is involved in every aspect of the creative process, especially in idea implementation. More precisely, cultural intelligence increases individual understanding of similarities, differences (Earley and Ang, 2003), and assessments in idea implementation between colleagues from the East and colleagues from the West, and therefore decreases social categorization processes (in other words, an 'us–them' distinction) for those who are collaborating. Given that cultural intelligence is contextual, it is reasonable to expect that whether the environment stimulates the potential of such capabilities influences how individuals with high cultural intelligence flourish. Accordingly, an interesting question emerges: In a culturally diverse organization would a culturally diverse work environment with high individual cultural intelligence lead to high individual idea implementation?

The aim of this chapter is thus to explore this question and provide insight into this understudied process of how cultural intelligence can enhance idea implementation at the individual level in a culturally diverse work environment. We begin the chapter with the theoretical background of understanding cultural intelligence and how it can help individuals decrease social categorization processes based on cultural differences, and in turn enhance idea implementation in a culturally diverse environment. Thus, we aim to first contribute to innovation research by examining the conditions under which cultural diversity stimulates employee idea implementation with the help of individual capability (Anderson et al., 2014). Second, we advance the cultural intelligence theory and research by proposing that not only cultural intelligence as a whole but also each dimension of cultural intelligence is a cornerstone of idea implementation in a culturally diverse environment. In doing so we answer a recent call by Van Dyne and colleagues (2012) in order to provide a more in-depth examination of each cultural intelligence dimension. We end the chapter by providing some practical examples of how individuals can increase their cultural intelligence in order to better implement creative ideas in a culturally diverse environment.

INDIVIDUAL CULTURAL INTELLIGENCE AND IDEA IMPLEMENTATION IN A CULTURALLY DIVERSE ENVIRONMENT

Idea implementation is a key distinction between employees' creativity and organizational innovation. Whereas creativity mainly encompasses only the generation of novel and useful ideas (Amabile, 1996), innovation is a much broader concept (Axtell et al., 2000) and involves not only the generation phase but also the adoption and implementation of new ideas (Van de Ven et al., 1989). Thus, idea implementation is the last stage of the innovation process in which individuals successfully implement creative ideas within an organization (Shalley et al., 2009).

In line with Van der Vegt and Janssen (2003, p. 730), we argue that individual idea-implementation behavior as part of the innovation process is a 'product of a person's relationships with fellow team members and the team context'. For example, research from Axtell et al. (2000) found that individual implementation is associated with a supportive group and organizational environment; that is, management support, participation in decision-making and team support for innovation. The social context in which idea implementation occurs is therefore seemingly a salient factor to its success. In particular, a culturally diverse environment may stimulate an individual's capabilities derived from his or her cultural intelligence to effectively handle unfamiliar ideas suggested by colleagues from different cultural backgrounds and subsequently implement them. The empirical evidence linking culturally diverse environments and implementation of ideas as part of the innovation process is equivocal (Van der Vegt and Janssen, 2003; Anderson et al., 2014). For example, Anderson et al. (2014, p. 1310) stated that diversity as such 'is a problematic variable with regard to innovativeness – with either unclear findings, findings in either direction, or findings suggesting effects at different phases in team innovation'.

Drawing on social categorization theory (Tajfel and Turner, 1986), we argue that a culturally diverse environment can have a negative impact on individual idea implementation, because when cultural diversity increases in the work environment, a social categorization process emerges (Richard et al., 2004). Thus, individuals start to compare themselves based on similarities and differences to other team members to reduce uncertainty (Tajfel and Turner, 1986; Van Knippenberg et al., 2004). We broadly define cultural diversity as differences in visible characteristics such as ethnicity and race and in national culture (Chua, 2013). It follows that culturally diverse environments motivate employees to generate new subgroups in the work environment based on cultural dissimilarities between similar in-group members and dissimilar out-group members (Van Knippenberg and Schippers, 2007). Scholars have identified that social categorization is negatively related to individual work performance (Pelled et al., 1999), group processes (Guillaume et al., 2013), and interactions in the diverse work group such as sharing and elaborating creative ideas (Van Knippenberg et al., 2004), while individuals tend to favor similar colleagues more than dissimilar colleagues (Williams and O'Reilly, 1998). As a result, the social process of categorizing people into in- and out-groups can have negative consequences on individual idea implementation.

Nevertheless, cultural intelligence can reduce these potentially negative consequences of the social categorization process and in turn enhance individual idea implementation in a culturally diverse environment. This is because cultural intelligence represents an individual ability to deal effectively with situations characterized by culturally diverse settings and with people from a culturally diverse environment (Earley and Ang, 2003). Earley and Ang (2003) conceptualized cultural intelligence as a multidimensional construct consisting of metacognitive, cognitive, motivational, and behavioral complementary dimensions or capabilities. Cultural intelligence as a whole and each dimension of cultural intelligence can provide more in-depth insight as to how to implement ideas in cross-cultural collaborations.

First, the metacognitive dimension of cultural intelligence reflects individual mental consciousness and awareness during intercultural interactions. More precisely, it determines how an individual plans his or her behavior before actual multicultural interactions, checks for assumptions during multicultural interactions, and makes mental adjustments when actual experiences differ from expectations (Ang et al., 2007). In particular, metacognitive cultural intelligence can help with idea implementation, while metacognitive skills are important triggers for creative thinking (Feldhusen and Goh, 1995). Furthermore, it is more likely that individuals with high metacognitive cultural intelligence create a fusion culture in the work environment and blend diverse cultural values into one culture (Crotty and Brett, 2012), which will in turn decrease negative aspects of the social categorization processes in diverse teams (Rockstuhl and Ng, 2008). If culturally diverse employees blend diverse cultural values into a common culture, they perceive themselves more as in-group members rather than out-group members. Common cultural values among culturally diverse individuals enhance social interaction among them that is crucial for the idea-implementation process. Thus, it is likely that individuals who have high culturally metacognitive skills should be better able to contribute to idea implementation than individuals who are less culturally metacognitive.

Second, cognitive cultural intelligence involves different aspects of knowledge that individuals in a particular culture possess about norms, practices, conventions, language, religious beliefs, as well as economic, legal, and social systems (Erez et al., 2013). Based on this knowledge, individuals anticipate and understand similarities and differences between themselves and colleagues from different cultural backgrounds (Ng et al., 2009a). This particular cognitive skill is useful in dampening the social categorization processes (Rockstuhl and Ng, 2008). Thus, individuals with high cognitive cultural intelligence overcome prejudices based on superficial cultural characteristics and, in turn, collaborate and effectively share knowledge with out-group members (Michailova and Hutchings, 2006; Ang and Van Dyne, 2008), which will stimulate individuals to implement more useful and appropriate ideas in a culturally diverse work environment.

Third, motivational cultural intelligence is defined as an individual's capability to direct energy and effort toward learning and functioning in cross-cultural situations (Ang et al., 2007). High motivational cultural intelligence stimulates enjoyment and more confidence in individuals when they are interacting with culturally diverse coworkers. Consequently, individuals with high motivational cultural intelligence tend to be more engaged in intercultural interactions, and thus are more likely to overcome obstacles, setbacks, or failures due to cultural misunderstandings (Ang et al., 2006; Kim and Van Dyne, 2012). As Rockstuhl and Ng (2008) explain, individuals with high motivational intelligence may look for opportunities to interact with out-group members, which will reduce the likelihood of triggering the social categorization process within the group. Therefore, we predict that individuals with high motivational cultural intelligence will interact more with out-group members and thus the social categorization process, and this, in turn, will trigger individual idea implementation in a culturally diverse environment.

Fourth, behavioral cultural intelligence relates to an individual's capability to use appropriate verbal and non-verbal actions (for example, words, tones, gestures, and facial expressions) in intercultural interactions (Gudykunst et al., 1988; Ng et al., 2009b). Individuals with high behavioral cultural intelligence during interactions use appropriate words, gestures, and facial expressions that help them to be more easily accepted by out-group members (Ang et al., 2006; Lin et al., 2012). It follows that behavioral cultural intelligence can enhance interaction with culturally dissimilar out-group members. Idea implementation depends on the extent and quality of social interactions among the members in the group. Therefore, it is crucial to stimulate colleagues to interact with each other, especially when culturally diverse colleagues can bring different points of view into the process. Thus, cultural intelligence can help individuals increase their idea implementation capabilities while enhancing effective interactions and collaborations with culturally diverse colleagues.

To explore how cultural intelligence and its dimension can help implement novel and useful ideas in culturally diverse environments and multicultural collaborations, we conducted an experimental study with 80 international undergraduates (see Figure 4.1) in an elective course at a Slovenian university. We employed a two-by-one (that is, two conditions of cultural intelligence, low/high), between-subjects factorial design.

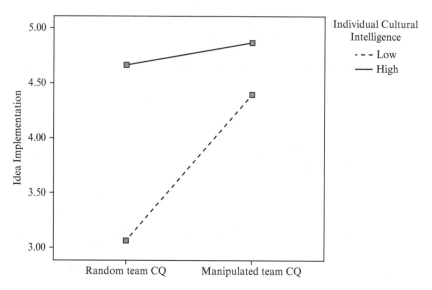

Note: CQ = cultural quotient/cultural intelligence.

*Figure 4.1   Relationship between idea implementation and individual level
of perceived cultural intelligence (experimental study)*

Therefore, we first measured individual cultural intelligence of the participants and, based on their results, put them into two groups. Individuals
with low cultural intelligence were our control group, and those with
high cultural intelligence were our experimental group. Participants then
randomly formed multicultural teams of four to design a prototype of a
new coffee shop in a foreign country. This task was part of the students'
design-thinking training to enhance their problem-solving ability, creative
confidence, and emotional well-being (Likar et al., 2014). We used the
design-thinking method, as it 'provided value to any process requiring creativity and innovation' (Ulibarri et al., 2014, p. 252). Rauth and Nabergoj
explain in more detail about the design-thinking method and development
of shared sensemaking of creative ideas in Chapter 16.

Participants in the experimental task went through all five distinct stages
of the design-thinking innovation process. Our experimental task started
with the 'empathize' stage, where we introduced students to techniques for
investigating the nature of a given problem, and the underlying emotions
or needs influencing it, through explaining and talking about the given task
(Ulibarri et al., 2014). Second, in the 'define' stage, we helped them identify
the core of the problem and participants were asked to choose a country in

which to implement their coffee shops. In the 'ideate' stage, students first brainstormed different ideas and possible solutions to the given task, and then chose one idea to implement. In the end, in the 'prototype' and 'test' stages, teams had to build and present their prototypes to two independent raters (experts in the field of creativity and innovation) who assessed them on a scale from 1 (absolutely inappropriate and innovative idea implementation) to 7 (absolutely appropriate and innovative idea implementation). All participants worked in multicultural teams that consisted of 'three or more people who had different nationalities' (Crotty and Brett, 2012). The results of the experiment are shown in Figure 4.1.

The ANOVA revealed that cultural intelligence has a direct impact on idea implementation (F[18,24] = 2.49, $p < 0.05$, Figure 4.1). As we can see in Figure 4.1, idea implementation was highest when we manipulated and put individuals with high cultural intelligence in a team to collaborate together. On the other hand, idea implementation was lowest when individuals had low cultural intelligence. As mentioned, we also observed them as they implemented their creative ideas in the prototypes and found that different dimensions of cultural intelligence influence individual cross-cultural collaborations.

Specifically, the results from observing the participants during the experimental task also replicated our indication that individuals with high motivational, behavioral and metacognitive cultural intelligence will adapt their enthusiasm and communicate better with their culturally diverse team members, which will decrease social categorization and consequently individuals will implement the best idea in their prototype. For example, participants mostly communicated in English, yet for most of them English was a foreign language. Therefore, second-language English participants had some problems sharing their ideas with their team members. Yet, throughout the observation we saw that in groups where individual cultural intelligence of the members was high, individuals changed their behavior and started to speak more slowly, used short sentences, and visual representations (drawings, tables, etc.) so second-language English participants would understand their ideas. This is a textbook example of how individuals with high behavioral and metacognitive cultural intelligence observe and adapt their behavior to culturally diverse team members (Livermore, 2009) to enhance communication and sharing of ideas, which in this case did stimulate idea implementation. The control group did not show this adaptation. Furthermore, from observing participants in experimental tasks, we also noticed that those with high motivational cultural intelligence were more engaged, made more intense effort, and persisted longer. Those who lacked motivational, behavioral, and metacognitive cultural intelligence more frequently appeared to struggle to explain and share ideas about the task to their team members.

The observations also suggest that cognitive and motivational cultural intelligence can stimulate idea implementation among culturally diverse individuals. Specifically, we noticed that individuals with high cognitive cultural intelligence showed more knowledge of the symbols, history, and costumes of a particular country. For example, the team that decided to represent the coffee shop in Spain used the sign of the bull and red and yellow stripes in their coffee shop prototype. Moreover, the team that decided to represent the coffee shop in Tajikistan, based on their knowledge about the country, redesigned their coffee shop as a tea shop; they showed in their presentation of their prototype that in Tajikistan people drink more tea than coffee. This evidence indicates that individuals who have high cognitive cultural intelligence (knowledge about a country's history and customs) implement ideas that are more creative and appropriate.

This finding suggests that, as predicted, cultural intelligence indeed helps people implement ideas in a culturally diverse work environment. Nevertheless, we are aware that providing evidence for our question as to whether in a culturally diverse organization a culturally diverse work environment with high individual cultural intelligence would lead to high individual idea implementation is not enough for organizations and their managers. As such, we propose that individuals can increase their cultural intelligence through different types of cross-cultural experience (Erez et al., 2013; Li et al., 2013; Rosenblatt et al., 2013). We therefore provide managers and their employees with practical examples of how they can increase the cultural intelligence of employees to stimulate their own idea implementation in a culturally diverse environment.

DEVELOPING INDIVIDUAL CULTURAL INTELLIGENCE

In today's globalized work environment, managers should be highly motivated to understand how to develop employees' cultural intelligence potential in order to stimulate employees' innovative idea implementation (Elenkov and Manev, 2009; Livermore, 2009). In this chapter, we provide theoretical and empirical evidence that employees with high cultural intelligence tend to be more valuable than their colleagues with low cultural intelligence when individuals implement creative ideas in a culturally diverse work environment. Thus, Livermore (2011) implies that high individual cultural intelligence doesn't come automatically, yet individuals can improve and develop their cultural intelligence (Erez et al., 2013).

Therefore, we first propose that in order for individuals to boost their idea implementation and cultural intelligence it is crucial that they interact with culturally diverse colleagues. For example, recent research (Erez et al., 2013; Rosenblatt et al., 2013) shows that MBA students developed and increased their cultural intelligence by being exposed to a cross-cultural interaction or having an optimal cross-cultural contact. Similarly, cross-cultural interactions can be beneficial for idea implementation because during different cross-cultural interactions employees can be stimulated to supply additional ideas while they are exposed to different concepts, scripts, and perspectives (Van der Vegt and Janssen, 2003; Madjar, 2005; Leung et al., 2008). As research from Leung and colleagues (2008) has shown, the exposure to multiple cultures is positively related to recruitment of ideas from unfamiliar cultures for creative idea expansion. Therefore, we suggest that in order to improve cultural intelligence and individual idea implementation, employees need to be exposed to intercultural inter-actions, during which they will gain information about new ideas, points of cultural differences and will in turn better implement ideas and develop their cultural intelligence.

Second, we suggest that employees need to be exposed to concrete cross-cultural experience in order to enhance their cultural intelligence, and that will in turn help them to boost their implementation capabilities in a culturally diverse environment. Recent research from Li and colleagues (2013) has shown not only that overseas work experience is positively related to the level of individual cultural intelligence, but also that the length of overseas experience is important. More precisely, they found that the longer employees spend in foreign countries, the more individual cultural intelligence they may develop. Thus, we agree with Thomas and Inkson (2004) that true individual cultural intelligence development requires learning only from real life cross-cultural experiences. Furthermore, individuals who lived abroad can better implement ideas when they can recruit ideas from diverse cultures and are 'fostering synthesis of seemingly incompatible ideas from diverse cultures' (Leung et al., 2008, p. 173). Therefore, we suggest that leaders and managers need to expose their employees to intercultural collaborations as much as possible in order to increase their cultural intelligence and idea implementation capabilities with culturally diverse colleagues.

REFERENCES

Amabile, T. (1996), *Creativity in Context*, Boulder, CO: Westview Press.

Anderson, N. and N. King (1991), 'Managing innovation in organisations', *Leadership and Organization Development Journal*, **12**(4), 17–21.

Anderson, N., K. Potočnik and J. Zhou (2014), 'Innovation and creativity in organizations: A state-of-the-science review, prospective commentary, and guiding framework', *Journal of Management*, **40**(5), 1297–333.

Ang, S. and L. van Dyne (2008), 'Conceptualization of cultural intelligence: Definition, distinctiveness, and nomological network', in S. Ang and L. van Dyne (ed.), *Handbook of Cultural Intelligence: Theory, Measurement, and Applications*, New York: M.E. Sharpe, pp. 3–15.

Ang, S., L. van Dyne and C. Koh (2006), 'Personality correlates of the four-factor model of cultural intelligence', *Group and Organization Management*, **31**(1), 100–123.

Ang, S., L. van Dyne, C. Koh, K.Y. Ng, K.J. Templer and C. Tay et al. (2007), 'Cultural intelligence: Its measurement and effects on cultural judgment and decision making, cultural adaptation and task performance', *Management and Organization Review*, **3**(3), 335–71.

Axtell, C.M., D.J. Holman, K.L. Unsworth, T.D. Wall and P.E. Waterson (2000), 'Shopfloor innovation: Facilitating the suggestion and implementation of ideas', *Journal of Occupational and Organizational Psychology*, **73**(3), 265–85.

Chua, R.Y.J. (2013), 'The costs of ambient cultural disharmony: Indirect intercultural conflicts in social environment undermine creativity', *Academy of Management Journal*, **56**(6), 1545–77.

Chua, R.Y.J., M.W. Morris and S. Mor (2012), 'Collaborating across cultures: Cultural metacognition and affect-based trust in creative collaboration', *Organizational Behavior and Human Decision Processes*, **118**(2), 116–31.

Cox, T.H. and S. Blake (1991), 'Managing cultural diversity: Implications for organizational competitiveness', *The Executive*, **5**(3), 45–56.

Crotty, S.K. and J.M. Brett (2012), 'Fusing creativity: Cultural metacognition and teamwork in multicultural teams', *Negotiation and Conflict Management Research*, **5**(2), 210–34.

Earley, P. and S. Ang (2003), *Cultural Intelligence: Individual Interactions across Cultures*, Stanford, CA: Stanford University Press.

Elenkov, D.S. and I.M. Manev (2009), 'Senior expatriate leadership's effects on innovation and the role of cultural intelligence', *Journal of World Business*, **44**(4), 357–69.

Erez, M., A. Lisak, R. Hatush, E. Glikson, R. Nouri and E. Shokef (2013), 'Going global: Developing management students' cultural intelligence and global identity in culturally diverse virtual teams', *Academy of Management Learning and Education*, **12**(3), 330–55.

Feldhusen, J.F. and B.E. Goh (1995), 'Assessing and accessing creativity: An integrative review of theory, research, and development', *Creativity Research Journal*, **8**(3), 231–47.

Gudykunst, W.B., S. Ting-Toomey and E. Chua (1988), *Culture and Interpersonal Communication*, Newbury Park, CA: Sage.

Guillaume, Y.R., J.F. Dawson, S.A. Woods, C.A. Sacramento and M.A. West (2013), 'Getting diversity at work to work: What we know and what we still don't know', *Journal of Occupational and Organizational Psychology*, **86**(2), 123–41.

Homan, A.C., J.R. Hollenbeck, S.E. Humphrey, D. van Knippenberg, D.R. Ilgen and G.A. van Kleef (2008), 'Facing differences with an open mind: Openness to experience, salience of intragroup differences, and performance of diverse work groups', *Academy of Management Journal*, **51**(6), 1204–22.

Hülsheger, U.R., N. Anderson and J.F. Salgado (2009), 'Team-level predictors of innovation at work: A comprehensive meta-analysis spanning three decades of research', *Journal of Applied Psychology*, **94**(5), 1128–45.

Kim, Y.J. and L. van Dyne (2012), 'Cultural intelligence and international leadership potential: The importance of contact for members of the majority', *Applied Psychology*, **61**(2), 272–94.

Leung, A.K., W.W. Maddux, A.D. Galinsky and C. Chiu (2008), 'Multicultural experience enhances creativity: The when and how', *American Psychologist*, **63**(3), 169–81.

Li, M., W. Mobley and A. Kelly (2013), 'When do global leaders learn best to develop cultural intelligence? An investigation of the moderating role of experiential learning style', *Academy of Management Learning and Education*, **12**(1), 32–50.

Likar, B., F. Cankar and B. Zupan (2014), 'Educational model for promoting creativity and innovation in primary schools', *Systems Research and Behavioral Science*, **32**(2), 205–13.

Lin, Y.C., A.S.Y. Chen and Y.C. Song (2012), 'Does your intelligence help to survive in a foreign jungle? The effects of cultural intelligence and emotional intelligence on cross-cultural adjustment', *International Journal of Intercultural Relations*, **36**(4), 541–52.

Livermore, D. (2009), *Leading with Cultural Intelligence: The New Secret to Success*: New York: AMACOM/American Management Association.

Livermore, D. (2011), *The Cultural Intelligence Difference Special Ebook Edition: Master the One Skill You Can't Do Without in Today's Global Economy*, New York: American Management Association.

Madjar, N. (2005), 'The contributions of different groups of individuals to employees' creativity', *Advances in Developing Human Resources*, **7**(2), 182–206.

Michailova, S. and K. Hutchings (2006), 'National cultural influences on knowledge sharing: A comparison of China and Russia', *Journal of Management Studies*, **43**(3), 383–405.

Ng, K., L. van Dyne and S. Ang (2009a), 'Beyond international experience: The strategic role of cultural intelligence for executive selection in IHRM', in P.R. Sparrow (ed.), *Handbook of International Human Resource Management: Integrating People, Process, and Context*, Chichester, UK: Wiley, pp. 97–113.

Ng, K., L. van Dyne and S. Ang (2009b), 'From experience to experiential learning: Cultural intelligence as a learning capability for global leader development', *Academy of Management Learning and Education*, **8**(4), 511–26.

Pelled, L.H., K.M. Eisenhardt and K.R. Xin (1999), 'Exploring the black box: An analysis of work group diversity, conflict, and performance', *Administrative Science Quarterly*, **44**(1), 1–28.

Richard, O.C., T. Barnett, S. Dwyer and K. Chadwick (2004), 'Cultural diversity in management, firm performance, and the moderating role of entrepreneurial orientation dimensions', *Academy of Management Journal*, **47**(2), 255–66.

Rockstuhl, T. and K.Y. Ng (2008), 'The effects of cultural intelligence on interpersonal trust in multicultural teams', in S. Ang and L. van Dyne (eds), *Handbook of Cultural Intelligence: Theory, Measurement, and Applications*, New York: M.E. Sharpe, pp. 206–20.

Rosenblatt, V., R. Worthley and B. MacNab (2013), 'From contact to development in experiential cultural intelligence education: The mediating influence of expectancy disconfirmation', *Academy of Management Learning and Education*, **12**(3), 356–79.

Shalley, C.E., L.L. Gilson and T.C. Blum (2009), 'Interactive effects of growth need strength, work context, and job complexity on self-reported creative performance', *The Academy of Management Journal Archive*, **52**(3), 489–505.

Tajfel, H. and J.C. Turner (1986), 'The social identity theory of intergroup behavior', in S. Worchel and W. Austin (eds), *Psychology of Intergroup Relations*, Chicago, IL: Nelson-Hall, pp. 7–24.

Thomas, D.C. and K. Inkson (2004), *Cultural Intelligence: People Skills for Global Business*, San Francisco: CA: Berrett-Koehler Publishers.

Ulibarri, N., A.E. Cravens, M. Cornelius, A. Royalty and A.S. Nabergoj (2014), 'Research as design: Developing creative confidence in doctoral students through design thinking', *International Journal of Doctoral Studies*, **9**, 249–70.

Van de Ven, A., H. Angle and M. Poole (eds) (1989), *Research on the Management of Innovation: The Minnesota Studies*, New York: Harper and Row.

Van der Vegt, G.S. and O. Janssen (2003), 'Joint impact of interdependence and group diversity on innovation', *Journal of Management*, **29**(5), 729–51.

Van Dyne, L., S. Ang, K.Y. Ng, T. Rockstuhl, M.L. Tan and C. Koh (2012), 'Sub-dimensions of the four factor model of cultural intelligence: Expanding the conceptualization and measurement of cultural intelligence', *Social and Personality Psychology Compass*, **6**(4), 295–313.

Van Knippenberg, D. and M.C. Schippers (2007), 'Work group diversity', *The Annual Review of Psychology*, **58**, 515–41.

Van Knippenberg, D., C.K.W. de Dreu and A.C. Homan (2004), 'Work group diversity and group performance: An integrative model and research agenda', *Journal of Applied Psychology*, **89**(6), 1008–22.

Williams, K.Y. and C.A. O'Reilly (1998), 'Demography and diversity in organizations: A review of 40 years of research', in B.M. Staw and R. Sutton (eds), *Research in Organizational Behavior*, Vol. 20, Greenwich, CT: JAI Press, pp. 77–140.

PART II

What can we do about it as teams?

5. This idea rocks! Idea championing in teams

Matej Černe, Robert Kaše and Miha Škerlavaj

The aim of this chapter is to shed more light onto the often-overlooked process between idea generation and idea implementation: idea championing. We begin with defining idea championing and then move on to describe how it manifests itself at the team level as an explanatory mechanism of idea generation in teams, and how it influences team-level idea-implementation outcomes. Schön (1963) was the first to point out the importance of product champions – advocates of an implementation of a particular product – for the success of technological innovation. Idea championing is a contemporary descending construct with an emphasis on the creative process.

A commonly used definition for idea championing is: 'A role where individuals are strong advocates for a project and generate positive behavioral support for an innovation during its development or work on behalf of the project in the face of organizational neutrality or opposition' (Markham et al., 1991, p. 219). In essence, idea championing represents a position in an organization when someone creates, defines and adopts an idea (Maidique, 1980). However, it can also be understood more broadly, as definitions of idea championing vary, and also includes influencing others using any means necessary to succeed in promoting an idea (Schön, 1963), possessing and exhibiting political and sales skills in order to convince the opposition of the quality of an idea (Day, 1994), or linking an idea to experts with knowledge on how to implement it (Chakrabarti and Hauschildt, 1989). While we do adopt Markham et al.'s (1991) definition of idea championing, we acknowledge and highlight the fact that idea championing cannot occur in isolation and thereby examine it in a team context. Nonetheless, we do not view political and sales skills as an integral part of the construct, but rather as antecedents of successful idea championing.

Idea championing is needed in the innovation process to overcome organizational barriers and resistance. According to Schön (1963), a new idea 'either finds a champion or dies'. Since then, plenty of studies have recognized the presence of idea champions as a relevant factor in innovation

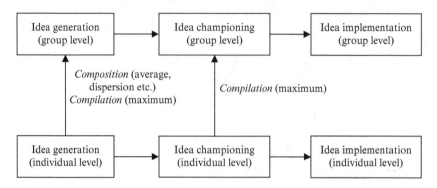

Figure 5.1   Conceptual model of team-level idea championing

process effectiveness (for example, Markham et al., 1991; Markham and Griffin, 1998). However, rigorous empirical investigation of the role of idea champions in the process has often been lacking. This is particularly (and surprisingly!) true for the micro-level (individual- and team-level) creativity and innovation research. Therefore, with this chapter, we aim first to contribute to micro- (individual- and team-level) innovation research by considering elements from multi-level theory (emergence; Rousseau, 1985, 2011; Mathieu et al., 2014) to offer insight into the emergence of idea generation and idea championing in team innovation process. Specifically, we examine idea championing as an overlooked missing link between idea generation and implementation in teams (see Figure 5.1). We also contribute to multi-level theory; we do so by discussing different emergence types in a specific setting (in other words, team innovation process). In practical terms, this chapter helps to illustrate special cases of idea championing, and the explanatory mechanisms underlying the manifestation of this process.

EMERGENCE OF IDEA CHAMPIONING

We first focus on operationalizing and measuring employee idea championing (using an item from the Zhou and George, 2001 creativity scale: 'I frequently champion ideas to others'). Our three studies (of employees of two large Slovene companies and 12 Chinese SMEs) have indicated that supervisor-reported idea championing of their employees (direct reports) correlates strongly with employees' self-reported idea generation (0.47, $p < 0.01$) at the individual level (of the very same individual who champions ideas).

We extend this research in another field study within the largest Slovene insurance company (200 employees divided into 53 work groups with immediate supervisors), who evaluated employee individual idea championing and team idea implementation (of all their direct reports), where we examined different emergence types of idea championing in a group setting.

We first tested and compared dispersion-composition models of emergence from individual to the team level (Rousseau, 1985, 2011; Mathieu et al., 2014) for idea generation and idea championing. Starting with idea generation, of the general composition aggregation types only average was significantly positively related to team-level idea implementation, whereas of the compilation aggregation types, maximum was an even stronger predictor of idea implementation at the team level. These results are in line with expectations and previous research (Gong et al., 2013). From the assortment of dispersion models (standard deviation, within-group agreement etc.), none exhibited a significant relationship with team-level idea implementation. The takeaway is that it is better (in a team-level idea-implementation process) if someone from the team stands out from other team members in terms of their idea generation.

This finding is aligned with previous research on idea generation in groups, which has demonstrated that although idea sharing in groups is important (Woodman et al., 1993; Taggar, 2002), particularly in diverse groups (McLeod et al., 1996), it involves a relatively inefficient process (Paulus and Yang, 2000). In addition, cultural values research has shown that individualism is beneficial even in group creative processes, as individualistic values encourage uniqueness when creativity is a salient goal (Goncalo and Staw, 2006). Our findings, on the other hand, are not completely in line with existing team-level creativity research, which suggested that team creativity at a particular point in time could be described as either the average or a weighted average of team members' creativity (Pirola-Merlo and Mann, 2004). They are, however, aligned with another finding of Pirola-Merlo and Mann (2004) who argue that creativity of project outcomes is explained by either the maximum of or the average of team creativity across time points, along with the aforementioned finding of Gong et al. (2013) that had the maximum score of individuals' creativity in teams more positively related to team-level outcomes.

A step further could be found in network creativity research, which has indicated that it is crucial that creative individuals are well connected with other group members in order to foster better results in terms of group creativity (Björk and Magnusson, 2009). Therefore, it may be imperative for these highly creative individuals in teams to connect to other team members effectively. As the results supported that for a team to champion an idea it still needs a strong champion in its midst, another important question emerges. Why do the others follow? Is it still because of the idea or because of the champion that they join in the championing?

In phase two of our field study, we added team-aggregated idea championing (all forms: average, dispersion, maximum etc.) as explanatory mechanisms (mediators) between idea generation (average and maximum) and idea implementation at the team level. No form of aggregated idea championing exhibited a mediating effect when the predictor was average creativity. Alternatively, when the predictor was maximum creativity, maximum idea championing was a significant mediator. This leads to the conclusion that the teams with strong idea generators also have stronger idea implementation. The very extraordinary idea generator is likely the same person who then also stands out from the rest of the team members in championing these ideas. Such a finding supports one (quite small and definitely not prevailing) stream of previous research on idea or innovation champions that emphasized the inevitable connection between creating and championing ideas (for example, Maidique, 1980).

Our field study is a reflection of corporate reality and as such provides external validity to our claims. By presenting a brief summary of results from empirical studies we hope to have stimulated additional research on the boundary conditions of the relationship between idea championing and team-level idea implementation that would focus on the moderating variables that could improve the likelihood of idea championing actually resulting in higher versus lower levels of team-level idea implementation.

Similarly, we would also like to stimulate practitioners' thinking about these issues. Therefore, we now focus our attention away from academic theorizing and testing towards practical cases that will account for the above-made point by representing different ways of idea championing and highlighting the fact that most are individually focused and reflect team-level dynamics that occur in order to manifest in successful championing.

SPECIAL CASES OF IDEA CHAMPIONING

Why You Would Not Champion Ideas: Early Birds Finishing Last

Can you think of an occurrence, when you came up with a brilliant creative idea (perhaps a bit distant from the regular working process) and your boss was fast to assign you to the majority of its realization? Sounds familiar? Well, we bet you thought twice the next time you had a groundbreaking thought about whether or not to share it with others. And this is exactly what we focus on in this special case: how employees who generate creative ideas and champion it to others (usually the most creative and proactive individuals) often end up carrying the large chunk of implementation activities. This in turn leads to them not coming up with creative ideas the next time, for fear of their boss/supervisor/leader giving them too much work and adding to their already busy schedules. Of course, this is how team supervisors in effect 'shoot themselves in the foot' as they no longer obtain high-quality creative ideas that could potentially result in groundbreaking innovations.

Next, we theorize what the supervisor can do to prevent this – with a particular, more democratic, inclusive leadership style, team activity management or employee voice hearing, by ensuring team support for implementation, by providing some guarantee in advance that the team as a whole will do it, or by rewarding employees who generate or champion ideas. The subsequent 'silence' of ideas could also depend on how the employee perceives the assignment of the implementation task and to what cause he or she attributes this development (for example, has this been done by the supervisor on purpose, or was it simply negligence of keeping in mind all the employees' tasks and duties etc.?).

Internal Agents of Change

In the management innovation literature, there is a lot of discussion about internal agents of change who push for and eventually implement managerial innovations. Their actions, which are based on sponsorship and acquiring coalitions in order to overcome resistance, are a manifestation of idea championing. Birkinshaw et al. (2008) define management innovation as 'everything the managers do'. In practice, it usually consists of generating an idea for a managerial innovation, promoting (championing) it to others in an organization in order to obtain support required for the implementation (such as top management; cf. Vaccaro, 2010), overcoming resistance to change (cf. Battilana and Casciaro, 2013), and finally, implementing new managerial solutions.

Consistent with a cultural perspective on management innovation, which examines how new managerial solutions are constructed inside organizations (cf. Zbaracki, 1998), this is a socially constructed change process, usually containing change in ways of working and perpetuation of existing power relations (Birkinshaw et al., 2008). This means that idea championing is crucial. In particular, internal agents of change champion ideas by theorizing and labeling a new managerial solution, which is a social process whereby individuals inside and outside the organization make sense of and validate the management innovation to build its legitimacy (ibid.).

Creative Bootlegging and Stealth Innovation

To develop innovations, especially in large, mature organizations, individuals often have to resort to underground, 'bootleg' research and development (R&D) activities that have no formal organizational support (Criscuolo et al., 2013). Such bootlegging is defined as the process by which individuals take the initiative to work on ideas that have no formal organizational support and are often hidden from the sight of senior management, but are undertaken with the aim of producing innovations that will benefit the company (Augsdorfer, 2005). This process also involves idea-championing activities. Research has in fact found that individuals' bootleg efforts are associated with achievement of high levels of innovative performance (Criscuolo et al., 2013). Bootlegging allows individuals to explore divergent research directions that fall outside the remit of formal projects (O'Connor and McDermott, 2004) and provides the individual with more freedom to explore uncharted territory and to attain explorative advantage over colleagues who do not bootleg. Although bootlegging counts as an illegitimate activity, it can function as a channel through which unconventional ideas may be realized (Criscuolo et al., 2013).

Bootlegging also allows individuals to delay the moment of monitoring and assessment by the organization until an idea is reasonably developed (Cheng and van de Ven, 1996). In more extreme cases, bootlegging may even involve continuing to work on projects rejected by top management and re-presenting them to the organization when the time and circumstances are more appropriate (Mainemelis, 2010). Ultimately, the engagement of individuals in the formally deviant activity of bootlegging depends heavily upon their proactivity, but also the organizational context; that is, the autonomy individuals are given and the enforcement of organizational norms in terms of innovation. Namely, the benefits of an individual's bootlegging efforts are enhanced in work units with high levels of innovative performance that include members who are also engaged in bootlegging; however, during periods of organizational change involving formalization of the R&D process, individuals who increase their bootlegging activities are less likely to innovate (Criscuolo et al., 2013).

So-called stealth innovation is a similar process defined as innovating under the radar; when employees in companies engage in innovative processes without their supervisors knowing about it (Miller and Wedell-Wedellsborg, 2013). It is beneficial because in certain circumstances it is better to ask for forgiveness than ask for permission in the first place. In particular, resistance or myopic reward systems are likely to be the reason for failure of a creative idea if this idea is highly unusual and novel. Therefore, it might at times be more practical to champion ideas (that is, obtain support and help) and innovate without top management consent. Miller and Wedell-Wedellsborg (2013, p. 92) describe the case of PfizerWorks: 'a human resources manager in Pfizer created the productivity initiative to allow employees to outsource "grunt work" and other routine parts of their jobs, giving them more time to focus on important tasks and allowing Pfizer to make better use of its highly skilled (and highly paid) employees'. PfizerWorks was launched in 2008. It rapidly became a noted success story, and the HR manager (Jordan Cohen) was featured in many outlets, such as *Business Week*. Miller and Wedell-Wedellsborg (2013, p. 92) continue:

> Cohen didn't bring his idea to fruition by going straight to the top. To the contrary, he stayed under the radar for more than a year, developing the service, accumulating evidence, and gaining allies. When he finally pitched it to Pfizer's top executives, he was able to show them much more than an idea: He presented existing users who were passionate about the project, outlined a proven business case, and pointed to the backing of several senior managers. Pfizer's decision to support the project came quickly, and Cohen received not just a budget for it but a new job as the head of PfizerWorks.

A crucial question emerges when discussing stealth innovation – when to reveal your idea? The practice and literature on idea championing support the notion of under-radar championing (Criscuolo et al., 2013) and obtaining support and 'critical mass' of your idea's propagators. This depends on the organizational culture and procedures, while it is very important for the evaluation of the context (whether or not an idea will be supported) to be accurate.

Tea Lempiälä, researcher at Aalto University in Finland describes idea champions as individuals who stand against the opposition of others and confidently push their ideas through the organization, acting as icons of change, embodying the risk-taking and perseverance necessary to gain acceptance for ideas that disrupt the status quo. However, she asserts that there is also another side to idea champions, one that involves subtle means of gaining acceptance for one's ideas. Here, ideas are smuggled rather than championed, in practice transforming idea champions into 'corporate smugglers' and in many situations, assertive championing might not be the best way to go: 'Pushing too hard and too fast can generate resistance in an organization and the champion might end up with less support than she began with' (Lempiälä, 2011, p. 1).

A better approach would be to test the ground and present an idea in an experimental, trial-and-error manner; playfully even, not to stir up too much opposition. Even letting go of an idea for a while (even few years) and waiting for the appropriate opportunity when the organizational context is ready is a viable option:

Many champions who choose to take up a smuggling strategy feel by letting go of some of their ideas they are able to secure a position where they can get more of their ideas accepted over a longer time period. Smugglers thus demonstrate perseverance, but in a different form from the one we are accustomed to linking to champions. (Lempiälä, 2011, p. 1)

This Finnish study also speaks to the importance of involving others (as opposed to only exhibiting self-confidence and head-on persuasion) to the process of construction of ideas in order to create commitment and obtain support:

The genuine inclusion of others is not easy, however, since it requires allowing someone else to actually have a say in the larger vision. And this openness includes the disclosure of uncertainty and ambiguity – qualities, which are often seen to undermine the credibility of champions. Yet, when building acceptance through collaborative construction these are fundamental components in making the co-champion feel that she has a genuine possibility to contribute. (Ibid.)

This would include implanting the idea into the minds of other employees, correcting it in during the process, and improving it even before it is officially presented to the broader context. Obtaining support must not necessarily be an intentional effort, although the study indicates that this approach is efficient in generating both acceptance and support for the idea: 'By making compromises to the original vision and disclosing uncertainty, the smuggler is able to generate deeper commitment toward the idea that might have been possible through more assertive championing tactics' (ibid.).

There are a couple of prerequisites of successful idea championing under the radar, corporate smuggling or stealth innovation (Miller and Wedell-Wedellsborg, 2013): (1) you need to marshal allies (who you champion your idea to) who can help you operate off the grid and make sure that you don't lose perspective as you do so; (2) you need to build proof of concept so that when you're ready to make your case to the higher-ups, you have hard evidence to support you; (3) you must obtain access to funds and other resources to keep your project afloat. On the other hand, early exposure can 'kill' or shut down the probability that a creative idea would ever get implemented if the innovators would present it to the top management immediately. Consider a company that Miller and Wedell-Wedellsborg (2013, pp. 92–3) called RedTec Media, whose European division came up with an idea for a potentially game-changing consumer product aimed at the luxury market:

Excited about the idea's potential, the European team presented it to leaders at corporate headquarters. The response was much less enthusiastic than the team had expected. While the executives didn't kill the idea outright, they questioned the project's technical feasibility and expressed strong doubts about whether there was a market for it. The European team members, recognizing that their enthusiasm was not contagious, set out to make a better case for the idea.

Over the next few months, they built support for the idea. They built a working prototype and had it tested (rigorously and reliably) with the consumers, who provided positive feedback, and generated awareness and support among the retailers, who were similarly excited and even suggested a higher price than the European team had hoped. The key seemed to be in documenting all the positive responses (Miller and Wedell-Wedellsborg, 2013). Nonetheless, the top management stood firmly and did not change their minds, deciding to kill the project:

> To be fair, there were legitimate reasons to oppose the project, but we also got the feeling that the leadership made an early judgment call based on their gut feelings about the first presentation, and then pretty much stuck by that call irrespective of all the evidence we sent them subsequently. (Miller and Wedell-Wedellsborg, 2013, p. 93)

Therefore, idea championing must be conducted with caution and consider who and when to include in the implementation activities. What can management do in order to foster beneficial outcomes of underground innovation activities? Criscuolo et al. (2013) offer two suggestions. First, instead of formal R&D management systems managers use monitoring mechanisms, such as R&D management, as a form of 'soft power' to provide guidelines and incentives for alignment and coordination of creative efforts without invoking the organization's 'hard power' (in other words, the enforcement of norms through sanctions and punishment), which may crush independent initiative. Second, even in organizations where there is no explicit free time, unofficial R&D efforts frequently take place. By providing dedicated free time, organizations might actually reduce the allure of these hidden creative efforts since they are no longer forbidden. Criscuolo et al. (2013, p. 16) wonder and then conclude: 'Does the forbidden nature of the "fruit" increase its sweetness? Or, alternatively, is it the formally provided autonomy that counts, or is it the autonomy that individuals achieve informally through underground activities?' Ultimately, it might be more productive for organizations to impose restrictions on the free time of would-be innovators and idea champions in order to heighten its allure while tolerating the existence of bootlegging and enabling the integration of its outputs into the organization's formal management processes (Criscuolo et al., 2013).

REFERENCES

Augsdorfer, P. (2005), 'Bootlegging and path dependency', *Research Policy*, **34**(1), 1–11.

Battilana, J. and T. Casciaro (2013), 'Overcoming resistance to change: Strong ties and affective cooptation', *Management Science*, **59**(4), 819–36.

Birkinshaw, J., G. Hamel and M.J. Mol (2008), 'Management innovation', *Academy of Management Review*, **33**(4), 825–45.

Björk, J. and M. Magnusson (2009), 'Where do good innovation ideas come from? Exploring the influence of network connectivity on innovation idea quality', *Journal of Product Innovation Management*, **26**(6), 662–70.

Chakrabarti, A.K. and J. Hauschildt (1989), 'The division of labour in innovation management', *R&D Management*, **19**(2), 161–71.

Cheng, Y.-T. and A.H. van de Ven (1996), 'Learning the innovation journey: Order out of chaos?' *Organization Science*, **7**(6), 593–614.

Criscuolo, P., A. Salter and A.L. Ter Wal (2013), 'Going underground: Bootlegging and individual innovative performance', *Organization Science*, **25**(5), 1287–305.

Day, D.L. (1994), 'Raising radicals: Different processes for championing innovative corporate ventures', *Organization Science*, **5**(2), 148–72.

Goncalo, J.A. and B.M. Staw (2006), 'Individualism–collectivism and group creativity', *Organizational Behavior and Human Decision Processes*, **100**(1), 96–109.

Gong, Y., T.-Y. Kim, J. Zhu and D.R. Lee (2013), 'A multi-level model of team goal orientation, information exchange, and creativity', *Academy of Management Journal*, **56**(3), 827–51.

Lempiälä, T. (2011), 'Corporate smugglers: Championing ideas under the radar', *Fast Company*, accessed 1 July 2014 at http://www.fastcompany.com/1736968/corporate-smugglers-championing-ideas-under-radar.

Maidique, M.A. (1980), 'Entrepreneurs, champions, and technological innovation', *Sloan Management Review*, **21**(2), 59–76.

Mainemelis, C. (2010), 'Stealing fire: Creative deviance in the evolution of new ideas', *Academy of Management Review*, **35**(4), 558–78.

Markham, S.K. and A. Griffin (1998), 'The breakfast of champions: Associations between champions and product development environments, practices and performance', *Journal of Product Innovation Management*, **15**(5), 436–54.

Markham, S.K., S.G. Green and R. Basu (1991), 'Champions and antagonists: Relationships with R&D project characteristics and management', *Journal of Engineering and Technology Management*, **8**(3), 217–42.

Mathieu, J.E., S.I. Tannenbaum, J.S. Donsbach and G.M. Alliger (2014), 'A review and integration of team composition models moving toward a dynamic and temporal framework', *Journal of Management*, **40**(1), 130–60.

McLeod, P.L., S.A. Lobel and T.H. Cox (1996), 'Ethnic diversity and creativity in small groups', *Small Group Research*, **27**(2), 248–64.

Miller, P. and T. Wedell-Wedellsborg (2013), 'The case for stealth innovation', *Harvard Business Review*, **91**(3), 90–97.

O'Connor, G.C. and C.M. McDermott (2004), 'The human side of radical innovation', *Journal of Engineering and Technology Management*, **21**(1), 11–30.

Paulus, P.B. and H.-C. Yang (2000), 'Idea generation in groups: A basis for creativity in organizations', *Organizational Behavior and Human Decision Processes*, **82**(1), 76–87.

Pirola-Merlo, A. and L. Mann (2004), 'The relationship between individual creativity and team creativity: Aggregating across people and time', *Journal of Organizational Behavior*, **25**(2), 235–57.

Rousseau, D.M. (1985), 'Issues of level in organizational research: Multi-level and cross-level perspectives', in L. Cummings and B. Staw (eds), *Research in Organizational Behavior*, Vol. 7, Greenwich, CT: JAI Press, pp. 1–37.

Rousseau, D.M. (2011), 'Reinforcing the micro/macro bridge: Organizational thinking and pluralistic vehicles', *Journal of Management*, **37**(2), 429–42.

Schön, D. (1963), 'Champions for radical new inventions', *Harvard Business Review*, **41**(2), 77–86.

Taggar, S. (2002), 'Individual creativity and group ability to utilize individual creative resources: A multi-level model', *Academy of Management Journal*, **45**(2), 315–30.

Vaccaro, I.G. (2010), 'Management innovation: Studies on the role of internal change agents', PhD thesis, Rotterdam: Erasmus University.

Woodman, R.W., J.E. Sawyer and R.W. Griffin (1993), 'Toward a theory of organizational creativity', *Academy of Management Review*, **18**(2), 293–321.

Zbaracki, M.J. (1998), 'The rhetoric and reality of total quality management', *Administrative Science Quarterly*, **43**(3), 602–38.

Zhou, J. and J.M. George (2001), 'When job dissatisfaction leads to creativity: Encouraging the expression of voice', *Academy of Management Journal*, **44**(4), 682–96.

6. Should our heart rule our head? Team innovation through intuition and rationality

Jana Krapež Trošt and Miha Škerlavaj

Peter F. Drucker (1909–2005), who was considered the top management thinker of his time, once said: 'Every decision is a risk-taking judgment'. In today's economy (great recession, rapid technological changes, and dynamic environment) innovation is more than ever the lifeblood of business (Amabile, 1993). According to Drucker, managing risk is managing uncertainty of the outcome from current actions, yet every day companies let innovation slip away and countless ideas and opportunities are lost. Innovation concerns those processes where individuals, groups, or organizations seek to achieve desired changes, or avoid the penalties of inaction (West, 2002). Therefore, no organization can survive and prosper without a constant focus on innovation (Anderson and King, 1991).

The aim of this chapter is to gain a deeper insight into the often-overlooked process of idea generation and idea implementation at the team level. Innovation concerns those processes where individuals and groups seek to achieve desired changes. We begin with describing both types of decision-making processes – intuitive and analytical – and then explain how they may influence team-level innovation outcomes. This chapter integrates topics of decision-making and innovation management.

Innovation is the introduction of new and improved ways of doing things at work (Anderson and King, 1993). Despite the prominence of the innovation construct in recent research, numerous innovations in practice often fail because innovators do not take into account the importance of the effect that individual traits have on them (Rogers and Shoemaker, 1971). Innovation's success relies strongly on the people who are most likely to be present when an innovative idea occurs. However, these employees are often ignored. How many of them are able to capture innovation when it occurs, or to ensure it has the best possible opportunity to succeed?

Identifying which thinking mode, intuitive or analytical, yields better decisions has been a major subject of inquiry by decision-making researchers (Rusou et al., 2013). There is considerable agreement among researchers that information in decision-making involves two qualitatively different thinking modes but there are different viewpoints regarding the ways in which these two thinking modes interact. Some authors (for example, Kahneman and Frederick, 2002) have argued that the two modes operate sequentially, yet other researchers (Epstein, 1994) have suggested that the two thinking modes work in parallel and are used to different extents depending on the decision environment. Identifying the circumstances under which each thinking mode is preferable might help in understanding the advantages of each mode.

In order to fully understand the factors that could facilitate or inhibit team innovation, we outline and test a multilevel model by building on dual process theory (DPT). The core assumption of DPT is that reasoning and decision-making are accomplished by the joint action of two types of process, differing in the degree to which they are characterized as fast and automatic or slow and conscious (for example, Sloman, 2002; Kahneman, 2003). One of the DPTs is cognitive-experiential self-theory (CEST), which was developed as a global theory of personality with two parallel systems (Epstein, 1990). According to CEST, information in decision-making involves two qualitatively different thinking modes: (1) an intuitive mode and (2) a deliberative/analytical mode (Epstein, 1994). As Albert Einstein said: 'The intuitive mind is a sacred gift and the rational mind is a faithful servant'. The analytical part was developed when we first acquired speech and cognition around its neural architecture. In fact, the human story is the story of the development of our species' left brain and its thinking role in self and group. The intuitive hemisphere (right side of the brain) indicates orientation towards the senses (direct sensory input) or towards the higher cognitive functioning.

Pacini and Epstein (1999) developed the CEST, which posits that personalities may be understood as comprising two separate, parallel, and interactive fundamental information-processing systems: a preconscious experiential system and a conscious rational system. Isenberg (1984) believed that intuition is not the opposite of rationality; instead, it is based on extensive experience both in analysis, problem-solving, and implementation. Intuition may therefore be positioned as being interdependent with rational analysis rather than in opposition to it (Sadler-Smith and Shefy, 2007). 'Intuitive and rational approaches both have their own validity and may be more or less appropriate in different contexts' (Sinclair and Ashkanasy, 2005, p. 359). The experiential system functions in a way that is preconscious, automatic, fast, effortless, concrete, associative, and minimally demanding of cognitive resources (Epstein, 1990). According to CEST, the experiential system not only leads behavior in expected ways to achieve pleasurable outcomes and to avoid unpleasurable ones, but the cognitions themselves are influenced by affect. In line with the development of research, intuition has been conceptualized in several ways and we use a broadly accepted theoretical definition of intuition, which is defined in CEST as the 'accumulated tacit information that a person has acquired by automatically learning from experience' (Epstein, 2008, p. 29). Therefore, decisions that are based on intuition are frequently implemented on the basis of unconscious reasoning without analytically comparing strengths and weaknesses of individual options (Dayan and Elbanna, 2011). Leybourne and Sadler-Smith (2006) found support for the fact that the earlier experience leads to quick decisions, which may incorporate an affective component, such as 'gut feel' or 'hunch'.

Existing research proposes that organizations perceive intuition as a guide in helping managers make fast, accurate decisions (Dane and Pratt, 2007), when important indicators are missing for rational analyses, when high uncertainty exists, and when decision-makers are facing tasks that are loosely structured (Leybourne and Sadler-Smith, 2006). Team intuition can be beneficial for rapidly solving problems in innovation. There is a strong reason to believe that development of intuition is not isomorphic at the individual and team level as team intuition involves drawing advice and experience from colleagues and making the individuals' implicit knowledge more available to the team. What is more, daily interactions help team members to develop shared experiences. Hence, due to repeated interactions, team intuition becomes homogeneous within the team and members are likely to be a part of the same processes, share experiences, and gather similar information (Hinsz et al., 1997). For example, Raab and Laborde (2011) investigated whether a preference for intuition results in faster and better choices in team handball attack situations. The results show that athletes who made intuitive decisions performed faster and better than those taking a more analytical approach.

We propose that team intuition emerges as a shared referent-shift consensus construct and can be measured using aggregated responses from multiple team members. It has been suggested that intuitive problem-solving may play a fundamental role in fostering creative ideas because of its holistic and associative thinking features (Dane et al., 2011). During the learning mode individuals will make their own perceptions more important than group perception. However, with time the team as a whole begins to integrate and think intuitively together. Therefore, individuals' perceptions of team-level intuition can be viewed as a mechanism through which team idea generation is influenced.

In contrast to the experiential system, the rational system is a system that operates according to a person's understanding of the rules of reasoning and of evidence. The rational system operates primarily at the conscious level, is relatively slow, affect-free, intentional and analytic (Epstein, 1990). Cacioppo and Petty (1982) defined the need for cognition (NFC) as the tendency to engage in thinking. Individuals high in NFC will more probably organize and assess the information to which they are exposed to, since they want to structure situations in meaningful ways (Cacioppo et al., 1983).

Individuals who achieve high levels of NFC often engage in situations with high risk that are complex and unusual to them (Cacioppo et al., 1996). As a consequence, they seek new information from their environment (Evans et al., 2003). They are therefore more likely to recognize problems, develop a strong and positive attitude toward them (Wu et al., 2014) and toward achieving their goal (Cacioppo et al., 1986).

Many types of teams learn and improve through time while working together. A football team, for example, gets better through the sheer act of practice without ever discussing how and what; the same holds true for a surgical team or a cockpit crew. Space crews have to undergo a diverse set of activities and should also show adequate responses to unforeseen situations, for example, system failures. Astronauts, who are part of the same crew, are highly educated individuals with complementary education. Human exploration of space requires astronauts to maintain consistently high levels of team cognitive performance to ensure mission safety and success, and prevent potential errors and accidents.

NFC is mostly researched at the individual level and less attention has been paid to team-level NFC. There are only a few studies that focus on team members' NFC (for example, Kearney et al., 2009). Our main assumption is that the team NFC can be conceptualized by using the summary index model (Chen et al., 2005) as there is no requirement for sharedness of experience or consensus, nor any required interdependence. In the summary index model, the team-level construct is defined as the mean of the individual characteristics and represents an average of the individuals' NFC regardless of the variance among these units. Also teams can be described as being comparatively high or low in NFC, therefore team NFC has important effects on types of tasks in which the team enjoys engaging in (Park et al., 2008). Team members' tendency to enjoy learning new ways to think and coming up with new solutions to problems may help to make the right decisions regarding innovations. We propose that team-level NFC will be positively associated with team innovative behavior.

The first phase of innovation, the generation (initiation) mode, is characterized by creative and intuitive thought, whereas the implementation is characterized by rational and stabilizing thought (Van de Ven, 1986; Glynn, 1996; Sadler-Smith, 1998). In the generation stage, ideas occur in

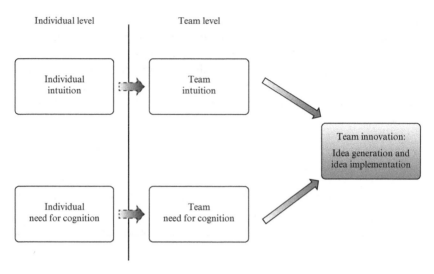

Figure 6.1   Intuition, need for cognition and team innovation

a non-evaluative context, whereas in the implementation stage alternatives need to be evaluated in order to decide which to proceed with (Paulus, 2002). Agrell and Gustafson (1996) argued that although innovation starts with individuals and their ideas, it is extremely important that the whole team accepts them, otherwise they can be discarded and hence team members have an essential role in the innovation process because of their diverse knowledge, expertise, and perspectives.

Based on the considerations above, we expect a positive relationship between individuals' perceptions of team intuition, team-level NFC and team innovation. Furthermore, the relationship will be stronger between individuals' perceptions of team intuition and team idea generation and team-level NFC and team idea implementation (Figure 6.1).

RESEARCH METHOD AND SUMMARY OF RESULTS

Complete data were obtained from 185 team members and 64 team leaders of R&D teams in four companies located in Germany and Slovenia, where average team size in the final sample was 3.28 (range = two to six members per team).

Individual perception of team intuition was measured using seven items adapted by Dayan and Elbanna's (2011) measurement scale. *Individual perception of team-level need for cognition* was measured using 18 items adapted from Cacioppo et al.'s (1996) measurement scale. We operational-ize *team innovation* as the combination of the quantity and quality of ideas that are developed and implemented and we measure it with Eisenbeiss et al.'s (2008) measurement scale. We controlled for team-aggregated values of members' gender, age, country of residence, level of education, tenure (years in the company).

We analyzed the data using multivariate hierarchical regression analysis. We first tested for positive relationship between individuals' perceptions of team intuition, need for cognition, and team innovation. Results indi-cate positive and statistically significant relationships between three vari-ables (see Table 6A.1 in the Appendix). Second, we tested whether team intuition more strongly relates to team idea generation and individuals' perceptions of team NFC more strongly relate to team idea implementa-tion. The effects of individuals' perception of intuition and NFC on team idea generation and on team idea implementation were positive and sta-tistically significant. However, according to results (see Table 6A.2 in the Appendix) team intuition more strongly relates to team idea generation than team NFC does and team NFC more strongly relates to team idea implementation than team intuition does.

DISCUSSION

In the competitive business environment innovation is increasingly desired as an employee's work outcome because industries are being transformed through fast-paced changes in technology. And the latter not only applies to young high-tech companies, but also to more traditional businesses. This brings to mind the anecdote of the 'boiling frog'. The idea is that if a frog is placed in boiling water, it will jump out, but if it is placed in cold water that is slowly heated, it won't perceive the danger and will be cooked to death. The story is used as a metaphor for the inability or unwilling-ness of people to react to significant changes that occur gradually. This is when the ability to be creative (generation of new ideas) and innovate (implementation of these ideas) becomes crucial to future success in any industry.

Our study highlights the importance of both individual and team contri-butions when managing team-level innovation. Specifically, it suggests that team innovation is impacted by teams' perceptions and/or individual per-sonalities. For example, think about a basketball team. Observe how each player is trained individually but they also continue practicing as a team. After a while, they will begin performing as a team too and joint ability becomes as great as the individual's. The individual player starts using his or her intuition (based on past experience) to predict the move and game of other players and rational decisions that were made prior to the game in order to outperform the opposing team. Our model can therefore help inform managers how to successfully employ and train individual team members and teams as a whole in order to achieve higher levels of team innovation. For employees to become better informed and more aware of intuition, organizations should create the conditions for employees' intuitive awareness to prosper so that they may make more effective and intelligent use of the intuitions they experience in their professional and personal lives (Sadler-Smith and Shefy, 2007).

The typical rational manager relies on 'hard' evidence from the past to conduct logical analyses and to make plans and predictions about the future (Sadler-Smith and Shefy, 2004). When the problems are structured, simple and routine, the necessary facts are often available and can be used. Rationality helps employees solve problems based upon knowledge that is explicit. However, intuition allows people to 'think outside the box' and make the association of new combinations of means and ends. Research by Dane et al. (2005) indicates that analytical decision-making is best suited to highly structured tasks, while intuitive decision-making is more effective when decision-makers are facing tasks that are poorly structured. Moreover, they may sometimes be required to act quickly and on limited data.

We found that both team intuition and NFC are positively related to team innovation. Furthermore, we compared the effects of rational versus intuitive problem-solving on different phases of team innovation. We argued that the relative effectiveness of these approaches depends upon an individual's typical thinking style such that individuals will be more innovative when they adopt a problem-solving approach that fits better with a certain phase of team innovation (for example, individuals who avoid rational thinking will exhibit higher idea generation and individuals who rely on rational thinking will exhibit higher success in idea implementation). According to our results, team intuition more strongly relates to team idea generation, whereas individuals' perceptions of team NFC more strongly relate to team idea implementation. Hence, organizations need to recruit intuitive and rational employees and provide a supportive environment where they have an opportunity to seek continuous improvement and search for innovative solutions. Both intuition and rationality have limits and each can sometimes lead to bad decisions (Dane and Pratt, 2007). Hence, it is far more productive to consider intuition and rationality as being at the heart of an important dynamic in team members' cognition (Sadler-Smith and Shefy, 2004) in which both have the potential to balance each other. As Arthur Fry, Co-creator of the Post-it note, once said: 'I back away from conscious thought and turn the problem over to my unconscious mind. It will scan a broader array of patterns and find some new close fits from other information stored in my brain'.

REFERENCES

Agrell, A. and R. Gustafson (1996), 'Innovation and creativity in work groups', in M.A. West (ed.), *Handbook of Work Group Psychology*, Chichester, UK: Wiley, pp. 314–43.

Amabile, T.M. (1993), 'Motivational synergy: Toward new conceptualizations of intrinsic and extrinsic motivation in the workplace', *Human Resource Management Review*, **3**(3), 185–201.

Anderson, N. and N. King (1991), 'Managing innovation in organizations', *Leadership and Organization Development Journal*, **12**(4), 17–21.

Anderson, N. and N. King (1993), 'Innovation in organizations', in C.L. Cooper and I.T. Robertson (eds), *International Review of Industrial and Organizational Psychology*, Chichester, UK: Wiley, pp. 1–34.

Cacioppo, J.T. and R.E. Petty (1982), 'The need for cognition', *Journal of Personality and Social Psychology*, **42**(1), 116–31.

Cacioppo, J.T., R.E. Petty and K. Morris (1983), 'Effects of need for cognition on message evaluation, recall, and persuasion', *Journal of Personality and Social Psychology*, **45**(4), 805–18.

Cacioppo, J.T., R.E. Petty, J.A. Feinstein and W.B.G. Jarvis (1996), 'Dispositional differences in cognitive motivation: The life and times of individuals varying in need for cognition', *Psychological Bulletin*, **119**(2), 197–253.

Cacioppo, J.T., R.E. Petty, C.F. Kao and R. Rodriguez (1986), 'Central and peripheral routes to persuasion: An individual difference perspective', *Journal of Personality and Social Psychology*, **51**(5), 1032–43.

Chen, G., J.E. Mathieu and P.D. Bliese (2005), 'A framework for conducting multi-level construct validation', in F.J. Yammarino and F. Dansereau (eds), *Multilevel Issues in Organizational Behaviour and Process*, Amsterdam: Elsevier, pp. 273–303.

Dane, E. and M.G. Pratt (2007), 'Exploring intuition and its role in managerial decision making', *The Academy of Management Review*, **32**(1), 33–54.

Dane, E., K. Rockmann and M.G. Pratt (2005), 'Should I trust my gut? The role of task characteristics in intuitive and analytical decision-making', paper at the 2005 Academy of Management Annual Meeting, Honolulu.

Dane, E., M. Baer, M.G. Pratt and G.R. Oldham (2011), 'Rational versus intuitive problem-solving: How thinking "off the beaten path" can stimulate creativity', *Psychology of Aesthetics, Creativity, and the Arts*, **5**(1), 3–12.

Dayan, M. and S. Elbanna (2011), 'Antecedents of team intuition and its impact on the success of new product development projects', *Journal of Product Innovation Management*, **28**(S1), 159–74.

Eisenbeiss, S.A., D. Van Knippenberg and S. Boerner (2008), 'Transformational leadership and team innovation: Integrating team climate principles', *Journal of Applied Psychology*, **93**(6), 1438–46.

Epstein, S. (1990), 'Cognitive-experiential self-theory', in L. Pervin (ed.), *Handbook of Personality Theory and Research*, New York: Guilford Press, pp. 165–92.

Epstein, S. (1994), 'Integration of the cognitive and the psychodynamic unconscious', *American Psychologist*, **49**(8), 709–24.

Epstein, S. (2008), 'Intuition from the perspective of cognitive-experiential self-theory', in T. Betsch (ed.), *Intuition in Judgment and Decision Making*, Oxford, UK: Psychology Press, pp. 23–38.

Evans, C.J., J.R. Kirby and L.T. Fabrigar (2003), 'Approaches to learning, need for cognition, and strategic flexibility among university students', *British Journal of Educational Psychology*, **73**(4), 507–28.

Glynn, M.A. (1996), 'Innovative genius: A framework for relating individual and organisational intelligences', *Academy of Management Review*, **21**(4), 1081–111.

Hinsz, V.B., R.S. Tindale and D.A. Vollrath (1997), 'The emerging conceptualization of groups as information processors', *Psychological Bulletin*, **121**(1), 43–64.

Isenberg, D.J. (1984), 'How senior managers think', *Harvard Business Review*, **62**(6), 81–90.

Kahneman, D. (2003), 'A perspective on judgment and choice: Mapping bounded rationality', *American Psychologist*, **58**(9), 697–720.

Kahneman, D. and S. Frederick (2002), 'Representativeness revisited: Attribute substitution in intuitive judgment', in T. Gilovich, D. Griffin and D. Kahneman (eds), *Heuristics of Intuitive Judgment: The Psychology of Intuitive Judgment*, New York: Cambridge University Press, pp. 49–81.

Kearney, E., D. Gebert and S.C. Voelpel (2009), 'When and how diversity benefits teams: The importance of team members' need for cognition', *Academy of Management Journal*, **51**(3), 581–98.

Kvasnytaska, M. (2013), 'Left–right brain Magento theory', *Magento Store Manager Blog*, 14 August 2013, accessed 24 March 2015 at http://blog.mag-manager.com/2013/08/left-right-brain-magento-theory.html.

Leybourne, S. and E. Sadler-Smith (2006), 'The role of intuition and improvisation in project management', *International Journal of Project Management*, **24**(6), 483–92.

Pacini, R. and S. Epstein (1999), 'The relation of rational and experiential information processing styles to personality, basic beliefs, and the ratio-bias phenomenon', *Journal of Personality and Social Psychology*, **76**(6), 972–87.

Park, H.S., C. Baker and D.W. Lee (2008), 'Need for cognition, task complexity, and job satisfaction', *Journal of Management in Engineering*, **24**(2), 111–30.

Paulus, P.B. (2002), 'Different ponds for different fish: A contrasting perspective on team innovation', *Applied Psychology: An International Review*, **51**(3), 395–400.

Raab, M. and S. Laborde (2011), 'When to blink and when to think: Preference for intuitive decisions results in faster and better tactical choices', *Research Quarterly for Exercise and Sport*, **82**(1), 89–98.

Rogers, E.M. and F.F. Shoemaker (1971), *Communication of Innovations: A Cross-cultural Approach*, New York: The Free Press.

Rusou, Z., D. Zakay and M. Usher (2013), 'Pitting intuitive and analytical thinking against each other: The case of transitivity', *Psychonomic Bulletin and Review*, **20**(3), 608–14.

Sadler-Smith, E. (1998), 'Cognitive style: Some human resource implications for managers', *The International Journal of Human Resource Management*, **9**(1), 185–202.

Sadler-Smith, E. and E. Shefy (2004), 'Developing intuition: Becoming smarter by thinking less', *Academy of Management Conference Proceedings*, August.

Sadler-Smith, E. and E. Shefy (2007), 'Developing intuitive awareness in management education', *Academy of Management Learning and Education*, **6**(2), 186–205.

Sinclair, M. and N.M. Ashkanasy (2005), 'Intuition: Myth or decision making tool?' *Management Learning*, **36**(3), 353–70.

Sloman, S.A. (2002), 'Two systems of reasoning', in T. Gilovich, D. Griffin and D. Kahneman (eds), *Heuristics and Biases: The Psychology of Intuitive Judgment*, New York: Cambridge University Press, pp. 379–96.

Van de Ven, A.H. (1986), 'Central problems in the management of innovation', *Management Science*, **32**(5), 590–607.

West, M.A. (2002), 'Sparkling fountains or stagnant ponds: An integrative model of creativity and innovation implementation in work groups', *Applied Psychology: An International Review*, **51**(3), 355–87.

Wu, C.-H., S.K. Parker and J.P.J. de Jong (2014), 'Need for cognition as an antecedent of individual innovation behavior', *Journal of Management*, **40**(6), 1511–34.

APPENDIX

Table 6A.1 Descriptive statistics and inter-item correlation matrix

	Mean	St. Dev.	Reliabilities (Cronbach Alpha)	1.	2.	3.	4.	5.	6.	7.	8.	9.	10.	11.
1. Gender	1.85	0.35	n.a.	1										
2. Country	1.43	0.50	n.a.	0.23**	1									
3. Age	2.01	0.63	n.a.	00.01	0.42**	1								
4. Education	4.17	0.75	n.a.	00.14	0.59**	0.24**	1							
5. Tenure	3.15	1.06	n.a.	−00.01	0.44**	0.65**	0.18*	1						
6. Team size	3.28	1.20	n.a.	00.02	0.44**	0.25**	0.15*	0.26**	1					
7. Team intuition	3.28	0.73	0.92	00.01	0.35**	00.05	00.13	0.21**	0.15*	1				
8. Team NFC	3.77	0.72	0.93	00.04	0.15*	−00.11	−00.07	−00.09	00.01	0.67**	1			
9. Team innovation	4.25	0.97	0.96	00.04	00.02	−00.11	−00.02	−00.08	00.06	0.60**	0.65**	1		
10. Team idea generation	3.99	1.01	0.92	00.09	00.12	−00.01	−00.01	00.04	0.17*	0.59**	0.57**	0.93**	1	
11. Team idea implementation	4.51	1.06	0.93	−00.02	−00.09	−0.19**	−00.03	−0.18*	−00.06	0.53**	0.64**	0.93**	0.75**	1

Notes: N = 185; *correlation is significant at the $p < 0.05$ level, **correlation is significant at the $p < 0.01$ level.

Table 6A.2   *Results of multivariate hierarchical regression analysis*

		Team Idea Generation is the Dependent Variable		Team Idea Implementation is the Dependent Variable	
		Model 1	Model 2	Model 1	Model 2
1.1.1.1.1	1. Gender	0.19 (0.22)	00.33 (0.17)	−0.07 (0.23)	0.06 (0.16)
1.1.1.1.2	2. Country	0.27 (0.23)	−00.44* (0.19)	0.24 (0.24)	−0.79 (0.18)
1.1.1.1.3	3. Age	−0.16 (0.16)	00.06 (0.12)	−0.24 (0.17)	−0.01** (0.12)
1.1.1.1.4	4. Education	−0.13 (0.13)	00.05 (0.10)	0.03 (0.13)	0.27 (0.10)
1.1.1.1.5	5. Tenure	0.03 (0.09)	00.02 (0.08)	−0.09 (0.10)	−0.09* (0.08)
1.1.1.1.6	6. Team size	0.12 (0.07)	00.16* (0.05)	0.01 (0.07)	0.04 (0.05)
1.1.1.1.7	7. Team intuition		00.57** (0.12)		0.47** (0.11)
1.1.1.1.8	8. Team NFC		00.47** (0.12)		0.71** (0.11)

Notes: N = 185; values are standardized coefficients, with standard errors in parentheses. *correlation is significant at the *p* < 0.05 level, **correlation is significant at the *p* < 0.01 level.

7. Fueling, curating, connecting and fascinating: why and how creativity provokes curiosity

Spencer Harrison

Why generate mystery when a creative idea is fully mature and ready to be implemented? Why does Apple generally rely on stealth development, tight security, and secrecy prior to any product launch (indeed, Apple sells a t-shirt that reads 'I VISITED THE APPLE CAMPUS. BUT THAT'S ALL I'M ALLOWED TO SAY')? Why did Nine Inch Nails, the rock band, hide thumb drives loaded with new songs in a stadium where they are performing a concert (Wikipedia, 2015)? Why did the director of the film *Cloverfield* release a teaser trailer for the film that did not provide the name of the film, a plot, or even much of a sense of the genre (Wikipedia, 2015b)? The common theme across these disparate examples is the generation of mystery, the slow, controlled reveal of secrets, inviting customers to solve a puzzle. Put simply, they point to the importance of curiosity in unveiling a creative product.

The common assumption is that curiosity is an important precursor to creativity. Curiosity can be defined as the desire for new information that catalyzes exploration (Litman, 2005). Because curious individuals are more likely to encounter new information and because creativity is the generation of novel (read: new) and useful ideas, researchers have often assumed that curiosity sparks creativity. As an aside, it is worth noting that there is limited direct empirical evidence of curiosity as an antecedent to creativity and future research could do far more to establish this link rather than relying on the broader literature on intrinsic motivation as a an empirical catch-all. This chapter takes the relationship between curiosity and creativity and turns it on its head. In this chapter, I tackle a reversal of the relationship between curiosity and creativity by asking: '*Why* and *how* might creativity spark curiosity?'

In tackling this question, I reveal that curiosity plays a role as a sort of 'through-line' or motivational backbone that goes beyond the generation of an idea and strongly influences how others adopt and disperse a new creative product. That is, curiosity is not just important for catalyzing creativity; curiosity is also critical for transforming a creative product from an uncertain, risky notion to a viral, popular product. As a preview, to answer the 'why?' portion of the question, I suggest that curiosity is an important outcome of creativity because it taps into the personalities and ultimately the identities of the individuals that are most likely to be the early adopters of the creative product. Individuals with a curious identity, like any other identity, are drawn to symbols that signify who they are. As a result, in aggregate, curious individuals become a sort of living, collective 'curiosity cabinet': their identities and their drive to adopt new identity symbols serve as signals of what is new and interesting in the world. Capturing the attention of these individuals is critical for the success of a creative endeavor because they serve as gatekeepers and broadcasters of new ideas. I then turn to the 'how?' portion of the question and propose that curiosity encourages interest, generates contagion, and induces collaboration. These activities provide a network of dispersion that helps creativity make the transition from radical to excitingly acceptable, from discontinuous to developmental, from ingenious yet inaccessible to easily implementable. I conclude with observations about how research should further attend to the relationship between curiosity and creativity and a summary of practical implications that emerge from these insights.

WHY MIGHT CREATIVITY SPARK CURIOSITY?

Imagine sixteenth-century Europe. Although this time period might seem far removed from the modern world, it shares the contemporary dynamic of the increasing movement of information, the willingness to cross boundaries. State and national boundaries were being crossed via travel, and boundaries in types of knowledge – science, religion, art, and so on – were being crossed as well. And so this time period evokes many of the dynamics of our own time. In a popular essay on 'The American Condition' Richard Goodwin envisions the result of all this movement by describing a summer scene in Florence, Italy:

> Now at Florence, when the air is red with the summer sunset and the campaniles begin to sound vespers and the day's work is done, everyone collects in the piazzas. The steps of Santa Maria del Fiore swarm with men of every rank and every class. . . a thousand minds, a thousand arguments; a lively intermingling of questions, problems, news of the latest happening, jokes; an inexhaustible play of language and thought, a vibrant curiosity. (Cited in Oldenburg, 1989, p. 27)

Evidence of this curiosity and explosion of knowledge was made material by the travelers who collected artifacts during their journeys abroad:
objects that to them seemed rare, strange, or odd. Travelers showcased
these 'curios' in *Wunderkammer* – curiosity cabinets. These collections generated a great deal of interest because they allowed individuals a visceral
experience with novelty: they could see, touch, and discuss or try to make
sense of something they had never seen before. Curiosity cabinets also
served as the predecessor for the modern museum. In those early days, as
curators attempted to define the curios they found to an interested public,
the story of acquiring the object was often the best way of explaining the
curio. As Margocsy explains:

> [W]ritten and human museum guides spiced up their tours by telling hair-
> raising, curious stories about certain specimens, or waxed lyrically about their
> potential to reform the national economy. Such anecdotal information was
> helpful because they made sense of otherwise baffling specimens, and also
> increased their worth, and, as a result, many museum curators made a special
> effort to collect these stories. (Margocsy, 2013, p. 391)

It is worth highlighting that these stories not only helped to define the
object but it also increased the value – a theme I will revisit shortly.

If the above is true, and modern society bears some similarity to the age of
the Renaissance, it bears asking, where are our modern curiosity cabinets?
The answer: everywhere! Twitter, Facebook, Instagram, Pinterest – much
of social media is constructed in a way to relay information about the odd,
unusual, and new. Indeed, the instinct to share novelty via the Internet is so
engrained that early Earthlink, an early Internet provider, once published
a 'curiosity manifesto' (EarthLink, 2000), hackers see themselves as driven
to open the Internet by their 'curiosity' (Jordan and Taylor, 1998), and
YouTube has been described as a modern *Wunderkammer* (Gehl, 2009).
The result is that consumers have access to the largest curiosity cabinet
ever assembled in the form of digital media, particularly the Internet, but
also other venues like television and print media.

Innovative companies know this. Rather than seeing themselves as care-
takers of a portfolio of products, innovative companies see themselves as
curators of curios. Hence, their goal is not just to use curiosity as fuel for
generating creative products; they also want to curate these products in
a way that allows them to connect to potential consumers. Consider this
anthropological description of following a museum curator setting up a
new exhibit:

> Curators. . . [are] involved in the manipulation of practical circumstances in the
> various situations of art installation. They are constantly providing accounts of

the installation process, thus producing their own 'indigenous' rules in situation and their own attitudes to objects. Thus, by following the [curators] and their 'management devices' for mastering the practical circumstances, for thinking about, discussing and calculating an object's transformations, you will see their specific ways of making the transformation of an ordinary object into artwork. (Yaneva, 2003, p. 124)

This modern description of museum curators aligns nicely with the earlier description of museum guides with curiosity cabinets: individuals in these roles maintain interest by telling the story of finding the object. This is exactly what happens when automakers release concept cars, when technology firms 'leak' prototypes of devices, and when companies tease new products with surprising or mysterious advertising campaigns. By releasing bits of the narrative around the design and generation of these products, these curators of new products are highlighting the 'novelty' in the 'novel and useful' definition of creativity. They are introducing a narrative that makes the new newer and more interesting.

Such narratives are critical because they provide potential consumers with the raw material for them to engage in identity work. To explain the need for identity work, let me step back and explain a bit more about consumers of highly creative products. Potentially creative products tend to attract a very specific type of consumer: early adopters. Research on the lifecycles of innovative products and the diffusion of new ideas shows that early adopters often act as gatekeepers to mainstream success. Research on the personalities of early adopters and opinion leaders strongly suggests that they see themselves as motivated by an innate interest or curiosity about the things they buy (Dickerson and Gentry, 1983; Chan and Misra, 1990; Mahajan et al., 1990; Fisher and Price, 1992; Ram and Jung, 1994; Chau and Hui, 1998; Goldsmith et al., 2003). Because personalities and identities are self-constituting – one informs the other – it is likely this curiosity and search for newness is strongly bound to a sense of self. Hall (1996) has described individuals with identities that constantly seek novelty and change as 'protean identities': what is stable about the identity is the search for change, the need to continually construct a personal narrative that epitomizes a curiosity for newness.

Jay Rounds's anthropological research on museum visitors helps to illustrate why early adopters – individuals likely to have strongly protean identities – search for new objects and how this search informs their sense of self. He writes:

They absorb the orderliness of the museum environment without feeling obligated to plumb the depths of the systems of order presented. They take advantage of the heightened intensity of the environment to enact identities, through performances in which the exhibit's explicit contents are a supporting cast, rather than a protagonist. And they sample a wide variety of experiences, learning only a little of each, as a kind of cognitive hedge fund to build their capacity for rapid adaptation in an unforeseeable future. The exhibit, and all it has to show and tell, are used as tools for identity construction, maintenance and exploration. (Rounds, 2006, p. 148)

In the same way as individuals exploring a museum, for early adopters, a new creative product is not important so much for what it does, but for what it signals about the consumers' identities. Creative products provide early adopters with material objects that symbolize their identities but the symbolism is not innate in the product itself; it is woven into the narrative that is tied to the product. Hence, creativity sparks curiosity when new products are curated in a way that provides potential early adopters with product narratives that allow consumers to validate and enact their own curiosity, and thereby, their own identities.

HOW MIGHT CREATIVITY SPARK CURIOSITY?

Continuing with the museum metaphor, when people leave museums they leave with new stories to tell. Again, Rounds explains: 'the curiosity-driven museum visitor. . . seeks to maximize the "Total Interest Value" of her visit, rather than maximizing mastery of a domain of knowledge' (2006, pp. 134–5). Early adopters are the same: they now have a product, but more importantly, they have narratives that maximize interest or curiosity. This is incredibly important for the potential success of a new product. One of the reasons is that stories that spark interest are more memorable and more enjoyable.

Brewer's work (Brewer and Lichtenstein, 1982; Brewer, 1996) on the impact of the structure of narrative on reader's enjoyment is informative in this regard. Brewer suggests that stories that are structured to induce curiosity generate a strong, positive emotional response, lead to more reader enjoyment, and are more identifiable as stories (as opposed to lists of events or bare description) (see also Oatley, 1994; Hoeken and Van Vliet, 2000; Knobloch et al., 2004). Specifically, a curiosity structure for a narrative is one that begins with a significant fact, for example, 'a bomb under a table exploded killing three men' (Brewer, 1996, p. 112), which begs for further explanation. What caused the event? Why did it happen? For example, Brewer and Ohtsuka (1988) analyzed readers' reactions as they read the famous short story 'The Lottery' by Shirley Jackson. This story features a town meeting with a mysterious drawing for a lottery and ends when the reader discovers that the 'winner' of the lottery is stoned to death by the other town members. The researchers found that the mystery of the story made readers extremely curious and that this peak in curiosity predicted 'liking' the story.

While there are differences between buying a new, creative product before it is widely known and a carefully crafted short story, the similarities are what are important here. First, early adopters often initiate a curiosity narrative because they tend to prominently display new products they have acquired (Baumgarten, 1975; Nisbet and Kotcher, 2009). This causes individuals in their social network to wonder and ask, 'Why did you buy that? What is it? What does it do?' In effect, displaying the product initiates a curiosity narrative. If the firm producing the product has curated it appropriately by providing a discovery narrative that explains the generation of the product then the early adopter has a ready-made explanation for what the product is. However, this explanation is made more powerful because the early adopter has already integrated aspects of this narrative into their identity. So, in providing answers about the product, the early adopter is inherently personalizing the answers, making the description of the product more intimate and personal.

The passing of information about new products in this way is important not only because narratives that induce curiosity are better liked, but also they are more memorable, and perhaps more importantly, they seem to be contagious. For example, in a study of automotive engineering (Terwiesch et al., 2002), the curiosity of the researchers made the leaders of the auto company curious. Similarly, research on Hollywood pitch meetings shows that successful pitches often occur when the writer's curiosity generates curiosity in the executives (Elsbach and Kramer, 2003). The result is that the early adopter's curiosity is transmitted through their network to others, making them curious about the new product. In thinking about the sort of viral nature of the spread of new products in this way, it is helpful to consider that, to some degree, every identity is protean. While, individuals with strongly protean identities are more likely to be early adopters, individuals with weaker protean orientation look to them to understand what is safe and what identity changes might be needed in the future. They follow once things seem safe. So the curiosity narratives that early adopters transmit serve as an impetus for others to engage in their own identity work.

CONCLUSION

This chapter examined research on creativity and the implementation, or in this case, the acceptance by consumers of new creative products by exploring the role of curiosity. While acknowledging that curiosity fuels

1. Fueling: Catalyzing creativity with curiosity

2. Curating: Enhancing a creative product with a discovery narrative

3. Connecting: Helping individuals tie a creative product to identity

4. Fascinating: Enabling contagion by sharing creative product as an identity symbol

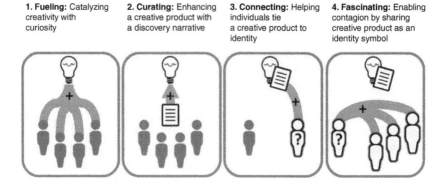

Figure 7.1   Curiosity in creativity: fueling, curating, connecting and fascinating

creative work, I have argued that perhaps the more beneficial outcome of curiosity is not in generating the raw creative idea. Instead, curiosity provides a narrative that allows organizations to curate their products, binding the product to a discovery narrative. This narrative then provides an opportunity for early adopters to connect with the product with regard to identity work. Once connected with the creative product, these early adopters then fascinate individuals in their networks by sharing now personalized narratives that induce curiosity in others, creating a cascade of contagion and paving the way for greater market entry of the new product. I have summarized this process of fueling creative work, curating new products by fusing them with a narrative, connecting early adopters via identity work, and fascinating other potential consumers with curiosity narratives in Figure 7.1.

One of the important implications in the figure is highlighted by the use of 'plus signs' in each stage of the process. Whether it is associating ideas between creative workers, bonding a narrative to a product, relating a product with an individual, or joining the individual with others, curiosity serves not just as an individual motivation, but as a connective tissue that not only catalyzes creative thought but carries creativity through from a nascent idea to a widely accepted product. Hence, curiosity is about much more than individual motivation, it is a social resource, a crucial mechanism for connecting individuals interested in pushing the boundaries of what is known.

Many of the ideas presented here are widely accepted. The literature on innovation lifecycles, the diffusion of innovation, and early adopters, taste-makers, and opinion leaders have all suggested that some individuals are more likely to collect new products and that their habits have a large impact on the purchasing decisions of others. However, by suggesting curiosity as a through-line in this process, I have revealed several connections that have been largely ignored and that promise important theoretical and practical implications. One very obvious theoretical implication is that by looking at curiosity as both fuel for creativity and as fodder for narratives that help to 'sell' creative products, the model presented here helps to link the literature on creativity and innovation. Researchers have long lamented the theoretical disconnect between these two literatures whilst the two words – creativity and innovation – are largely seen as synonyms outside of academia. Following curiosity as a motivation during the generation of the idea and as a narrative residue that remains with the product during implementation provides a new way of connecting the literature.

Perhaps a more important contribution provided here, in terms of both theory and practice, is highlighting the narrative deficit that creativity, especially the 'novelty' intrinsic in creativity, creates. That is, how do you describe something new? If it is really new, then are there words, metaphors, or stories that can adequately communicate what the new thing is and why it exists? This suggests that for both creative workers and potential consumers, there is a significant challenge in making sense of what a potential creative product might be and, more importantly, what it means. What I have suggested in this chapter is that rather than describing the product itself, it may be more important to describe the process that leads to discovering the product. Moreover, I have suggested that this discovery narrative needs to become connected to the product itself so as to provide early adopters with the necessary raw material to help them integrate the product into their protean identity. This suggests that there is a significant opportunity to better understand the narrative and identity implication of creativity – how these narratives are constructed, what audiences they serve, and how they reflect the creative process. Future work could even begin to consider how these narratives might also have certain costs, especially considering how these narratives might constrain future creativity.

In sum, curiosity and creativity are inherently linked, and yet, curiously, little research has critically examined the nature of these linkages. Given the considerable practical benefits of understanding the link between curiosity and creativity, more work needs to be done in this area. As I have suggested here, some of the relationships between curiosity and creativity are likely different than we assume and it is possible if not likely, that curiosity plays a bigger role in the implementation and acceptance of a creative product than in the generation of the product in the first place.

REFERENCES

Baumgarten, S.A. (1975), 'The innovative communicator in the diffusion process', *Journal of Marketing Research*, **12**(1), 12–18.

Brewer, W.F. (1996), 'The nature of narrative suspense and the problem of rereading', in P. Vorderer, H.J. Wulff and M. Friedrichsen (eds), *Suspense: Conceptualizations, Theoretical Analyses, and Empirical Explorations*, Mahwah, NJ: Lawrence Erlbaum Associates, pp. 107–28.

Brewer, W.F. and E.H. Lichtenstein (1982), 'Stories are to entertain: A structural-affect theory of stories', *Journal of Pragmatics*, **6**(2), 473–83.

Brewer, W.F. and K. Ohtsuka (1988), 'Story structure, characterization, just world organization, and reader affect in American and Hungarian short stories', *Poetics*, **17**(4–5), 395–415.

Chan, K.K. and S. Misra (1990), 'Characteristics of the opinion leader: A new dimension', *Journal of Advertising*, **19**(3), 53–60.

Chau, P.Y.K. and K.L. Hui (1998), 'Identifying early adopters of new IT products: A case of Windows 95', *Information and Management*, **33**(5), 225–30.

Dickerson, M.D. and J.W. Gentry (1983), 'Characteristics of adopters and non-adopters of home computers', *The Journal of Consumer Research*, **10**(2), 225–35.

EarthLink (2000), 'Mission & values', *Earthlink*, accessed 2 December 2015 at http://www.earthlink.net/about/corp/values.faces.

Elsbach, K.D. and R.M. Kramer (2003), 'Assessing creativity in Hollywood pitch meetings: Evidence for a dual-process model of creativity judgments', *Academy of Management Journal*, **46**(3), 283–301.

Fisher, R.J. and L. Price (1992), 'An investigation into the social context of early adoption behavior', *Journal of Consumer Research*, **19**(3), 477–87.

Gehl, R. (2009), 'YouTube as archive: Who will curate this digital Wunderkammer?' *International Journal of Cultural Studies*, **12**(1), 43–60.

Goldsmith, R., L. Flynn and E.B. Goldsmith (2003), 'Innovative consumer and market mavens', *Journal of Marketing Theory and Practice*, **11**(4), 54–64.

Hall, D.T. (1996), 'Protean careers of the 21st century', *Academy of Management Executive*, **10**(4), 8–16.

Hoeken, H. and M. van Vliet (2000), 'Suspense, curiosity, and surprise: How discourse structure influences the affective and cognitive processing of a story', *Poetics*, **26**(4), 277–86.

Jordan, T. and P. Taylor (1998), 'A sociology of hackers', *The Sociological Review*, **46**(4), 757–80.

Knobloch, S., G. Patzig, A. Mende and M. Hastall (2004), 'Affective news: Effects of discourse structure in narratives on suspense, curiosity, and enjoyment while reading news and novels', *Communication Research*, **31**(3), 259–87.

Litman, J.A. (2005), 'Curiosity and the pleasures of learning: Wanting and liking new information', *Cognition and Emotion*, **19**(1), 793–814.

Mahajan, V., E. Muller and R. Srivastava (1990), 'Determination of adopter categories by using innovation diffusion models', *Journal of Marketing Research*, **27**(1), 37–50.

Margocsy, D. (2013), 'The fuzzy metrics of money: The finances of travel and the reception of curiosities in early modern Europe', *Annals of Science*, **70**(3), 381–404.

Nisbet, M.C. and J.E. Kotcher (2009), 'A two-step flow of influence? Opinion-leader campaigns on climate change', *Science Communication*, **30**(3), 328–54.

Oatley, K. (1994), 'A taxonomy of the emotions of literary response and a theory of identification in fictional narrative', *Poetics*, **23**(1), 53–74.

Oldenburg, R. (1989), *The Great Good Place: Cafes, Coffee Shops, Community Centers, Beauty Parlors, General Stores, Bars, Hangouts and How They Get You Through the Day*, New York: Marlowe and Company.

Ram, S. and H. Jung (1994), 'Innovativeness in product usage: A comparison of early adopters and early majority', *Psychology and Marketing*, **11**(1), 57–67.

Rounds, J. (2006), 'Doing identity work in museums', *Curator*, **49**(2), 133–50.

Terwiesch, C., C.H. Loch and A. de Meyer (2002), 'Exchanging preliminary information in concurrent engineering: Alternative coordination strategies', *Organization Science*, **13**(4), 402–19.

Wikipedia (2015a), 'Cloverfield', accessed 29 November 2015 at http://en.wikipedia.org/wiki/Cloverfield.

Wikipedia (2015b), 'Year Zero (album)', accessed 29 November 2015 at http://en.wikipedia.org/wiki/Year_Zero_(album).

Yaneva, A. (2003), 'When a bus met a museum: Following artists, curators and workers in art installation', *Museum and Society*, **1**(3), 116–31.

8. Social-contextual forces and innovative work: a motivational climate perspective

Christina G.L. Nerstad

INTRODUCTION

There has been a common belief that individual creativity and innovation are primarily dependent on talent. However, the role of talent might have been overestimated, as research evidence has shown that hard work and intrinsic motivation, or doing an activity for the pleasure it gives in itself, are at least as important for creative success (Amabile, 2001). The social environment also plays a significant role in supporting or undermining creativity and the implementation of creative ideas (Andersen et al., 2014). Therefore, creativity and innovation researchers have more recently adopted an interactional approach, in which both personal and situational factors contribute to the innovation process, which consists of creative idea generation and implementation. Situational factors, such as the organizational context, are important because they shape the meaning and salience of organizational events for employees (Kuenzi and Schminke, 2009). Work environments are suggested to have an influence on the innovation process by affecting mechanisms that contribute to creative idea generation and the implementation of these ideas (for example, Andersen et al., 2014). The work climate is considered to be just such an essential factor that influences individuals' generation of creative ideas and the effective implementation of them at work (Hammond et al., 2011).

The purpose of this chapter is to emphasize the relevance of the perceived motivational climate, as defined by achievement goal theory (AGT; for example, Nicholls, 1989; Ames, 1992b), and how it may influence the curvilinear relationship between frequent idea generation and implementation at work. According to AGT, the motivational climate refers to employees' perceptions of the extant criteria of success and failure in the work context. There are two sub-climates that represent the motivational climate. A mastery climate rewards and emphasizes the value of learning, development, effort, and cooperation. A performance climate, rather, rewards and stresses the value of normative ability and a demonstration of competence. Empirical evidence has shown that a mastery climate is typically associated with adaptive outcomes (for example, higher work performance), while a performance climate is typically associated with maladaptive outcomes (for example, turnover intentions) (Nerstad et al., 2013).

In the following, I will argue that these climates are relevant for the understanding of why idea implementation in certain circumstances may fail or succeed. Mastery and performance climates are particularly relevant to the innovation process because they reflect different value orientations. These result in different ways of attending to and processing various meanings attached to failure and success, performance information, and diverse action strategies (Ames and Ames, 1984a).

Previous research has shown that social contextual aspects conveying control (for example, external evaluation) typically are detrimental to both intrinsic motivation and creativity (Amabile and Pillemer, 2012). A performance climate is an example of such a contextual force. On the other hand, factors that support individuals' autonomy, learning, skill development, and task engagement can, rather, enhance intrinsic motivation and creativity (Amabile, 2001). A mastery climate represents such a contextual structure. However, a single focus on one motivational climate dimension may conflict with practical organizational realities; therefore, the two motivational climates are likely to coexist (DeShon and Gillespie, 2005). An interesting question is, therefore, how do mastery and performance climates interplay to affect the innovation process?

The intended contribution of this chapter is to the micro-innovation literature by describing the joint role of mastery and performance climates regarding hindering or enhancing innovative behavior. Creativity is a complex phenomenon that is subject to numerous individual, social, and contextual influences (Agars et al., 2008). The theoretical lens of AGT is particularly relevant because idea work is a core of the business process of many organizations (Carlsen et al., 2012), where success and failure in idea realization is pertinent. Given the focus on criteria of success and failure and its relevance for achievement behavior at work, mastery and performance climates may have a significant influence on innovative behavior.

THE PERCEIVED MOTIVATIONAL CLIMATE

According to AGT, achievement behavior concerns a goal of being, or appearing to be, competent rather than incompetent (Nicholls, 1984). The goal–reward structure put forth by AGT, which is also conceptualized as the motivational climate, plays an important role with respect to this because it elicits achievement cues to employees. Their interpretation of these cues may affect or even direct their behavior (cf., Roberts, 2012). The motivational climate is defined as employees' individual and/or shared perceptions of the extant criteria of success and failure that is accentuated through the practices, policies, and procedures of the work achievement context (Nerstad et al., 2013). Although many characteristics of the work climate exist that may influence employees' motivation and achievement behavior at work, the motivational climate, as defined by AGT, delineates the goals that employees are to achieve, how employees are to relate to tasks and each other, and how employees are to be evaluated (Ames and Ames, 1984b).

The motivational climate is multi-dimensional and comprises two different goal–reward structures: a mastery climate and a performance climate. A mastery climate is evident when the extant criteria of success and failure are task involving, self-referenced, and when the individual perceives that the demonstration of learning, mastery, and cooperation are valued.

On the other hand, a performance climate is evident when the extant criteria of success and failure are ego involving, other referenced, and when individuals perceive that the demonstration of normative competence is valued and rewarded (Ames, 1992a). Accordingly, mastery and performance climates represent different value systems. One is focused on values that enhance individual growth, learning, and cooperation, while the other is focused on values enhancing egoistic motivation in which normative comparison information is important.

THE INTERDEPENDENCY OF MASTERY AND PERFORMANCE CLIMATES

In the AGT literature, it is commonly argued that mastery criteria are beneficial in facilitating individual growth, which most likely will enhance performance (for example, DeShon and Gillespie, 2005). Such a perspective may conflict with organizational realities where employees are required to focus on end results and performance instead of learning, growth, and exploring tasks (Poortvliet and Darnon, 2010). Consequently, mastery and performance climates are likely to be interdependent (Ames, 1992b). This means that the work-task structure may be mastery involving (for example, through a focus on sharing ideas, cooperation, and discussion to generate ideas), while the evaluation structure may be performance involving (for example, public recognition and/or rewards according to how many creative ideas are implemented). The mastery and performance climate interdependency at work is salient when, for example, a leader is very effective in designing tasks that are meaningful, offer variety, and are appropriately challenging to employees. The same leader might also use evaluation practices that encourage intra-team competitions and social comparison (for example, public recognition or rewarding the best performers with incentives). Ommundsen and Roberts (1999) conducted a study among athletes in which they investigated mastery and performance climate profiles, achievement, and socially related cognitions. Their findings indicated that a high-mastery climate moderates the influence of being in a high-performance climate, where perceiving a performance climate may not be motivationally maladaptive when accompanied by a mastery climate. This finding led them to conclude that 'introducing mastery oriented criteria *in addition* to the extant performance oriented criteria seems to be a desirable motivational strategy to follow' (Ommundsen and Roberts, 1999, p. 396; original emphasis). How may this be relevant for innovation behavior at work?

THE MOTIVATIONAL CLIMATE AND THE CREATIVITY–INNOVATION PROCESS

Creativity and innovation refer to a process, outcomes, and products of attempts to develop and introduce novel ways of doing things (Andersen et al., 2014). Creativity represents the first stage of this process, namely, idea generation and development. Innovation represents the following stage of idea implementation. For organizations to innovate, it is necessary to adopt contrasting climates as they move from the initiation to the implementation stages of innovation (Zampetakis et al., 2014).

In the following section, I will discuss how mastery and performance climates may interact with the frequency of idea generation in predicting idea implementation. Consistent with a study that my colleagues and I recently conducted on this issue (Škerlavaj et al., 2014), I will present four different scenarios.

Scenario One

In our study we expected that the multiplicative combination of low levels of idea generation, mastery climate, and performance climate would be associated with low levels of idea generation. This was anticipated because when team members rarely engage in creative idea generation, there is little or no creative material available for implementation despite the levels of the motivational climates.

Scenario Two

When team members frequently generate creative ideas and share their perceptions of a high-mastery climate and a low-performance climate, we expected that fewer of the team members' ideas would be implemented. This is mainly because the climate rewards and encourages employees to focus on cooperation, learning, and mastery to such an extent that it can becomes a 'learning trap' in which creativity implementation is diminished (for example, Hirst et al., 2009). Specifically, cooperative reward structures, which have some aspects in common with a mastery climate, have been found to negatively influence teams' speed of performance, although the teams' focus on accuracy stays intact (Beersma et al., 2003). A possible explanation for this finding may be that taking the time to cooperate on tasks, share knowledge, and engage in discussion can slow down the team (ibid.). Accordingly, too much emphasis on learning can compromise efficiency, particularly for teams that have been performing well (Bunderson and Sutcliffe, 2003). This challenges the 'more-is-always-better' assumption and teams overemphasizing learning may, rather, end up suffering.

Therefore, the focus on learning and development may 'consume time without assurance of results' and may, accordingly, 'reduce efficiency and detract from performance' (Edmondson, 1999, p. 354). By being mainly focused on personal growth, team members can end up overlooking alternative solutions and favor exploration and novelty over practicality (for example, Bunderson and Sutcliffe, 2003). Therefore, team members can end up lacking the extra push that is needed for action.

However, for mastery-oriented individuals and, to a lesser degree, performance-oriented individuals, team learning behavior (a concept that is, to some extent, similar to a mastery climate) enhanced their creative tendencies (Hirst et al., 2009). In sum, a mastery climate can be beneficial in terms of promoting knowledge sharing, discussions, and cooperation on frequent idea generation. Nevertheless, it may be a disadvantage with respect to speed of performance in the idea implementation process.

Scenario Three

In conditions where team members more frequently generate ideas and perceive high levels of a performance climate and low levels of a mastery climate, they are expected to perform and deliver results instantly, in terms of idea implementation. Thus, when employees are placed in a motivational climate that is characterized by normative comparison, control, and public evaluation, employees' focus goes from initially intrinsic to more extrinsic motives (Amabile and Pillemer, 2012). This prediction aligns with the findings of Beersma and colleagues (2003), who found that competi-tive reward structures, which have some aspects in common with a perfor-mance climate, enhanced the teams' speed of performance, although it did not promote accuracy. Rather, a performance climate is likely to speed up the implementation of ideas while being a liability in the cooperative process of frequent idea generation (cf., Beersma et al., 2003).

When the goal–reward structure is mainly focused on whether or not employees deliver end results, learning, development and cooperation may become underemphasized and individuals can become inhibited from exploring or pursuing alternative approaches in the innovation process (cf., Bunderson and Sutcliffe, 2003). Given the criteria of success in a performance climate, team members are likely to become more sensitive to external cues to maximize the likelihood for public recognition and extrinsic rewards, while avoiding punishment or sanctions. Although suc-cessful idea implementation is dependent upon resources in the form of social connections and interactions (Van de Ven, 1986), team members are not likely to direct their energy toward cooperation and personal growth because they are unlikely to be rewarded for such behavior. Since the social process of creativity may become underutilized in high-performance, low-mastery climate conditions, we expected that the link between frequent idea generation and idea implementation would be attenuated.

Scenario Four

Last, under high conditions of idea-generation mastery and perfor-mance climates, we expected that the curvilinear relationship between the frequency of idea generation and idea implementation should become linear and reach its highest levels. A high-performance climate may not negatively influence the idea generation–idea implementation relation-ship when accompanied by a high mastery climate. In their initial study, Ames and Archer (1988) found that the degree to which a goal–reward structure emphasized mastery criteria rather than performance criteria was predictive of how individuals decided to approach tasks and engage in learning. Consequently, the presence of performance cues might not inhibit achievement behavior, as long as mastery cues are salient. This aligns with the findings of Jagacinski and Nicholls (1984), who found that the presence of social comparison information did not reduce the self-evaluation of students who were mastery involved. Both a focus on effectiveness and end results, as well as securing team members' growth and positive social interaction, can enhance the link between frequency of idea generation and implementation because a greater motivation for both is energized. A performance climate may play an important role in keeping team members' performance efforts channeled toward the desired outcome (for example, idea implementation) (cf., Van Yperen et al., 2011). However, simultaneously expecting and rewarding positive interactions and cooperation among team members is needed in order to balance the negative aspects of a performance climate (cf., Ames and Archer, 1988). Multiple criteria of success may help team members to better cope with the competitive elements that are inherent in their work situation because it can give them a broader basis for experiencing success (Ommundsen and Roberts, 1999). Under conditions of high-mastery and high-performance climates, team members are likely to be able to balance their resources with respect to frequent idea generation and idea implementation. This creates a so-called well-adjusted ambidexterity (cf., Cao et al., 2009), where a mastery climate is a necessity to balance the negative aspects of a performance climate.

EMPIRICAL FINDINGS

To test the predictions presented above, we conducted two field studies in non-Western countries (China and Slovenia) (Škerlavaj et al., 2014). The results revealed that the interplay between a mastery and performance climate seemed to determine whether the frequency of idea generation is likely to be associated with idea implementation. When employees' perceptions of both a mastery climate and a performance climate were high, we found the most positive association between the frequency of creative idea generation and idea implementation. Therefore, we found support for our predictions, although there were some minor differences between the two countries. In the Slovenian sample, the relationship between frequent idea-generation behavior and idea-implementation behavior was U-shaped under high-mastery/high-performance climate conditions. In the Chinese samples, the relationship was linear. In the Slovenian sample, rarely generating creative ideas is linked with higher levels of implementation behavior. A possible explanation for these differences may be uncertainty avoidance, which is a characteristic of both Chinese and Slovenian cultures. Uncertainty avoidance is significantly more prevalent in Slovenia because Slovenians seem more prone to avoiding risks (Škerlavaj et al., 2014).

Based on our results, we suggest that creative processes benefit from emphasizing multiple criteria of success. Introducing mastery climate criteria is found to be suitable for stimulating idea implementation from creative ideas and for balancing the maladaptive aspects that might result from a performance climate. In other words, concerning the development of frequent novel and useful ideas and their implementation, social contextual forces conveying both mastery and performance criteria of success appear to be equally effective.

DISCUSSION

The findings of our study have important implications for practice. First, organizations and their leaders need to consider both mastery and performance climates. We found support for their interdependence and that their simultaneous co-existence plays an important role with respect to whether generated ideas actually become implemented. Regarding frequent idea generation and implementation behaviors, the interplay between a mastery and a performance climate is indicated to function better. Although a mastery climate is advocated in the AGT literature, the emphasis on multiple criteria of success (in other words, a focus on growth and delivering end results) may help employees to better cope with organizational realities that typically already have an inherent competitive element (DeShon and Gillespie, 2005).

Still, our findings should not be misinterpreted. A performance climate is mainly associated with maladaptive outcomes and would not be beneficial, pertaining to performance or employee well-being, to recommend that leaders create such a climate. Given that a performance climate and the competitive behavior that comes with it is of rather high salience in many business contexts, leaders are well advised to focus on increasing the facilitation of mastery cues. In conditions of a high-performance climate, a high-mastery climate is, according to our findings, a necessity for creative generated ideas to become implemented.

To illustrate such a climate interplay, the world-renowned architecture company Snøhetta, which is based in Oslo and New York City, may serve as a good example. With the ambition to integrate landscape architecture and architecture, Snøhetta was launched in the late 1980s with success by winning the competition for designing the Alexandria Library in Egypt. The company is also known for projects such as the 9/11 Memorial Museum in New York, the renovation of Times Square, and the new Opera House in Oslo.

The competitive element is clearly present within Snøhetta, given the winner-takes-all surroundings of architectural competitions (Carlsen et al., 2012). The end results and their quality, therefore, do matter. Given the reputation of the company, performance pressure regarding what and how it delivers exists. Certain performance standards are likely to be expected from both customers and management. Again and again Snøhetta has managed to implement its ideas, although the firm wins about one in ten of the competitions in which it participates (ibid.). The failures it experiences are viewed as important for learning and what they dare to imagine in other situations (Carlsen et al., 2012). Snøhetta not only celebrates its successes but it also celebrates the efforts made by each individual in the projects that it did not win. Both success and failure are viewed as collective accomplishments from which employees may learn.

According to research conducted by social anthropologist Aina L. Hagen, the aim of Snøhetta is to develop the creative potential in each and every employee (Khazaleh, 2014). With the intention to facilitate a free float of ideas across topics, age, experience and nationality, no employee belongs to a permanent department or workspace. The furniture in the company is on wheels to enable necessary flexibility and foster employee cooperation. This flexibility is an important tool for collective creativity. All employees are viewed as important assets. Even administrative employees are expected to give their input and are therefore situated between the architects. The intention of this is to showcase that the input and ideas of each and every employee are equally important. Further, there is no such thing as bad ideas. The purpose of emphasizing this concept is to reduce the fear of sharing new thoughts and ideas. Employees are not given any grades for their performance and there is no count on the models they have built. Rather, employees are encouraged to be autonomous and are not told what they should do.

These characteristics of Snøhetta represent several of the criteria of success to be found in both mastery and performance climates. However, the flexibility that a high-mastery climate offers (for example, learning from failure, developing creative potential, autonomy, rewarding effort) seems to be a necessity for continuous creative and innovative processes.

The Snøhetta example gives some indications on how a mastery climate can be fostered, which aligns with empirical evidence. Based on work presented by Epstein (1988, 1989), Ames (1992a, 1992b) initially provided practices, represented by the acronym TARGET (tasks, authority, recognition, grouping, evaluation and time), that were aimed at creating a mastery climate in classrooms. These practices could also be relevant for the work setting and, in particular, idea work, given their focus on facilitating aspects that are typically creativity initiating. Table 8.1 illustrates the motivational focus of TARGET in each of the two motivational climates.

According to TARGET, a first important feature of a mastery climate is to design meaningful tasks that include challenge, variety, diversity, and self-determination. Employees then find intrinsic motivation in the task (for example, idea generation) and can develop their own ability, which is not dependent on social comparison. Second, team members must feel that they have the authority to choose the strategies they want to use to

Table 8.1   Elements of mastery and performance climates

Mastery Climate		Performance Climate	
1.1.1.1.1 Element	1.1.1.1.2 Description	1.1.1.1.3 Element	1.1.1.1.4 Description
Tasks	Challenging and diverse Active involvement Help to set realistic and short-term goals	Tasks	Absence of variety and challenge
Authority	Employees are involved in decision-making and leadership roles Help employees to develop self-management skills	Authority	Employees do not take part in decision-making processes
Recognition	Private and based on individual progress and improvement Equal opportunities for rewards Focus on the self-worth of each employee	Recognition	Public and based on social comparison
Grouping	Promotion of cooperative learning and coworker interaction Flexible and heterogeneous grouping	Grouping	Teams are formed on the basis of ability
Evaluation	Based on mastery of tasks and on individual progress Involve employees in self-evaluation Evaluation is private	Evaluation	Based on 'winning' or outperforming coworkers
Time	Time requirements are adjusted to personal capabilities Provide time and opportunities for improvement	Time	Time allocated for learning is uniform to all employees

Sources: Adapted from Ames (1992a, p. 267) and Ntoumanis and Biddle (1999, p. 644).

complete a task (for example, idea generation and implementation). Third, team members' effort and progress should be recognized privately, and not in comparison to colleagues. Failure should be viewed as an opportunity to learn. Fourth, treating employees similarly and accepting individual

differences by giving the same encouragement, opportunities, and attention to everyone, is vital. Finally, some employees need more time to
develop their potential. In essence, the important goal of a mastery climate
is equal fulfillment of potential, meaning that all employees should be able
to achieve the best that is possible for them (Nicholls, 1979).

The leader has been identified as an important facilitator and architect of the motivational climate. This is because the leader sends signals
to employees concerning the behavior that is expected, supported, and
rewarded (Dragoni, 2005). These signals give employees a perception
of the criteria of success in the specific work situation. To illustrate the
role of the leader regarding mastery and performance climate interplay,
Marit Breivik, the former coach of the Norwegian women's national handball team from 1994–2009, serves as a good example.

The national handball team received 13 medals in international championships (at the European, World, and Olympic championships) during
the years that Breivik was the head coach. Breivik was named 'Best Coach'
during the Norwegian Sports Gala in 2001, 2004, 2007, and 2009. In 2008,
she was awarded the Olav statuette, she was 'Name of the Year' in the
newspaper *VG*, and she was awarded the 'The Art of Leadership' prize by
HR Norway (the member organization for HR professionals in Norway).
On 16 March 2009, the Royal Court announced that the Norwegian king
had appointed Breivik Knight First Class of the Royal Norwegian Order
of St. Olav for her efforts as a role model in Norwegian sport.

Among her team members and colleagues, Breivik is known for being
a team-focused person who is good at team building and focusing on
developing potential of each individual. She has been characterized as
extremely participative, clear in her communication, patient and flexible.
As a coach she was particularly good at building valuable internal and
external relationships. Year after year, she led, developed, and innovated a
high-performing team of players and managers. She created the conditions
for good self-management and she helped others to develop their ability
to perform well under pressure. Breivik was famous for taking care of and
developing competency. She did so by creating an environment for growth
through the facilitation of realistic challenges, good humor, and by being a
supportive coach who cared for the welfare of her team members. Still, one
should not forget that although Breivik facilitated a mastery climate for
her team players, the inherent structure of elite sports is competitive and
focused on end results. Although the example is from the sport domain, it
has implications for work because it illustrates that, although competitive
elements are present, a team can excel and perform at high levels as long
as mastery cues are inherent. These particular characteristics seem to be
success factors that align considerably with those of Snøhetta.

However, when employees are offered choices, participate in decision-making, and work with meaningful and challenging tasks but, at the same time the evaluation criteria are normative, employees' motivation outcomes may become confused (cf., Ames, 1992b). Therefore, the climate structures need to be both coordinated and work in concert (ibid.), otherwise the positive contribution of a mastery climate may become undermined by inappropriate strategies in a performance climate. Marit Breivik and Snøhetta are good examples of how it may be possible to coordinate the climates and make them work in such concert to facilitate creativity, innovation, and high performance.

REFERENCES

Agars, M.D., J.C. Kaufman and T.R. Locke (2008), 'Social influence and creativity in organizations: A multilevel lens for theory, research, and practice', in M.D. Mumford, S.T. Hunter and K.E. Bedell-Avers (eds), *Multi-level Issues in Organizational Innovation*, Amsterdam: JAI Press, pp. 3–61.

Amabile, T.M. (2001), 'Beyond talent: John Irving and the passionate craft of creativity', *American Psychologist*, **56**(4), 333–36.

Amabile, T.M. and J. Pillemer (2012), 'Perspectives on the social psychology of creativity', *Journal of Creative Behavior*, **46**(1), 3–15.

Ames, C. (1992a), 'Achievement goals, motivational climate, and motivational processes', in G.C. Roberts (ed.), *Motivation in Sport and Exercise*, Champaign, IL: Human Kinetics, pp. 161–76.

Ames, C. (1992b), 'Classrooms: Goals, structures, and student motivation', *Journal of Educational Psychology*, **84**(3), 261–71.

Ames, C. and R. Ames (1984a), 'Goal structures and motivation', *The Elementary School Journal*, **85**(1), 39–52.

Ames, C. and R. Ames (1984b), 'Systems of student and teacher motivation: Toward a qualitative definition', *Journal of Educational Psychology*, **76**(4), 535–56.

Ames, C. and J. Archer (1988), 'Achievement goals in the classroom: Students' learning strategies and motivation processes', *Journal of Educational Psychology*, **80**(3), 260–67.

Andersen, N., K. Potocnik and J. Zhou (2014), 'Innovation and creativity in organizations: A state-of-the-science review, prospective commentary, and guiding framework', *Journal of Management*, **40**(5), 1297–333.

Beersma, B., J.R. Hollenbeck, S.E. Humphrey, H. Moon, D.E. Conlon and D.R. Ilgen (2003), 'Cooperation, competition, and team performance: Toward a contingency approach', *Academy of Management Journal*, **46**(5), 572–90.

Bunderson, J.S. and K.M. Sutcliffe (2003), 'Management team learning orientation and business unit performance', *Journal of Applied Psychology*, **88**(3), 552–60.

Cao, Q., E. Gedajlovic and H. Zhang (2009), 'Unpacking organizational ambidexterity: Dimensions, contingencies, and synergistic effects', *Organization Science*, **20**(4), 781–96.

Carlsen, A., R. Gjersvik and S. Clegg (2012), 'Daring to imagine: How great ideas result from cutting into the rock, celebrating your dusters, and cheerleading', in A. Carlsen, S. Clegg and R. Gjersvik (eds), *Idea Work*, Oslo: Cappelen Damm, pp. 120–39.

DeShon, R.P. and J.Z. Gillespie (2005), 'A motivated action theory account of goal orientation', *Journal of Applied Psychology*, **90**(6), 1096–127.

Dragoni, L. (2005), 'Understanding the emergence of state goal orientation in organizational work groups: The role of leadership and multilevel climate perceptions', *Journal of Applied Psychology*, **90**(6), 1084–95.

Edmondson, A. (1999), 'Psychological safety and learning behavior in work teams', *Administrative Science Quarterly*, **44**(2), 350–83.

Epstein, J. (1988), 'Effective schools or effective students? Dealing with diversity', in R. Haskins and B. MacRae (eds), *Policies for America's Public Schools*, Norwood, NJ: Ablex, pp. 89–126.

Epstein, J. (1989), 'Family structures and student motivation: A developmental perspective', in C. Ames and R. Ames (eds), *Research on Motivation in Education*, Vol. 3, New York: Academic Press, pp. 259–95.

Hammond, M.M., N.L. Neff, J.L. Farr, A.R. Schwall and X.Y. Zhao (2011), 'Predictors of individual-level innovation at work: A meta-analysis', *Psychology of Aesthetics Creativity and the Arts*, **5**(1), 90–105.

Hirst, G., D. van Knippenberg and J. Zhou (2009), 'A cross-level perspective on employee creativity: Goal orientation, team learning behavior, and individual creativity', *Academy of Management Journal*, **52**(2), 280–93.

Jagacinski, C.M. and J.G. Nicholls (1984), 'Conceptions of ability and related affects in task involvement and ego involvement', *Journal of Educational Psychology*, **76**(5), 909–19.

Khazaleh, L. (2014), 'Magi får fart på kreativiteten i Snøhetta' [Magic gets the juices flowing in Snøhetta], accessed 11 March 2014 at http://forskning. no/arkitektur-arbeid-ledelse-og-organisasjon-innovasjon-sosialantropologi-data/2014/03/magi-far-fart-pa [in Norwegian].

Kuenzi, M. and M. Schminke (2009), 'Assembling fragments into a lens: A review, critique, and proposed research agenda for the organizational work climate literature', *Journal of Management*, **35**(3), 634–717.

Nerstad, C.G.L., G.C. Roberts and A.M. Richardsen (2013), 'Achieving success at work: The development and validation of the motivational climate at work questionnaire (MCWQ)', *Journal of Applied Social Psychology*, **43**, 2231–50.

Nicholls, J.G. (1979), 'Quality and equality in intellectual development: The role of motivation in education', *American Psychologist*, **34**(11), 1071–84.

Nicholls, J.G. (1984), 'Conceptions of ability and achievement motivation', in C. Ames and R. Ames (eds), *Research on Motivation in Education: Goals and Cognitions*, Vol. 3, San Diego, CA: Academic Press, pp. 39–73.

Nicholls, J.G. (1989), *The Competitive Ethos and Democratic Education*, Cambridge, MA: Harvard University Press.

Ntoumanis, N. and S.J.H. Biddle (1999), 'A review of motivational climate in physical activity', *Journal of Sport Sciences*, **17**(8), 643–65.

Ommundsen, Y. and G.C. Roberts (1999), 'Effect of motivational climate profiles on motivational indices in team sport', *Scandinavian Journal of Medicine and Science in Sports*, **9**(6), 389–97.

Poortvliet, P.M. and C. Darnon (2010), 'Toward a more social understanding of achievement goals: The interpersonal effects of mastery and performance goals', *Current Directions in Psychological Science*, **19**(5), 324–8.

Roberts, G.C. (2012), 'Motivation in sport and exercise from an achievement goal theory perspective: After 30 years, where are we?' in G.C. Roberts and D. Treasure (eds), *Advances in Motivation in Sport and Exercise*, Vol. 3, Champaign, IL: Human Kinetics, pp. 5–58.

Škerlavaj, M., A. Dysvik, M. Černe, C.G.L. Nerstad and C. Su (2014), 'Riding two horses at once: The combined roles of mastery and performance climates in implementing creative ideas', paper submitted, BI Norwegian Business School.

Van de Ven, A. (1986), 'Central problems in the management of innovation', *Management Science*, **32**(5), 590–607.

Van Yperen, N.W., M.R.W. Hamstra and M. van der Klauw (2011), 'To win, or not to lose, at any cost: The impact of achievement goals on cheating', *British Journal of Management*, **22**(S1), 5–15.

Zampetakis, L.A., M.L. Gruys and T. Dewett (2014), 'Ideas and implementation: The effective implementation of novel marketing programmes in small- to medium-sized Greek firms', *Creativity and Innovation Management*, **23**(2), 168–82.

PART III

What can we do about it as leaders?

9. Supportive supervision: a crucial factor for unlocking the potential of highly creative ideas perspective

Matej Černe, Miha Škerlavaj and Anders Dysvik

Perceived supervisor support is formally defined as the degree to which employees in organizations believe their supervisors value their contributions and care about their well-being (Kottke and Sharafinski, 1988; Eisenberger et al., 2002). According to Amabile et al. (2004), there are two views on supervisor support. A perspective that includes both task- and relationship-oriented leadership behaviors is more common in the creativity literature, whereas leadership literature usually adopts a narrower view that only deals with relationships. In this chapter, we decided to follow the broader definition of perceived supervisor support. It encompasses both instrumental and socio-emotional support (Amabile et al., 2004), such as helping other employees who had been absent, orienting new employees to their jobs, helping others when their workload increases, and assisting others with their duties (Shanock and Eisenberger, 2006).

Perceived supervisor support is important in relation to a range of beneficial organizational outcomes. First, at the unit level, a perceived supervisor support climate has been positively associated with unit performance (Dysvik and Kuvaas, 2012) and negatively associated with post-traumatic stress (Bacharach and Bamberger, 2007). At the individual level, perceived supervisor support has been found to relate positively to perceived organizational support, in-role performance, organizational citizenship behavior and negatively related to turnover intention (Eisenberger et al., 2002; Shanock and Eisenberger, 2006). Employees that feel supported by their supervisors have also been found to go beyond their formal job duties (Shanock and Eisenberger, 2006).

The aim of this chapter is to explore a crucial boundary condition in the relationship between idea generation and implementation at the individual level – the extent to which employees feel supported by their group/ team supervisors. By doing so we seek to extend previous research on

moderating influences on the idea generation–idea implementation relationship that has thus far focused on team-level climate or individual characteristics (cf. Baer, 2012; Somech and Drach-Zahavy, 2013). Specifically,
we propose and test whether the extent to which immediate leaders/line
managers are perceived as supportive affects the idea generation–idea
implementation relationship. This chapter significantly builds upon our
own previous experimental work on the role of perceived supervisor
support in implementing creative ideas (Škerlavaj et al., 2014) by extending
its theoretical underpinnings and demonstrating its practical value using
illustrative case studies.

First, we present an overview of theoretical ideas tested in Škerlavaj
et al. (2014) that was based on the resource allocation framework.
Second, this chapter extends the theoretical background of understanding the implementation of creative ideas of followers supported by
their supervisors, with two complementary views: self-determination
theory (Deci and Ryan, 1985; Deci et al., 1989; Gagné and Deci, 2005)
and management innovation literature that examines leaders as role
models in enhancing creative-idea implementation (Vaccaro et al., 2012).
Finally, we present our findings with practical examples and mini-case
studies.

SUPERVISOR SUPPORT FOR CREATIVE-IDEA IMPLEMENTATION – THEORETICAL CHOICES AND EMPIRICAL FINDINGS

Resource Allocation Framework: Too-much-of-a-good-thing Effect in Creative-idea Implementation

In our mixed-method study (field: 165 employees and their 24 direct
supervisors from a Slovene steel manufacturing firm; and experimental:
123 second-year undergraduate student participants; Škerlavaj et al.,
2014), we explored how perceived supervisor support (PSS) represents
a crucial contingency that enables higher levels of idea implementation
from creative-idea generation. According to the job demands-resources
model (Demerouti et al., 2001) and empirical research (see Rhoades and
Eisenberger, 2002 for a review), PSS is a resource at the interpersonal
level, and represents an important factor for connecting employees to
the resources and supporters they need, both in general and in particular
for the implementation of creative ideas. Drawing on a resource allocation framework (Becker, 1965; Hockey, 1997), we initially observed a
curvilinear inverse U-shaped relationship between employee creative-idea

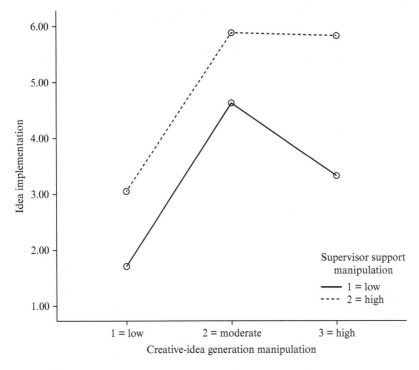

Source: Škerlavaj et al. (2014).

Figure 9.1 *Relationship between idea generation and implementation by level of perceived supervisor support (experimental study)*

generation (both in terms of frequency and creativity of generated ideas) and implementation (Škerlavaj et al., 2014).

We then examined perceived supervisor support as a moderator and found that higher levels of perceived supervisor support dampen the curvilinear relationship between creative-idea generation and idea implementation (ibid.). By recognizing usefulness and accepting novel ideas generated by highly creative individuals, immediate supervisors act as resources at the interpersonal level (cf. Demerouti et al., 2001), and provide employees with access to resources and support needed for idea implementation, making highly creative ideas (both in terms of frequency and creativity of generated ideas) more implementable (Figure 9.1).

Self-determination Theory: Focus on Supervisors' Interpersonal Style

In what follows, we draw on self-determination theory (SDT; Deci and Ryan, 1985, 1991; Ryan, 1995) to suggest that PSS stimulates employees' perceptions of competence and relatedness and can help in harvesting high-level creativity results in terms of superior innovation through employees' psychological motivational states that should yield optimal functioning. In conceptualizing the ways to stimulate self-determination, we draw on the extant literature that has shown the importance of supportive supervision for self-motivation (Deci et al., 1989). SDT concurs that job characteristics are one way of stimulating motivation, but the interpersonal style of supervisors is even more important (Deci et al., 1989; Gagné and Deci, 2005). This is also consistent with findings from creativity and innovation literature. Contextual factors, in particular team leader and management support, were shown to be more important for implementation than for idea suggestion (Oldham and Cummings, 1996; Axtell et al., 2000). We propose that supervisor support is the key to enhancing employees' perceptions of competence and relatedness.

We conducted an experiment with 117 second-year undergraduates within a human resource management (HRM) course at a Slovenian university. The experiment used a three-by-two (low/moderate/high creative-idea generation by low/high supervisor support) between-subjects factorial design. The MANOVA revealed a significant interaction effect of the creative-idea generation and supervisor support manipulations on innovation ($F[2,115] = 5.87, p < 0.01$). Both competence and relatedness mediated the moderating effect of supervisor support on the relationship between creativity and innovation.

Leaders as Role Models: Management Innovation at the Team Level

A third view that we study in this chapter examines leaders as role models with respect to management innovation at the team level. A field study on two Slovene manufacturing companies (steel manufacturing and steel constructions) has shown a positive relationship between team leaders' management innovation at the team level on challenge stressors ($\beta = 0.17$, $p < 0.05$). Based on status characteristics theory (Bunderson, 2003), innovative supervisors induce a positive type of stress, which in turn influences individual idea implementation. In other words, when managers exhibit innovative behavior in their managerial work, employees are likely to follow the lead and do the same in their tasks. Job complexity was indicated to be an important control in the examined relationships.

HOW DOES THE INFLUENCE OF PERCEIVED SUPERVISOR SUPPORT FUNCTION IN PRACTICE?

In what follows, we present three practical short cases with scenarios and vignettes for each of them, with a clear focus on explaining the mechanisms of how perceived supervisor support helps transforming highly creative ideas into implemented innovations at the individual level. The cases are organized in a way that they follow the three theoretical explanatory arguments presented above: the first one presents the mechanism of resource allocation framework in transforming idea generation into idea implementation; the second portrays psychological self-determination as the key; the third examines leaders as role models for fostering innovative behavior. In the second step, we explain how one can work on building the capacity of supportive supervision in order to stimulate capitalizing on creative ideas.

Case 1: Resource Allocation – Providing Employees with (Access to) Resources

Leaders directly influence whether or not individuals can innovate. To close the innovation gap (between how the companies want to innovate and how they actually do so), executive leaders must clarify what they want to achieve with innovation, and understand the specific issues that can prevent individuals and teams from innovating in their organization. They need to make innovation a core priority for the organization and for key departments; assign credible senior people to lead the implementation; and fully resource their innovation initiatives (Legrand and Weiss, 2011).

Take, for example, employees in the company that we examined in our field study, which produces steel construction components. They provide constant emphasis on innovation and sustainable development. Innovation is one of their most important corporate values, which is evident from their 'slogans of the year'. Past slogans have included 'Show what you can do', 'Innovation for a balanced growth and development', and 'Increasing competitiveness through innovative processes'. However, ideas rated as the most highly innovative (for example, a robotic manipulator for the assembly of facade elements; a fluorescent nanotube-based wall coating filled with zinc; self-supporting, insulating, fireproof modular panels; a modular facade system; iridescent paint [changing color as the angle of view changes]; and the development of an anti-corrosion implant) would never become implemented if it were not for the influence of direct supervisors who are involved in day-to-day individual-level innovation activities.

In practice, this occurs by providing the employees with sufficient time, which can be viewed as a resource – but not too much, as there should be a moderate level of time pressure for the implementation of creative ideas. Studies have indicated that some amount of time pressure might be beneficial for actual innovative performance so that creative individuals do not get carried away in creative thought (Baer and Oldham, 2006). What is even more important is for the leaders to provide their employees (direct reports) with access to other resources. For example, providing advice when the employees' thinking becomes too little or too creative, connecting them to other employees with relevant knowledge for solving their problems, and providing them with actual practical resources (funds, equipment etc.).

Let's take a look at how popular manufacturer of plastic construction toys LEGO does it (based on Crawford and Robertson, 2008). In the first years of the 2000s, only one or two of ten new product ideas actually made it to the market, indicating serious problems in idea implementation. In addition to being slow, the product development process suffered from bringing radically new ideas to market. In order to address this, LEGO had created a so-called Concept Lab with the aim of developing revolutionary breakthrough products. The Lab was seen as a free resource to development teams, and Concept Lab employees often became involved in the development of more incremental product concepts, providing crucial resources in the idea implementation phase that the developers previously did not have access to.

The logic of resource allocation was also nicely illustrated in our qualitative study following up the student experiment. Although the final implementation output was individual based, group dynamics that we simulated by dividing the participants into groups and instructing them to comment on others' ideas played an important role. Critique and opposition of creative ideas by others prevented many participants from persevering in implementing their ideas. As per one participant's opinion: 'After a couple of put-downs from my team members, I was simply afraid of proposing another highly creative idea. I knew that we were not going to implement it anyway. There was so much negativity'. Or, in another participant's opinion: 'After a while, you just don't bother anymore, you just don't care'.

Supportive supervision represents an important means of overcoming these issues – the supervisors are in a position to better explain the value of a particular creative idea to other group members. Such an example is also the concept of stewardship or servant leadership – leading with the purpose of helping and enabling the employees. Forbes's Kevin Cashman (2013) writes:

> While many publishing companies have closed their doors during the last 20 years, Berrett-Koehler (BK) has been thriving. Steve Piersanti, founder and

president, established BK on a stewardship model. He explained, 'When you choose the context of stewardship, the language of the model influences your entire perception from how you make decisions about what books to publish to how you regard all the stakeholders.' Stewardship brings people together around a common purpose and a spirit of innovation generated by an intense desire to serve in new ways.

The lack of confidence and perseverance to carry out implementation was the most prevalent of the individual-level characteristics, especially when the supervisor failed to provide support for the ideas and work. Therefore, providing socio-emotional support is an equally important task (as is providing access to resources) for the supervisors, which we explain in the next case study.

Case 2: Self-determination – Stimulating Competence and Relatedness

The logic here is similar to the one presented above. When supervisors connect the employees with other team members that can help them, or even provide advice themselves, this stimulates perceptions of relatedness and thereby higher levels of self-determination and optimal functioning.

An example of applying self-determination in leading for innovation is the case of Kelvingrove Art Gallery and Museum (based on Liedtka and Salzman, 2009). The new director Mark O'Neill came on board in 2003 to renovate the historic Victorian building, which reopened in 2006 only to surpass Edinburgh Castle as Scotland's most popular tourist destination in July 2007. He has done so by utilizing an innovative style of management that he describes as 'maze behavior' – trial-and-error learning. It involved moving from the traditional discipline-bound museum into a cross-disciplinary, visitor-oriented experience. He has done so by engaging the curators (through a number of personal briefing meetings) into creating exhibits based on stories rather than professional classification, putting a premium on interdisciplinary stories. Even though they had never been trained to tell stories, O'Neill's belief that he can make a difference has thereby spilled over to his colleagues at the museum. The newly acquired Leadership Team certainly helped – opting for assertive, responsible, and resilient senior leaders to help him spread the innovation vibe. Throughout the process, he had several major setbacks but never quit and was able to bring the staff along by building upon their self-perceptions of confidence and relating them into a joint community by remaining consistent over time. Nevertheless, self-determination focus put aside, he claims that '[innovation] is often about removing obstacles [including those in people's minds] and securing resources'.

To support the above point, Jane Stevenson, Vice Chairman, Korn/ Ferry's Board & CEO Services group, and coauthor of *Breaking Away: How Great Leaders Create Innovation That Drives Sustainable Growth–and Why Others Fail*, shared:

> It starts at the top, but innovation is a team sport. Each person needs to feel that they matter, that the outcome wouldn't be the same without their contribution. One of the key jobs of leaders is to make sure each person has a clear sense of purpose and value in connection to the larger mission. . . In this kind of collaborative, abundance mentality, there is a limitless mentality about what can be achieved. (Cited in Cashman, 2013)

Case 3: Leaders as Role Models

Complex issues present in contemporary organizations are ambiguous, uncertain, and represent unique problems or opportunities. Leaders themselves need to apply innovative thinking to gain insight into the complexities and to discover innovative solutions (Legrand and Weiss, 2011). Leaders also must demonstrate their strong commitment in their actions, not just their talk.

Ultimately, this notion can be related to management innovation – 'generation and implementation of a management practice, process, structure or technique that is new to the state of the art and is intended to further organizational goals' (Birkinshaw et al., 2008, p. 829). This ultimately refers to what managers do and how they do it (Hamel, 2006). In our field study, this is most reflected in the tools that support ideation, which arise from highly creative ideas of the management. There is an innovation contest for the employees called 'The Boldest Idea', in which coming up with the most creative ideas results in equally creative rewards, such as a chance to drive a Formula 1 car at Silverstone, a visit to a nuclear submarine, a tour of CERN's accelerator complex, and an astronaut-training session at NASA (floating in zero gravity).

Vaccaro (2010) presented a longitudinal (2001–10) case study of Procter and Gamble (P&G) and its self-managing teams as a management innovation. An overhaul of new management practices (employees became in charge of setting their own goals and deciding when and how tasks were going to be performed), processes (overhaul of promotion and reward systems where pay and promotion were determined in relation to skill as evaluated by fellow team members), and structures (hierarchical layers were removed to allow team autonomy), conducted by the top management team and the immediate supervisors, resulted in role modeling and higher levels of individual idea implementation.

Please note that even though the management innovation itself was the installment of self-managing teams, the role of leadership/supervisors was still very important. While keeping to the principles of self-managing teams, supervisors were primarily concerned with gaining compliance from operators by clearly specifying targets and rewards and intervening when the achievement of these goals seemed compromized (ibid.). As one respondent (employee) said (p. 85), 'He [the plant manager] is responsible for everything at the end. He is the one looking down. . . he will come and tell somebody or the entire group "it's going the wrong way, we have to do this or we have to do that"'. In order to achieve this, quite a lot of supportive supervision behavior was done at the supervisor–subordinate level. As for another employee's opinion (ibid.), 'His [the supervisor's] role is management too, but in a way of trying to give a message to employees. . . It is not formal. It has its ups and downs, but in a way. . . you talk to him and go back to your seat and want to try and do it'.

Such a leader is capable of inspiring and stimulating employees to look for new solutions, experiment and challenge assumptions, and implement them. These initiatives (management innovations by the leaders/supervisors) were shown to stimulate 'good' kinds of stressors, challenge stressors (as opposed to hindrance stressors). The employees are 'kept on their toes' and are constantly challenged to produce and implement creative innovations themselves. They are more likely to be stimulated to do so because of the leaders' role modeling – 'walking the talk', not just communicating the importance of innovating.

BUILDING THE CAPACITY OF SUPPORTIVE SUPERVISION

To improve the implementation of highly novel and potentially useful ideas, team leaders/immediate supervisors should exhibit high levels of both instrumental and socio-emotional support. In practice, supervisors should care about opinions and the well-being of their employees, and consider their goals and values when engaged in the individual innovation process. In order to ensure this to the largest extent possible, organizations should thus strive to recruit or develop supervisors with the potential of being perceived as supportive. This can be achieved by formal training programs based on established research findings from the longstanding tradition of leadership research. In addition, organizations can hire to management positions based on candidates' history of helping their coworkers thrive and perform. But as recent research shows (Kuvaas et al., 2014) research and developmental processes alone may be insufficient. In addition, organizations should enable line managers to have a greater say in the implementation of HR practices and adapt these to the individual needs of their subordinates. As Kuvaas et al. (2014) found, the more the line managers perceive HR practices to be enabling, the more supportive they were perceived by their followers. As such there are important boundary conditions that could influence how effective the line managers are allowed to be. This way, supportive supervisors can help to provide both the intangible (psychological support) and tangible resources (for example, training, idea championing, and access to resources) needed for effective idea implementation.

REFERENCES

Amabile, T.M., E.A. Schatzel, G.B. Moneta and S.J. Cramer (2004), 'Leader behaviors and the work environment for creativity: Perceived leader support', *The Leadership Quarterly*, **15**(1), 5–32.

Axtell, C.M., D.J. Holman, K.L. Unsworth, T.D. Wall, P.E. Waterson and E. Harrington (2000), 'Shopfloor innovation: Facilitating the suggestion and implementation of ideas', *Journal of Occupational and Organizational Psychology*, **73**(3), 265–85.

Bacharach, S.B. and P. Bamberger (2007), 'Organizational context and post-event distress: 9/11 and the New York City firefighters', *Academy of Management Journal*, **50**(4), 849–68.

Baer, M. (2012), 'Putting creativity to work: The implementation of creative ideas in organizations', *Academy of Management Journal*, **55**(5), 1102–19.

Baer, M. and G.R. Oldham (2006), 'The curvilinear relation between experienced creative time pressure and creativity: Moderating effects of openness to experience and support for creativity', *Journal of Applied Psychology*, **91**(4), 963–70.

Becker, G.S. (1965), 'A theory of the allocation of time', *The Economic Journal*, **75**(299), 493–517.

Birkinshaw, J., G. Hamel and M.J. Mol (2008), 'Management innovation', *Academy of Management Review*, **33**(4), 825–45.

Bunderson, J.S. (2003), 'Recognizing and utilizing expertise in work groups: A status characteristics perspective', *Administrative Science Quarterly*, **48**(4), 557–91.

Cashman, K. (2013), '7 ways leaders can foster innovation', *Forbes*, 21 August, accessed 2 December 2015 at http://www.forbes.com/sites/kevincashman/2013/08/21/7-ways-leaders-can-foster-innovation/.

Crawford, R. and D. Robertson (2008), 'Innovation at the LEGO group', *IMD Case Study*, Lausanne: Institute for Management Development.

Deci, E.L. and R.M. Ryan (1985), *Intrinsic Motivation and Self-determination in Human Behavior*, New York: Plenum.

Deci, E.L. and R.M. Ryan (1991), 'A motivational approach to self: Integration in personality', in R. Dienstbier (ed.), *Perspectives on Motivation: Nebraska Symposium on Motivation*, Vol. 38, Lincoln, NE: University of Nebraska Press, pp. 237–88.

Deci, E.L., J.P. Connell and R.M. Ryan (1989), 'Self-determination in a work organization', *Journal of Applied Psychology*, **74**(4), 580–90.

Demerouti, E., A.B. Bakker, F. Nachreiner and W.B. Schaufeli (2001), 'The job demands-resources model of burnout', *Journal of Applied Psychology*, **86**(3), 499–512.

Dysvik, A. and B. Kuvaas (2012), 'Perceived supervisor support climate, perceived investment in employee development climate, and business-unit performance', *Human Resource Management*, **51**(5), 651–64.

Eisenberger, R., F. Stinglhamber, C. Vandenberghe, I.L. Sucharski and L. Rhoades (2002), 'Perceived supervisor support: Contributions to perceived organizational support and employee retention', *Journal of Applied Psychology*, **87**(3), 565–73.

Gagné, M. and E.L. Deci (2005), 'Self-determination theory and work motivation', *Journal of Organizational Behavior*, **26**(4), 331–62.

Hamel, G. (2006), 'The why, what, and how of management innovation', *Harvard Business Review*, **84**(2), 72–84.

Hockey, G. (1997), 'Compensatory control in the regulation of human performance under stress and high workload: A cognitive-energetical framework', *Biological Psychology*, **45**(1), 73–93.

Kottke, J.L. and C.E. Sharafinski (1988), 'Measuring perceived supervisory and organizational support', *Educational and Psychological Measurement*, **48**(4), 1075–9.

Kuvaas, B., A. Dysvik and R. Buch (2014), 'Antecedents and employee outcomes of line managers' perceptions of enabling HR practices', *Journal of Management Studies*, **51**(6), 845–68.

Legrand, C. and D.S. Weiss (2011), 'How leaders can close the innovation gap', *Ivey Business Journal* (July/August), accessed 30 November 2015 at http://ivey-businessjournal.com/publication/how-leaders-can-close-the-innovation-gap/.

Liedtka, J.M. and R. Salzman (2009), *Leading Innovation at Kelvingrove*, Los Angeles, CA and Charlottesville, VA: J. Paul Getty Trust and The University of Virginia Darden School Foundation.

Oldham, G. and A. Cummings (1996), 'Employee creativity: Personal and contextual factors at work', *Academy of Management Journal*, **39**(3), 607–34.

Rhoades, L. and R. Eisenberger (2002), 'Perceived organizational support: A review of the literature', *Journal of Applied Psychology*, **87**(4), 698–714.

Ryan, R.M. (1995), 'Psychological needs and the facilitation of integrative processes', *Journal of Personality*, **63**(3), 397–427.

Shanock, L.R. and R. Eisenberger (2006), 'When supervisors feel supported: Relationships with subordinates' perceived supervisor support, perceived organizational support, and performance', *Journal of Applied Psychology*, **91**(3), 689–95.

Škerlavaj, M., M. Černe and A. Dysvik (2014), 'I get by with a little help from my supervisor: Creative-idea generation, idea implementation, and perceived supervisor support', *Leadership Quarterly*, **25**(5), 987–1000.

Somech, A. and A. Drach-Zahavy (2013), 'Translating team creativity to innovation implementation: The role of team composition and climate for innovation', *Journal of Management*, **39**(3), 684–708.

Vaccaro, I.G. (2010), 'Management innovation: Studies on the role of internal change agents', PhD thesis, Rotterdam: Erasmus University.

Vaccaro, I.G., J.J.P. Jansen, F.A.J. van den Bosch and H.W. Volberda (2012), 'Management innovation and leadership: The moderating role of organizational size', *Journal of Management Studies*, **49**(1), 28–51.

10. Economic and social leader–member exchange, and creativity at work

Robert Buch and Bård Kuvaas

Since its inception over 40 years ago, a growing body of scholarly literature has accumulated on the leader–member exchange (LMX) relationship. LMX theory began as an alternative to average leadership style (Graen and Uhl-Bien, 1995) and is based on the notion that leaders do not treat all subordinates alike, but rather develop high-quality relationships with some (that is, the 'in-group'), and low-quality relationships with others (that is, the 'out-group'). Unlike traditional leadership theories, LMX theory is unique in its adoption of the relationship itself as the level of analysis as opposed to explaining leadership as a 'a function of personal characteristics of the leader, features of the situation, or an interaction between the two' (Gerstner and Day, 1997, p. 827). While high-quality LMX relationships are long term, based on trust and mutual liking, low-quality LMX relationships are limited to the transactional part of the employment contract (Bernerth et al., 2007).

To date, several meta-analytical reviews demonstrate positive associations between high-quality LMX relationships and outcomes such as performance ratings, objective performance, job satisfaction, and organizational commitment (for example, Graen and Uhl-Bien, 1995; Gerstner and Day, 1997; Ilies et al., 2007; Dulebohn et al., 2012; Rockstuhl et al., 2012). Although creativity has not been a central topic in this research, studies suggest that LMX is important for the generation of creative ideas (Tierney et al., 1999; Atwater and Carmeli, 2009; Pan et al., 2012; Volmer et al., 2012) and their actual implementation (Liao et al. 2010; Olsson et al., 2012). The LMX framework is important because it links the role of the leader and the social context to the emergence of creativity in the workplace (Tierney, 2008; Pan et al., 2012).

The objective of this chapter is to review and extend the existing literature regarding the association between LMX and the generation and implementation of creative ideas. The chapter is organized as follows. First, we review a few existing studies on LMX and creative idea generation and implementation. We then explore the distinction between social and economic LMX relationships and their associations with work outcomes. Finally, we explore ways in which social and economic LMX relationships may be differentially linked with the generation and implementation of creative ideas in the workplace.

LEADER–MEMBER EXCHANGE RELATIONSHIPS AND FOLLOWER CREATIVITY

Creativity, understood as the development of novel and useful ideas (Amabile, 1996) is recognized as a source of competitive advantage (Shalley, 1991; Pan et al., 2012). However, for an idea to lead to organizational success it has to be successfully implemented. Accordingly, researchers have started distinguishing between the generation of and implementation of creative ideas. Although creative idea generation does not always result in innovation implementation, the former is widely recognized as a necessary antecedent to the latter (Škerlavaj et al., 2014). We would like to point out, however, that most studies on LMX and creativity do not explicitly distinguish between idea generation and implementation. Still, existing research indicates that a high-quality LMX relationship constitutes an important driver of not only creative idea generation, but also creative idea implementation.

First, with respect to creative idea generation, researchers have argued that followers in high-quality LMX relationships are typically allowed greater autonomy (for example, Graves and Luciano, 2010), which has been suggested to be crucial to creative processes. Basu and Green (1997), for instance, argued that by 'providing members in such dyads with autonomy, leaders can create an environment that encourages free thinking, exchange of information, and the latitude to explore and examine new ways of handling old problems' (p. 480). Furthermore, followers in high-quality LMX relationships typically enjoy more challenging tasks (Graen and Scandura, 1987), and are thus also probably able to advance their own expertise as well as their cognition and motivation to generate and promote creative ideas (Atwater and Carmeli, 2009). In line with these arguments, a recent meta-analysis (Hammond et al., 2011) suggests a link between LMX and creative idea generation. It should be noted, however, that operationalizations of creativity have varied and that separate results for creative idea generation and implementation have not always been reported.

One study examining the LMX–creative idea generation link was conducted by Volmer et al. (2012), using a sample of 144 followers in a high-technology firm in Germany. Specifically, using a longitudinal field study with a three-month time lag, they uncovered a positive relationship between LMX and creative work involvement (including items such as 'I took risks in terms of producing new ideas in doing my job'). In addition they sought to uncover the moderating role of job autonomy based on the premise that LMX may interact with job design characteristics to influence creativity. Interestingly, while they found that job autonomy accentuated the positive relationship between LMX and creative work involvement, they also found that for followers who experienced low levels of job autonomy, LMX was unrelated to creative work involvement. This implies that job autonomy represents a boundary condition for the LMX–creativity association, and points to the importance of considering the interplay between the social context (that is, the leader–follower relationship) and job design (that is, job autonomy) with respect to creative idea generation. Still, they did also report a positive correlation between LMX and job autonomy ($r = 0.28$, $p < 0.01$), which may also indicate that, in addition, LMX increases followers' autonomy as suggested by Basu and Green (1997).

Second, with respect to creative idea implementation, social exchange theory (Blau, 1964) – which has been widely applied to the study of LMX – posits that followers who experience a high-quality social exchange relationship with their supervisors feel an obligation to reciprocate by means of a range of productive behaviors in the workplace (for example, Bernerth et al., 2007). Such an obligation is probably particularly important when it comes to the implementation of creative ideas. In accordance with these arguments, recent research suggests that social exchange-oriented felt obligation is responsible for translating LMX into creative idea implementation. Specifically, Pan and colleagues (2012) investigated the mediating roles of felt obligation and psychological empowerment in relationships between LMX and follower creativity among 367 followers in three manufacturing companies located in China. The measure they used did not differentiate between idea generation and idea implementation, as they had supervisors rate followers using items such 'This employee is creative'. They also argued that followers in high-quality LMX relationships should feel more empowered, confident, and efficacious, and be equipped with more information and resources, and thus be more likely to act innovatively in their work. Furthermore, they argued that LMX should elicit a felt obligation to engage in creativity if this was valued by their leader and their organization. In accordance with their hypotheses, Pan et al. (2012) found that the relationship between LMX and follower creativity was fully mediated by (1) motivation-oriented psychological empowerment and (2) social exchange-oriented felt obligation. Not being afraid to make mistakes can be hypothesized to be an additional mediator. Implementing new ideas is a risky venture (for example, Khazanchi and Masterson, 2011) and a high-quality LMX relationship involves trust, implying that followers should expect support from the leader even if creative idea implementation fails.

Another mediator of the association between LMX and creative idea implementation that has been identified is self-efficacy, defined as 'an individual's belief in one's capability to organize and execute the courses of action required to produce given attainments' (Bandura, 1997, p. 3). Using longitudinal, multisource data from 828 followers and 116 teams in a Chinese iron and steel manufacturing company, Liao et al. (2010) investigated the mediating role of self-efficacy in the relationship between LMX and the implementation of creative ideas, as measured by the amount of bonuses received for creative idea implementation. In line with their expectations, Liao and colleagues found a unique indirect relationship from LMX to creative idea implementation via self-efficacy, thus indicating that high-quality LMX relationships increase followers' self-judgment of their ability, which is essential to the implementation of creative ideas (Tierney and Farmer, 2002; Liao et al., 2010). Liao et al. (2010) additionally sought to determine if this indirect relationship was moderated by LMX differentiation. LMX differentiation can be defined as the degree of variability in the LMX quality between a leader and various team members (ibid.). For instance, a low LMX differentiation would mean that the leader treats individual team members more or less the same (in other words, the quality of the exchange relationships does not vary to a large extent). Interestingly, Liao and colleagues found that a high LMX differentiation (that is, a leader develops relationships of highly varying quality with the team members) attenuated the indirect relationship between LMX quality and follower creativity via self-efficacy. According to Liao and colleagues, this finding suggests that LMX may not effectively operate as a positive catalyst for followers' self-efficacy, and in turn creative idea implementation, when leaders allocate resources differentially among followers – perhaps because LMX differentiation is disadvantageous to the development of shared team justice perceptions (Liao et al., 2010).

In sum, these studies suggest that when leaders develop high-quality LMX relationships with their followers they respond by way of both creative idea generation and implementation. Furthermore, these studies suggest that LMX facilitates creative idea implementation in at least three ways. That is, LMX seems to elicit (1) a motivation-oriented feeling of psychological empowerment that may make followers *want to* implement creative ideas, (2) a social exchange-oriented felt obligation that makes them feel they *should* implement creative ideas, and (3) efficacy beliefs in their ability to actually do so (that is, self efficacy). However, the findings of these studies also suggest that these mechanisms may be influenced by job design characteristics (that is, job autonomy), and the social context (for example, LMX differentiation). In addition, and as a potential avenue for future research, LMX may also create an environment where followers are less afraid to fail, which may be particularly important for the implementation of creative ideas.

DISTINGUISHING BETWEEN ECONOMIC AND SOCIAL LMX RELATIONSHIPS

High-quality LMX relationships are typically identified in the LMX literature as social exchange relationships (Wayne et al., 2009), and low-quality transactional LMX relationships are typically identified as economic exchange relationships (Wayne et al., 2009). Most scholars investigating LMX relationships have assumed that LMX falls on a continuum from low to high quality. An economic leader–member exchange (ELMX) relationship, however, is not by definition the exact opposite of a social leader–member exchange (SLMX) relationship (cf., Blau, 1964; Shore et al., 2006). Therefore, ELMX and SLMX relationships should be portrayed as relationships with different qualities, as opposed to merely relationships with different levels of quality (Kuvaas et al., 2012). Although scholars have investigated multidimensional approaches to LMX (Liden and Maslyn, 1998; Greguras and Ford, 2006; Olsson et al., 2012), these still focus on the social part of the LMX dimension. As a result, knowledge about ELMX relationships and its outcomes was until recently seriously underdeveloped.

Kuvaas et al. (2012) addressed this gap in the literature by directly investigating the economic exchange dimension of dyadic LMX relationships among 552 followers and 78 leaders in a gas station chain in Norway. Kuvaas et al.'s (2012) exploratory study supported the two-dimensional nature of LMX relationships and demonstrated that an ELMX relationship related negatively to outcomes such as work performance and organizational citizenship behavior (OCB), or their willingness to 'go beyond that which is required' (Organ, 1990, p. 43). As expected, positive associations were revealed for an SLMX relationship and work performance and OCB. In a similar study, Buch et al. (2011) investigated the associations between ELMX and SLMX relationships and job satisfaction, affective commitment, and turnover intention among 716 Norwegian followers from ten organizations. They found that whereas an SLMX relationship was associated with greater job satisfaction, affective commitment, and lower turnover intentions, an ELMX relationship was associated with lower commitment and job satisfaction and greater turnover intentions (Buch et al., 2011).

In a third study, Buch et al. (2014) explored the possibility that LMX relationships are not equally important to all followers in terms of inducing beneficial follower outcomes, and that intrinsic motivation, or the motivation to carry out an activity for its own sake, so as to experience the satisfaction and pleasure inherent in the activity (Deci et al., 1989; Vallerand, 1997), is an important moderator of the associations between social and economic LMX and work effort. Specifically, they argued that followers with low intrinsic motivation might benefit more from social exchanges with their leader (that is, SLMX) to motivate them to increase their work effort, because such exchanges counterbalance followers' lack of interest in and enjoyment of the work itself. Furthermore, they argued that intrinsic motivation may have a neutralizing effect on the ELMX–effort association because intrinsically motivated followers should be less prone to the negative influences of the instrumental and contractual nature of ELMX relationships. Therefore, intrinsically motivated followers should perform well independently of the level of ELMX. While Buch et al. (2014) received support for an interaction between SLMX and intrinsic motivation in a study among 352 followers from the public health sector in Norway, the interaction between ELMX and intrinsic motivation was only marginally significant ($p = 0.08$). Nonetheless, their study suggests that intrinsic motivation may represent an important moderator of LMX–follower outcomes associations.

The moderating roles of SLMX and ELMX relationships have also been investigated. In a fourth study, Buch (2015) conceptualized employee–organization and leader–member exchange relationships as interdependently connected in the sense that the exchange of resources in one exchange relationship can have implications for the exchange of resources in the other exchange relationship (Coyle-Shapiro and Conway, 2004). The main finding, from a study of 341 followers from two financial companies in Norway, was that SLMX relationships reduce the negative link between organizational economic exchanges and affective organizational commitment. This indicates that SLMX relationships may play a crucial role by reducing the unintended 'side-effects' of economic employee–organization exchange relationships. Accordingly, organizations emphasizing economic exchanges such as pay-for-performance can benefit from promoting SLMX relationships among their employees.

In a final recent study, Dysvik et al. (2015) distinguished between knowledge donating (communicating knowledge to others) and knowledge collecting (actively consulting others for their intellectual capital; De Vries et al., 2006) and investigated the moderating roles of ELMX and SLMX on the association between followers' knowledge donating and leaders' knowledge collecting. They hypothesized that even though active knowledge donating by followers should make the leader more inclined to actively collect what is donated, knowledge sharing is a relational act. As such, the exchange of knowledge should depend upon the qualities of the relationship between followers and their leader. In this respect, they argued that the likelihood that the leader seeks to learn (collect) from followers in response to their communicated (donated) knowledge increases the higher the level of SLMX, and decreases the higher the level of ELMX. The hypotheses were tested using a sample of 227 leader–member dyads from four Norwegian organizations. In line with Dysvik et al.'s (2015) expectations, moderation analysis revealed a positive relationship between knowledge donating and knowledge collecting for high (but not low) levels of SLMX. Contrary to their expectations, however, an ELMX relationship did not moderate the association between the follower's knowledge donating and the leader's knowledge collecting.

SOCIAL AND ECONOMIC LMX RELATIONSHIPS AND FOLLOWER CREATIVITY

Even though the linkages between social and economic LMX relationships are still in the early stages of theory development, theoretical arguments presented below and the studies reviewed above collectively suggest that the characteristics of SLMX may be beneficial, and the characteristics of ELMX may be detrimental, for the generation and implementation of creative ideas.

More specifically, with respect to SLMX relationships, they align well with the traditional conceptualization and measurements of high-quality LMX (Kuvaas et al., 2012). Therefore, and based on studies that have focused on the association between high-quality LMX and creative idea implementation (for example, Liao et al., 2010; Olsson et al., 2012), SLMX should be positively related to the generation and implementation of creative ideas in the workplace:

Proposition 1: There is a positive association between SLMX relationships and creative idea generation and implementation

On the one hand, ELMX involves economic exchange behavior that may motivate the follower by providing a link between creative idea implementation and tangible rewards (Vroom, 1964). ELMX relationships may further provide the followers with a clear understanding of their precise responsibilities and their work status (Waldman et al., 1990), which in turn may serve to increase creative idea implementation to the extent that their organization emphasizes creativity and innovation. Furthermore, research reviewed by Wayne et al. (2002) concludes that 'a large body of research suggest[s] the importance of contingent rewards for leadership effectiveness' (p. 596).

On the other hand, the nature of the ELMX relationship is *quid pro quo* and the exchanges are limited to the fulfillment of basic requirements. Followers should feel only a minimum of emotional attachment to their leader when reciprocating, and be less interested in contributing above and beyond the necessary requirements. These characteristics of ELMX make it less likely that such relationships will foster the commitment and trust necessary for the generation and implementation of creative ideas. For example, creative idea generation and subsequent implementation can be quite demanding and stressful for followers, despite their potential benefits (for example, Janssen, 2004; Khazanchi and Masterson, 2011). As pointed out by Khazanchi and Masterson (2011, p. 92) 'taking the risk to offer new ideas that may have uncertain or unknown outcomes can cause feelings of anxiety'. While social exchange relationships may foster followers' perceptions that the leader is supportive of creative behaviors, has trust in them, and is there to support them when faced with stressful situations (Khazanchi and Masterson, 2011), ELMX relationships are more instrumental in nature with a lower level of mutual trust, obligation and investment in the relationship itself (Buch et al., 2014). As previously noted, the trust and support involved in SLMX relationships may be even more important for creative idea implementation.

Furthermore, creative behaviors in organizations conceptually overlap with discretionary organizational citizenship behaviors that are intended to help the organization and/or its members (Unsworth and Clegg, 2010), and as argued by Organ (1990) and echoed by Shore et al. (2006) social exchange is 'the best theoretical explanation for organizational citizenship' (p. 846), whereas 'economic exchange with the emphasis on a narrow set of economic obligations should be unrelated to citizenship' (ibid.). After all, a widespread assumption in the LMX literature is that transactional-based LMX relationships involve little more than what is stipulated in the employment contract (for example, Bernerth et al., 2007), and creative idea implementation is probably difficult to stipulate, measure, and monitor.

In addition, with a minimum of emotional attachment to their leader, followers in ELMX relationships experience lower job satisfaction (Buch et al., 2011) and thus probably fewer positive emotions, which help facilitate the capacity to think and act in the moment and thus their creativity (Dutton, 2003).

Finally, while Dysvik et al. (2015) did not obtain support for the proposition that ELMX increases the likelihood that the leader seeks to learn (collect) from followers in response to their communicated (donated) knowledge, they did report a negative correlation between ELMX and follower knowledge donating ($r = -0.18$, $p < 0.01$), suggesting that followers in ELMX relationships are significantly less willing to share knowledge. The lack of willingness to share knowledge is, in turn, likely to reduce creative idea generation, which in an organizational context is typically the result of information and knowledge sharing (Montuori and Purser, 1999; Khazanchi and Masterson, 2011). Taken as a whole, the above theoretical arguments and prior research suggest that there is a negative association between ELMX and creative idea generation and implementation:

Proposition 2: There is a negative association between ELMX relationships and creative idea generation and implementation.

CONCLUSION

In conclusion, research suggests that the leader–member exchange relationship plays a critical role for creative idea generation and implementation. We offered a proposition suggesting that economic exchange relationships among leaders and followers should be avoided, although we acknowledge that the ELMX–creative idea implementation association is not clear-cut, but rather complex and in need of more research. Nonetheless, it is probably safe to argue that organizations should strive to facilitate social exchange relationships among leaders and followers if they value creative idea generation and implementation. In this respect, research suggests that the development of high-quality, or social leader–member exchange relationships can be aided by relationship-oriented behaviors such as such as recognizing, supporting, delegating, and consulting (Yukl et al., 2009).

REFERENCES

Amabile, T.M. (1996), *Creativity in Context*, Boulder, CO: Westview.
Atwater, L. and A. Carmeli (2009), 'Leader–member exchange, feelings of energy, and involvement in creative work', *The Leadership Quarterly*, **20**(3), 264–75.
Bandura, A. (1997), *Self-efficacy: The Exercise of Control*, New York: Freeman.
Basu, R. and S.G. Green (1997), 'Leader–member exchange and transformational leadership: An empirical examination of innovative behaviors in leader–member dyads', *Journal of Applied Social Psychology*, **27**(6), 477–99.
Bernerth, J.B., A.A. Armenakis, H.S. Feild, W.F. Giles and H.J. Walker (2007), 'Leader–member social exchange (LMSX): Development and validation of a scale', *Journal of Organizational Behavior*, **28**(8), 979–1003.

Blau, P.M. (1964), *Exchange and Power in Social Life*, New York: John Wiley.

Buch, R. (2015), 'Leader–member exchange as a moderator of the relationship between employee–organization exchange and affective commitment', *The International Journal of Human Resource Management*, **26**(1), 59–79.

Buch, R., B. Kuvaas and A. Dysvik (2011), 'The measurement and outcomes of economic leader–member exchange relationships', paper presented at the Annual Meeting for the Academy of Management, San Antonio, TX.

Buch, R., B. Kuvaas, A. Dysvik and B. Schyns (2014), 'If and when social and economic leader–member exchange relationships predict follower work effort: The moderating role of work motivation', *Leadership and Organization Development Journal*, **35**(8), 725–39.

Coyle-Shapiro, J.A.M. and N. Conway (2004), 'The employment relationship through the lens of social exchange', in J.A.M. Coyle-Shapiro, L.M. Shore, S.M. Taylor and L.E. Tetrick (eds), *The Employment Relationship: Examining Psychological and Contextual Perspectives*, Oxford, UK: Oxford University Press, pp. 5–28.

De Vries, R.E., B. van den Hooff and J.A. de Ridder (2006), 'Explaining knowledge sharing: The role of team communication styles, job satisfaction, and performance beliefs', *Communication Research*, **33**(2), 115–35.

Deci, E.L., J.P. Connell and R.M. Ryan (1989), 'Self-determination in a work organization', *Journal of Applied Psychology*, **74**(4), 580–90.

Dulebohn, J.H., W.H. Bommer, R.C. Liden, R.L. Brouer and G.R. Ferris (2012), 'A meta-analysis of antecedents and consequences of leader–member exchange: Integrating the past with an eye toward the future', *Journal of Management*, **38**(6), 1715–59.

Dutton, J.E. (2003), *Energize your Workplace: How to Build and Sustain High-quality Relationships at Work*, San Francisco, CA: Jossey-Bass.

Dysvik, A., R. Buch and B. Kuvaas (2015), 'Knowledge donating and knowledge collecting: The moderating roles of social and economic LMX', *Leadership and Organization Development Journal*, **36**(1), 35–53.

Gerstner, C.R. and D.V. Day (1997), 'Meta-analytic review of leader–member exchange theory: Correlates and construct issues', *Journal of Applied Psychology*, **82**(6), 827–44.

Graen, G. and T.A. Scandura (1987), 'Toward a psychology of dyadic organizing', in L.L. Cummings and B.M. Staw (eds), *Research in Organizational Behavior*, Vol. 9, Greenwich, CT: JAI Press, pp. 175–208.

Graen, G. and M. Uhl-Bien (1995), 'Relationship-based approach to leadership: Development of leader–member exchange (LMX) theory of leadership over 25 years: Applying a multi-level multi-domain perspective', *The Leadership Quarterly*, **6**(2), 219–47.

Graves, L.M. and M.M. Luciano (2010), 'Effects of LMX on employee attitudes: The role of need satisfaction and autonomous motivation', *Academy of Management Proceedings*, **1**, 1–6.

Greguras, G.J. and J.M. Ford (2006), 'An examination of the multidimensionality of supervisor and subordinate perceptions of leader–member exchange', *Journal of Occupational and Organizational Psychology*, **79**(3), 433–65.

Hammond, M.M., N.L. Neff, J.L. Farr, A.R. Schwall and X. Zhao (2011), 'Predictors of individual-level innovation at work: A meta-analysis', *Psychology of Aesthetics, Creativity, and the Arts*, **5**(1), 90–105.

Ilies, R., J.D. Nahrgang and F.P. Morgeson (2007), 'Leader–member exchange and citizenship behaviors: A meta-analysis', *Journal of Applied Psychology*, **92**(1), 269–77.

Janssen, O. (2004), 'How fairness perceptions make innovative behavior more or less stressful', *Journal of Organizational Behavior*, **25**(2), 201–15.

Khazanchi, S. and S.S. Masterson (2011), 'Who and what is fair matters: A multi-foci social exchange model of creativity', *Journal of Organizational Behavior*, **32**(1), 86–106.

Kuvaas, B., R. Buch, A. Dysvik and T. Haerem (2012), 'Economic and social leader–member exchange relationships and follower performance', *The Leadership Quarterly*, **23**(5), 756–65.

Liao, H., D. Liu and R. Loi (2010), 'Looking at both sides of the social exchange coin: A social cognitive perspective on the joint effects of relationship quality and differentiation on creativity', *Academy of Management Journal*, **53**(5), 1090–109.

Liden, R.C. and J.M. Maslyn (1998), 'Multidimensionality of leader–member exchange: An empirical assessment through scale development', *Journal of Management*, **24**(1), 43–72.

Montuori, M. and R. Purser (1999), *Social Creativity*, Vol. 1, Cresskill, NJ: Hampton Press.

Olsson, L., S. Hemlin and A. Pousette (2012), 'A multi-level analysis of leader–member exchange and creative performance in research groups', *The Leadership Quarterly*, **23**(3), 604–19.

Organ, D.W. (1990), 'The motivational basis of organizational citizenship behavior', in B.M. Staw and L.L. Cummings (eds), *Research in Organizational Behavior*, Vol. 12, Greenwich, CT: JAI Press, pp. 43–72.

Pan, W., L.-Y. Sun and I.H.S. Chow (2012), 'Leader–member exchange and employee creativity: Test of a multilevel moderated mediation model', *Human Performance*, **25**(5), 432–51.

Rockstuhl, T., J.H. Dulebohn, S. Ang and L.M. Shore (2012), 'Leader–member exchange (LMX) and culture: A meta-analysis of correlates of LMX across 23 countries', *Journal of Applied Psychology*, **97**(6), 1097–130.

Shalley, C.E. (1991), 'Effects of productivity goals, creativity goals, and personal discretion on individual creativity', *Journal of Applied Psychology*, **76**(2), 179–85.

Shore, L.M., L.E. Tetrick, P. Lynch and K. Barksdale (2006), 'Social and economic exchange: Construct development and validation', *Journal of Applied Social Psychology*, **36**(4), 837–67.

Škerlavaj, M., M. Černe and A. Dysvik (2014), 'I get by with a little help from my supervisor: Creative-idea generation, idea implementation, and perceived supervisor support', *The Leadership Quarterly*, **25**(5), 987–1000.

Tierney, P. (2008), 'Leadership and employee creativity', in J. Zhou and C.E. Shalley (eds), *Handbook of Organizational Creativity*, New York: Erlbaum, pp. 95–124.

Tierney, P. and S.M. Farmer (2002), 'Creative self-efficacy: Its potential antecedents and relationship to creative performance', *Academy of Management Journal*, **45**(6), 1137–48.

Tierney, P., S.M. Farmer and G.B. Graen (1999), 'An examination of leadership and employee creativity: The relevance of traits and relationships', *Personnel Psychology*, **52**(3), 591–620.

Unsworth, K.L. and C.W. Clegg (2010), 'Why do employees undertake creative action?' *Journal of Occupational and Organizational Psychology*, **83**(1), 77–99.

Vallerand, R.J. (1997), 'Toward a hierarchical model of intrinsic and extrinsic motivation', in M.P. Zanna (ed.), *Advances in Experimental Social Psychology*, Vol. 29, San Diego: Academic Press, pp. 271–360.

Volmer, J., D. Spurk and C. Niessen (2012), 'Leader–member exchange (LMX), job autonomy, and creative work involvement', *Leadership Quarterly*, **23**(3), 456–65.

Vroom, V.H. (1964), *Work and Motivation*, New York: Wiley.

Waldman, D.A., B.M. Bass and F.J. Yammarino (1990), 'Adding to contingent-reward behavior – the augmenting effect of charismatic leadership', *Group and Organization Studies*, **15**(4), 381–94.

Wayne, S.J., L.M. Shore, W.H. Bommer and L.E. Tetrick (2002), 'The role of fair treatment and rewards in perceptions of organizational support and leader–member exchange', *Journal of Applied Psychology*, **87**(3), 590–98.

Wayne, S.J., J. Coyle-Shapiro, R. Eisenberger, R.C. Liden, D.M. Rousseau and L.M. Shore (2009), 'Social influences', in H.J. Klein, T.E. Becker and J.P. Meyer (eds), *Commitment in Organizations: Accumulated Wisdom and New Directions*, New York: Routledge, pp. 253–84.

Yukl, G.A., M. O'Donnell and T. Taber (2009), 'Influence of leader behaviors on the leader–member exchange relationship', *Journal of Managerial Psychology*, **24**(4), 289–99.

11. Everything in moderation: authentic leadership, leader–member exchange and idea implementation

Matej Černe, John Sumanth and Miha Škerlavaj

The notion of authenticity has deep roots, reaching back into the discourse of ancient Greek philosophers focused on their search of self-understanding ('knowing thyself') and being genuine ('being true to thyself'). Scholarly research on the topic of authentic leadership, however, has flourished in the past decade or so, and a considerable amount of academic work has emerged during this period. After it had first gained popularity through practitioner books, some even best-sellers (for example, George, 2003; Cashman, 2008), scholars have listed numerous definitions and conceptualizations of authentic leadership (see Gardner et al., 2011 for a comprehensive review). As a result, the study of this leadership approach is currently somewhat fragmented (Sumanth and Hannah, 2014) and many open questions loom over the field (cf. Gardner et al., 2005, 2011). However, consistent across the majority of these perspectives is a focus on the enhancement and development of employees' values, motives, emotions, and goals, and capitalizing on them for the benefit of the organization (Gardner et al., 2005). Consequently, many even consider authentic leadership foundational for any positive forms of leadership (May et al., 2003; Ilies et al., 2005).

The most recently used definition of authentic leadership (Walumbwa et al., 2008, p. 94) describes it as:

> [. . .]a pattern of leader behavior that draws upon and promotes both positive psychological capacities and a positive ethical climate, to foster greater self-awareness, an internalized moral perspective, balanced processing of information, and relational transparency on the part of leaders working with followers, fostering positive self-development.

Authentic leadership is comprised of four unique dimensions: (1) self-awareness, (2) balanced processing, (3) relational transparency, and an (4) internalized moral perspective. Self-awareness is related to self-reflection and learning about oneself. Through introspection, leaders who engage in authentic behaviors observe and analyze their own mental state, including their thoughts, feelings, and aspirations. Internal connection with one's true self is achieved by an individual delving into his or her own personality by recalling the important events in his or her life, and by examining his or her reactions and emotions during these milestones (Avolio and Gardner, 2005). Balanced processing means as objective and bias-free as possible, analyzing all relevant information before making a decision (Gardner et al., 2005). It includes precise and balanced perception and evaluation of oneself and others that are independent from ego-based defense mechanisms (Gardner et al., 2009).

The third authentic leadership dimension, internalized moral perspective, implies that managers possess and exhibit internal moral standards and values instead of allowing external pressures to influence their behavior. Individuals possessing high levels of moral perspective direct their own behavior to match moral standards (May et al., 2003; Begley, 2006; Novicevic et al., 2006). The fourth dimension, relational transparency, involves leaders exhibiting open, transparent relations with their coworkers. Managers show their true selves when they exhibit openness, engage in self-disclosure, and are willing to be vulnerable (that is, trust) to their followers (Gardner et al., 2005). Such behavior encourages trust building between leader and follower through sharing of information and expressing true thoughts and feelings (Kernis, 2003).

Based on these dimensions and their characteristics, authentic leadership is often characterized by transparency, consistency, and reliability, and has been shown to foster greater trust, emotional safety, and unconventional idea proposition within followers (Avolio et al., 2004). Because individuals who willingly engage in authentic leadership behaviors tend to be more tolerant of ambiguity and open to new experiences and change, they are often helpful catalysts for stimulating creativity and/or innovation in others (for example, Rego et al., 2012, 2014; Černe et al., 2013).

Yet, despite this acknowledgement that authentic leaders have a positive role to play in cultivating and supporting their followers' creative and innovative potential, many unanswered questions remain. Consistent with scholars' long operating under the implicit assumption that positive leadership behaviors yield perpetual benefits, without any downside or negative consequences, most previous studies exploring authentic leadership phenomena have neglected its potential pitfalls. Such an approach has been the norm for many years in organizational circles, leading to a host of studies being conducted with relationships hypothesized as purely linear functions. Sadly, this traditional linear-based approach to diagnosing leadership's impact disregards emerging conceptual and empirical work suggesting many organizational phenomena, including leadership, are far more complex and multifaceted than typically presented (Fleishman and Harris, 1962; Sumanth, 2011; Grant and Schwartz, 2012; Pierce and Aguinis, 2013; Škerlavaj et al., 2014). Speaking directly to this point in his review of the leadership literature, Yukl (2012) bemoaned the fact that leadership scholars have for too long approached the study of leadership from a romanticized, positivist perspective that fails to consider the possibility of non-linear relationships between leadership behavior and important individual, team, and organizational outcomes. Regrettably, this parsimonious mindset has 'obscured the prevalence and importance of non-monotonic inverted-U-shaped effects, whereby positive phenomena reach inflection points at which their effects turn negative' (Grant and Schwartz, 2012, p. 61).

The purpose of this chapter is to review recent research on authentic leadership that acknowledges the fact that this construct may not always provide positive benefits, and explicitly focuses on how leaders that are deemed 'too authentic' may in fact contribute heavily to their followers' plateauing returns on innovation (in other words, individual-level idea implementation).

A CURVILINEAR RELATIONSHIP OF AUTHENTIC LEADERSHIP WITH BOTH CREATIVITY (IDEA GENERATION) AND INNOVATION (IDEA IMPLEMENTATION)

In this chapter, we empirically explore the form of the relationship between authentic leadership and followers' idea implementation, paying specific attention as to how it may vary across different levels of authentic leadership behavior. The data were collected from 171 employees and their 24 direct supervisors in a Slovenian manufacturing and processing company that produces highly customized bathroom equipment and accessories. We measured idea implementation with three items (see Montag et al., 2012 for a discussion on selecting appropriate items from general creativity or innovation scales) from the research instrument developed by Zhou and George (2001). Using a series of hierarchical regression analyses, we found that leaders who are perceived as high on their authentic leadership behaviors contribute to their followers' diminished returns on idea implementation (β of the linear term of authentic leadership $= 0.29$, $p < 0.05$; quadratic term $= -0.25$, $p < 0.05$). Specifically, we find that the self-awareness dimension of authentic leadership is most closely associated with the curvilinear impact on idea implementation (β of the linear term of self-awareness $= 0.21$, $p < 0.05$; quadratic term $= -0.27$, $p < 0.05$) (Figure 11.1).

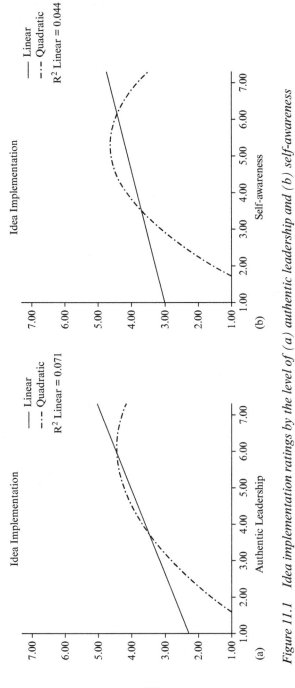

Figure 11.1 Idea implementation ratings by the level of (a) authentic leadership and (b) self-awareness

We tested the 'too-much-of-a-good-thing effect' recently articulated by Pierce and Aguinis (2013) and Grant and Schwartz (2012), and shed valuable theoretical insight into how authentic leadership may be inherently limited in terms of the positive benefits it is espoused to produce. Using the conceptual lens of social exchange (Blau, 1964), we found an inverted curvilinear U-shaped relationship between supervisors' authentic leadership and followers' idea implementation. These findings support the view that authentic leadership is generally a suitable leadership style for enhancing employee idea implementation, but also leads to diminishing or plateauing returns at very high levels.

We propose that this relationship is formed partly by the quality of the exchange relationship between leaders and their followers. Leaders perceived as too authentic by their followers risk stifling their followers' innovative output by causing them to disengage from the task, in part, because of a faulty belief that their efforts are no longer needed or valued. In line with Tierney's (2008) call to examine how leaders can suppress employees' innovative behaviors, our research indicates that under low levels of authentic leadership, followers can become emotionally detached from their leader due to their perceived lack of self-awareness and relational transparency.

On the other end of the spectrum, although a high level of self-awareness and certainty is a hallmark of a highly authentic leader, this may also come across as leaders 'having it all figured out', thus reducing followers' motivation to provide idea-implementation behavior. When individuals view their leaders as directly or indirectly lording power and moral superiority over them, they are likely to resist the leaders' efforts and seek ways to exit the healthy exchange relationship (Tepper et al., 2009; Kiazad et al., 2010). If such concerns remain unaddressed, followers may be more disinclined to form the strong relational bonds that can help to enhance their own energy and creativity (cf., Atwater and Carmeli, 2009). In this way, high leader authenticity can actually backfire by creating the perception amongst followers that they are superfluous and even hindrances. Authentic leadership apparently qualifies as one of the many positive-oriented leadership constructs that also seem to have a 'dark side'.

We further theorize about the underlying mechanism, explaining why high levels of authentic leadership may undermine and weaken the reciprocal bonds that characterize strong leader–follower relationships, and consequently diminish creative-idea implementation. Highly authentic leaders might also frequently be viewed as narcissistic, and this undermines their patterns of social exchange with their followers, resulting in decreased engagement in the idea implementation task. In striving to become more self-aware, morally focused, open-minded, and relationally transparent, leaders may unintentionally signal to observers that their own personal growth and leader development takes precedence over the wants and needs of others (Paulhus, 1998; Morf and Rhodewalt, 2001). Although leaders' efforts may be well intentioned and aimed at improving their followers' psychological resources and capabilities, by focusing on authentic actions leaders may inadvertently move the spotlight away from others (for example, leadership development) and upon themselves (for example, leader development). This subtle, but important shift in leader–member focus is likely to speak volumes to observers about the leader's priorities and interests (in other words, a disproportionate focus on self-development at the expense of others) and reinforce the psychological distance that naturally exists between leader and follower. Consequently, followers may come to see their leaders as self-absorbed and overly narcissistic in their leadership approach (Grijalva et al., 2014; Grijalva and Newman, 2015).

In general, research suggests that individuals who exhibit narcissistic tendencies tend to display greater self-confidence and efficacy in their abilities to perform at a high level, which helps them to emerge as leaders more often (Brunell et al., 2008). At the same time, however, narcissists have also been known to be destructive forces within organizations, noted for their Machiavellian attitudes, self-aggrandizement, and inability to work well with others (Maccoby, 2004; Rosenthal and Pittinsky, 2006). In situations where followers perceive their leaders' authentic behaviors as disingenuous or primarily self-serving, followers may be less motivated to provide their leaders with high-quality ideas because they lack faith in their leaders' motives and values, perceiving them as exceedingly independent, and having little need or value for others' contributions (Baer et al., 2003). This, in turn, further deteriorates the leader–member relationship (Padilla et al., 2007). By focusing sustained time and energy on their own authentic advancement, leaders may unwittingly create negative reputations as 'Lone Rangers', which leads followers to see themselves as superfluous to achieving their leaders' stated goals and objectives. Because highly authentic leaders, by definition, have a deep and intimate sense of their unique strengths and weaknesses, followers may misconstrue their leaders' heightened self-awareness as excessive self-reliance that equips them to act independently (Martin, 2004; Černe et al., 2014). For these reasons, behaving in a highly authentic manner and being perceived as narcissistic may short-circuit the relational process that enables followers to engage in the creative task, take risks, perform more effectively, and implement more and better creative solutions (Atwater and Carmeli, 2009; Liao et al., 2010). Thus, what started out on the leader's part as an honest effort to gain greater insight and self-understanding may ultimately backfire and lead to unintended negative consequences, such as diminished idea implementation output.

PRACTICAL EXAMPLES OF OVERLY AUTHENTIC AND CONSEQUENTLY, OVERLY NARCISSISTIC LEADERS

Most people think of narcissists in a primarily negative way; after all, Freud named the type after the mythical figure Narcissus, who died because of his pathological preoccupation with himself. However, narcissism in leadership may not necessarily be a bad thing per se. Moderate levels of narcissism may in fact prove to be beneficial for effective leadership. Too little narcissism and the leader will lack the confidence to do what it takes to get the position or to fulfill the negative responsibilities of the job (for example, firing people).

Major problems occur when there is too much narcissism. In such cases, the leader may believe that he or she is better than others, or even above the law (Burgemeester, 2013). Consider how an executive at Oracle described his narcissistic CEO Larry Ellison: 'The difference between God and Larry is that God does not believe he is Larry'. Leadership expert and psychoanalyst Michael Maccoby, co-author of *The Productive Narcissist: The Promise and Peril of Visionary Leadership* (2003), describes what he labels 'productive narcissists'. He believes it takes a healthy dose of narcissism for leaders of huge corporations to have great visions and achieve them. He argues that many of the revered leaders of the technological revolution, Bill Gates, the late Steve Jobs, Andy Grove, are productive narcissists (Maccoby, 2004).

Narcissism helps these leaders accomplish extraordinary things, but it can also be their ruin. Leaders who are too narcissistic are convinced they are right and are too sensitive to criticism, leading them to ignore legitimate warnings. Because they lack empathy, they are also insensitive to the impact of their behavior on others. Moreover, leaders with too much narcissism begin to believe that they are above the law and they may engage in illegal or unethical behavior – and that is the downfall of many narcissists (Burgemeester, 2013). Despite the pleasant feelings that charisma induces in others, narcissists suffer from looming weaknesses, such as being uncomfortable with own emotions, sensitive to criticism, poor listeners, and having lack of empathy (Burgemeester, 2013). They are known to possess 'egos the size of skyscrapers', arrogance, envy of others, having an intense desire to compete, distaste for mentoring, and reluctance to take blame or share credit (Maccoby, 2004). This indicates that narcissists are far from being team players, which shows in the idea implementation process.

Maccoby (2004) illustrates this notion in the Volvo case and discusses the manager Pehr Gyllenhammar, who tried to revolutionize the industrial workplace by replacing the traditional assembly line with a team-based approach. This novelty was embraced with enthusiasm among the employees and the broader public, making him very successful and internationally praised. However, Gyllenhammar started to feel he could ignore the concerns of his operational managers, and pursued chancy and expensive new business deals, which he publicized on television and in the press (ibid.). He overestimated himself, leading him to believe that others would want him to be 'the czar' of a multinational enterprise. This led to some misguided individual business decisions that eventually led to his resignation (ibid.).

OVERCOMING THE (MIS-)PERCEPTIONS OF NARCISSISM

In our field study, we found that authentic leadership at high levels, despite its inherent benefits, can be detrimental to followers' idea implementation because of the way in which it short-circuits the natural exchange process between leaders and followers and activates negative leader perceptions of narcissism.

In order to combat this potentially detrimental outcome, we first suggest that leaders engage in authentic leadership to the extent that it doesn't fuel negative perceptions of narcissism and doesn't jeopardize the pattern of leader–follower exchange that characterizes healthy, productive work relationships. Obviously, walking this tightrope of authenticity is easier said than done. In order to carry this out in practice, leaders must emphasize in their daily actions, communications with others and self-development work that the ultimate goal of this authentic transformation is the betterment of others and their organization. Rather than obsessing over their own characteristics and development, successful authentic leaders focus more on the relational aspects of their leadership and the needs of others (Dasborough and Ashkanasy, 2005). By openly sharing information and expressing their true thoughts and emotions in their central work relationships, leaders can strengthen the relational transparency dimension of their authentic leadership approach, which in our supplementary empirical tests, did not exhibit any negative curvilinear trends at high levels.

Furthermore, by engaging in behaviors that reflect a greater concern for others, as opposed to self, research suggests leaders may be able to effectively mitigate attributions of narcissism. In a recent set of studies, Giacomin and Jordan (2014) found that individuals who were induced to feel empathy and more interdependent, rather than independent self-construals, reported less state narcissism. Importantly, these changes in state narcissism were found to mediate changes in desire for fame and perceptions that others deserve help, giving greater weight to the possibility that narcissism may be more state-like and context-dependent than previously assumed. In this way, leaders may be able to foster positive and productive relationships with subordinates by creating a relational dynamic that encourages collegial collaboration (Novicevic et al., 2006) and that enables expressions of authentic leadership to flourish unadulterated.

From the practical perspective, Maccoby (2004) offers some explicit solutions, such as finding a sidekick or indoctrinating the organization. The first suggestion would be to find a trustworthy sidekick (Maccoby, 2004, p. 1), which speaks to the importance of social and practical support in implementing innovations:

> Bill Gates can think about the future from the stratosphere because Steve Ballmer, a tough obsessive COO, keeps the show on the road. At Oracle, CEO Larry Ellison can afford to miss key meetings and spend time on his boat contemplating a future without PCs because he has a productive obsessive COO in Ray Lane to run the company for him.

The second approach involves indoctrinating the organization as a whole (ibid.):

> GE's Jack Welch uses toughness to build a corporate culture and to implement a daring business strategy, including the buying and selling of scores of companies. Welch was able to transform his industry by focusing on execution and pushing companies to the limits of quality and efficiency, bumping up revenues and wringing out costs. In order to do so, Welch hammers out a huge corporate culture in his own image – a culture that provides impressive rewards for senior managers and shareholders.

A misunderstanding of Welch's approach to culture building is widely documented (Tichy and Cohen, 1997), and his techniques are often labeled as teaching. But Maccoby argues how Welch's approach involves a personal ideology that he indoctrinates into GE managers through speeches, memos, and confrontations. This in turn is successful in transforming merely ideas into implemented innovations:

> Rather than create a dialogue, Welch makes pronouncements (either be the number one or two company in your market or get out), and he institutes programs (such as Six Sigma quality), that become the GE party line. GE managers must either internalize his vision or they must leave. Welch does have the rare insight and know-how to achieve what all narcissistic business leaders are trying to do – namely, get the organization to identify with them, to think the way they do, and to become the living embodiment of their companies. (Ibid.)

To conclude, a discussion about 'true authenticity' is in order (see Černe et al., 2014 for a start), one that could make problems and challenges related to authentic leadership less problematic. The question that commonly emerges is: Can the leaders (or anyone, for that matter) be inauthentic? Is this labeling even appropriate? How about responsible leaders (including ethical etc.)? Wouldn't this be more in line with what the authentic leadership construct presents? If we stick to 'authenticity' per se, which is actually opposing some propositions in the authentic leadership model (see Cooper et al., 2005; Shamir and Eilam, 2005; Sparrowe, 2005 for discussions), it is bound to include something negative in some individuals, and frequent misperceptions of the meaning of authenticity, as our study has shown. We hope to have stimulated additional research on the very 'core' of authentic leadership and potential pitfalls it may possess, but also the possible remedies or boundary conditions aimed at making this leadership style the most effective.

REFERENCES

Atwater, L. and A. Carmeli (2009), 'Leader–member exchange, feelings of energy, and involvement in creative work', *The Leadership Quarterly*, **20**(3), 264–75.

Avolio, B.J., W.L. Gardner, F.O. Walumbwa, F. Luthans and D.R. May (2004), 'Unlocking the mask: A look at the process by which authentic leaders impact follower attitudes and behaviors', *The Leadership Quarterly*, **15**(6), 801–23.

Baer, M., G.R. Oldham and A. Cummings (2003), 'Rewarding creativity: When does it really matter?' *The Leadership Quarterly*, **14**(4), 569–86.

Begley, P. (2006), 'Self-knowledge, capacity and sensitivity: Prerequisites to authentic leadership by school principals', *Journal of Educational Administration*, **44**(6), 570–89.

Blau, P.M. (1964), *Exchange and Power in Social Life*, New York: Wiley.

Brunell, A.B., W.A. Gentry, W.K. Campbell, B.J. Hoffman, K.W. Kuhnert and K.G. DeMarree (2008), 'Leader emergence: The case of the narcissistic leader', *Personality and Social Psychology Bulletin*, **34**(12), 1663–76.

Burgemeester, A. (2013), 'Business leaders and narcissism', *The Narcissistic Life*, 5 May, accessed 24 June 2014 at http://thenarcissisticlife.com/business-leaders-and-narcissism/.

Cashman, K. (2008), *Leadership from the Inside Out: Becoming a Leader for Life*, 2nd edition, San Francisco, CA: Berrett-Koehler.

Černe, M., M. Jaklič and M. Škerlavaj (2013), 'Authentic leadership, creativity, and innovation: A multilevel perspective', *Leadership*, **9**(1), 63–85.

Černe, M., V. Dimovski, M. Mari, S. Penger and M. Škerlavaj (2014), 'Congruence of leader self-perceptions and follower perceptions of authentic leadership: Understanding what authentic leadership is and how it enhances employees' job satisfaction', *Australian Journal of Management*, **39**(3), 453–71.

Cooper, C.D., T.A. Scandura and C.A. Schriesheim (2005), 'Looking forward but learning from our past: Potential challenges to developing authentic leadership theory and authentic leaders', *The Leadership Quarterly*, **16**(3), 475–93.

Dasborough, M.T. and N.M. Ashkanasy (2005), 'Follower emotional reactions to authentic and inauthentic leadership influence', in W.L. Gardner, B.J. Avolio and F. Walumbwa (eds), *Authentic Leadership Theory and Practice: Origins, Effects and Development*, Oxford, UK: Elsevier, pp. 281–300.

Fleishman, E.A. and E.F. Harris (1962), 'Patterns of leadership behavior related to employee grievances and turnover', *Personnel Psychology*, **15**(1), 43–56.

Gardner, W.L., D. Fischer and J.G. Hunt (2009), 'Emotional labor and leadership: A threat to authenticity?' *The Leadership Quarterly*, **20**(3), 466–82.

Gardner, W.L., C.C. Cogliser, K.M. Davis and M.P. Dickens (2011), 'Authentic leadership: A review of the literature and research agenda', *The Leadership Quarterly*, **22**(6), 1120–45.

Gardner, W., B. Avolio, F. Luthans, D. May and F. Walumbwa (2005), '"Can you see the real me?" A self-based model of authentic leader and follower development', *The Leadership Quarterly*, **16**(3), 343–72.

George, W. (2003), *Authentic Leadership: Rediscovering the Secrets to Creating Lasting Value*, San Francisco, CA: Jossey-Bass.

Giacomin, M. and C.H. Jordan (2014), 'Down-regulating narcissistic tendencies: Communal focus reduces state narcissism', *Personality and Social Psychology Bulletin*, **40**(4), 488–500.

Grant, A.M. and B. Schwartz (2012), 'Too much of a good thing: The challenge and opportunity of the inverted U', *Perspectives on Psychological Science*, **6**(1), 61–76.

Grijalva, E. and D.A. Newman (2015), 'Narcissism and counterproductive work behavior (CWB): Meta-analysis and consideration of collectivist culture, big five personality, and narcissism's facet structure', *Applied Psychology*, **64**(1), 93–126.

Grijalva, E., P.D. Harms, D. Newman, B. Gaddis and R. Fraley (2014), 'Narcissism and leadership: A meta-analytic review of linear and non-linear relationships', *Personnel Psychology*, **68**(1), 1–47.

Ilies, R., F.P. Morgeson and J.D. Nahrgang (2005), 'Authentic leadership and eudaemonic well-being: Understanding leader–follower outcomes', *The Leadership Quarterly*, **16**(3), 373–94.

Kernis, M. (2003), 'Toward a conceptualization of optimal self-esteem', *Psychological Inquiry*, **14**(1), 1–26.

Kiazad, K., S.L.D. Restubog, T.J. Zagenczyk, C. Kiewitz and R.L. Tang (2010), 'In pursuit of power: The role of authoritarian leadership in the relationship between supervisors' Machiavellianism and subordinates' perceptions of abusive supervisory behavior', *Journal of Research in Personality*, **44**(4), 512–19.

Liao, H., D. Liu and R. Loi (2010), 'Looking at both sides of the social exchange coin: A social cognitive perspective on the joint effects of relationship quality and differentiation on creativity', *Academy of Management Journal*, **53**(5), 1090–109.

Maccoby, M. (2004), 'Narcissistic leaders: The incredible pros, the inevitable cons', *Harvard Business Review*, January, accessed 7 March 2015 at https://hbr.org/2004/01/narcissistic-leaders-the-incredible-pros-the-inevitable-cons.

Maccoby, M. and C. Conrad (2003), *The Productive Narcissist: The Promise and Peril of Visionary Leadership*, New York: Broadway Books.

Martin, M.G. (2004), 'The limits of self-awareness', *Philosophical Studies*, **120**(1), 37–89.

May, D.R., A.Y.L. Chan, T.D. Hodges and B.J. Avolio (2003), 'Developing the moral component of authentic leadership', *Organizational Dynamics*, **32**(3), 247–60.

Montag, T., C.P. Maertz and M. Baer (2012), 'A critical analysis of the workplace creativity criterion space', *Journal of Management*, **38**(4), 1362–86.

Morf, C.C. and F. Rhodewalt (2001), 'Unraveling the paradoxes of narcissism: A dynamic self-regulatory processing model', *Psychological Inquiry*, **12**(4), 177–96.

Novicevic, M., M. Harvey, M. Ronald and J. Brown-Radford (2006), 'Authentic leadership: A historical perspective', *Journal of Leadership and Organizational Studies*, **13**(1), 64–76.

Padilla, A., R. Hogan and R.B. Kaiser (2007), 'The toxic triangle: Destructive leaders, susceptible followers, and conducive environments', *The Leadership Quarterly*, **18**(3), 176–94.

Paulhus, D.L. (1998), 'Interpersonal and intrapsychic adaptiveness of trait self-enhancement: A mixed blessing?' *Journal of Personality and Social Psychology*, **74**(5), 1197–208.

Pierce, J.R. and H. Aguinis (2013), 'The too-much-of-a-good-thing effect in management', *Journal of Management*, **39**(3), 313–38.

Rego, A., F. Sousa and C. Marques (2012), 'Authentic leadership promoting employees' psychological capital and creativity', *Journal of Business Research*, **65**(3), 429–37.

Rego, A., F. Sousa, C. Marques and M. Pina e Cunha (2014), 'Hope and positive affect mediating the authentic leadership and creativity relationship', *Journal of Business Research*, **67**(2), 200–210.

Rosenthal, S.A. and T.L. Pittinsky (2006), 'Narcissistic leadership', *The Leadership Quarterly*, **17**(6), 617–33.

Shamir, B. and G. Eilam (2005), 'What's your story?' A life-stories approach to authentic leadership development', *The Leadership Quarterly*, **16**(3), 395–417.

Sparrowe, R.T. (2005), 'Authentic leadership and the narrative self', *The Leadership Quarterly*, **16**(3), 419–39.

Sumanth, J. (2011), 'Speak well not more: How highly inclusive leaders diminish upward communication quality, doctoral dissertation', Chapel Hill, NC: University of North Carolina.

Sumanth, J.J. and S.T. Hannah (2014), 'Developing leadership capacity: An integration and exploration of ethical and authentic leadership antecedents', in L.L. Neider and C.A. Schriesheim (eds), *Advances in Authentic and Ethical Leadership*, Charlotte, NC: Research in Management, pp. 25–74.

Škerlavaj, M., M. Černe and A. Dysvik (2014), 'I get by with a little help from my supervisor: Creative-idea generation, idea implementation, and perceived supervisor support', *Leadership Quarterly*, **25**(5), 987–1000.

Tepper, B.J., J.C. Carr, D.M. Breaux, S. Geider, C. Hu and W. Hua (2009), 'Abusive supervision, intentions to quit, and employees' workplace deviance: A power/dependence analysis', *Organizational Behavior and Human Decision Processes*, **109**(2), 156–67.

Tichy, N.M. and E. Cohen (1997), *The Leadership Engine*, New York: HarperCollins.

Tierney, P. (2008), 'Leadership and employee creativity', in J. Zhou and C.E. Shalley (eds), *Handbook of Organizational Creativity*, New York: Lawrence Erlbaum Associates, pp. 95–123.

Walumbwa, F., B. Avolio, W. Gardner, T. Wernsing and S. Peterson (2008),

'Authentic leadership: Development and validation of a theory-based measure', *Journal of Management*, **34**(1), 89–126.

Yukl, G. (2012), 'Effective leadership behaviors: What we know and what questions need more attention?' *The Academy of Management Perspectives*, **26**(4), 66–85.

Zhou, J. and J. George (2001), 'When job dissatisfaction leads to creativity: Encouraging the expression of voice', *Academy of Management Journal*, **44**(4), 682–96.

PART IV

What can we do about it as organizations?

12. Creativity that works: implementing discovery

Arne Carlsen and Liisa Välikangas

Upon returning from California to Finland in 2008, one of the authors was struck by the different attitude towards ideas at the two sets of industrial culture. In Silicon Valley, ideas were about the exploration of the new. The stranger the idea, the more opportunities it gave for thinking about what could be. In Finland, ideas were strictly about implementation. Indeed, upon voicing an idea, one was very soon charged with its execution. Not proceeding to such implementation meant personal failure.

These two attitudes at two sites across the Atlantic illustrate very different assumptions toward what ideas are and how one can capitalize on creativity in organizations. In this chapter we challenge implicit assumptions with regard to ideas as discrete, stable entities to be implemented in processes subsequent to and clearly separated from their generation. We differentiate between an orthodox view where implementation is a matter of execution and a more enlightened view where implementation is best understood as a process of discovery.

The orthodox view of creativity carries implicit assumptions of discreteness and reification of ideas. It implies a linear sequence to creative work and an atomistic view of the decisions of actors. We discuss why these assumptions are both theoretically flawed and impractical (or ineffective) and present tenets of a strong process-based view on creativity. Building on practice-based approaches to creativity and two sets of recent empirical research (Carlsen et al., 2012; Välikangas and Romme, 2013) we then present and illustrate the dynamics of 'implementation by discovery'. It is essential that we recognize that ideas are more or less always in flux and being worked upon. It is the processes where one's ideas come into contact with ideas of others, by adaptation, exploration, and connection that ultimately determine their potential for fruitful capitalization.

WHY A STRONG PROCESS VIEW OF CREATIVITY?

In a recent article on implementation of creative ideas in organizations, leading creativity researcher Markus Baer (2012, p. 1103) 'acknowledges' that 'idea generation and implementation are two clearly distinguishable elements of the innovation process'. Baer assumes that there are creative ideas that may be considered both novel and useful but are not implemented because they evoke uncertainty and are met with resistance. He further suggests that creative ideas may be disadvantaged over mundane ideas because the latter evoke less resistance. The assumption, made from the outset, is that ideas emerge in a state ready for implementation. Thus it is better to be mundane rather than creative for the sake of materialized outcomes (ibid., p. 1106).

To us, this way of talking about creativity provides a serious itch. Why so? It assumes that there is a distinct phase or decision point whereby people in organizations have circumscribed ideas in such a way that they are being presented and evaluated as graduate candidates for implementation. It also assumes that ideas stay more or less the same, and that the inherent qualities at the stage of their first expression as 'ideas' determine their outcomes. According to Baer (2012), a key element of implementation is convincing people to buy into something that is already made.

Baer's arguments are paralleled by the use of stage-gate models for handling implementation of innovations (Cooper, 2001). They seem to prevail despite denouncements of myths about the linearity of innovation (Kline and Rosenberg, 1986; Godin, 2006). The tendencies to reify ideas and talk about clearly demarcated stages of creativity are also evident in many leading management and organization journals (Kijkuit and van den Ende, 2007; Paulus et al., 2011; Sosa, 2011; Montag et al., 2012). Ideas are still considered as ready-to-use products rather than fluid explorations of what is possible or preferable.

Why is this problematic? The first problem is an uncritical reification of ideas, where the logics of practice (Sandberg and Tsoukas, 2011) and the complexities of judgments and participations in the messy circumstances of the everyday (Tsoukas and Shotter, 2014) are abstracted away. As researchers and practitioners interested in innovative efforts in organizations we more or less willingly inherit a language of ideas as nouns. It follows that ideas are typically talked of as varieties of entities and cognitive manifestations: conceptions, thoughts, principles, beliefs, plans – see any lexical definition of 'idea'. Theoretically, part of the problem is that from a strong process view (Sztompka, 1991; Pettigrew, 1997; Tsoukas and Chia, 2002) ideas do not exist outside their constitutive events. Ideas are nothing in themselves, as much as knowledge, identities or strategies are other social structures that only exist in the doing. Ideas are the acts of suggesting, visualizing, communicating, combining, remembering, and reshaping some imagined conception or proposition and only exist as idea work (Carlsen et al., 2012; Carlsen and Sandelands, 2012). When reifying ideas we may miss all these practices and micro-processes of their constitution, including the dynamics of their realization.

The second problem with the orthodox view is the belief that there are distinctly different practices for generating and implementing ideas. We do not negate that there are divergent and convergent phases of work processes, and that managerial control is more easily applied toward the implementation end. But that does not mean that ideas at some point are developed once and for all and that the work that follows is mere execution. Both research on innovation processes (Van de Ven et al., 1999; Garud et al., 2013) and creativity as collective practice (Hargadon and Bechky, 2006; Sawyer, 2007; Harvey and Kou, 2013) have shown that these processes are recursive and iterative and offer opportunities for continued creativity.

Consider IKEA: the famous business model of IKEA – selling design furniture in flat packs – required the insight of cost savings but then also the experimentation on 'implementation ideas' how to execute to the effect (Tuulenmäki and Välikangas, 2011). Making all furniture flat for packaging is no mean design feat! Thus, simply having the idea of such a business model is not sufficient, and often the original idea evolves significantly as it is explored and learned about. The idea work and the resulting discovery then focus on what it actually takes to sell furniture that people carry (or drive) home in flat packs directly from the warehouse. And oh yes, include tools in the flat packs so people can assemble the furniture at home. In addition, the furniture is designed to a particular price point to be cost competitive. Would you have thought of all that upfront, never having been to IKEA? In retrospect, it is an obvious combination of ideas, implemented at different stages and in different adaptations that together make it a highly competitive business model.

Thus we ask: Does the discovery process ever pass from mere 'idea generation' into 'idea execution'? Do ideas ever stay the same? More generally, when is it fruitful to refer to discrete ideas rather than ongoing processes when researching creativity in organizations? And what does it do to people's engagement in idea work if they are framed as merely executing ideas of others rather than taking on leading roles in idea discovery?

Such seemingly innocent questions are asked far too seldom in literature on innovation and creativity. Yet their answers may have profound implications for enabling creativity at work – *and* capitalizing on it. Another noteworthy aspect of this discussion is the potential that is simply foregone or willingly abandoned if only mundane ideas are attended to, for the sake of their presumably easier implementation. We would intentionally then sacrifice the creativity with regard to its radical potential at the altar of poor implementation skills – or flawed assumptions about what implementation is: 'As we do not know how to implement larger and really creative ideas, please do not bring them forward'. In what follows we suggest and illustrate with cases a more fruitful approach and a tentative set of answers to these questions in the form of dynamics for implementation.

IMPLEMENTATION THROUGH THE DISCOVERY OF EXPERIMENTATION

The first dynamic of discovery involves implementation of ideas through trial-and-error learning, sometimes in the form of prototyping. Successful prototyping allows for repeated interaction on half-worked solutions and results in proposals that are being judged as increasingly plausible and valuable as key sources of uncertainty are addressed from one trial to the next (Ford, 2009). This dynamic has parallel conceptions within literatures on experiential learning and design thinking (Beckman and Barry, 2007; Brown, 2009; Sims, 2013) and emphasizes how work on ideas is highly iterative and shuttles between processes of concrete experiences, reflective observation and abstract conceptualization on the one hand, and processes of solution design, prototyping and testing on the other. Solutions are incrementally discovered rather than pre-planned. In this dynamic it is evident that implementation in the form of prototyping and experimentation may both follow and precede idea generation. Moreover, variation may take place within a focal area of continuous experimentation rather than across multiple sets of independent ideas (Harvey and Kou, 2013). And efforts of prototyping may be double-looped back to revisions of problem space and questioning the purpose of creative efforts. Let us look at four examples – the ones from Statoil and Snøhetta are adapted from Carlsen et al. (2012).

Implementing the Sverdrup Field – Statoil

As an interpretive science, exploration of hydrocarbons is rife with stories of findings made in areas that others have abandoned. A typical example is the largest discovery of oil in the world in 2011, the Sverdrup field in the North Sea. Statoil's successful participation in that discovery came from a combination of five sets of information: (1) oil shows in the basement rock from an Exxon well in 1967; (2) a recent spectacular discovery by the small company Lundin (another main actor in the larger discovery); (3) an argument in a geoscience article from 2006; (4) new shows in the basement rock in a well completed for other purposes; and (5) the discovery of intriguing pressure dynamics. From these new insights, the team came up with a generative question for an area already perforated by wells, upon which a decision for further acreage acquisition was made. In the years that followed, other teams in Statoil developed the area for placement of the wells, showing that some of the assumptions behind the area acreage had actually been wrong. The area is at the time of writing still being developed after several high-impact wells, but also some that were dry. Well over 40 individuals have been involved. There are many heroes in that story, but still a certain controversy over who had the breakthrough ideas. There is no point in time one could say that the subsequent work was merely implementation by execution.

Implementing a Generous Concept at Snøhetta

When architects at the renowned architectural firm Snøhetta reflect on the practices behind the award-winning buildings that they design, a key term that emerges is 'generous concepts'. Generous concepts are desirable because they (1) can survive and assimilate continuously changing ideas, demands and constraints; and (2) evoke a broad range of interpretations and user experiences. Says one of the senior architects: 'If the project has that quality, that it is so generous to begin with, that it opens up for your own interpretations as you go – and generosity seems to be a very important theme – if you imagine that it is so, then it is as if the project develops itself'. The antithesis of a generous concept is one that is so tightly defined that there is not much more to add for those engaged in the detailed design and drawing. Architects working down the line could find it utterly boring. Users may not read their own proclivities and needs into it. A project that 'develops itself' is made open to co-discovery.

Implementing Pulse News – Creativity in the Hindsight

In their recent book on everyday creativity, the Kelley brothers (Kelley and Kelley, 2013) – two of the forefathers of the tradition of design thinking at IDEO and Stanford d.school – present a tantalizing example of innovation practice. The d.school students, Akshay Khotari and Ankit Gupta, embarked upon an adventure of developing an application for reading the daily news on the recently launched iPad. Their first functional prototype was built in four days. Ashkay and Ankit next set up camp in a centrally placed cool café where they could present rough prototypes to café patrons and get their feedback. Any given day could result in hundreds of small iterations – thousands of variations over the course of two months. The application, called Pulse News, reached the Apple App Store hall of fame as one of the original first 50 apps, and was later sold to LinkedIn for US$90 million. Said Ankit of the experience (Kelley and Kelley, 2013, p. 114): 'I learned that creativity is always in the hindsight. . . It's not just about coming up with the genius idea that solves the problem, but trying and failing at a hundred or other solutions before arriving at the best one'.

In all these examples, viewing implementation of ideas as mere execution of something presumably finished would be utterly wrong. The point is not to avoid or disregard any descriptive output from idea work but to place and arrange such output so that it is considered unfinished, or evolvable, and may engage people in its continued development and exploration. It is this entire *process of co-discovery* with the set of artifacts, thought trials, testing and rapid feedback in repeated bouts of interaction that determines the quality of implementation, not the quality of ideas as such. Ideas are not inherently creative or not. They are made creative through ongoing idea work, and their quality is found only through their experimentation.

It hardly makes sense to characterize the processes in these examples as a linear sequence of idea generation, testing/evaluation and implementation. The examples from IKEA and d.school suggest a reversal of the orthodox model: the ideas in question follow from implementation! This suggests that much idea work may take the form of sensemaking: we must first act to make sense of what we are doing (Weick, 1995). And the quality of ideas – good or bad, generous or repellent – is only emergent in their interacting with us as innovators.

Another commonality is the framing of participation in these processes. The Statoil and Snøhetta cases both speak to the importance of ownership in implementation, but ownership as something entirely different than being talked into lowering one's resistance to the ideas of others, as suggested in the conceptions from Baer (2012). Rather, we see an awareness of the importance of being regarded as a co-discoverer. At Snøhetta, generous concepts have precisely this quality. In the Sverdrup case, people in several companies and stages of exploration contributed to the breakthrough ideas. In implementation of Pulse News, the matter of ownership and participation also include the close involvement of users in experiential learning.

IMPLEMENTATION THROUGH THE DISCOVERY OF ZOOMING OUT

The second dynamic of implementation by discovery concerns the ongoing dialectic of zooming in and out between parts and their wholes. Ideas are always intertextually linked to other ideas that underpin them and follow from them and always set within larger wholes that determine what people consider right or new. There is in our view no such thing as atomistic ideas being assessed as discrete and singular entities. Ideas behind the iPad or Pulse News are developed as part of a larger ecology of technology and market systems and can only gain their footing within such a cluster of accompanying, divergent and complementary ideas.

The importance of processes for zooming out stems from what we can call the circular and interpretive nature of all understanding, and thus also idea work: the never-ending dialectic between parts and their wholes (Palmer, 1969; Klein and Myers, 1999). Every idea of something is colored by being placed in some larger and often implicit whole and vice versa – every whole is derived from its parts. To complicate things, there are many alternative wholes for every detail. Relative to practices of implementation, this is a type of discovery dynamics that is little explored in organization studies. Let us look at two sets of examples again – also taken from Carlsen et al. (2012).

Zooming Out in Hydrocarbon Exploration: What is the Larger Story?

Zooming out in hydrocarbon exploration means an ongoing interplay between attention to singular data from rock samples, seismic and well logs on one hand with the 'play models' (models for how reservoirs of oil and gas may be formed and trapped underground) and larger regional geological stories on the other. There are at least two elements in the discovery of the Sverdrup field that testifies to this dynamic. One is the reconsideration of an entire area previously thought to be mature and void of any remaining large discoveries. Another is the invocation of new play models resulting from the questioning of the geology of the area: if the assumed migration patterns of oil were deemed false, this opened up for new explanations of where oil and gas might be found. Both these sets of elements enable the zooming out from details to wholes not previously considered. Says one seasoned explorer (Carlsen et al., 2012, p. 69):

> Geology is like a puzzle where you need to get a grasp of the totality very early. An image one can use is that of a tablecloth that someone is pulling by its sides. The cloth will have folds in different places, and it's about understanding how

the whole cloth is moving. Then it can be useful to get help from someone who has data from another place, only remotely linked to your data. Perhaps they have a piece of the puzzle that you don't have access to and that can shed new light on your interpretation. The point is to see the big picture the entire time, but with a focus on where there is oil to be found.

Zooming Out in Architecture: What Really is an Opera?

Zooming out in architecture means an ongoing interplay between details of buildings and spaces on one hand, and the larger landscapes and cultural historical tales on the other. When the architects at Snøhetta worked to develop the winning concept behind the Oslo Opera House, the dynamics of discovery was triggered by fundamental questions that invite zooming out: What really is an opera? What kinds of user experiences do we want to create with an Opera House? What is the function of the new Opera House in the city landscape of Oslo? How can the new Opera House resonate in the larger stories of social democracy in Norway?

To the architects at Snøhetta and their clients, the culturally charged buildings placed in landscapes are successful in so far as they resonate with the larger stories of the land. The Alexandria Library in Egypt that the company designed carries many references to the ancient pyramids and to the role of the Middle East as the cultural cradle of civilization. Signs from over 500 languages are carved into the surface stone. The Opera House in Oslo is designed to incorporate the social-democratic notion of the common land – with a defining feature being a carpet-like open space available to the public free of charge. Its success was not anticipated but rather discovered by its users.

One may think that the questions of larger contexts are only relevant in the early phases of idea generation. Yet nobody attains full knowledge of any oil field. Renewed regional understanding may invigorate even near-field exploration. Likewise, the mark of a good architect is that he or she continuously asks the larger questions during the entire project. These questions have bearing on the handling of minutiae in the everyday.

Is zooming out particular to interpretive work like architecture and hydrocarbon exploration? Not so. Small ideas are always connected to larger ones. A good feature article connects to larger stories of culture, society, and life that people care deeply about. A potent legal strategy sees the long-term consequences for the client. The layers of larger contexts are part of what gives continued life to ideas during both early conception and implementation.

BUILDING A CULTURE OF DISCOVERY: ONE COMPANY'S EXAMPLE

Valio, a Finnish high-tech dairy company, exemplifies how organizations may work systematically with building a culture of discovery in innovation. Fours years ago the company engaged in a discovery journey to enlarge its ability to engage in non-adjacent innovation. Titled 'Inner Fire and Speedy Action', the program invited the participants first to reflect on their own assumptions regarding innovation. Is it something that only people in the R&D labs do or is it a right and privilege of everyone within a business unit? The first event that brought the participants together was to convene in a city theatre and literally sit on the stage, rather than form the audience. The explicit message was: You are the actor here. You are not sitting in the audience this time, merely observing and clapping. What does it feel like? The participants were invited to reflect on questions like: How do I perceive myself as an innovator? What is it like to have an active or strong voice in innovation? Interestingly, many of the people sitting on that stage are now, four years later, in leading executive roles, including an R&D director, a manufacturing director, and a director of blue-sky innovation.

The second phase in the discovery process was to learn from others. The participants visited companies and shared learnings with each other. Nothing particularly unusual here but the activity was explicitly framed as discovery, not copying of best practices. What do they do that Valio can learn from? What is surprising, intriguing, and potentially workable? How do these companies manage their innovation processes? How do they go about experimenting or coping with failure? The companies visited ranged from fashion and sports devices and clothes designers to industrial manufacturers and software and information technology firms. These insights were shared and discussed in a follow-up workshop. It was obvious that such discovery was highly motivating, there was a lot of energy in the room, and many people exhibited open curiosity as to what the learnings were and how the teams framed them for Valio.

The next, third phase was to experiment on the insights in a concrete, observable form. This required discovery again in that the teams had to be creative in how to implement the insights in the context of their own organization, and in a small enough scale, in the short time of four-to-six weeks and with no formal resources. This was to make the point that product development can be done much more lightly and in rapid iteration. Some participants created plays and TV news where they acted or broadcasted the storyline. Others moonlighted in the R&D laboratory and developed a dairy formula that they invited passers-by to taste. Not all idea experimentations were adopted company-wide of course, but the program did result in five major changes in the Valio innovation processes that were highly appreciated by the senior leadership.

The final workshop focused on the overall role of discovery in innovation. The participants engaged in the discussion on how to keep the discovery alive. A recent discussion with the director of blue-sky innovation described how the company is moving from 'special forces' for radical innovation to finding ways to give everyone a license to innovate, no matter where in the organization and in what position.

CONCLUSIONS – DISCOVERING THE RIGHT TO DISCOVER

In her book with the evocative title *The Future and its Enemies*, Virginia Postrel (1998) once pointed to the dangers of assuming too much knowledge without experimentation. In an article on her website, Postrel (1999) wrote:

> The biggest threat to a better life is the desire to keep the future under control – to make the world predictable by reining in creativity and enterprise. Progress as a neat blueprint, with no deviations and no surprise, may work in children's cartoons or utopian novels. But it's just a fantasy.

In this chapter we have tried to follow in Postrel's footsteps, using slightly different words, by emphasizing discovery over execution to combat orthodoxies related to implementation of creative ideas. We have identified and challenged assumptions about ideas as reified entities and rejected idea work as proceeding in linear and clearly separated stages of generation and execution. As an alternative conception we offered tenets of a process-based view on creativity and, furthermore, presented two sets of dynamics of implementation as discovery: discovery by experimentation and by zooming out.

Practically, this chapter suggests that implementation may be the most creative phase of all! Our point is: do not deprive your organization and your users of the continuous evolution of innovation that the discovery of implementation enables. In successful projects, implementation is much more than execution. Potent ideas never stay the same. They have many authors, editors, and publishers. Arbitrarily distinguishing ideation from execution is not only untrue to the nature of innovation processes but it also goes against our deeply held beliefs about equality: there are those with the privilege of idea generation and those who 'merely' execute. What would you yourself prefer – to execute the ideas of others or to take part in adventurous discoveries?

While our own discovery continues, and the ideas expressed in this chapter may be experimenting on us (Välikangas and Sevón, 2010) as well as us experimenting on them, we hope to have contributed to making discovery more pertinent in implementation. Not doing so has serious hazards in excluding radical ideas as non-implementable, excluding many people as mere execution laborers, and making organizational life generally much more boring and less generous than it deserves. Showing generosity means including people in the excitement of discovery.

REFERENCES

Baer, M. (2012), 'Putting creativity to work: The implementation of creative ideas in organizations', *Academy of Management Journal*, **55**(5), 1102–19.

Beckman, S.L. and M. Barry (2007), 'Innovation as a learning process: Embedding design thinking', *California Management Review*, **50**(1), 25–56.

Brown, T. (2009), *Change by Design*, New York: Harper Collins.

Carlsen, A. and L. Sandelands (2012), 'Living ideas at work', in T.S. Pitsis (ed.), *Handbook of Organizational and Managerial Innovation*, Cheltenham, UK and Northampton, MA, USA: Edward Elgar Publishing, p. 219.

Carlsen, A., S. Clegg and R. Gjersvik (2012), *Idea Work. Lessons of the Extraordinary in Everyday Creativity*, Oslo: Cappelen Damm.

Cooper, R.G. (2001), *Winning at New Products: Accelerating the Process from Idea to Launch*, New York: Basic Books.

Ford, C. (2009), 'Prototyping processes that affect organizational creativity', in R. Tudor, M.A. Runco and S. Moger, S. (eds), *The Routledge Companion to Creativity*, London: Routledge, pp. 317–26.

Garud, R., P. Tuertscher and A.H. van de Ven (2013), 'Perspectives on innovation processes', *The Academy of Management Annals*, **7**(1), 775–819.

Godin, B. (2006), 'The linear model of innovation: The historical construction of an analytical framework', *Science, Technology and Human Values*, **31**(6), 639–67.

Hargadon, A.B. and B. Bechky (2006), 'When collections of creatives become creative collectives: A field study of problem solving at work', *Organization Science*, **17**(4), 484–500.

Harvey, S. and C.-Y. Kou (2013), 'Collective engagement in creative tasks. The role of evaluation in the creative process in groups', *Administrative Science Quarterly*, **58**(3), 346–86.

Kelley, T. and D. Kelley (2013), *Creative Confidence: Unleashing the Creative Potential Within Us All*, New York: Random House.

Kijuit, B. and J. van den Ende (2007), 'The organizational life of an idea: Integrating social network, creativity and decision–making perspectives', *Journal of Management Studies*, **44**(6), 863–82.

Klein, H.K. and M.D. Myers (1999), 'A set of principles for conducting and evaluating interpretive field studies in information systems', *MIS Quarterly*, **23**(1), 67–93.

Kline, S.J. and N. Rosenberg (1986), 'An overview of innovation', in R. Landau and N. Rosenberg (eds), *The Positive Sum Strategy: Harnessing Technology for Economic Growth*, Washington, DC: National Academies Press, pp. 275–305.

Montag, T., C.P. Maertz and M. Baer (2012), 'A critical analysis of the workplace creativity criterion space', *Journal of Management*, **38**(4), 1362–86.

Palmer, R.E. (1969), *Hermeneutics: Interpretation Theory in Schleiermacher, Dilthey, Heidegger, and Gadamer*, Evanston, IL: Northwestern University Press.

Paulus, P., M. Dzindolet and N. Kohn (2011), 'Collaborative creativity: Group creativity and team innovation', in M. Mumford (ed.), *Handbook of Organizational Creativity*, Oxford, UK: Elsevier, pp. 327–57.

Pettigrew, A.M. (1997), 'What is a processual analysis?' *Scandinavian Journal of Management*, **13**(4), 337–48.

Postrel, V.I. (1998), *The Future and its Enemies: The Growing Conflict over Creativity, Enterprise, and Progress*, New York: Free Press.

Postrel, V.I. (1999), 'Our anxiety about what's to come is just the wish for things to stand still', from *The Philadelphia Enquirer*, 18 July, accessed 16 December 2015 at http://vpostrel.com/articles/our-anxiety-about-what-s-to-come-is-just-the-wish-for-things-to-stand-still.

Sandberg, J. and H. Tsoukas (2011), 'Grasping the logic of practice: Theorizing through practical rationality', *Academy of Management Review*, **36**(2), 338–60.

Sawyer, K. (2007), *Group Genius: The Creative Power of Collaboration*, New York: Basic Books.

Sims, P. (2013), *Little Bets: How Breakthrough Ideas Emerge from Small Discoveries*, New York: Simon and Schuster.

Sosa, M.E. (2011), 'Where do creative interactions come from? The role of tie content and social networks', *Organization Science*, **22**(1), 1–21.

Sztompka, P. (1991), *Society in Action: The Theory of Social Becoming*, Chicago, IL: University of Chicago Press.

Tsoukas, H. and R. Chia (2002), 'On organizational becoming: Rethinking organizational change', *Organization Science*, **13**(5), 567–82.

Tsoukas, H. and J. Shotter (2014), 'In search of phronesis: Leadership and the art of coming to judgement', *Academy of Management Learning and Education*, **13**(2), 224–43.

Tuulenmäki, A. and L. Välikangas (2011), 'The art of rapid, hands-on execution innovation', *Strategy and Leadership*, **39**(2), 28–35.

Välikangas, L. and G. Romme (2013), 'How to design for strategic resilience: A case study in retailing', *Journal of Organization Design*, **2**(2), 44–53.

Välikangas, L. and G. Sevón (2010), 'Of managers, ideas and jesters, and the role of information technology', *The Journal of Strategic Information Systems*, **19**(3), 145–53.

Van de Ven, A.H., D.E. Polley, R. Garud and S. Venkataraman (1999), *The Innovation Journey*, New York: Oxford University Press.

Weick, K.E. (1995), *Sensemaking in Organizations*, Thousand Oaks, CA: Sage.

13. Designing and implementing innovative business models

Ivan Župič and Alessandro Giudici

INTRODUCTION

The concept of business model gained popularity among managers and entrepreneurs during the dot-com boom in the late 1990s (Zott et al., 2011). A key tenet of the concept is that it connects the value creation and value capture sides of a firm's strategy. In other words, the business model must link the activities performed by the firm to create and capture value to outside actors such as customers, partners, and complementors (Baden-Fuller and Mangematin, 2013). In doing so, the business model plays three main roles (Spieth et al., 2014): it helps (1) to describe the business (that is, how the firm generates its profit); (2) to run the business (in terms of, for example, operational aspects like processes, linkages, and structures); and (3) to develop the business (in other words, as a support to the management in the strategy process). In addition, entrepreneurs can use the business model to generate and test working hypotheses about how their business creates and delivers value to customers (Eckhardt, 2013).

In this chapter we introduce the concept of business model and business model innovation and provide some guidelines for designing 'good' business models. Since this task is generally challenging in that it requires particularly creative reconfigurations, we will also discuss some of the key difficulties that firms may experience when trying to innovate their business model. Reflecting the richness of business model research, we will present three different perspectives. Next, we describe some real-world examples of different business models, and discuss the main reason why incumbents are often slow to react to new business models. We provide two illustrative cases. The first shows how Blockbuster found it very difficult to respond to severe disruption in its market created by the innovative business models introduced by new entrants. The second briefly presents the innovative business model of Naked Wines.

DESIGNING 'GOOD' BUSINESS MODELS

Business modeling is the managerial equivalent of the scientific method (Magretta, 2002). A working hypothesis (about customers, market, pricing, partners etc.) is put forward and then tested. If it works, it is adopted and the process is then iteratively repeated ad infinitum. The most powerful business models do not simply shift existing business among companies, but also create new demand and with it new markets (ibid.). One of the primary goals when designing models is to create customer stickiness (in the form of loyalty or lock-in) and barriers to entry for competitors (McGrath, 2011). Business models that create a recurring stream of revenues are more sustainable in the long run than those in which customers buy only once and never come back.

Effective business models have three main characteristics. First, they are aligned with the company's strategy and present a good fit with the industry's competitive landscape. Industry fit does not mean following the prevailing view about how 'things are done' within the industry, but requires a good dose of critical thinking about how to challenge existing assumptions. Often, innovative business models emerge when the industry environment changes (for example, a shift in technology or regulation), but most major players remain stuck in the old ways of doing things.

Second, the choices made within business model design should be self-reinforcing (Casadesus-Masanell and Ricart, 2011). They need to complement each other and seek synergies with feedback effects. These virtuous cycles continually strengthen the business model with network effects such as dynamic. For example, Ryanair's low-cost business model aims to achieve cost savings through high aircraft utilization. The consequence is low prices that attract even more customers and – to conclude the cycle – the high volume of customers enables even higher aircraft utilization.

Third, the business model should be robust, and its effectiveness should be sustained over time. This means that the firm should be able to counter four main threats: imitation (the ability of others to copy the business model), holdup (the value is captured by customers, suppliers or other players), slack (organizational complacency) and substitution (could similar value proposition be delivered by other products and services?).

Business Model Frameworks

Academics and practitioners alike have still to agree about an exact definition of the business model concept. What is common to most definitions is that the concept encompasses both the value creation and value capture sides of a firm's strategy and that it represents a holistic view of the business that outlines the firm's architecture of revenues, costs, and profits (Teece, 2010). Using the language of business models, complex relationships and interdependencies among different activities can be simplified into coherent stories (Arend, 2013).

Business models can be defined both objectively and subjectively (Doz and Kosonen, 2010). From an objective standpoint, they offer descriptions of the logic of the business and of the complex inter-relationships between the firm, its customers, suppliers, and other stakeholders. In this respect, the business model concept can be useful to classify what firms do into various taxonomies. However, from a subjective standpoint, the business model represents how a firm's senior management thinks of the complex interdependencies between their business and its environment (ibid.). It thus offers a cognitive structure that provides a theory of how to set the boundaries of the firm, create value, and choose the appropriate organization design.

Along the objective–subjective continuum, we can identify three perspectives on business models: (1) the business model canvas (Osterwalder and Pigneur, 2010); (2) business models as activity systems (Zott and Amit, 2010); and (3) the cognitive perspective (Baden-Fuller and Mangematin, 2013).

Arguably the most used framework in consultancy, the 'business model canvas' (Osterwalder and Pigneur, 2010), divides business models into nine building blocks: value proposition, customer segments, channels, customer relationships, revenue streams, key resources, key activities, key partnerships, and cost structure. Among these building blocks, the value proposition is the most central because it is tightly connected to customer segments. This framework is deeply enrooted in design thinking and its main purpose is to provide a powerful visualization tool that may aid the process of business model design. The business model canvas is often used in conjunction with the lean start-up process (Ries, 2011) as the hypotheses related to each different building block need to be tested based on feedback from potential customers. This framework suggests that firms should engage in an iterative process in which each block of the business model is tweaked and changed until a suitable level of fit with the external environment is reached.

A well-known alternative is that of the business model as an activity system. According to this view, an activity system is 'a set of interdependent organizational activities centered on a focal firm, including those conducted by the focal firm, its partners, vendors or customers' (Zott and Amit, 2010, 217). It is thus not limited just to the focal firm, but spans its boundaries to include external partners as value co-creators. This line of thinking echoes Porter's (1996) view on strategy, who suggested that the real sources of a firm's competitive advantage lie in its choices and configuration of activities. It suggests that business model innovation is primarily about innovating on the content, structure, and governance of the activity system (Amit and Zott, 2012). The content includes the set of activities that are performed within the business model and innovation might thus include the addition of new activities or the abandonment of old ones. The structure of an activity system describes instead how the activities are linked (ibid.), The governance of an activity system defines who performs which activity. In this respect, value can be created (and captured!) not only by the focal firm, but also by multiple firms within a given activity system.

This view also argues that there are four fundamental value drivers of business models: novelty (the degree of innovation within a given business model), efficiency (the potential for cost savings through a given activity system), lock-in (customers' level of ability and willingness to transfer to another activity system) and complementarities (the level of value-related interdependencies across activities within the system). Innovating the activity system requires therefore systemic and holistic thinking as the goal is to optimize the whole activity system and not just a particular activity.

Finally, Baden-Fuller and Haefliger (2013) see business models as cognitive devices. Their purpose is to make better business decisions by facilitating the explication of ideas in entrepreneurs' and managers' minds, thus allowing for an easier detection of potential inconsistencies (Abraham, 2013). According to this view, the business model does not describe 'reality', but it is independent of context and captures how the firm sees the world. In other words, rather than being a complete description of everything that the firm does, it offers a concise depiction of the cause–effect relationships between customers, the focal firm, outside partners and money (Baden-Fuller and Mangematin, 2013). Proponents of this perspective suggest that the business model can be analyzed along four basic dimensions: customer identification (who the customer groups are and which groups of customers actually pay for the product or service), customer engagement (often divided into 'taxi' – tailored approach – and 'bus' – scale-based approach with limited ability to offer flexibility in satisfying customer needs), value delivery and linkages (how value is delivered and who actually delivers it; this may not be the focal company but one of its partners) and monetization (which goes beyond just pricing and includes systems for collecting revenue and timings of payment).

Some Examples of Business Models

Arguably the longest-existing types of business models are those involving the manufacturing of products (for example, food, clothing, cars) or the delivery of services (for example, cleaning, legal advice) for which the company is paid a certain price. This type includes, for example, the 'no-frills' or 'low-cost' business models that provide products and services stripped down to essentials for low price. The essence of this model is to run an extremely efficient operation with low margins and make it up on volume. The most famous exemplars are no-frills airlines (for example, Ryanair, Southwest Airlines) and discount retailers (for example, Aldi).

The razor-blade business model is another classic type that involves pricing razors cheaply while earning a profit on the high-margin consumables (that is, razor blades) (Teece, 2010). A famous exemplar of a firm employing this business model is – of course – Gillette (razor/razor blades).

Platforms (sometimes also called two-sided markets) are unique in the sense that the platform provider connects two different customer groups. Credit cards (for example, MasterCard), which connect merchants with individual buyers, are common exemplars. Platform providers have two different customer groups to serve and have to decide whether they will charge both groups or have one group subsidize the other.

Free platform models normally mean that users get the service for free but some other party pays for them. This other party is most often advertisers. Good instances of companies employing this type of model are various types of online services and media (for example, Google Search, Huffington Post).

Freemium (free + premium) business models provide instead part of the service for free while charging for more advanced parts of service that customers are willing to pay for. The logic behind the freemium model is that the free offer serves as a loss leader for the premium offer where revenues are made. Dropbox is a prime exemplar of a freemium model. The company provides a service of storing digital files for free up to a certain limit, above which it charges a monthly subscription fee. Freemium business models are very popular but can also be very dangerous as the cost of supporting (perhaps millions) of free users may prove to be a very expensive marketing mechanism over time.

Internet retailing enabled so-called 'long-tail' business models. Physical stores have limited shelf space, meaning that each of the products needs to bring in large amounts of revenue. The long-tail model makes profit by selling lots of different items just a few times each, but aggregated revenue still brings in respectable profit. Online retailers (for example, Amazon) often employ this model to a certain degree.

Why Incumbents Fail to React to Disruptive Business Models

When presented by consultants, business model innovation sounds simple. However, it has been proven difficult for incumbents (that is, companies with an established powerful position in a certain market) to react to new, potentially disruptive business models.

The problem is that established companies often find new business models unattractive (Markides, 2008). The market around a new business model might be initially small and insignificant compared to the company's core customer groups already served by the existing model. In addition, the success factors and the resources and capabilities critical to success in the new market may be different than in the existing one and may often conflict. Finally, new markets need time to grow and this is often at odds with the expectations of immediate results so common in today's corporate world. Indeed, successful new businesses normally revise their business models several times before reaching profitability (Johnson et al., 2008) and this might prove too challenging for existing incumbents who might also suffer from a special kind of myopia (Tripsas and Gavetti, 2000). In other words, as Chesbrough and Rosenbloom (2002) demonstrated so aptly in the case of Xerox, existing business models limit the search for alternative models that differ from the current way of thinking within a company. New business models tend therefore to be evaluated through the lens of the existing business model, severely limiting the possibilities for innovation.

Change is Difficult: Blockbuster

The mini-case of Blockbuster will show how difficult it is for established companies to engage in business model innovation. A consequence of this was Blockbuster's bankruptcy.

Blockbuster was a video rental company established in 1985 in Dallas, Texas, whose main business was renting movies through its network of neighborhood stores. In 1988 Blockbuster became the top video retailer in the USA with more than 500 stores. Blockbuster had a very simple pricing scheme: $2.99 for two-day rental of new releases and the same price for five-day rental of old movies (Girotra et al., 2010). An important part of its revenues was derived from fees charged to customers who were late to return the movies. Blockbuster continued to grow both organically and through acquisitions. Viacom acquired Blockbuster in 1994.

Its business model was innovative at the time because it enabled the customization of the offerings to the demographic characteristics of the neighborhood where the store was located. It also used then-novel computer technology and applied 'big data' insights into its customer base well before the term 'big data' was even invented. At the height of its fortunes it owned 5000 retail stores and employed 60 000 people.

However, in 1997, Blockbuster found itself in crisis. At the time, inventory purchases of movies were the company's largest single cost and amounted to 36 percent of Blockbuster's revenue. With these payments Blockbuster contributed more revenue to the movie studios than the latter obtained through movie releases in theatres (ibid.) but failed to make adequate returns on capital itself. Blockbuster's top management then negotiated a new revenue-sharing deal with movie studios. Under this agreement Blockbuster would pay only $6–7 per movie (before $65) and split the revenue 60/40 with studios in favor of Blockbuster. With these changes, interests of movie studios and Blockbuster became better aligned. Blockbuster increased its market share and went public in 1999. The revenue-sharing model saved Blockbuster, but not for long since a number of Internet and mail subscription services emerged in just a few years, challenging Blockbuster's store network model. The best-known competitor was Netflix, which started a DVD-by-mail subscription service in 1997. Initially, Netflix had several tiers of rental plans that allowed customers to keep one to five videos as long as they wanted without paying late fees. It also developed a personal recommendation system that was based on user ratings and reviews, which increased the number of times each video was rented (ibid.). The DVD-by-mail model evolved into the Internet-streaming subscription model, which is the dominant model used today, with Netflix having the largest market share.

Even though Blockbuster soon launched its own version of the DVD subscription model, it was held back by concerns that this new service would cannibalize its brick-and-mortar operations (Teece, 2010). Patent protection also prevented Blockbuster from fully copying some important features of the Netflix service. Netflix was thus able to enjoy a long period without a full-blown competitive response. It was only in 2004 that Blockbuster launched its Blockbuster Online initiative, which was then extended in 2006 with its Blockbuster Total Access service, based on a combination of a subscription delivery model with its retail stores. At this point Blockbuster was imitating most of the Netflix business model and was able to offer some services that Netflix could not match. However, maintaining the commitment to its costly retail network proved fatal for Blockbuster.

Blockbuster was unable to fully change its business model from brick-and-mortar stores to a lean Internet approach. The company applied for Chapter 11 bankruptcy in 2010 and was subsequently acquired by Dish Network. The last Blockbuster stores closed in 2013.

How to Innovate on Business Models?

Business model innovation can be defined as the company's search for an improved business model in essentially the same business and market. We can speak of business model innovation every time a company changes one of its business model dimensions. However, sometimes just small reconfigurations of existing models are not enough, but the design of a completely new model is required. This 'new' business model could be new to the company or new to the industry and could commercialize a new product for a previously unmet need or find new ways of selling existing offerings (Magretta, 2002).

New technologies are generally commercialized through innovative business models (Chesbrough, 2010; see also Chapter 17 in this volume) because the technologies have no economic value themselves, unless the value is created and delivered through appropriate models. In this context, the business model is seen as the connection between a firm's (innovative) technology and customer needs (Zott et al., 2011). On the other hand, technology can be the enabler of novel business models. The business models could therefore be seen either as a vehicle for (technological) innovation or a subject of (business model) innovation.

There are three types of strategies for business model innovation (Giesen et al., 2007). First, business model innovation at the industry level involves innovating the 'industry value chain'. This could be done by bringing an existing business model from one industry to another (like Virgin uses its customer management expertise to enter new industries, for example, financial services and telecommunications), or by redefining existing industries (like Apple established the category of smart-phones with the iPhone, which then completely transformed the mobile phone industry). The most extreme version of this type of strategy develops entirely new industries or industry segments (for example, Google and other search engines).

A second type revolves instead on producing innovations in how firms generate revenues or by using new pricing models. A good example of this type of revenue-based innovation is the above-mentioned razor-blade model that was then adopted by HP and Epson to sell printers cheaply and make it up with expensive ink cartridges.

The third type of innovation is the enterprise model, which creatively changes the structure of the enterprise and its value chains. The focus is on redefining organizational boundaries. A case in point is the clothing retailer Zara, which introduced a novel information system with feedback loops to enable information flows from local stores to the headquarters and used local suppliers to cut delivery times for newly designed merchandise

(Giesen et al., 2007). Thanks to these choices, Zara has been consistently able to react to changing customer demands very quickly.

Innovative Business Model: Naked Wines

A second case will show the innovative business model of a UK firm, Naked Wines.[1] The model revolves around an online platform that links (1) quality independent winemakers around the world with limited production capabilities, and (2) end customers seeking to explore and enjoy a broad variety of quality wines at a much lower price than from existing brick-and-mortar retailers. The key element of the model is that customers can sign up as 'angel' investors by prepaying at least £20 on a monthly basis. The company then uses this money to fund independent winemakers in advance so that they can afford the risk of producing larger than usual quantities. In this way, and by selling directly with no other intermediaries, Naked Wines can enjoy heavy discounts that are passed onto end customers with discounts ranging between 25 and 50 percent on the full retail price, on top of being able to redeem all the money previously prepaid. The complementary aspects of the model include: (1) close monitoring of customer preferences via a detailed feedback system that can predict future purchases; (2) effective cash flow management since the company mainly invests money on behalf of end customers; (3) a pure marketplace section in which demand for new winemakers is tested with limited quantities and a bidding system until stock lasts.

The business model represented by Naked Wines mainly serves two groups of customers. A minority of customers are not subscribers of the 'angel' system based on monthly payments and simply use the website to source good wines when needed (without additional discounts). Through a recent fine wine bond emission, Naked Wines is also testing the possibility to appeal to customers more interested in traditional investment opportunities rather than wines as mere products.

The value proposition is twofold. On the one hand, Naked Wines offers customers interested in quality wines the possibility to buy from a large number of independent winemakers around the world with home delivery and at a substantial discount. Customer engagement is also achieved via the above-mentioned crowd-funding mechanism that makes customers feel as they are proactively supporting independent winemakers, with characteristics similar to fair trade certifications. These customers also enjoy a sense of exclusivity – that is, the same wine is not available elsewhere – and of being part of a creative winemaking process – that is, each customer can interact with winemakers and provide feedback online – within a like-minded community. On the other hand, it offers these independent winemakers crowd-funded investments (generally in the region of £50 000) to reduce the risk of increasing their production volumes in exchange of very low prices that are then partly passed onto end customers. Winemakers can also enjoy the possibility of being connected to their customers – an important aspect for small producers in this sector.

To maintain quick delivery time, Naked Wines uses a network of warehouses throughout the UK (and the USA/Australia). Winemakers thus ship to these warehouses and then Naked Wines delivers them to the final customer. In this way, the company can also use its stock to create pre-mixed cases, thus increasing product rotation and keeping inventory costs down. Its standard delivery is £4.99 for next business day (£6.99 for Saturday deliveries) to almost everywhere in the UK if an order is placed before 5pm. However, delivery is also free to most UK postcodes for orders above £80. From spring 2014, the company has been testing a same-day delivery service in London for £14.99.

The latest financial information about the company suggests that Naked Wines closed 2013 with around £50 million in revenues and additional funding from investors. The fine wine bond emission in Autumn 2013 was also successful: the company hoped to raise at least £1 million, set an upper limit of £5 million and received offers for £6.2 million, with two-thirds of subscribers opting for the 10 percent return in wine credit. Although the company does not disclose its marginality, information released to the public for the bond emission suggests it enjoyed between approximately 30 percent gross profit on wine purchases, with selling/distribution costs amounting to 13–16 percent and other operating expenses between 11 and 13 percent, for a total pre-tax profit in the region of 4–6 percent. At the beginning of 2015, Naked Wines was acquired by Majestic Wines, the UK's largest wine distributor, for £70 million. Naked Wines' founder and CEO Rowan Gormley has been appointed at the helm of both companies to facilitate backend integration while keeping the two customer-facing value propositions independent.

CONCLUSION

Business models encourage systemic and holistic thinking (Amit and Zott, 2012). Entrepreneurs and managers should thus consider particular choices in the context of the overarching business model. The business model concept provides a common language that enables entrepreneurs and managers to focus on the forest, rather than individual trees. The core guiding principles common to most definitions of business models focus on both value creation and value capture. They emphasize the inter-dependencies between different parts of each business model and provide a framework to relate the activities performed within a firm to its outside environment.

While technological innovation is championed in advanced economies, much less attention is given to business model innovation. Nevertheless, the true potential of technological inventions often needs to be released through proper commercialization strategies. To be achieved, these strategies require the design of appropriate business models. Creative ideas in the form of innovative business models are then the primary vehicles for the diffusion of novel products and services. Finding the right combination of business model parts is the crucial task of true innovators and needs to be completed over time, again and again.

NOTE

1. The case is reproduced and partly adapted with permission of the authors under a Creative Commons 'Attribution – Non-Commercial – No Derivatives' 4.0 International License. © C. Baden-Fuller; S. Haefliger; A. Giudici, Cass Business School, London 2015. It was written as part of the 'Building Better Business Model' project supported by the UK EPSRC (EP/K039695/1) grant with matching funding from Cass Business School, City University London, and the Mack Institute, Wharton Business School, University of Pennsylvania.

REFERENCES

Abraham, S. (2013), 'Will business model innovation replace strategic analysis?' *Strategy and Leadership*, **41**(2), 31–8.

Amit, R. and C. Zott (2012), 'Creating value through business model innovation', *MIT Sloan Management Review*, **53**(3), 41–9.

Arend, R.J. (2013), 'The business model: Present and future – beyond a skeumorph', *Strategic Organization*, **11**(4), 390–402.

Baden-Fuller, C. and S. Haefliger (2013), 'Business models and technological innovation', *Long Range Planning*, **46**(6), 419–26.

Baden-Fuller, C. and V. Mangematin (2013), 'Business models: A challenging agenda', *Strategic Organization*, **11**(4), 418–27.

Casadesus-Masanell, R. and J.E. Ricart (2011), 'How to design a winning business model', *Harvard Business Review*, **89**(1/2), 100–107.

Chesbrough, H. (2010), 'Business model innovation: Opportunities and barriers', *Long Range Planning*, **43**(2–3), 354–63.

Chesbrough, H. and R.S. Rosenbloom (2002), 'The role of the business model in capturing value from innovation: Evidence from Xerox Corporation's technology spin-off companies', *Industrial and Corporate Change*, **11**(3), 529–55.

Doz, Y.L. and M. Kosonen (2010), 'Embedding strategic agility: A leadership agenda for accelerating business model renewal', *Long Range Planning*, **43**(2–3), 370–82.

Eckhardt, J.T. (2013), 'Opportunities in business model research', *Strategic Organization*, **11**(4), 412–17.

Giesen, E., S.J. Berman, R. Bell and A. Blitz (2007), 'Paths to success: Three ways to innovate your business model', *IBM Global Business Services*, accessed 2 December 2015 at http://www-01.ibm.com/common/ssi/cgi-bin/ssialias?infotype=PM& subtype=XB&htmlfid=GBE03170USEN.

Girotra, K., S. Netessine and M. Coluccio (2010), 'From Blockbuster to video on demand: Distribution channel innovation in the U.S. video-rental indus-try', *Case Centre*, accessed 3 December 2015 at http://www.thecasecentre.org/educators/products/view?id=97741.

Johnson, M., C.M. Christensen and H. Kagermann (2008), 'Reinventing your busi-ness model', *Harvard Business Review*, December.

Magretta, J. (2002), 'Why business models matter', *Harvard Business Review*, May.

Markides, C.C. (2008), *Game-changing Strategies: How to Create New Market Space in Established Industries by Breaking the Rules*, San Francisco, CA: Jossey-Bass.

McGrath, R.G. (2011), 'When your business model is in trouble', *Harvard Business Review*, January–February, 96–8.

Osterwalder, A. and Y. Pigneur (2010), *Business Model Generation: A Handbook for Visionaries, Game Changers, and Challengers*, Hoboken, NJ: Wiley.

Porter, M.E. (1996), 'What is strategy?' *Harvard Business Review*, November–December, 61–78.

Ries, E. (2011), *The Lean Startup: How Today's Entrepreneurs Use Continuous Innovation to Create Radically Successful Businesses*, New York: Crown Business.

Spieth, P., D. Schneckenberg and J.E. Ricart (2014), 'Business model innovation – state of the art and future challenges for the field', *R&D Management*, **44**(3), 237–47.

Teece, D.J. (2010), 'Business models, business strategy and innovation', *Long Range Planning*, **43**(2–3), 172–94.

Tripsas, M. and G. Gavetti (2000), 'Capabilities, cognition, and inertia: Evidence from digital imaging', *Strategic Management Journal*, **21**(10–11), 1147–61.

Zott, C. and R. Amit (2010), 'Business model design: An activity system perspec-tive', *Long Range Planning*, **43**(2), 216–26.

Zott, C., R. Amit and L. Massa (2011), 'The business model: Recent developments and future research, *Journal of Management*, **37**(4), 1019–42.

14. Idea implementation as a relational phenomenon: a social network perspective

Saša Batistič and Robert Kaše

CREATIVITY, INNOVATION AND SOCIAL NETWORKS

> You're not just looking at one [social network] diagram. You're looking at who communicates with whom, who trusts whom, who goes to whom for new and innovative ideas, who gets information from whom, who goes to whom for decision making. (Kate Ehrlich, IBM)

There is an increasing awareness among practitioners that social networks – a set of actors and relationships such as friendships, communication or advice that connect them (Kilduff and Tsai, 2003) – are very important for fostering creativity and driving innovation (for example, Pugh and Prusak, 2013). McGregor (2006) identifies various pharmaceutical and ICT companies that actually map informal relations to understand and sparkle innovation. For instance, IBM uses social network analysis (SNA) as a management tool to explore informal interactions between various groups of employees and promote the creation of novel and useful ideas accordingly. Examining the same company, Ehrlich (2006) indicates that companies can streamline innovation and collaboration by using SNA for exploring three major phases of innovation: generating ideas, translating ideas, and delivering ideas. The emphasis of this chapter is thus on how SNA can be used to provide valuable insight about the second part of the innovation process; that is, idea implementation.

The main advantage of using SNA to explore idea implementation in organizations lies in that it helps to identify opportunities and restraints for implementing ideas that are present in the social context in which organizational members are embedded (Borgatti and Foster, 2003). Innovation is an inherently social phenomenon because it necessitates social connections between people who are the carriers of ideas and resources for producing useful and novel solutions (for example, Woodman et al., 1993; Obstfeld,

2005). As Baer (2012, p. 1114) pointed out: 'the motivation to implement one's ideas and the ability to network – or, alternatively, the strength of one's actual network relationships – serve as moderating factors that jointly determine the extent to which creative ideas are eventually realized'.

Recognizing the importance of interactions for innovation, contemporary organizations emphasize teamwork and various other forms of interactive work designs such as job sharing to ensure that knowledge workers have sufficient social interaction to be able to implement ideas and get their job done. Nevertheless, a systematic analysis of idea implementation, as a process driven by work and social relationships within organizations (Monge et al., 1992; Perry-Smith, 2006) is still rather an exception than a rule. The purpose of this chapter is thus to provide a simple practical example of how SNA can be used to explore an organization's idea implementation network by looking at its formal and informal social structure.

IDEA IMPLEMENTATION AND THE SOCIAL NETWORK PERSPECTIVE

Social network research uses two distinctive, yet complementary approaches – the structural and the relational perspectives (Raider and Krackhardt, 2002; Galaskiewicz, 2007; Kilduff and Brass, 2010). The structural perspective focuses on the structural form of social networks; that is, the patterns of relationships and the position of actors within it. In doing so, this perspective attributes attitudes, behaviors, or beliefs to the position of an actor in their social network. By addressing patterns of network structure, social network analysis allows us to study the whole and the smaller parts of the social network simultaneously (Wellman, 1998). For example, when people interact, they may represent not only themselves, but also any formal or informal group or even organization of which they are considered to be a member (for example, Zaheer and Soda, 2009). On the other hand, the relational perspective puts the focus on the content of relationships; that is, on the quality of network relationships or ties (Raider and Krackhardt, 2002). In most cases both approaches complement each other and allow the researcher to get a more comprehensive picture of the phenomena studied.

Network literature suggests that in addition to the formal organizational structure, there is also an informal structure, which is at least as important as the formal one (for example, Cross et al., 2001; Cross and Prusak, 2002). Moreover, literature on network communications and creativity (Monge et al., 1992; Amabile, 1996; Monge and Contractor, 2003) points out that to stimulate creativity an employee should have an 'optimally' sized network predominately composed of heterogeneous contacts reaching to different social circles within and outside the organization.

We approach idea implementation from a behavioral perspective (Perry-Smith and Shalley, 2003) acknowledging that implementing ideas requires cooperation with others, and when this happens it becomes a social process (King, 1990). Idea implementation, in contrast to creativity, is primarily a social-political process. Consequently, people – provided they are motivated to engage in the risky process of pursuing their ideas, and they possess the social abilities that allow them to involve other supporters in their organization – should be able to influence this social-political process, thereby improving their odds that their ideas will be eventually implemented.

To operationalize idea implementation we adopted the 'taking charge' perspective (Morrison and Phelps, 1999) and defined it as voluntary and constructive efforts by individual employees to effect organizationally functional change with respect to how work is executed within the contexts of their jobs, work units, or organizations. This suggests that employees who take charge go beyond the boundaries of their jobs to bring about positive change. This complements Van Maanen and Schein's (1979) view that organizations need change and innovations to survive in the long term. In this respect, taking charge does not assume seeing the actual situation in the company as a negative one, but rather one that needs to be improved. As a consequence such behaviors are motivated by positive outcomes, or what is calculated to be of personal benefit, and top management openness to suggestions (Morrison and Phelps, 1999; Baer, 2012). Taking charge thus focuses more on the narrower idea implementation process rather than on the innovation process more generally and is dependent on the individual but also on the context, fitting in with the social network perspective, where the relationship between individuals is the key mechanism through which innovative ideas can be implemented. Individuals will be more likely to engage in idea implementation activities if they perceive that there is a 'climate' for idea implementation, or in other words if their organization supports new idea implementation and change (Somech and Drach-Zahavy, 2013).

Taking charge is different from issue selling – an organization's attention to key trends, developments, and events that have implications for its performance – as it is not focused on strategic issues (Dutton et al., 2001) but rather on internal means for accomplishing organizational goals, and it offers suggestions on how to address those problems or opportunities. Furthermore, when compared to idea championing (see Chapter 5 in this volume) it is broader: every individual can take charge to promote functional change, rather as a person who emerges and employs various strategies to get the members of the organization to support the idea (Shane et al., 1995).

METHODS AND DATA ANALYSIS

To show how idea implementation can be studied with SNA we recruited a medium-sized knowledge-intensive firm headquartered in Slovenia. At the time of the study this information and communication technology firm employed around 120 people and provided its business clients (B2B) with comprehensive solutions for system integration of telecommunication networks. It is an increasingly international market player, which sees the innovation process as a key source of its competitive advantage. The workflow in the company unfolds by means of a team-based process structure with centralized administrative, technical, and business support. Leadership style is hands-on through a cohesive extended top management team, whereas its organizational culture features extensive cooperation, openness to change, information sharing and devotion to enhancing knowledge.

Demographic and sociometric data about employees were gathered in the company. The average age of employees in our sample was 36.1 years (average tenure was 5.9 years), 78 percent of whom were male. Further, 67 percent of employees in our sample held a university degree, and 13 percent held a Master's degree or higher. Major employee competencies covered: electrical engineering/electronics, telecommunications, IT and computer science, software programming, and business administration.

Sociometric data were first gathered with a name generator – a data collection device for eliciting the names of the respondents' contacts that correspond to a specific relational content (Marsden, 1987). The respondents generated contact names that matched the following description: 'During your everyday work you probably often have new ideas. Select coworkers (you can select any number of them) who helped your creativity and ideas formulation in the last year (for example, during a conversation with them you got a new idea)'. We then assessed each of the contacts provided with a name interpreter – a device for evaluating the quality/intensity of respondents' relations (Marsden, 1987, p. 123). In our case this was worded: 'To what extent were or will be the ideas provided by this coworker helpful in developing a new solution for the customer?' The number of coworkers the respondent could nominate was not restricted and was done using the nominalist approach – the respondents were provided with a list prepared by researchers from which they selected coworkers that matched the description. For each selected coworker the respondents then answered the name interpreter question using a five point scale, ranging from 'not relevant at all' to 'essential'. After reminders and follow-up procedures, 110 employees reported and evaluated their contacts, which corresponded to a response rate of 92 percent.

The exploratory social network analysis (SNA) was done using Pajek (Batagelj and Mrvar, 1998). This software package allowed us to transform the network, determine its density and visualize and measure various structural positions of the individuals within this network. Two measures were selected to examine individuals' positions in the idea implementation network – ingoing degree centrality and betweenness centrality (for example, Wasserman and Faust, 1994; Nooy et al., 2011). To illustrate, the ingoing degree centrality of an individual is the number of all ingoing relations (ties) from other organizational members. In our case this means that the individual was a stronger source of idea implementation as found by his or her colleagues. Betweenness centrality of an individual on the other hand measures the proportion of all shortest paths between pairs of individuals in the network that pass through the focal organizational member. An individual with a high betweenness centrality can control a greater proportion of viable and useful ideas flowing through the network.

RESULTS

We first present the visualization of the idea implementation network in a company and structural positions of individual organizational members within it (Figure 14.1).

The more central is the individual the more centrally positioned he or she is in Figures 14.1 and 14.2. On the other hand, network density is defined as the proportion of the actual number of ties between all actors in a network relative to all possible ties between all actors in the network (Wasserman and Faust, 1994). In our case, the network density of idea implementation is 0.022, which suggests a relatively sparse network as only 2.2 percent of all possible relationships between individuals of the organization are present.

Moreover, it appears that the presented network is quite centralized and cohesive. However, some individuals (for example, v26, v32) are isolated, while four of them are connected with one other organizational member (v1 and v90, and, v14 and v34). Figure 14.1 also depicts peripheral individuals (for example, v23, v29). A group of core employees that cooperate intensively with all other employees and a group of peripheral employees that mostly cooperate with the core can be identified – showing a core-periphery model. In the sociogram (see Figure 14.1) one can see that there

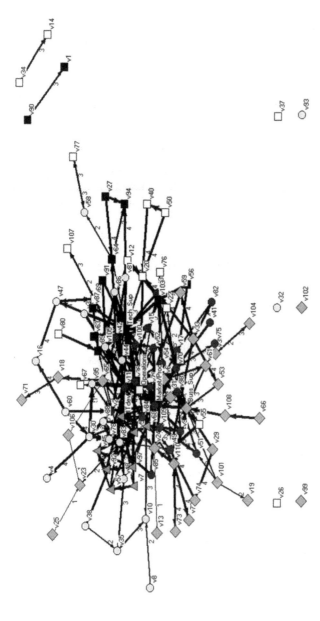

Note: Each of the 110 individuals is labeled with an identification number, which is the same in all presented network pictures (sociograms). Individuals differently labeled represent the formal manager of different departments. The individual identified with 'Operations' is the head of Operations department in the company, the one labeled 'Dev' is the head of the Development department, the one with 'Tech. Sup' is in charge of the Technical Support department, 'Buss_Sup' shows the formal manager of the Business Support unit, 'ITdev' is the head of the development unit of the company, last, 'Market/Prod' has a dual role, as a head of Marketing and as a head of Products. In the visualizations members of different departments are colored and shaped as follows: Operations is shown as a white box, IT Development is gray triangle, Technical Support is depicted black box, Business Support is shown as a gray diamond, Marketing is shown as a dark circle, and finally, Products is depicted as a lighter circle. The value or relationships between (in other words, the strength of the relationship) can be observed in Figures 14.1 and 14.2 by their thickness, where higher values of the relationships are presented by thicker lines (1 is the lowest one, 5 is the highest one). Arrows illustrate idea implementation flows.

Figure 14.1   Idea implementation network

is a very dense center of the network, whereas most of the ties from the margins are directed into the center of the network. It can be also noted that employees in the core of the idea implementation network are connected with multiple organizational units. Thus, the core-periphery model of idea implementation in this company stretches beyond formal organizational unit boundaries. Finally, this also suggests that the central (groups of) individuals may play a brokerage (translator) role in the idea implementation process within this firm.

All of the formally appointed managers play an important role in the idea implementation process as they are highly centrally positioned in the examined network. This is especially true for managers labeled 'Operations', 'ITdev' and 'Market/Prod'. The other two appointed managers 'Tech_Sup' and 'Buss_Sup' are less central and mostly have strong intra-departmental relationships. When looking at the department membership, it appears that the most centrally positioned individuals are the members from Marketing, followed by the IT Developers. On the other hand, most peripheral individuals come from the Business Support and Products departments.

These observations are supported by calculations of centrality measures (not reported here). Among the most central individuals (in-degree centrality) we find formal department managers. On the other hand, when we look at the betweenness, we can see that the most prominent roles are played by only three managers ('Market/Prod', 'ITdev' and 'Buss_Sup'), who serve as bridges between various clusters or departments of the firm. Nevertheless, we can confirm our observation from the previous section based on the network visualization. When looking at brokerage roles this position is taken by formal managers and a greater proportion of other individuals from various departments, thus effectively controlling the idea implementation process.

We further explored the firm's idea implementation network with clustering algorithms in Pajek to see if this process generates clusters of individuals and who their members are. We carried out the analysis with the Louvain algorithm (Blondel et al., 2008). Results are presented in Figure 14.2.

Figure 14.2 shows seven clusters with 96 members. Some of them are more homogeneous in terms of departmental affiliation than others, again advocating for observation that the social side of idea implementation goes beyond formal organizational units. The most homogeneous cluster appears to mimic the Operations department (second cluster in second row). The most diversified one appears to be the second in the first row, which consists of members from all five departments, but the majority are from Technical Support, Products, and Marketing. This cluster could be

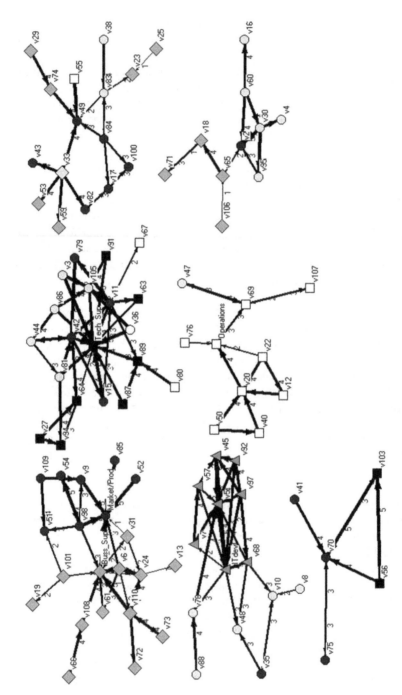

Figure 14.2   Clustering of idea implementation network

seen as the core of the interdepartmental idea implementation process. If we further exclude low-valued relations (relations with intensity equal to or below the value of 3) (not shown in Figure 14.2), the IT Development department appears to form its own cluster, whereas other departments form more heterogeneous ones. Very similar pattern to the one depicting IT Development unit can also be observed in the Operations department. However, when excluding low-valued relations, the majority of the Operations department form one strong cluster, yet some of them still belong to other clusters (for example, second and third in the first row). This is not the case with the IT unit as they form one homogeneous cluster. In general we can observe that most of the units' formal memberships span beyond their boundaries and individuals form heterogeneous clusters. The units most likely involved with other units are (being situated respectively in six and five clusters out of seven) Marketing and Products.

DISCUSSION AND IMPLICATIONS

The purpose of this chapter was to show a practical example of how SNA can be used to explore formal and informal networks of idea implementation in a knowledge-intensive firm. The results suggest that formal structure plays an important role in the idea implementation network, especially when it is related to the control of the idea implementation process (for example, Kleinbaum and Stuart, 2014; McEvily et al., 2014).

In more detail, our results show that formally appointed managers occupy a central role in the idea implementation network, thus they have the ability to execute the innovation process as others probably see them as sponsors. This is consistent with previous findings that suggest that central roles are usually taken by formally appointed managers and as a consequence this has benefits in the innovation process (Van de Ven, 1986; Ibarra, 1993; Morrison and Phelps, 1999). From a discussion with the firm's top management we could not identify such problems, thus we suspect that such composition of the top individuals provides benefits to the firm's idea implementation network.

Second, authors suggest that for creativity to flourish individuals should have connections outside their department, thus companies should facilitate interactions across work groups (Perry-Smith and Shalley, 2003; Oh et al., 2006; Liu et al., 2010). As suggested by Oh et al. (2006) the best results are achieved when there are moderately strong relationships present in the working group and a high-level of bridging conduits between groups – providing individuals with access to more varied resources and innovative information. In our case this is true to a certain degree;

especially employees in the Marketing and Products departments exhibit strong connections with other departments. These departments are key to the flow of idea implementation process and provide most structural bridges in this company. Quite surprising is the fact that IT department is very internally oriented, yet based on our results it may well be the case that the contribution of this unit strongly relies on the brokering of their appointed manager. This again supplements the literature, which suggests that weak ties between individuals of different departments are very important for the creative process (Perry-Smith, 2006).

Research has shown the value of simultaneously considering informal and formal relations in organizations (for example, Kleinbaum and Stuart, 2014; McEvily et al., 2014). This example extends this observation to the idea implementation process and implies that researchers and practitioners might get a more comprehensive picture of a firm's social network regarding creativity and innovation if both aspects are explored at the same time. In this way, possible organizational actions towards shaping optimal social networks in order to promote idea implementation should be easier to identify. It also suggests that SNA should be used more extensively (if possible by spanning different levels of analysis; Stadler et al., 2014) when exploring creativity and innovation in organizations. Practitioners should be aware that SNA is a useful tool for mapping relationships in creativity and innovation networks as this research has shown. Exploring structural positions of key individuals in the innovation process (such as managers or idea generators) provides useful information for firms and allows them to target specific individuals with personalized interventions that could potentially increase their effectiveness in this process.

When insight into the idea implementation (network) is obtained, activities for development and consolidation of the idea implementation network can be initiated. For example, managers could minimize imposing formal policies and focus on activities that provide initiatives for the innovation and implementation process. Helping organizational members accessing crucial social resources (that is, access to information, knowledge) about how to implement ideas is essential and SNA provides management with a powerful tool to explore where such process can be improved (Cross and Thomas, 2009). In addition, managers should be aware of the organizational context and develop human resource management (HRM) practices (for example, training) that could facilitate access to social resources (Kaše et al., 2009), lessen bureaucratic procedures, and provide a broader organizational culture that fosters idea implementation (Škerlavaj et al., 2010). As key idea generators can be socially independent (Martindale, 1989), using SNA could provide information of their social positioning and help the organization to develop specific socialization initiatives to help these creative individuals become more integrated (Morrison, 2002) along with linking them to translators to foster idea implementation.

REFERENCES

Amabile, T.M. (1996), 'Creativity and innovation in organizations', *Harvard Business School Background Note*, No. 396–239.

Baer, M. (2012), 'Putting creativity to work: The implementation of creative ideas in organizations', *Academy of Management Journal*, **55**(5), 1102–19.

Batagelj, V. and A. Mrvar (1998), 'Pajek – a program for large network analysis', *Connections*, **21**(2), 47–57.

Blondel, V.D., J.-L. Guillaume, R. Lambiotte and E. Lefebvre (2008), 'Fast unfolding of communities in large networks', *Journal of Statistical Mechanics: Theory and Experiment*, **2008**(10), P10008.

Borgatti, S.P. and P.C. Foster (2003), 'The network paradigm in organizational research: A review and typology', *Journal of Management*, **29**(6), 991–1013.

Cross, R. and L. Prusak (2002), 'The people who make organizations go – or stop', *Harvard Business Review*, **80**(6), 104–12.

Cross, R.L. and R.J. Thomas (2009), *Driving Results Through Social Networks: How Top Organizations Leverage Networks for Performance and Growth*, 1st edition, San Francisco, CA: Jossey-Bass.

Cross, R., A. Parker, L. Prusak and S.P. Borgatti (2001), 'Knowing what we know: Supporting knowledge creation and sharing in social networks', *Organizational Dynamics*, **30**(2), 100–120.

Dutton, J.E., S.J. Ashford, R.M. O'Neill and K.A. Lawrence (2001), 'Moves that matter: Issue selling and organizational change', *Academy of Management Journal*, **44**(4), 716–36.

Ehrlich, K. (2006), 'IBM: Untangling office connections', *BusinessWeek Online*, 17 February, accessed 3 December 2015 at http://www.ufpa.br/cdesouza/teaching/topes/6-IBM-Untangling%20Office%20Connections.pdf.

Galaskiewicz, J. (2007), 'Has a network theory of organizational behaviour lived up to its promises?' *Management and Organization Review*, **3**(1), 1–18.

Ibarra, H. (1993), 'Network centrality, power, and innovation involvement – determinants of technical and administrative roles', *Academy of Management Journal*, **36**(3), 471–501.

Kaše, R., J. Paauwe and N. Zupan (2009), 'HR practices, interpersonal relations, and intrafirm knowledge transfer in knowledge-intensive firms: A social network perspective', *Human Resource Management*, **48**(4), 615–39.

Kilduff, M. and D.J. Brass (2010), 'Organizational social network research: Core ideas and key debates', *The Academy of Management Annals*, **4**(1), 317–57.

Kilduff, M. and W. Tsai (2003), *Social Networks and Organizations*, London: Sage.

King, N. (1990), 'Innovation at work: The research literature', in M.A. West and J.F. Farr (eds), *Innovation and Creativity at Work: Psychological and Organizational Strategies*, New York: Wiley, pp. 15–59.

Kleinbaum, A.M. and T.E. Stuart (2014), 'Inside the black box of the corporate staff: Social networks and the implementation of corporate strategy', *Strategic Management Journal*, **35**(1), 24–47.

Liu, C.-H., S.-C. Chiu and C.L. Chiu (2010), 'Intranetwork relationships, creativity, knowledge diversification, and network position', *Social Behavior and Personality: An International Journal*, **38**(9), 1173–90.

Marsden, P.V. (1987), 'Core discussion networks of Americans', *American Sociological Review*, **52**(1), 122–31.

Martindale, C. (1989), 'Personality, situation, and creativity', in J.A. Glover, R.R. Ronnings and C.R. Reynolds (eds), *Handbook of Creativity*, New York: Plenum. pp. 211–32.

McEvily, B., G. Soda and M. Tortoriello (2014), 'More formally: Rediscovering the missing link between formal organization and informal social structure', *The Academy of Management Annals*, **8**(1), 299–345.

McGregor, J. (2006), 'The office chart that really counts', *Bloomberg Business*, 26 February, accessed 3 December 2015 at http://www.bloomberg.com/bw/stories/2006-02-26/the-office-chart-that-really-counts.

Monge, P.R. and N.S. Contractor (2003), *Theories of Communication Networks*, New York: Oxford University Press.

Monge, P.R., M.D. Cozzens and N.S. Contractor (1992), 'Communication and motivational predictors of the dynamics of organizational innovation', *Organization Science*, **3**(2), 250–74.

Morrison, E.W. (2002), 'Newcomers' relationships: The role of social network ties during socialization', *The Academy of Management Journal*, **45**(6), 1149–60.

Morrison, E.W. and C.C. Phelps (1999), 'Taking charge at work: Extrarole efforts to initiate workplace change', *The Academy of Management Journal*, **42**(4), 403–19.

Nooy, W., A. Mrvar and V. Batagelj (2011), *Exploratory Social Network Analysis with Pajek*, 2nd edition, New York: Cambridge University Press.

Obstfeld, D. (2005), 'Social networks, the *tertius iungens* orientation, and involvement in innovation', *Administrative Science Quarterly*, **50**(1), 100–130.

Oh, H., G. Labianca and M.-H. Chung (2006), 'A multilevel model of group social capital', *The Academy of Management Review*, **31**(3), 569–82.

Perry-Smith, J.E. (2006), 'Social yet creative: The role of social relationships in facilitating individual creativity', *The Academy of Management Journal*, **49**(1), 85–101.

Perry-Smith, J.E. and C.E. Shalley (2003), 'The social side of creativity: A static and dynamic social network perspective', *Academy of Management Review*, **28**(1), 89–106.

Pugh, K. and L. Prusak (2013), 'Designing effective knowledge networks', *MIT Sloan Management Review*, **55**(1), 79–88.

Raider, H. and D. Krackhardt (2002), 'Intraorganizational networks', in J.A.C. Baum (ed.), *The Blackwell Companion to Organizations*, Malden: Blackwell Publishing, pp. 59–74.

Shane, S., S. Venkataraman and I. MacMillan (1995), 'Cultural differences in innovation championing strategies', *Journal of Management*, **21**(5), 931–52.

Škerlavaj, M., J.H. Song, and Y. Lee (2010), 'Organizational learning culture, innovative culture and innovations in South Korean firms', *Expert Systems with Applications*, **37**(9), 6390–403.

Somech, A. and A. Drach-Zahavy (2013), 'Translating team creativity to innovation implementation: The role of team composition and climate for innovation', *Journal of Management*, **39**(3), 684–708.

Stadler, C., T. Rajwani and F. Karaba (2014), 'Solutions to the exploration/exploitation dilemma: Networks as a new level of analysis', *International Journal of Management Reviews*, **16**(2), 172–93.

Van de Ven, A.H. (1986), 'Central problems in the management of innovation', *Management Science*, **32**(5), 590–607.

Van Maanen, J. and E.H. Schein (1979), 'Toward a theory of organizational socialization', in B.M. Staw (ed.), *Research in Organizational Behavior*, Vol. 1, Greenwich: JAI Press, pp. 209–64.

Wasserman, S. and K. Faust (1994), *Social Network Analysis: Methods and Applications*, Cambridge, UK: Cambridge University Press.

Wellman, B. (1998), 'Structural analysis: From method and metaphor to theory and substance', in B. Wellman and S.D. Berkowitz (eds), *Social Structures: A Network Approach*, New York: Cambridge University Press, pp. 19–61.

Woodman, R.W., J.E. Sawyer and R.W. Griffin (1993), 'Toward a theory of organizational creativity', *The Academy of Management Review*, **18**(2), 293–321.

Zaheer, A. and G. Soda (2009), 'Network evolution: The origins of structural holes', *Administrative Science Quarterly*, **54**(1), 1–31.

15. Proactive employee behaviors and idea implementation: three automotive industry cases

Janez Hudovernik, Miha Škerlavaj and Matej Černe

The purpose of this study is to examine innovation processes (specifically focusing on idea implementation) in three companies based in Slovenia that are operating within the automotive industry. This chapter thus focuses on identifying predictors of innovation performance beyond position of company, level of autonomy and ownership types, and even individual-level innovation predictors that stem from employee personal characteristics. Specifically, we took an evidence-based grounded theory–building approach (Eisenhardt, 1989) on the foundations of multiple case studies (Yin, 2009) to contribute to the literature on the drivers of employee proactive behavior as an antecedent of innovation performance. The extant literature on proactive behavior across different research domains (cf. Crant, 2000) focuses in depth on its predictors at the individual level, such as personality characteristics, job design, and employee motivation (Parker et al., 2006). Within this chapter we take a broader approach and attempt to identify additional antecedents of proactive behavior (beyond the individual level) and its role in idea implementation. We suggest a guiding framework on proactive behavior and idea implementation that could be used both for future research on these topics as well as for practice.

We selected three companies as our case studies, which share some similarities but also have quite distinctive different positions. The first one is a locally owned company (with employees as majority shareholders) positioned in the global market – Domel d.o.o. The second is part of a multinational company with moderate levels of autonomy in decision-making – GKN Driveline Slovenija, d.o.o. The third is also a branch of an international operation with the least autonomy – Sumida Slovenija, d.o.o. They were chosen because we wanted to make generalizable claims about innovation processes above and beyond their ownership type (Hoskisson et al., 2002; Aghion et al., 2009), position of company in terms of its market (Blundell et al., 1999; Agarwal et al., 2003) and level of autonomy (Wissema and Euser, 1991), and on the other hand we also wanted to focus on firms that share some similarities. They are operating in the same industry (automotive), and all three companies are employing similar competency profiles from almost the same pool of people (Slovene labor market) and do their business in the same socio-political environment, but they are different than others. They capitalize on their innovation strategies and practices and transform them into business performance. In what follows, we examine what these companies do in terms of engaging their employees to be proactive and not only generate more ideas, but also implement them.

COMPARATIVE CASE STUDY ANALYSIS

The Innovation Enhancement Processes at Sumida Slovenija, d.o.o.

Problems are the easiest way toward improving ideas. (Janez Ločniškar, general manager of Sumida Slovenija, d.o.o.)

In order to get an overview of the current state of affairs in terms of innovativeness in Sumida Slovenija, d.o.o., we first conducted a quantitative multi-level study (of leaders and followers). The added value of this study is that it enabled some cross-company and also cross-national comparisons with companies that had participated in our similar studies in the past. Here is a brief overview of the results.

In Sumida Slovenija, d.o.o., the quality of its mastery climate, which is generally posited as beneficial for stimulating idea generation (Černe et al., 2014), is generally higher than in other surveyed companies (in Slovenia, Norway, and China). It is also quite positive that employees perceive 'knowledge hiding' in their organization to be at very low levels – the values in Sumida Slovenija, d.o.o. are lower than in all the companies we have surveyed so far.

In terms of transforming creative ideas into implemented innovations at the individual and group levels (often translated to the company level), the employees were shown to possess quite high levels of task-related self-efficacy and self-monitoring. The survey also showed rather high levels of creativity and individual innovation, whereas the radicalness of ideas that are implemented is relatively lower than in other surveyed firms – indicating that Sumida Slovenija, d.o.o. bases its competitive advantage on incremental innovations. In what follows, we portray some best practices in Sumida Slovenija, d.o.o. that allow it to score highly with regard to creativity and innovation.

Idea generation workshops (*Brihtalnice*/smart thinking room)
Sumida Slovenija, d.o.o. has a well-organized system of obtaining ideas and suggestions from employees and it runs regular guided problem-solving sessions. It calls them *Brihtalnice*, which translates as 'idea generators', a well-structured process of problem-solving. Team leaders have the opportunity and an obligation to involve their team in a guided workshop. For example, in a first session, they will brainstorm for problems and cluster them. Next they will look for solutions to these problems, and then they will evaluate and improve on these ideas, and brainstorm on ways to implement them. No session takes longer than 45 minutes. The result – an average of eight realized ideas per employee per year.

When employees were gathered for the first time in the idea-generating process there were a lot of objections, such as: 'I do not have any ideas, I only work here, what do you want from me?' However, when asked specifically about their problems the picture was different. We know that idea generation and problem-solving are basically the same processes with different starting points. In Sumida Slovenija, d.o.o. they discovered that people identify problems much faster than generate ideas.

The five-steps process
According to those findings Sumida Slovenija, d.o.o. developed the five-steps process. First, a working group goes into a special room equipped with equipment for the problem-solving process. This meeting lasts up to one hour, of which the first 45 minutes is problem storming and writing down all problems that the working group can identify. Each member of the group identifies a problem and a trained facilitator writes it down. This problem can be a spark for related problems and other problems pop up. The facilitators are trained to motivate and support problem storming and to stop any critical evaluation of the problems at this stage. Rules similar to the well-known brainstorming process apply here.

After 30–45 minutes or so, the team looks at the written problems and groups them into clusters. Facilitator and group leader then decide which problems are the main issues. They make a selection of the problem clusters. The second step is defining the problem. Here they can use tools for further defining the problems. Most common are the 'fishbone diagram' (devised by Kaoru Ishikawa, 1968, also known as '4M/6M diagram': Man, Machine, Method, Materials, Measurement, Mother Nature) and 'Asking Five W's and One H' (What, Where, When, Who, Why and How). With these tools selected problems are dissected into causes and effects. More light is shed on the problem and areas that contribute to that problem that are out of the control of participants are eliminated. After the proper definition of the problems, the biggest causes are selected and are the starting point for next step.

The third step is idea generation. The prominent causes are presented and participants generate ideas. Lots of different tools and processes are used here. Choice depends on the problem as well as on participants. The most used process is brainstorming with different variations, such as brainwriting, reverse brainstorming, and so on. Again, the facilitator supports the process and emphasis is put on *not* evaluating the ideas. This is a crucial point. After 45 minutes ideas are grouped together and prepared for evaluation.

The fourth step is idea evaluation. There are several methods that can be used. Mostly they use two-dimensional tables where ideas are evaluated first based on implementability (x axis; low–high) and then on their effect on the results (similar to radicalness or contribution: y axis; low–high) – the implementability/results (IR) matrix. The ideas generated in these workshops are basically improvements on the current production process and they are deliberately kept simple. The IR principle can be built upon to devise a more complex evaluation matrix.

The fifth step is project planning. The best ideas are turned into projects. A plan for implementation is devised: who, when, where, how, and resources are assigned.

So, five steps from problems to improvements – a process that is not so difficult to implement, but is still not a common practice. Nevertheless, according to the managers in this company, this or similar systematic processes are necessary to educate people in generating ideas and continuous improvements. After they know the process they can and will use it on their own. And with time, ideas and suggestions will come from individuals arising from their everyday work. And what is more surprising, they are achieving these results with simple innovation tools. Everybody can do this, but not all of them are. And this, as we have discovered, is one of the (and most important) essences of success.

In Sumida Slovenija, d.o.o., additional improvements were made in the process of implementation. Employees were given the authority and opportunity to implement their own ideas. Do-it-yourself opportunities were introduced, meaning that an employee could both generate and implement a new, creative idea, so doubling the rewards. Also, the realization of ideas often requires teamwork so in the process team rewards were introduced.

Systematic Process of Generating and Implementing Ideas – Domel, d.o.o.

Innovation was one of Domel's core values a decade ago. One of the authors of this chapter was involved in this process and can speak from first-hand experience. Out of this came a strong incentive from top management towards innovation. They came up with the slogan: 'In Domel we plan for innovation'. This slogan was a hot discussion topic in the beginning because it stirred up certain beliefs first among top management and later in employees. It was myth breaking, clearly going against the general notion that 'Innovation cannot be planned, innovation is spontaneous' (Dyer et al., 2011). Research shows, however, that innovators can be made and are not just born. If you teach people creative problem-solving techniques you can dramatically improve results in this area. Such myths still persist in a lot of companies though and all too often innovative ideas are left to spontaneity. But fortunately the slogan survived and they started with an asystematic approach toward the innovation and continuous improvements. Recently they have changed the slogan to include 'sustainable innovative solutions', which reflects their high social and environmental responsibility.

Domel, d.o.o. has its own R&D department, the only one of all three studied companies. Domel, d.o.o. won a gold award from the Slovenian Chamber of Commerce for its blower designed for the German company J. Wagner GmbH. The new blower for the hand paint sprayer operates at 65000 rpm and achieves excellent results through highly dynamic switching. Due to its innovative design, the blower has been patented.

Although only a decade ago the company was highly dependent on one product line (more than 80 percent of revenue and with no more than five customers), today it has a goal that 40 percent of revenue must come from products younger than three years. This too is one of its key innovation goals (key performance indicators). In a decade of supporting innovation it has come a long way and the company knows now that it has to keep on innovating.

IT platform
Domel, d.o.o. has developed a special software program for tracking ideas and their implementation. In addition you can see how many ideas each employee has contributed and how much saving this idea has produced. This system allows them a good overview and quick feedback, which is very important. What you can measure, you can improve.

Where intention goes, energy flows and results show
Domel, d.o.o. first started with one big action for generating ideas in October every year. Results from the first year were positive, and that encouraged leadership to continue. They prepared posters, visual reminders and even greater emphasis than usual was put into innovation,

new ideas, and suggestions for improvement. Year by year results were better and that encouraged them to introduce another action in March.

Reward structure

What you reward you will get more of. This is true for ideas as well. All companies have a specific reward structure, using both practical and financial rewards. For the best innovators Domel, d.o.o. offers more practical rewards. The one that works best offers an experience such as a dream vacation. This practical reward is always known in advance and employees can choose between certain options.

For bigger innovations, employees get the percentages from savings or revenue according to internal rules. All companies offer the highest amount allowed by existent laws in Slovenia. If the innovation was great and substantial savings or revenue were generated out of the innovation the employee can benefit from a financial reward. It is critical to emphasize the difference between intrinsic or base-pay/non-tangible and extrinsic variable-pay/tangible rewards. Rewards tend to increase creative and innovative performance if they are creativity contingent, when individuals are given more positive, contingent, and task-focused performance feedback, and are provided more choice (autonomy). On the other hand, performance- or completion-contingent rewards actually tend to have a slightly negative effect on creative and innovative performance (Byron and Khazanchi, 2012).

Lean workshops

Both GKN Driveline Slovenija, d.o.o. (see below) and Domel, d.o.o. use similar approach, called 'lean workshops', to ensure continuous improvement process. In GKN Driveline Slovenija, d.o.o., workshops are planned on a yearly basis. They are conducted by trained internal champions, mostly leaders. In workshops, specialists from maintenance and manufacturing engineering and also from other functions are involved. The problems are discussed and several tools are used to get the most out of the employees in a short period of time.

They use different tools, among others five-sigma, visual management, standard work checklists, and lost time analysis (LTA). These workshops are ad hoc – when needed. According to our source this is a great idea generation process as well as a good education opportunity. They estimate that at least 70 percent of employees are familiar with the structure and content of these workshops. Employees who regularly go to these workshops produce more ideas during their everyday work, because they are familiar with the process and tools.

Daily Innovation Activities at GKN Driveline Slovenija, d.o.o.

Info meetings

GKN has a very useful approach toward generating ideas, or detecting problems, the by-product of daily 'info meetings'. In the company they have organized a special room where on the wall you can see the elements of the workflow process depicted in pictures and diagrams. Each group stands by their own part of the process and has a visual reminder of who their suppliers are and who are their customers (internal or external). Representatives of each working group participate, not only Production but also HR, Technology, Finance, Quality, and so on. These meetings have a time limit of 20 minutes and a fixed agenda. Every meeting starts with three reports about (1) health and safety, (2) quality and (3) people. Afterwards each representative informs others of current events. All interesting topics are written down and later processed.

In these meetings they share information about serious accidents and near-misses from other companies in the GKN Driveline. The last issue of this short daily information meeting is recognition of the day, which is then communicated through the company by defined communication channels. 'Could there be a similar danger in your work area?' This information is well documented and this prevents occurrences of similar events in the company.

Daily audits

In GKN they have established a 'daily audit' of the whole company called RADAR, based on the system that every square meter must be audited at least twice a year. A monthly plan is formulated following 'RADAR audits': Health/Safety Radar, Quality Radar, and Eco Radar. Each member of the audit team uses a checklist and camera so certain circumstances are immediately documented. Special emphasis is on near-misses – a great prevention method.

According to the yearly plan, the management team performs the so-called 'Gemba Walk'.[1] The aim of this management visit is to recognize improvements from the previous walk and give feedback to the working teams. Results of the weekly Gemba Walks are shown to all employees on Information Screens in the canteen and in the Info Room.

Info tables

Another good practice that we identified is the use of 'info tables', which we find in all three companies. You can find them in all work units. They have whiteboards where they use the write-and-wipe system. This allows them quick feedback and everyone is encouraged to write down suggestions or ideas. There are also visual reminders about mistakes, good practices, and feedback. How are we doing? This quick feedback allows for quick corrections. What was especially admirable in GKN was the one in the meeting room where the board of directors and other important meetings takes place (Figure 15.1). You can see suggestions for improvement for example board meeting written from last meetings. They are sharing the leadership of meetings and evaluations with everyone as soon as meetings finish.

DISCUSSION – COMPARATIVE ANALYSIS AND GROUNDED THEORY–BUILDING OF THE FRAMEWORK OF MULTI-LEVEL ANTECEDENTS OF PROACTIVE BEHAVIOR

Top Management Philosophy and Support

We will start our discussion from the top and present our findings and how they relate to theory, accompanied with practical evidence in Figure 15.2. The bottom left gray box represents individual-level antecedents of proactive behavior identified in the existing literature. Text in white boxes is a summary of our evidence-based grounded theory–building based on the results of our case studies. Two of the companies have innovation written into their vision statement. In all three, innovation is one of the core values or it is written into strategic plans. Top management supports innovation and continuous improvement. They have set strategic and yearly goals in this area and they measure and follow up rigorously. They have all adopted the philosophy that innovation is everyone's job and they not only declare this but they truly live it. This is related to Parker et al. (2010)'s proactive goal generation, but is much more generalistic and spans across the company as a whole, not only at the individual level. In all three cases this was not one day's work; it was a hard and laborious process for more than two decades. There is no overnight success and no spontaneity, only hard and systematic work and lots of trials and mistakes in the process as well. We can illustrate this with an interesting story:

All three studied companies have strong support from top management. Top management is either directly involved in the improvement or innovation processes or they strongly support it. But this, they find, is not enough. This important area for development and success of the company has to be reinforced throughout the whole system. And who runs the system? People do. However, as we have shown, the crucial point is not in selecting the people with particular characteristics beneficial for innovation, but rather in organizing them in a way to maximize their innovative potential.

Capitalizing on creativity at work

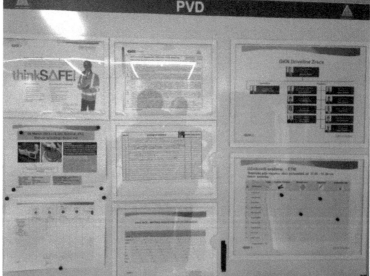

Figure 15.1   Visual representation of GKN Driveline strategy to become 'the best engineering company in the world' and info table in management meeting room

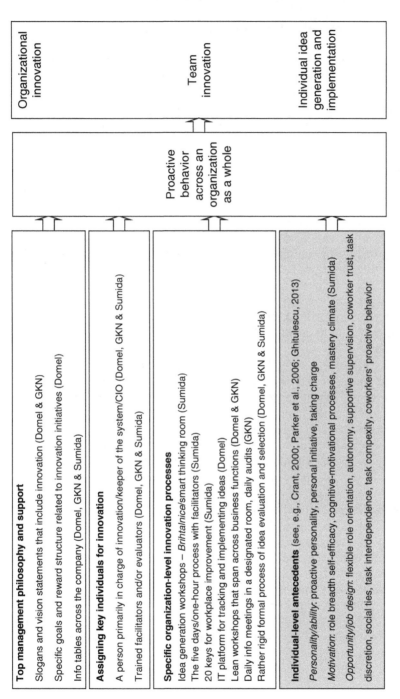

Top management philosophy and support

Slogans and vision statements that include innovation (Domel & GKN)

Specific goals and reward structure related to innovation initiatives (Domel)

Info tables across the company (Domel, GKN & Sumida)

Assigning key individuals for innovation

A person primarily in charge of innovation/keeper of the system/CIO (Domel, GKN & Sumida)

Trained facilitators and/or evaluators (Domel, GKN & Sumida)

Specific organization-level innovation processes

Idea generation workshops – *Brihtalnice*/smart thinking room (Sumida)

The five days/one-hour process with facilitators (Sumida)

20 keys for workplace improvement (Sumida)

IT platform for tracking and implementing ideas (Domel)

Lean workshops that span across business functions (Domel & GKN)

Daily info meetings in a designated room, daily audits (GKN)

Rather rigid formal process of idea evaluation and selection (Domel, GKN & Sumida)

Individual-level antecedents (see, e.g., Crant, 2000; Parker et al., 2006; Ghitulescu, 2013)

Personality/ability: proactive personality, personal initiative, taking charge

Motivation: role breadth self-efficacy, cognitive-motivational processes, mastery climate (Sumida)

Opportunity/job design: flexible role orientation, autonomy, supportive supervision, coworker trust, task

discretion, social ties, task interdependence, task complexity, coworkers' proactive behavior

Proactive behavior across an organization as a whole

Organizational innovation

Team innovation

Individual idea generation and implementation

Figure 15.2   A model of proactive behavior antecedents that expands existing research on its individual-level drivers

187

Assigning Key Individuals for Innovation

These companies soon discovered that they had to establish a system with different roles. All three assigned a person who is primarily in charge of innovation. This person is responsible for targets set in this area and for mobilizing others towards achieving these goals. He or she regularly reports to the board of directors about current events and status of improvement projects.

Creativity is our inherent trait; just as in the process of education and growing up, this ability is often suppressed (Torrance, 1962). And we have to create the right environment so that this trait surfaces again. People need to be trained in this respect. Our studied companies have decided to train chosen employees how apply to creative-thinking tools and problem-solving processes. They have trained facilitators how to use these tools and how to lead the process of idea generation. More on that later when describing the innovation process. Some facilitators also have another role and that is to help employees write down a suggestion. Why is this particularly important on the production floor where low-qualified employees are in the majority? Because these employees who run machines have the most profound knowledge of their processes and products, so their input is crucial.

All three companies also have a person who is responsible for the system – the keeper of the system. By the system we don't mean the person in charge of innovation processes, but rather IT support and idea capture. Companies need to have goals for innovation. They use different indicators from a number of suggestions per employee to percentages of generated revenue from new innovative products. We often heard: 'What you measure you can improve' (Thompson, 1883). What is measured gets done. This can sound like an old cliché but it is important to emphasize.

Specific Organization-level Innovation Processes

Where do creative ideas come from in these companies? They have identified and established many different sources and this guarantees lots of suggestions and ideas.[2] We found that these companies heavily rely on processes, that is, they established daily or ad hoc processes for generating ideas and then for their implementation. The processes are supported by IT technology. All three companies have their own software for managing process and ideas. They use this system for tracking ideas throughout the innovation process.

Idea selection and implementation

At first all three companies started with a rigid formal process of evaluating. Ideas were written down in special formulas and given to the committee. This group of people would meet once a month and look through suggestions. Sometimes these suggestions were not written clearly so they were often given back to the employee. This could then take a couple of months before an idea was evaluated. Feedback was slow and too formal. Lots of obstacles were generated on the way.

After the idea was approved there were new obstacles when implementing. People who worked in the maintenance department often saw this as additional work and were not very motivated to participate. Lots of ideas were killed in the process. So they sought a better solution, which they found: a selection of people called evaluators. These people were trained in evaluating ideas and were given the authority to decide on the spot. So the process was cut from an average of two months to two days for the implementation of small improvements. If evaluators see that potential suggestions or ideas could have a much higher impact, then this idea is still submitted to the committee, which is summoned ad hoc. Introducing evaluators is an example of process innovation itself. It has improved feedback, hastening implementation and results. Feedback is particularly crucial for idea implementation (Škerlavaj et al., 2014).

When an employee sees that his or her suggestion has been implemented, this acts as a boost to self-esteem, self-confidence, and self-efficacy. This in turn increases motivation and engagement, as research shows. Teresa Amabile (2011) clearly found that the progress at work is key to satisfaction and engagement, and we concur after examining the best practices in all three case studies.

CONCLUSION

The key premise of this chapter, based on the comparative analysis of three cases studies, is that innovation needs a system. The results indicate that innovation is not crucially dependent upon employees' personal (pre)dispositions, but rather about transforming those predispositions into proactive behavior that leads to creativity and innovation. Those organizational-level antecedents were in our cases not even constrained by being owned by a foreign mother-firm. Systems in the companies are like boxes with certain rules. Marissa Mayer, current president and CEO at Yahoo likes to say: 'Creativity Loves Constraints. People think of creativity as this sort of unbridled thing, but engineers thrive on constraints. They love to think their way out of that little box' (Salter, 2008). This reflects many successful innovators' (such as Google, Yahoo, Apple etc.) general approach toward innovation: creativity is encouraged, but only within certain predetermined and fairly rigid confines, which allow for creative ideas to become implemented.

The main message of the chapter is that the implementation of creative ideas should not be left to coincidence and spontaneity. Companies should strive to demystify the innovation process. As CEO of Sumida Janez Ločniškar said: 'I hate it when I hear employees saying, we have done everything. You could never do everything. There is always something you can do. The biggest obstacle in the innovation processes is in our heads'. Our research has revealed a set of organizational-level antecedents of engaging employees in proactive behavior that can serve as a basis for future research as well as for practice. We have identified three sets of such factors that go beyond the traditionally examined antecedents of proactive behavior at the individual level: top management philosophy and support, assigning key individuals for innovation, and specific organizational-level innovation practices that engage employees in proactive behavior. Implementing those ideas and best practices can potentially be very useful for firms trying to implement their creative efforts and enhance their innovation performance.

NOTES

1. Linus Pauling, American chemist, biochemist, peace activist, author, and educator once said if you want to have good ideas you have to have a lot of bad ideas (Goodreads.com, 2014).
2. Personal observation walk, from the Japanese word *gembutsu* or 'real thing'.

REFERENCES

Agarwal, S., M.K. Erramilli and C.S. Dev (2003), 'Market orientation and performance in service firms: Role of innovation', *Journal of Services Marketing*, **17**(1), 68–82.
Aghion, P., J. van Reenen and L. Zingales (2009), 'Innovation and institutional ownership', *CEP Discussion Papers No. 911*, London: LSE.
Amabile, T. (2011), *The Progress Principle, Using Small Wins to Ignite Joy, Engagement and Creativity at Work*, Boston, MA: Harvard Business Review Press.
Blundell, R., R. Griffith and J. van Reenen (1999), 'Market share, market value and innovation in a panel of British manufacturing firms', *The Review of Economic Studies*, **66**(3), 529–54.
Byron, K. and S. Khazanchi (2012), 'Rewards and creative performance: A meta-analytic test of theoretically derived hypotheses', *Psychological Bulletin*, **138**(4), 809–30.

Crant, J.M. (2000), 'Proactive behavior in organizations', *Journal of Management*, **26**(3), 435–62.

Černe, M., C.G.L. Nerstad, A. Dysvik and M. Škerlavaj (2014), 'What goes around comes around: Knowledge hiding, motivational climate, and creativity', *Academy of Management Journal*, **57**(1), 172–92.

Dyer, J., H. Gregersen and C.M. Christensen (2011), *The Innovator's DNA: Mastering the Five Skills of Disruptive Innovators*, Boston, MA: Harvard Business Review Press.

Eisenhardt, K.M. (1989), 'Building theories from case study research', *Academy of Management Review*, **14**(4), 532–50.

Ghitulescu, B.E. (2013), 'Making change happen: The impact of work context on adaptive and proactive behaviors', *The Journal of Applied Behavioral Science*, **49**(2), 206–45.

Goodreads.com (2014), 'Linus Pauling quotes', accessed 12 August 2014 at http://www.goodreads.com/author/quotes/52938.Linus_Pauling.

Hoskisson, R.E., M.A. Hitt, R.A. Johnson and W. Grossman (2002), 'Conflicting voices: The effects of institutional ownership heterogeneity and internal governance on corporate innovation strategies', *Academy of Management Journal*, **45**(4), 697–716.

Ishikawa, K. (1968), *Guide to Quality Control*, Tokyo: JUSE.

Parker, S.K., H.H. Williams and N. Turner (2006), 'Modeling the antecedents of proactive behavior at work', *Journal of Applied Psychology*, **91**(3), 636–52.

Parker, S.K., U.K. Bindl and K. Strauss (2010), 'Making things happen: A model of proactive motivation', *Journal of Management*, **36**(4), 827–56.

Salter, C. (2008), 'Marissa Mayer's 9 principles of innovation', *Fast Company*, accessed 3 December 2015 at http://www.fastcompany.com/702926/marissa-mayers-9-principles-innovation.

Škerlavaj, M., M. Černe and A. Dysvik (2004), 'I get by with a little help from my supervisor: Creative-idea generation, idea implementation, and perceived supervisor support', *Leadership Quarterly*, **25**(5), 987–1000.

Thompson, W. (Lord Kelvin) (1883), 'Lecture on "electrical units of measurement"', in *Popular Lectures and Addresses*, Vol. 1, London: Macmillan, p. 73.

Torrance, E.P. (1962), *Guiding Creative Talent*, Englewood Cliffs, NJ: Prentice-Hall.

Wissema, J. and L. Euser (1991), 'Successful innovation through inter-company networks', *Long Range Planning*, **24**(6), 33–9.

Yin, R.K. (2009), *Case Study Research: Design and Methods*, Thousand Oaks, CA: Sage Publications.

16. Design thinking workshops: a way to facilitate sensemaking and idea development across organizational levels

Ingo Rauth and Anja Svetina Nabergoj*

For an idea to thrive and be capitalized on, it must make sense to a variety of internal and external stakeholders, including managers, engineers, designers, marketers, and most importantly users. Addressing these groups in a way that resonates with all of them, while leveraging everyone's creativity, allows an idea to progress from its creation to its successful implementation. In light of this need, making sense of conflicting viewpoints in relation to idea development is an essential, complex social undertaking that has yet to be the subject of robust study (Drazin et al., 1999; Maitlis, 2005), particularly in the context of large companies (for example, Ravasi and Stigliani, 2012). The presence of conflicting views in collaborative work raises the question of how to engage functionally and hierarchically diverse individuals and external stakeholders (for example, users, experts) in a collaborative innovation process.

Design thinking (DT) is a recent approach that has sought to involve functionally diverse individuals in a collaborative innovation process (Brown, 2008). DT is often described as an iterative creative problem-solving process that fosters creativity and multi-actor sensemaking. Several large organizations, including GE Healthcare, Kaiser Permanente, JetBlue and SAP (for example, Carlgren, 2013; Carlgren et al., 2014; Liedtka, 2014), have utilized the DT approach in their innovation processes, claiming that the DT process leads to the generation and successful implementation of creative ideas (for example, Brown, 2008).

However, little is known about the ways in which DT can facilitate sensemaking and idea development across multiple organizational levels. Consequently this chapter reports the findings from a study that investigated three DT projects at Consumer Products Company (CCo), a multinational firm with over 100 000 employees and a multibillion US dollar annual turnover. CCo has been using DT in the format of design thinking workshops (DTWs) since 2001. As a result, CCo is considered to be one of the first and most experienced adopters of DT. DTWs are two- to three-day workshops that bring together 30–40 functionally and hierarchically diverse employees, external experts, and users to participate in the creative problem-solving process with the goal of innovation.

From a sensemaking perspective, in this chapter we investigate three DTWs that led to CCo being able to successfully capitalize on creative ideas. We identify six practices that foster sensemaking, idea development, and capitalization on ideas across multiple organizational levels, namely: the engagement of functionally and hierarchically diverse individuals, the establishment of heterogeneous teams, the iterative involvement of individuals, and the exposure to, engagement in, and acting upon conflicting views. The identified practices not only contribute to the understanding of sensemaking and design thinking, but also show how DT can increase the probability of capitalizing on ideas.

SENSEMAKING

In *Sensemaking in Organizations*, Karl Weick (1995) identified sensemaking as the process through which individuals in organizations engage in conflicting views by structuring them. More recently, Maitlis and Christianson (2014, p. 57) described sensemaking as the 'process through which people work to understand issues or events that are novel, ambiguous, confusing, or in some way violate expectations'. For some, sensemaking enables the accomplishment of key organizational processes, including innovation (Hill and Levenhagen, 1995; Glynn et al., 2010). Despite the fragmented state of the current literature on sensemaking (Maitlis and Christianson, 2014), we interpret sensemaking as a discursive, and therefore inherently social process (for example, Weick, 1995; Weick et al., 2005; Maitlis, 2005; Maitlis and Christianson, 2014). Consequently we define sensemaking according to Maitlis and Christianson's (2014, p. 67) description of 'a process, prompted by violated expectations [conflicting views] that involves attending to and bracketing cues in the environment, creating intersubjective meaning though cycles of interpretation and action and thereby enacting a more ordered environment from which future cues can be drawn'.

According to Maitlis (2005), most studies have focused on the sensemaking of individual actors (for example, Westley, 1990; Dutton and Ashford, 1993; Rouleau and Balogun, 2011) and sensemaking under extreme circumstances, such as crisis situations (for example, Weick, 1993).

Given this focus, only a small but growing body of research (Maitlis and Christianson, 2014) has investigated sensemaking across organizational levels (for example, Drazin et al., 1999) and in relation to creativity and innovation (for example, Drazin et al., 1999; Abolafia 2010).

In their review of the literature on creativity and innovation, Maitlis and Christianson (2014, p. 93) sought to establish a consistent pattern as to how sensemaking enables creativity and innovation, pointing to a series of six central practices:

1. *Exposing actors* to conflicting views (for example, company vs user opinions), allowing disruptive ambiguity to surface and facilitate individuals' engagement in sensemaking (Weick, 1995).
2. *Engaging* actors with conflicting views.
3. *Acting upon* conflicting views, thereby creating a more ordered physical (for example, prototypes, ideas) and social environment (for example, common idea ownership) that triggers and facilitates further innovation at the organizational level.
4. Ensuring the cyclic or *iterative involvement* of individuals in these three steps.
5. Bringing together a group of *functionally and hierarchically diverse individuals* with competing and disparate views.
6. Establishing and maintaining *social roles* and relationships.

The latter two practices are considered to be crucial for enabling sensemaking to work in social settings (Maitlis, 2005; Ravasi and Stigliani, 2012; Maitlis and Christianson, 2014). Overall, social practices seem to have been largely ignored by previous research (Maitlis, 2005).

DESIGN THINKING

Earlier studies have defined DT in numerous ways. In general, practitioners have defined DT as an approach 'that uses the designer's sensibility and methods to match people's needs with what is technologically feasible and what a viable business strategy can convert into customer value and market opportunity' (Brown, 2008, p. 86). Although the exact meaning and usage of DT seems to be largely context dependent (for example, Lindberg et al., 2012; Carlgren, 2013), it has often been described as an iterative, five-step process comprising the following phases (Figure 16.1): (1) empathizing: observing and interviewing users to better understand how they think and feel; (2) defining: (re)framing the problem based on research; (3) ideating: generating new ideas through brainstorming; (4) prototyping: building or

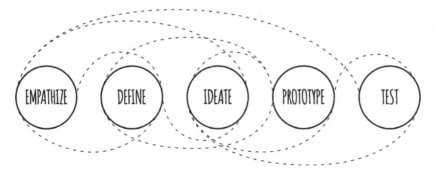

Source: Based on d.school (2010).

Figure 16.1 Design thinking process

acting out ideas, such as new products and services; (5) testing these ideas to learn more about them and the users.

The DTWs studied generally followed this five-step process, although the first step often included user research in order to gain a deeper understanding of users' experience prior to the DTW. The results of such research established the starting point for the workshops, which could then focus on cross-departmental and hierarchical idea development and sensemaking.

THE RESEARCH PROCESS

Being an early adopter of DT, CCo's multiple successes have been featured in the business press and in company presentations. In order to examine these successes, one of the authors and another researcher visited CCo for two weeks. Through interviews with the manager responsible for the company's DT initiative, we identified three DTWs that had led to the successful implementation of ideas over the previous year. To obtain a deeper understanding of what occurred in the workshops, we conducted interviews with the sponsor, the project manager, one participant, and one facilitator of each DTW. These 40–90-minute interviews covered the interviewee's professional background, his or her perception of DT, what happened during the workshop, the final results, and the idea development that occurred after the workshop's conclusion. In addition to the interviews, we obtained the workshop planning materials (for example, time tables and lists of participants) along with publically available documents (for example, business press articles, CCo website articles, and annual reports) and general information about CCo's use of DT and the results of the DTWs.

Next, we analyzed the interview transcripts and additional documents using NVIVO 10 software. This allowed us to identify information related to six sensemaking practices: the engagement of functionally and hierarchically diverse individuals, the establishment of heterogeneous teams, the iterative involvement of individuals, and the exposure to, engagement in, and acting upon conflicting views. After analyzing the workshops, we determined that we should have addressed additional topics in our analysis. As a result, we performed a second round of analysis on the DTWs, paying particular attention to the following topics: DT techniques used with respect to the various sensemaking practices, the reasons for their use, workshop preparation, environmental conditions (for example, organizational culture) and workshop results. These additional results allowed for a more robust comparison and discussion.

In the process of comparing and contrasting the topics of the DTWs and their content ('axial coding'; see Eisenhardt, 1989), we identified six central practices (outlined in the next section). In addition we were able to map all the relevant information on a time line (Yin, 2009; Knowlton and Phillips, 2012). We then compared these data to the workshop schedule received from CCo. Mapping the workshop practices and timings provided additional information regarding the setting (team or group) in which the activities took place and the order in which sensemaking practices occurred (see the Appendix at the end of this chapter). To solidify our understanding of how the cases unfolded, we concluded our analysis by writing up case studies for each of the DTWs.

Because the analyzed workshops followed a similar process, we will outline this process by describing one of the case studies in more detail in the next section.

IDEAS TO COUNTER COUNTERFEIT: A DTW EXAMPLE

All DTWs took place at the CCo headquarters (USA). During these two- to three-day workshops, functionally and hierarchically diverse groups of participants worked together on predefined challenges. Workshop sponsors strove to encourage personal connections between participants and to foster idea development that would continue after the workshop was over.

We will use the counterfeit workshop as an illustrative case. For this DTW, the company sought to address the illegal mass production and distribution of unlicensed replicas (counterfeit products) of their branded products. Counterfeiting has caused billions of US dollars in damage to the company. Because many employees were unaware of the significance of this issue, the counterfeit manager engaged a group of internal DT facilitators to conduct a two-day DTW with the following objectives: to develop ideas that would 'frustrate counterfeiters such that they stop trying to copy [CCo] brands' and to 'increase awareness. . . about the counterfeit problem among [CCo] employees'. In this DTW, the facilitators selected 26 participants from the company's diverse business branches and hierarchy levels based on their respective functions and personal level of motivation. These 26 individuals were grouped into five teams, each of which had at least one designer, one or more employees from brand protection, and one or more government officials from the US Department of Justice and US Customs and Border Protection. Five DT professionals facilitated and managed both the teams and the larger group.

The first day of the workshop focused on raising awareness about the problem and generating ideas to address the issue. The DTW began with a presentation by the global brand protection leader, exposing participants to the counterfeiting challenges faced by CCo. Next, participants engaged in a group Q&A session, discussing 'what the problem was' and 'how it affected them' professionally. This discussion 'dispelled some of the myth' around counterfeiting. Indeed, most of the participants were 'really shocked to find out that counterfeits were prevalent in modern markets like Western Europe and the US' and that this illegal activity extended to more than just 'designer handbags'. After this Q&A session, participants dispersed into their teams and discussed their personal experiences with regard to a specific, team-assigned counterfeiting challenge (for example, developing ideas for counterfeit items such as packaging, coupons, etc.). Next, each team received a brief introduction to user research and interview techniques. These newly learned techniques were immediately put to use in two rounds of interviews with invited users who had purchased counterfeit products. These interviews exposed employees to users' attitudes, values, behaviors, and views on counterfeiting, which the employees then shared and discussed in the larger group. In the words of the DTW participants, the 'surprising result' was a new understanding of the user and the 'realiz[ation]' that one group of customer [user] didn't really care while another one deeply cared and was "horrified" by the thought of buying counterfeits'. Guided by facilitators, the teams then acted on their user research by brainstorming different ways to address these specific challenges. By the end of first day, 'post-it notes with these ideas covered the walls of the workshop room'. In closing, each team selected and presented their top three ideas to the larger group.

The second day opened with a group review of the events of the first day, immersing participants in a discussion of how to take their ideas further (for example, product form, assembly). Next, the teams sprung into action by engaging in three rounds of idea development, during which they built prototypes, exposed them to users, discussed and shared user feedback (with the team and with the larger group), and acted on their findings by iterating and improving their prototypes. One participating manager noted that the interactions with users 'really served to energize the group [and to] bring the topics that we were discussing to life'. Reconvening in the larger group, teams discussed and presented the steps required to make their prototypes a physical reality, taking into account user expectations and company requirements. This sharing event was followed by a final refinement of presentations and prototypes, after which the teams delivered a fourth and final ten-minute presentation and a five-minute feedback session with senior management. The day concluded with a final group discussion with all of the participants and three of the facilitators. Meanwhile, two of the facilitators and the top managers discussed which ideas should be pursued after the workshop.

At the close of the DTW, top-management officials shared their decisions on which ideas to take forward, reinforcing the seriousness of the problem and the importance of pursuing the various ideas generated in the workshop. In the words of one participant, 'everybody seemed to unite as one team, and then, after our leadership debrief had finished. . . we felt like we'd achieved something together that was really worthwhile'. Similarly, a legal department manager spoke on idea development, explaining that the workshop 'cement[ed] the relationship with the design community. And they now see us as true partners. . . it made not just connections between projects, but connections between people that were working on similar possibilities'. Furthermore, participants described the feedback from management and experts as resulting in a 'bullet point list to take back to your managers [as] to why you should be allowed to go and do this and to develop this [idea]'.

FINDINGS AND DISCUSSION

In this chapter, we have identified six practices related to sensemaking that we discuss in detail below. Through our research, we found that the activities involved in the planning and execution of DTWs followed a pattern similar to the six sensemaking practices. As such, we will first focus on the engagement of functionally and hierarchically diverse individuals and the establishment of heterogeneous teams, before focusing on iterative involvement, and the exposure to, engagement in, and acting upon conflicting views.

Engagement of Functionally and Hierarchically Diverse Individuals

Prior to each workshop, the DTW facilitators identified and interviewed a diverse group of external experts, users, and employees representing various hierarchical levels (for example, top management) and functions (for example, marketing, human resources). These interviews provided the basis for selecting workshop participants according to their expertise, interpersonal relations, organizational influence and personal motivation. These criteria helped to ensure that (1) the workshop participants would be willing and able to develop their ideas following the workshop; (2) they had the necessary expertise and influence to develop an idea further; (3) motivated participation would occur through the engagement of top management; and (4) a shared viewpoint and new knowledge regarding idea development would be disseminated across organizational levels.

Interviewees also stressed that diverse teams were an important aspect of 'anchoring decisions in the organization to allow for ideas being taken forward'. This view is in line with research that has identified the engagement of multidisciplinary individuals as an important aspect of strategic change (Maitlis and Christianson, 2014, p. 89).

Establishment of Heterogeneous Teams

Facilitators selected functionally and hierarchically diverse teams, paying special attention to individual personalities and existing relationships. This vital step enabled cross-departmental exchanges and relations, and reduced the potential for conflicts within the teams. Moreover, a heterogeneous team setup encouraged a shared sense of purpose, idea ownership, and responsibility by incorporating different functions into the idea development steps and thereby enabling the continuation of the process after the workshop's conclusion. Scholars have argued what the interviewees confirmed: that a joint engagement of individuals in sensemaking can create a shared viewpoint (Weick and Roberts, 1993) by shifting individuals' perspectives from 'I' to 'we' (Drazin et al., 1999, p. 293). This suggests that working in heterogeneous teams might not only be important in terms of developing ideas, but also essential in terms of establishing collective idea ownership and securing further idea development.

DT literature has frequently stressed the need to engage functionally diverse individuals in idea creation (for example, Brown, 2009; Martin, 2009). However, the literature has not specifically addressed the importance of hierarchically diverse groups for establishing shared meaning. Furthermore, the literature has not paid much attention to cross-departmental and hierarchical relationships or to the shared respon-sibility of these groups in developing ideas.

Iterative Involvement

We discovered that DTWs did not follow a linear process, but rather iteratively involved individuals in different group constellations. Indeed, the analysis of the DTWs revealed a highly intentional and structured approach that iteratively engaged individuals by exposing them to con-flicting views. Moreover, participants were required to engage with and act upon these conflicting views. Although these approaches resemble the sensemaking processes of professional designers (Ravasi and Stigliani, 2012), this research identified two important differences.

First, participants engaged iteratively with a limited number of conflict-ing views at a time (for example, expert presentation, user interviews, and the perspectives of other employees). This reduced the level of ambiguity and allowed the group to establish some shared viewpoints before moving on to investigate other issues involving conflicting views. One interviewee verbalized this phenomenon, stating that 'when you do this [DT], every-one's right there. The solution is what everyone thought of, not just what one person thought of, so I found that to be the most rewarding part of it'. As such, lowering the amount of ambiguity through iterative involvement might be key to allowing non-professional designers to engage in otherwise complex and ambiguous sensemaking processes.

Second, individuals were iteratively involved in team and group settings. Presentations and discussions in group settings exposed all participants to the user research results and the ideas developed by individual teams. This interaction helped to establish a shared viewpoint among all partici-pants and facilitated idea development through the following emphases: a common understanding of the problem and the solution in terms of the user and the organization, the individual's role with regard to the proposed idea, and a set of redefined relationships between individuals and groups with respect to the idea and the user.

Consequently the whole process of these workshops can be described as iteratively involving individuals in various settings and views by establishing a shared viewpoint on the problem, the possibilities and the solutions.

Exposure to Conflicting Views, One at a Time

Throughout the workshop, participants negotiated conflicting views through user interviews and testing, discussions in heterogeneous teams, and presentations by experts. For example, the participants' exposure to user research showed them that counterfeiting happens in the United States, contradicting their common assumption that such crimes only occur in Asia. These findings confirm previous research, as scholars have found that exposure to conflicting views creates ambiguity, which encourages individuals' engagement in the creative process as they seek to resolve the conflicting views (Drazin et al., 1999, p. 293; Weick et al., 2005).

Engagement in Conflicting Views

After they had been exposed to conflicting views, participants were put in situations in which they had to engage with those views through activities, such as group and team discussions, Q&A sessions with experts and user testing. This facilitated engagement increased the participants' awareness of the conflicting views. As they engaged jointly with these contradictions, they reinforced their sincerity and group resolve (Maitlis and Christianson, 2014, p. 93). These qualities further motivated participants to engage in conflicting views, with some describing their participation as a 'very wide eye-opening experience'.

This finding is in line with Hoever et al. (2012) who found that merely putting together heterogeneous teams is not enough to foster creativity let alone idea implementation. Rather, Hoever et al. argued that a facilitated, active engagement is essential for fostering team creativity. As such, DTWs can be seen as one way to encourage this type of engagement.

In the CCo DTWs, as individuals participated in their teams and groups they established a shared viewpoint about the given challenge and their individual roles in relation to it. One participant described this experience in the following statement:

> One of the things that's very important to [CCo] is delivering to the consumer what the consumer wants. So the consumer is like god to us; therefore, we joined forces as a group, so we were no longer design, brand protection, legal and all those different people that we've been before. And we very much became [CCo], and they [interviewed users] were the consumer. It's a very healthy thing, I think.

This statement further highlights that interviewees experienced similar levels of sincerity and a shared understanding of the problem, which resulted in their joint desire to act upon their resolve. This collective desire forged a link between individual and group sensemaking, thereby serving as the initial step toward fostering a 'collective mind' (Weick and Roberts, 1993).

Acting Upon Conflicting Views

To resolve the potential conflicts arising from such conflicting views (for example, counterfeiting in the USA), participants acted upon these views through activities such as brainstorming and prototyping. These activities bridged conflicting views by developing new alternatives and capitalizing on participants' diversity and creativity. In the words of one participant:

> I think we all believe in our team; we all collaborate. . . We have a lot of different learners, people who use more right brain. . . I think this process takes everyone on [an] even playing field. And there are tools in which you kind of engage every type of person.

Furthermore, the intense collaboration during the DTWs created a helpful ambiguity with regard to identifying each participant's individual contributions. This ambiguity positively reinforced the interrelatedness felt by group members. One interviewee described this ambiguity as leading to 'more engagement and enrollment amongst more people [and] less of a not-invented-here [syndrome], because everybody has been involved'.

Given these findings, the identified practices resemble actions that Dougherty and colleagues (2000, p. 342) suggested are characteristic of innovative organizations; innovative organizations harness these actions to 'construct, bracket, interpret, and rethink the right kinds of market and technology knowledge in the right way for innovation'. However, since Dougherty et al.'s research did not include interviews with managers regarding their personal strategies for innovation, Dougherty et al.'s findings do not answer the question of 'how these sensemaking systems might emerge' (ibid., p. 326). As such, the DTW process can be seen as one way of combining the identified practices into a sensemaking process that in turn influences the larger sensemaking system.

CONCLUSION

In this chapter, we identified six practices related to sensemaking that were central to idea development across organizational levels at CCo: the engagement of functionally and hierarchically diverse individuals, the establishment of heterogeneous teams, the iterative involvement of individuals, and the exposure to, engagement in, and acting upon conflicting views. We determined that engaging not only functionally but also hierarchically diverse individuals was an essential prerequisite for multi-actor collaborative sensemaking and idea development across organizational levels. In addition, iteratively involving individuals in attending to, engaging in and acting upon one conflicting view at a time promoted more productive, actionable results. Together, these practices led to a multilevel understanding and collective feeling of ownership over the new ideas and their implementation. This mutuality positively affected continuous idea development and ultimately facilitated the organization's ability to capitalize on the ideas developed in the workshop.

In identifying these practices, this research expands on the understanding of design thinking from a sensemaking perspective by emphasizing iterative involvement. We highlight the iterative involvement of individuals in sensemaking practices and work settings as a central mechanism that facilitates sensemaking across organizational levels (see Appendix). Furthermore, this chapter also provided a detailed account of the ways in which large companies can use DTWs to capitalize on their employees' creativity and to drive idea development across multiple functions and organizational levels.

While not central to this chapter, facilitation was key to the success of the DTWs. Future research should consider the role of the workshop facilitator, as previous studies have not addressed this function specifically. Facilitation seems to reduce process- and problem-related ambiguity and complexity. As such, it could be key to allowing non-designers to work in ways similar to professional designers (Ravasi and Stigliani, 2012). Consequently researchers concerned with design thinking should further explore facilitation from a sensemaking perspective in a variety of contexts.

This chapter contributes to this book by presenting the DTW as a multi-actor, collaborative approach to idea development and implementation. As such, it highlights the importance of recruiting and involving functionally and hierarchically diverse individuals and engaging them in a facilitated, collaborative innovation process. Given the participants' diverse nature and their limited experience in collaborative idea development, facilitation may be an essential requirement for the success of the workshop. Two facilitation practices have proven to be of crucial importance. First, iteratively involving participants in team and group settings is critical for creating a shared viewpoint and laying a strong foundation for further idea development after the workshop. Second, iterative engagement in a limited number of conflicting views at a time is essential for reducing ambiguity and uncertainty. Based on the findings of our study, we are convinced that DTWs can be used to engage diverse individuals in sensemaking practices and, in turn, enable organizations to capitalize on creative ideas.

NOTE

* We gratefully acknowledge the gracious support provided by CCo employees during this study. We would also like to express our gratitude to VINNOVA and the Center for Business Innovation at Chalmers University of Technology, Göteborg, Sweden for funding this research. Finally, we want to extend our personal thanks to Professor Maria Elmquist for her support and constructive feedback when conducting this research.

REFERENCES

Abolafia, M.Y. (2010), 'Narrative construction as sensemaking: How a central bank thinks', *Organization Studies*, **31**(3), 349–67.

Brown, T. (2008), 'Design thinking', *Harvard Business Review*, **86**(6), 84–92.

Brown, T. (2009), *Change by Design: How Design Thinking Transforms Organizations and Inspires Innovation*, New York: Harper Business.

Carlgren, L. (2013), 'Design thinking as an enabler of innovation: Exploring the concept and its relation to building innovation capabilities', PhD thesis, Göteborg: Chalmers University of Technology.

Carlgren, L., M. Elmquist and I. Rauth (2014), 'Exploring the use of design thinking in large organizations: Towards a research agenda', *Swedish Design Research Journal*, **1**(14), 47–56.

Dougherty, D., L. Borrelli, K. Munir and A. O'Sullivan (2000), 'Systems of organizational sensemaking for sustained product innovation', *Journal of Engineering and Technology Management*, **17**(3), 321–55.

Drazin, R., M.A. Glynn and R.K. Kazanjian (1999), 'Multilevel theorizing about creativity in organizations: A sensemaking perspective', *Academy of Management Review*, **24**(2), 286–307.

d.school (2010), *bootcamp bootleg*, Stanford, CA: Stanford d.school, accessed 3 December 2015 at http://dschool.stanford.edu/wp-content/uploads/2011/03/BootcampBootleg2010v2SLIM.pdf.

Dutton, J.E. and S.J. Ashford (1993), 'Selling issues to top management', *Academy of Management Review*, **18**(3), 397–428.

Eisenhardt, K.M. (1989), 'Building theories from case study research', *Academy of Management Review*, **14**(4), 532–50.

Glynn, M.A., R. Kazanjian and R. Drazin (2010), 'Fostering innovation in complex product development settings: The role of team member identity and interteam interdependence', *Journal of Product Innovation Management*, **27**(7), 1082–95.

Hill, R.C. and M. Levenhagen (1995), 'Metaphors and mental models: Sensemaking and sensegiving in innovative and entrepreneurial activities', **21**(6), 1057–74.

Hoever, I.J., D. van Knippenberg, W.P. van Ginkel and H.G. Barkema (2012), 'Fostering team creativity: Perspective taking as key to unlocking diversity's potential', *Journal of Applied Psychology*, **97**(5), 982–96.

Knowlton, L.W. and C.C. Phillips (2012), *The Logic Model Guidebook: Better Strategies for Great Results*, Thousand Oaks, CA: Sage.

Liedtka, J. (2014), 'Innovative ways companies are using design thinking', *Strategy and Leadership*, **42**(2), 40–45.

Lindberg, T., E. Köppen, I. Rauth and C. Meinel (2012), 'On the perception, adoption and implementation of design thinking in the IT industry', in H. Plattner, C. Meinel and L. Leifer (eds), *Design Thinking Research: Studying Co-Creation in Practice*, Berlin/Heidelberg: Springer, pp. 229–40.

Maitlis, S. (2005), 'The social processes of organizational sensemaking', *Academy of Management Journal*, **48**(1), 21–49.

Maitlis, S. and M. Christianson (2014), 'Sensemaking in organizations: Taking stock and moving forward', *The Academy of Management Annals*, **8**(1), 57–125.

Martin, R. (2009), *The Design of Business: Why Design Thinking is the Next Competitive Advantage*, Boston, MA: Harvard Business School Press.

Ravasi, D. and I. Stigliani (2012), 'Product design: A review and research agenda for management studies', *International Journal of Management Reviews*, **14**(4), 464–88.

Rouleau, L. and J. Balogun (2011), 'Middle managers, strategic sensemaking, and discursive competence', *Journal of Management Studies*, **48**(5), 953–983.

Weick, K.E. (1993), 'The collapse of sensemaking in organizations: The Mann Gulch disaster', *Administrative Science Quarterly*, **38**(4), 628–52.

Weick, K.E. (1995), *Sensemaking in Organizations (Foundations for Organizational Science)*, Thousand Oaks, CA: Sage.

Weick, K.E. and K.H. Roberts (1993), 'Collective mind in organizations: Heedful interrelating on flight decks', *Administrative Science Quarterly*, **38**(3), 357–81.

Weick, K.E., K.M. Sutcliffe and D. Obstfeld (2005), 'Organizing and the process of sensemaking', **16**(4), 409–21.

Westley, F.R. (1990), 'Middle managers and strategy: Microdynamics of inclusion', *Strategic Management Journal*, **11**(5), 337–51.

Yin, R.K. (2009), *Case Study Research: Design and Methods*, Vol. 5, Thousand Oaks, CA: Sage.

APPENDIX

Table 16A.1   Exemplary two-day workshop process

Practice	Activity	Work setting
DAY 1		
	Breakfast and check-in exercise[a]	Group
	Welcome and introduction to agenda[a]	Group
Exposing	Presentation of the challenge by experts	Group
Engaging	Q&A with experts	Group
Engaging	Discussing team challenge and sharing perspectives	Team
Exposing	Interviews with users	Team
Engaging	Team discussions	
	Lunch[a]	
Acting	Two rounds of brainstorming	Team
Exposing	Each team presents top three ideas	Group
Engaging	Final group discussion	Group
DAY 2		
Exposing	Breakfast and check-in exercise	Group
Exposing	Welcome and exchange of 'overnight ah-has'	Group
Engaging	Develop a to-do list for the day	Team
Acting	Develop physical prototypes	Team
Exposing	User testing (two rounds)	Team
Engaging	Discussion on how to take ideas forward	Team
Acting	Further developing prototypes	Team
Exposing	Discussion on user views vs. internal (company) views	Group
Engaging	Discussion on how to take ideas forward within the organization	Team
Acting	Improve prototypes	Team
	Lunch[a]	
Exposing	Present prototypes to group	Group
Engaging	Teams get feedback from group	Group
Acting	Develop prototypes and prepare final presentations for senior managers	Team
Exposing	Presentation to top management and get feedback form senior managers	Group and Senior Managers
Engaging	Discussion on how to take ideas forward	Senior Managers and Facilitator
Engaging	Wrap up and Close	Group

Notes:
The workshop process iteratively involving participants in three practices (exposing, engaging, acting) and two work settings (group and team).
a. These activities were not facilitated. However, participants were expected to continue their engagement, hence a blend of all three practices likely took place.

17. Business model evolution and the growth of innovative new ventures: evidence from the Italian system*

Andrea Tracogna, Bernardo Balboni and Guido Bortoluzzi

INTRODUCTION

It is well acknowledged that a non-negligible number of new business ventures, of any industry and country, are short-lived and do not generate satisfactory economic performances or significant growth (Walker, 2005; Brusoni et al., 2006). Such poor outcomes, which apply to both traditional and innovative start-ups, are caused by several intrinsic limitations and weaknesses, pertaining to the entrepreneurial, strategic, and organizational levels. While these factors have been amply discussed – even if mostly in isolation – in the managerial literature (Goffin and Mitchell, 2005; Dodgson et al., 2008; Von Stamm, 2008; Tidd and Bessant, 2013), our claim is that, by considering them in an integrated perspective, we can shed new light on the deep causes of the above-mentioned 'innovation failures'.

In particular, the central idea of this study is that the performance gap of innovative new ventures mostly refers to a lack of adaptation and evolution of their initial business models (Zott and Amit, 2007, 2008). To support our claim, we analyze the business model evolution of four innovative new ventures over their first years of life. Our analysis reveals that, for all of the cases, the initial business models have significantly changed to cope with unexpected issues and negative feedback from the market. However, our findings also highlight that this adaptation to new contingent factors and to assure a better match with the market demand and the entrepreneurial objectives has not yet completely paid off (even after several years since the start of activities) and that most of the new ventures examined are still looking for a sustainable and scalable business model.

In sum, contrary to the well-rooted idea that the market potential of innovative start-ups is reflected in its initial business model, our findings emphasize the importance of business model reconfiguration and of its continuous adaptation and fine-tuning to the uncertain competitive land-scapes faced by such new ventures.

Our conclusions are consistent with the basic assumption of this book, whereby the innovation process is a complex and long-lasting phenomenon. It takes a lot of adaptation and fine-tuning to bring to the market new and creative ideas. Along this path, idea generation and implementation do not necessarily proceed in a linear fashion, but take place interchangeably (Anderson et al., 2004; Van de Ven and Sun, 2011). It is the nature of this recursive process that sets the directions of business model reconfiguration and eventually determines the success of innovation.

THE BUSINESS MODEL AS THE KEY ENABLER OF NEW VENTURE GROWTH

High-tech and science-based start-ups are considered the 'diamond edge' of any country's innovation system and one of the most important engines of economic development. This favorable view of innovative new ventures is based on the assumption that, when it comes to fostering the long-term growth of entrepreneurial systems, the firms who master radically new products and technologies matter more than those operating in traditional industries (Piccaluga and Chiesa, 2000; Zott et al., 2011). It is not surprising, then, that for the last decades such firms have been receiving plenty of attention from scholars of different disciplines (economics of innovation, entrepreneurship, strategic management) and strong support by policy-makers.

Yet, despite such long-standing favor, mounting literature also highlights the relatively poor performances of innovative start-ups (Song et al., 2008; Lazzeri and Piccaluga, 2011). Scholars point to the fact that while a handful of such firms achieve amazing performance in a very short time (Facebook, Amazon, Intuitive Surgical, to name a few), the vast majority of high-tech and science-based new ventures show very low growth rates, if any at all, and poor economic performance in general.

Thus, the available evidence contradicts the theoretical assumption that radically new products will automatically find their market and generate superior performance. In particular, as most scholars emphasize, such pro-innovation bias ignores the key role of entrepreneurial decisions, as reflected in a new firm's business model, in turning good innovations into superior economic performers (Baden-Fuller and Morgan, 2010).

Although we still lack a generally agreed definition of what a business model is, we can claim that this concept refers to a set of decisions that relate to the firm's market strategy, its organizational structure, and the activities it performs both inside the firm and within the business environment, through a network of transactions (Amit and Zott, 2001). As such, the concept builds on the extant literature on business strategy, on organization design, on transaction theory and on business networks.

Chesbrough and Rosenbloom (2002) define a business model as 'the heuristic logic that connects technical potential with the realization of economic value' (p. 529). They also offer an operational definition of a business model based on six elements: value proposition, market segment, value chain structure, cost and profit structure, value network, and competitive strategy. Johnson et al. (2008) define the concept by the following four interlocking elements: customer value proposition, profit formula, key resource, and key processes. Similarly, Baden-Fuller and Haefliger (2013) develop a typology with four main dimensions: customer identification, customer engagement, value delivery, and monetization.

In our study, we rely on the definition provided by Morris et al. (2005), whereby a business model refers to a set of six fundamental components: value offering, market segment/s, core competencies, external positioning, the cost and revenue model, and the entrepreneur's motivations. Value offering is mainly concerned with the decisions related to the nature of the product/service mix and the firm's role in value delivery. Market segments refer to the nature and scope of the market to which the firm's offerings are addressed. Core competencies represent the internal resources and capabilities enabling a firm to perform better than its competitors. External positioning (competitive strategy in our study) delineates how to achieve an advantage over competitors by relying on these core competencies. The cost and revenue model reflects the economic logic for expenses, earnings, and profits. The entrepreneur's motivations capture the entrepreneur's ambitions, in terms of time, size, and business scope.

As we have pointed out in the introduction, the business model should not be considered a set of decisions to be taken *una tantum*, at the time of the new venture start-up. On the contrary, it must be continuously adapted and reconfigured to ensure the alignment of the firm with the competitive landscape and the market opportunities and feedback. In this respect, this evolving business model can be considered a key dynamic capability of a new firm. In their seminal paper, Teece et al. (1997) define dynamic capabilities as 'the firm's ability to integrate, build and reconfigure internal and external competences to address rapidly changing environments. [Such capabilities] thus reflect an organization's ability to achieve new and innovative forms of competitive advantage given path dependencies and market positions' (p. 516) and to achieve congruence with the changing business environment, with the understanding that 'certain innovative responses are required when time-to-market and timing are critical, the rate of technological change is rapid and the nature of future competition and markets difficult to determine' (p. 515).

In the same vein, although from a slightly different conceptual perspective, Chesbrough (2010) underlines that new innovative ventures are forced to develop a discovery planning process based on experimentation, effectuation, and organizational leadership. This experimental process, which provides the business model with a dynamic, adaptive nature, leverages a set of dynamic capabilities that enable firms to develop novel value offerings, implement new value chain structures, and reconfigure their revenue models (ibid.).

We can then formulate our research question in the following way: How do the business models of innovative new ventures change over time? Are there any typical change patterns related to high levels of innovation performance? To answer these questions, we develop four case studies of business model reconfigurations, with the aim of isolating those elements that support the new ventures' growth. The exploratory nature of our study is aimed at deriving common patterns that will be developed into research propositions in future phases of our research project.

METHODOLOGY

Our chapter is based on a multiple case study design (Yin, 1994). We adopt this methodology in order to analyze and compare a select number of innovative new ventures, with the aim of developing theoretical insights from the analysis of the complex dynamics of decision-making processes (Eisenhardt and Martin, 2000).

Data on such new ventures were collected through direct interviews with the founders/entrepreneurs and a collection of company documents and newspaper articles. At least two interviews per company were conducted to describe the firms' initial and current business model configurations and the drivers that led to the business model changes.

While the selected firms can be considered significantly interesting from an investment standpoint (as demonstrated by the presence of external investors in their equity capital), they also share the common feature of not yet having fully turned their economic potential into accomplished performances, both in terms of sales growth and profitability (Table 17.1).

Table 17.1 Case studies: selected data

	MilkyWay	modeFinance	O3 Enterprise	DQuid
Year of establishment	2010	2009	2008	2011
Sales (euros) (2013)	125 000	294 000	479 000	311 000
Employees (2013)	6	5	6	7
Total investments (euros) (2013)	345 000	406 000	446 000	1 334 000
External investors	TT Venture (VC fund) Atlante Seed (VC fund)	Friulia S.p.A. (regional fund) Servizi C.G.N. (customer/ reseller)	Insiel Mercato S.p.A. (customer/ reseller)	Re:Lab Srl (75%) Mobivia (25%)

Source: Aida – Bureau Van Dijk.

CASE STUDIES

Case 1: MilkyWay

MilkyWay is a new Italian venture focused on the design, manufacture, and online sales of trial bikes and action-sport equipment. It was established in 2010 from the initial idea of a mechanical engineer, Jacopo Vigna, who had previous experience in the biomedical field and in the racing departments of two leading motorbike manufacturers. The start-up could leverage on the capital provided by an angel investor and on the support of a technology-transfer center at the University of Modena. In 2012, Vigna was selected to participate in the SeedLab acceleration program. This experience permitted him to enhance and better focus on the MilkyWay's business model. In 2013, two venture capital (VC) funds invested in the company's equity with a total of EUR 720 000.

MilkyWay's initial business idea was based on transferring technological innovations from the motorsport industry to the trial bike sector. Bikes and bike parts and components were targeted towards a specific 'tribe', the trial-bikers, and sold through an e-shop. In order to create a community-based marketplace and expand the 'long-tail' demand, in late 2012 MilkyWay became a reseller of products and devices connected to action sports (skate boarding, surfing, kite-surfing, parkour) and started investing in the development of a proprietary platform (community + e-commerce). At the time of the interview (2014), the overall assortment was based on 31 categories and more than 16 000 references, with a diminished incidence of MilkyWay's proprietary assembled products.

Case 2: modeFinance

ModeFinance is a new Italian venture operating in the financial consulting sector. Launched as a university research project in 2003, the company was established in 2009 and is currently located in the business incubator of AREA Science Park in Trieste. Its business is based on a proprietary technology for credit risk analysis. In detail, the firm provides its clients (firms, banks, insurance companies rank among its most important ones) with various reports aimed at evaluating the overall economic sustainability of a firm and its creditworthiness.

In the very beginning, the company only produced credit reports for a single client (a multinational company offering credit rating and business intelligence services and financial databases), which was, in turn, also its sole supplier of primary data. This activity is still part of the firm's business and currently accounts for some 30 percent of its actual turnover.

Soon the company decided to also develop a market for its proprietary products, software targeted at banks and bigger firms to help them assess the credit standing of its clients. Today, the weight of this activity in the company's total revenue is still marginal. In the following years (2010–13), the company started to directly sell credit reports to big firms. Currently, the majority of the revenue comes from this activity, which has been standardized. In parallel, the firm started producing more complete reports, combining qualitative (strategic, organizational) and quantitative (financial) data and information, especially in connection to mergers and acquisition (M&A) processes.

In 2012, the company launched an application (app) for mobile devices (S-peek) that allows users to get standardized credit reports. The product was launched with the intention of increasing business scalability. At the moment, S-peek generates a marginal part of the company's total revenue.

To compete in a sector dominated by big players, modeFinance has chosen to adopt a cost-leadership strategy. Prices are, on average, 30 percent lower than its competitors'. To sustain such price positioning, the company has been forced to gradually standardize its offering.

Case 3: O3 Enterprise

O3 Enterprise is a new Italian venture providing digital imaging services for the medical sector. In particular, it provides solutions for the visualization and management of patients' clinical data. The idea originates from an academic research project completed in 2004. The company was established in January 2008.

The company started its operations as a provider of open-source solutions for the visualization of patients' clinical data (especially images). The importance of this 'product' in the company's offering was prominent at that time. Recently, the company completely revised its strategy and now offers a cloud-based integrated solution for archiving, visualizing, and reporting clinical data (images, videos, and signals). The importance of the main product has diminished, while the importance of (and the revenue coming from) complementary services, such as project design, installation, and maintenance, has increased.

Starting from an initial partially incorrect definition of its target market (too broad and partly inaccessible to the firm because of regulatory constraints), the company has progressively narrowed its focus on the market of medium-sized private hospitals. It started, in parallel, a process of progressive internationalization.

In order to quickly achieve market share, the company initially opted for penetration prices (up to 50–60 percent below its competitors). The prices were eventually revised, especially the prices of ancillary services, and the price gap with its competitors has been reduced to 30 percent.

As the CEO said in an interview: 'The first years have been the ones of technological exploration. Now have come the years of market exploitation'. Indeed, the company has been growing around its technological capabilities in the first years. The turning point can be positioned in 2013, when O3 Enterprise decided to accelerate sales. It did so by hiring a sales manager who started boosting the revenue from foreign markets.

Case 4: DQuid

DQuid is a new ICT venture based in Reggio Emilia, Italy. It originated as a spin-out of an academic spin-off (University of Modena and Reggio Emilia), named Re:Lab. While the mother company is focused on interface-machinery software development, DQuid has developed and patented a full stack platform made up of hardware units and application programming interfaces (APIs), which uniquely simplify the communication between devices (tablets, smartphones, PCs), objects and people. In this vein, DQuid aims at providing an Internet of Things (IoT) ecosystem addressed to multi-industries' innovative companies and makers.

The initial main customers came from the automotive industry. The focus on this industry, derived from Re:Lab experience, provided the company with specific knowledge and led to the development of the first patent, BLU Dash, that was implemented within three products developed for specific customers: Xee (Eliocity), Piaggio Multimedia Platform (Piaggio) and Conti Dongle (Continental). Currently, DQuid is enlarging the spectrum of IoT to high-potential industries, such as home automation and household and to makers/digital craftspeople.

In 2013, a big automotive industrial group (Mobivia, which controls Eliocity) invested in the firm's equity for a total of EUR 1 000 000.

RESULTS

In this section, for the four innovative ventures examined, we compare the business models (BMs) adopted at the time of their establishment (T1) and the business models implemented at the time of the interviews (T2: June–July 2014). To describe such models, we relied on the components identified by Morris et al. (2005): value offering, market segment/s, core competencies, external positioning, the cost and revenue model, and the entrepreneurs' motivations. We asked the entrepreneurs to provide, for any identified difference in the business model in T1 and T2, the main change drivers (as represented by needs to serve, the goals pursued, the opportunities captured, etc.). The business model components and their drivers of change are described in Tables 17.2 to 17.5.

DISCUSSION

The four cases examined provided us with a rich array of different business model adaptations. While it can obviously be claimed that each and every case is unique, upon closer examination we could also identify a series of common patterns of business model reconfiguration.

Standardization and Modularization of Serial Products and Services

Transaction efficiency gains are enabled by the standardization and modularization of serial solutions (Amit and Zott, 2001; Brusoni and Prencipe, 2001). In particular, MilkyWay shifted its offering from customized trial bikes and trial-bike parts and components to standardized products and devices connected to action sports (skate boarding, surfing, kite-surfing, parkour). ModeFinance developed an app for mobile devices (s-peek) and expressed its intention to further enlarge its assortment of standardized products. O3 Enterprise completely revised its offering towards a cloud-based solution for the archiving, visualization, and reporting of clinical data (images, videos, and signals). This standardized platform is also

Table 17.2   *MilkyWay*

Building Blocks		BM Design T1	Drivers of BM Design Reconfiguration	BM Design T2
1. Value offering	1.1 Solution (product/service combination)	Customized trial bikes Customized trial-bike parts	Search for economies of scale	More standardized offer
	1.2 Standardization vs adaptation	Full customization	Efficiency gains	High standardization Limited customization of proprietary products
	1.3 Customer engagement	Direct interaction (e-shop)	Preserving customer experience despite standardization Developing a community-based marketplace	Platform-mediated interaction E-community (MilkyWay tribe)
	1.4 Product portfolio	Narrow. Unlimited customization	Cross-selling. Increase sales per customer	Broad, but standardized: 35 categories and 16000 references
2. Market segments	2.1 Customer segment	Trial bikers	Extending customer base	Action-sport lovers
	2.2 Segmentation strategy	Professional athletes	Extending customer base	Multiple small segments
	2.3 Customer portfolio	Around 200 (80% at the domestic level)	Market expansion	Around 2000 (80% at the domestic level)
	2.4 Channels	Online shopping without e-commerce	Developing cross-selling opportunities	E-commerce E-community

Table 17.2 (continued)

Building Blocks		BM Design T1	Drivers of BM Design Reconfiguration	BM Design T2
3. Competitive strategy	3.1 Key success factors	Focus on technology In-the-field experience (as a biker)	Proprietary platform Lock-in effect Community building	User interface/experience Social media marketing Cross-related product categories
	3.2 Price positioning	Premium price	Market penetration/expansion	Medium/high price
4. Core competencies	4.1 Internal resources and competencies	Technological capabilities Market needs knowledge No staff	ICT capabilities development Integration between ICT and logistics Value chain integration	ICT competence (user interface) SCM logistics Social media marketing and communication Internalization of human capital
5. Revenue source and cost structure	5.1 Revenue model	Revenue generated by sales of product/services Seed capital	Long-tail revenue model New investments needed in ICT	Diversification of revenue streams (bikes, technological devices, action sport equipment) VC investment
	5.2 Outsourcing	Internal R&D and e-shop Outsourcing of prototyping and manufacturing	Drop shipping strategy for resold products Higher control of value-added activities	Small warehouse and stocks Outsourcing of manufacturing
6. Growth orientation	6.1 Motivation	Lifestyle Excellence in sports performance	Business sustainability	Growth Profitability

Table 17.3 modeFinance

Building Blocks		BM Design T1	Drivers of BM Design Reconfiguration	BM Design T2
1. Value offering	1.1 Solution (product/ service combination)	Rating score under license agreements	Development of proprietary products Market expansion	Advanced rating reports Quick and mobile rating systems
	1.2 Standardization vs adaptation	Full standardization	Market expansion	Addition of new customized services
	1.3 Customer engagement	No interaction	Need to customize the service	Growing interaction with some customers
	1.4 Product portfolio	Narrow	Cross-selling. Increase sales per customer	Broad
2. Market segments	2.1 Customer segment	Single-customer (business intelligence multinational)	Multi-segments strategy (banks, SMEs)	Several customers
	2.2 Segmentation strategy	None	Marketing orientation	Based on customer size
	2.3 Customer portfolio	Highly concentrated	Enlargement of customer base Risk sharing	300+ in traditional channel Several thousand in mobile channel
	2.4 Channels	Indirect	Diversification of channels	Indirect Direct Mobile

Table 17.3 (continued)

Building Blocks		BM Design T1	Drivers of BM Design Reconfiguration	BM Design T2
3. Competitive strategy	3.1 Key success factors	Technology	Efficiency in operations / New market orientation	Operations / Technology / Marketing and sales
	3.2 Price positioning	Below the average	Market penetration	Below the average
4. Core competencies	4.1 Internal resources and competencies	Credit risk analysis / Technological capabilities	Marketing capabilities development / ICT capabilities development / Value chain integration	Technological capabilities / Operations management skills / Sales and marketing capabilities
5. Revenue source and cost structure	5.1 Revenue model	Revenues are generated by sales of product/services / Public funds	Search for business sustainability	Increased reliance on market sales / Public funds
	5.2 Outsourcing	Full internalization of core activities	Value chain integration	Full internalization of core activities
6. Growth orientation	6.1 Motivation	Growth	Acceleration of growth	Growth with entrance of new investors

Table 17.4　O3 Enterprise

Building Blocks		BM Design T1	Drivers of BM Design Reconfiguration	BM Design T2
1. Value offering	1.1 Solution (product/service combination)	Special purpose software (with open-source license) for image management	Product bundling Modularize software solutions	Software (with open-source license) and related services (installation, maintenance, etc.) Meta-product for storing and sharing of images between units, departments, hospitals
	1.2 Standardization vs adaptation	High customization	Efficiency gains Scale economies	High standardization (more than 70%)
	1.3 Customer engagement	High in the early stages and diminishing in the following stages	Long-term relationship Lock-in effect	Relative importance of complementary services
	1.4 Product portfolio	Narrow	Exploit complementarities	Product: narrow Services: multitude of related services
2. Market segments	2.1 Customer segment	B2B (medical operating units)	Market penetration in a global segment	B2B (medical units, hospitals): integrated management and sharing of diagnostic images
	2.2 Segmentation strategy	Both public and private hospitals	Avoid excessive focus on regulated markets Simplification of customer relations management	Private hospitals, both small and big

Table 17.4 (continued)

Building Blocks		BM Design T1	Drivers of BM Design Reconfiguration	BM Design T2
2. Market segments	2.3 Customer portfolio	Narrow	Focus on customer size and profitability	Stable (preference for big customers)
	2.4 Channels	Domestic market accounted for 95% of sales	Expansion in international markets	Growth in international markets
3. Competitive strategy	3.1 Key success factors	Operations Technology	Efficiency gains in operations Value chain integration	Operations Technology Sales Marketing
	3.2 Price positioning	Below the market average by 50%	Higher profitability Stronger market positioning	Below the market average by 30%
4. Core competencies	4.1 Internal resources and competencies	Technological capabilities Operations management skills	Sales capabilities development Value chain integration	Technological capabilities Operations management skills Sales and marketing capabilities
5. Revenue source and cost structure	5.1 Revenue model	Product Open-source model	Exploit complementarities and lock-in effects	Product + service Razor-and-blade model
	5.2 Outsourcing	Full internalization of core activities	Value chain integration	Full internalization of core activities
6. Growth orientation	6.1 Motivation	Growth	Faster growth New investments	Growth with possible entrance of new investors

Table 17.5   DQuid

Building Blocks		BM Design T1	Drivers of BM Design Reconfiguration	BM Design T2
1. Value offering	1.1 Solution (product/service combination)	Hardware device + software interfaces R&D services and prototyping for custom solutions	Hardware + apps bundling (libraries/ SDK + cloud services)	Full stack and modular technology to connect any object Semantic data storage to control a platform addressed to developers/ final users
	1.2 Standardization vs adaptation	Modular hardware device	Complementary effect	Modular hardware devices Customization of the firmware, and libraries/ SDK
	1.3 Customer engagement	Direct interaction with major customers	Long-term partnership with OEMs Lock-in effect	Direct interaction with major customers Free access to the libraries for developers Crowdfunding campaign for makers
	1.4 Product portfolio	Patented device licensed in three products (automotive industry)	IP development for multiple applications/ products	Three patented devices New product development for specific customers and for makers/developers

Table 17.5 (continued)

Building Blocks		BM Design T1	Drivers of BM Design Reconfiguration	BM Design T2
2. Market segments	2.1 Customer segment	OEMs within automotive and off road industries	Market expansion in selected segments and industries	OEMs SMEs in home automation and household industry Makers/developers
	2.2 Segmentation strategy	OEMs selected on the basis of their value network role	Customer penetration	Multi-segments and multi-industries
	2.3 Customer portfolio	3 OEMs		4 OEMs
	2.4 Channels	B2B		B2B (OEMs) and B2C (makers)
3. Competitive strategy	3.1 Key success factors	Internal object functioning know-how Human-machine interaction experience	Differentiated products (and prices) for different segments/industries	SDK development to allow makers/developers to create smart applications
	3.2 Price positioning	Premium price	Big-data management	High level price

222

4. Core competencies	4.1 Internal resources and competencies	Human–machine interface development Market needs knowledge Network capabilities	Marketing and sales capabilities development	Human–machine interface development Customer relationship management (OEMs + users/makers)
5. Revenue source and cost structure	5.1 Revenue model	Royalties for units sold Revenues generated by services	Diversification of revenue streams Exploit complementarities and lock-in effects New investments needed in ICT	Razor and blade revenue model (low cost hardware, free SDK, pay for use of APIs) Corporate venture capital
	5.2 Outsourcing	Internal R&D Outsourced manufacturing proximately localized	Higher control of value-added activities	Internal R&D Outsourced manufacturing proximately localized Commercial subsidiary in San Francisco Bay
6. Growth orientation	6.1 Motivation	To develop IoT full-stack platform relying on human–machine interaction experience	Creating a new ecosystem in the IoT industry	Global player in the IoT industry

combined with several complementary services, such as project design, installation, and maintenance that generate most of the revenue. DQuid focused on full stack and modular technologies to connect any object and create an IoT ecosystem. This ecosystem draws on a main object, which is a board equipped with sensors or actuators, that allows for connecting to physical objects and, in turn, connects to the Internet.

Bundling Solutions

The four cases suggest that each innovative venture is leveraging the potential for value creation by offering bundles of complementary products and services to their customers (Amit and Zott, 2001). These bundling solutions may rely on both vertical complementarities, that is, products and services characterized by a high vertical integration in the value chain and horizontal complementarities, that is, different solutions connected by cross-selling opportunities. MilkyWay developed a wide assortment in order to exploit horizontal cross-selling opportunities in the action sport segment. In fact, 'extreme' athletes usually perform different disciplines. ModeFinance broadened its product assortment not only to explore new segments (SMEs), but also to better horizontally fulfill the needs of its main customers (banks). O3 Enterprise revised its product strategy and now offers a cloud-based integrated solution for archiving, visualizing, and reporting clinical data connected to other vertical complementary services, such as project design, installation, and after-sales. DQuid exploited its experience in the human–machine interface to develop software interfaces able to vertically enrich its hardware devices.

The cases further suggest that these complementary solutions may not be directly related to the core transactions. MilkyWay is investing in community building in order to exploit its user base through a mix of e-business activities, such as direct marketing and sales promotions. DQuid attracts developers and digital makers by offering an array of free complementary libraries (SDK) and cloud services to create apps and software for their devices. This further development will enable DQuid to control and manage data about app users, thus becoming its future main source of revenue.

Fine-tuning of the Target Market

The target market has been continuously fine-tuned by the observed firms, with the aim of intercepting the needs expressed by different customer segments (Demil and Lecocq, 2010). The firms have also been focused on international markets/customers/niches and multiple channels of distribution. In particular, MilkyWay enlarged its target market from trial bikers to action-sport lovers, in order to exploit the existence of a long-tail demand composed of many sub-segments. O3 Enterprise has progressively shifted its focus to a broader target market consisting of medium-sized private hospitals. In parallel, it started a process of progressive internationalization through the establishment of a new channel of distribution (based on foreign distributors). ModeFinance tried hard to escape the 'deadly hug' of the single customer. Nowadays, three different channels are used to distribute its services. DQuid is trying to enlarge its application domain, focusing on high-potential original equipment manufacturers (OEMs) and to explore a new customer segment that encompasses makers and digital craftspeople.

Development of Market-oriented Competencies

The firms' initial focus on technological know-how and product development capabilities has been supplemented by a strong effort directed towards the development of sales and marketing competencies, aimed at supporting the firms' competitive strategies and growth sustainability (Colombo and Grilli, 2005). MilkyWay is currently investing in the implementation of an integrated platform (e-commerce and e-community), with a focus on enhancing the user's experience. ModeFinance, after having grown mainly around its technological and supply chain capabilities, is today directing its attention to sales and marketing competencies. O3 Enterprise is also trying to move from technological exploration to market exploitation. In this vein, a sales manager has been hired in order to boost revenue from foreign markets. DQuid is also shifting its focus from core technological competencies to marketing and sales-oriented capabilities. A subsidiary was established in Silicon Valley (within the Plug and Play Startup Accelerator Program) at the beginning of 2013 and specific market competencies have been internalized, including the hiring of a local marketing manager, to better penetrate the US market and develop long-term relationships with local OEMs.

Attraction of External Investors

The firms' credible commitment to growth has attracted several external investors (Davila et al., 2003). In particular, MilkyWay was initially leveraged on a business angel's investment and then participated in a first round of investment with two VC funds. ModeFinance has been oriented towards the systematic growth of the business aimed at attracting external investors, such as a regional investment fund and a private firm. As regards

O3, the strong entrepreneurial motivations towards growth have attracted an external industrial investor (a big customer who decided to invest in this new firm). DQuid aims at creating a standard for programming language in the IoT industry to enable developers to create smart applications spanning several heterogeneous objects. This orientation towards excellence has attracted the interest of its main customer, Mobivia, who decided to invest in the firm's equity.

CONCLUSIONS

Our analysis reveals that, since their establishment, all four of the examined start-ups have been involved in significant revisions of their business model to adapt to new contingent factors and to assure a better match with market demands. Despite the limited size of our sample, which does not allow for any attempt at generalization, some common patterns of evolution (described above) have arisen and can represent interesting benchmarks for other new ventures. Furthermore, we testified that the business model evolution has been strongly influenced by the evolution of the governance model and, in particular, by significant changes in the equity composition.

Contrary to the well-rooted idea that the market potential of innovative start-ups is reflected in their initial business model, our findings emphasize the importance of business model reconfiguration. The ability to detect new technological potential, more precise customer needs and market misalignments have been the major common drivers in the dynamics of the examined business models (Mezger, 2014).

Indeed, the cases of MilkyWay, modeFinance, O3 Enterprise, and DQuid reveal that these long, complex, and risky business model dynamics are as important as the innovation *per se* in determining a new firm's economic success. This evolution is far from over for all of the examined new ventures, as they are still involved in the complex process of reconfiguring key capabilities (Zahra, 2008; Teece, 2010). Nevertheless, in their first years since establishment and despite several difficulties in fine-tuning their ideas in alignment with the target markets, such firms have been able to continuously spot new opportunities, effectively manage external risks, and significantly evolve their internal resource base.

Our study supports the claim that to implement innovation the business models require significant revisions over time. This is particularly challenging for the new ventures from high-tech and science-based sectors. Pisano (2006, 2010) recently addressed the issue of designing viable business models for such innovative new ventures that confront three fundamental challenges: (1) the need to encourage and reward profound risk-taking over long time horizons ('the risk management problem'); (2) the need to integrate knowledge across highly diverse disciplinary bodies ('the integration problem'); and (3) the need for cumulative learning ('the learning problem'). While each of these challenges – risk, integration, and learning – are present in varying degrees in most business settings, in high-tech and science-based businesses they appear in far greater force and often simultaneously.

As the four cases analyzed in this chapter demonstrate, innovative new ventures must be aware that it takes not only great creative ideas, but also a lot of adaptation and fine-tuning to bring innovation to the market. Along this path, a recursive process of idea generation and implementation sets the directions of a firm's business model reconfiguration.

NOTE

*   This research has been supported by the Italian Ministry of Education, University and Research (MIUR) through the PRIN 2010-11 project, 'Scientific research and competitiveness. Variety of organizations, support systems and performance levels' prot. 2010744K3S.

REFERENCES

Amit, R. and C. Zott (2001), 'Value creation in e-business', *Strategic Management Journal*, **22**(6–7), 493–520.
Anderson, N., C. de Dreu and B. Nijstad (2004), 'The routinization of innovation research: A constructively critical review of the state of the science', *Journal of Organizational Behavior*, **25**(2), 147–73.
Baden-Fuller, C. and S. Haefliger (2013), 'Business models and technological innovation', *Long Range Planning*, **46**(6), 419–26.
Baden-Fuller, C. and M.S. Morgan (2010), 'Business models as models', *Long Range Planning*, **43**(2), 156–71.
Brusoni, S. and A. Prencipe (2001), 'Unpacking the black box of modularity: Technologies, products and organizations', *Industrial and Corporate Change*, **10**(1), 179–205.
Brusoni, S., E. Cefis and L. Orsenigo (2006), 'Innovate or die? A critical review of the literature on innovation and performance', *CESPRI-Bocconi Working Paper No. 179*, August.
Chesbrough, H. (2010), 'Business model innovation: Opportunities and barriers', *Long Range Planning*, **43**(2), 354–63.
Chesbrough, H. and R.S. Rosenbloom (2002), 'The role of the business model in capturing value from innovation: Evidence from Xerox Corporation's technology spin-off companies', *Industrial and Corporate Change*, **11**(3), 529–55.
Colombo, M.G. and L. Grilli (2005), 'Founders' human capital and the growth of

new technology-based firms: A competence-based view', *Research Policy*, **34**(6), 795–816.

Davila, A., G. Foster and M. Gupta (2003), 'Venture capital financing and the growth of startup firms', *Journal of Business Venturing*, **18**(6), 689–708.

Demil, B. and X. Lecocq (2010), 'Business model evolution: In search of dynamic consistency', *Long Range Planning*, **43**(2), 227–46.

Dodgson, M., A. Salter and D. Gann (2008), 'The management of technological innovation', 2nd edition, Oxford, UK: Oxford University Press.

Eisenhardt, K.M. and J.A. Martin (2000), 'Dynamic capabilities: What are they?', *Strategic Management Journal*, **21**(10–11), 1105–21.

Goffin, K. and R. Mitchell (2005), *Innovation Management*, London: Pearson.

Johnson, M.W., C.M. Christensen and H. Kagermann (2008), 'Reinventing your business model', *Harvard Business Review*, **86**(12), 57–68.

Lazzeri, F. and A. Piccaluga (2011), 'Le imprese spin-off della ricerca pubblica: convinzioni, realtà e prospettive future' [The spin-off of public research: beliefs, reality and future prospect], *Scuola Superiore Sant'Anna Working Paper*, Pisa: Istituto di Management.

Mezger, F. (2014), 'Toward a capability-based conceptualization of business model innovation: Insights from an explorative study', *R&D Management*, **44**(5), 429–49.

Morris, M., M. Schindehutte and J. Allen (2005), 'The entrepreneur's business model: Toward a unified perspective', *Journal of Business Research*, **58**(6), 726–35.

Piccaluga, A. and V. Chiesa (2000), 'Exploitation and diffusion of public research: The case of academic spin-off companies in Italy', *R&D Management*, **30**(4), 329–39.

Pisano, G.P. (2006), *Science Business: The Promise, the Reality and the Future of Biotech*, Boston, MA: Harvard Business School Press.

Pisano, G.P. (2010), 'The evolution of science-based business: Innovating how we innovate', *Industrial and Corporate Change*, **19**(2), 465–82.

Song, M., K. Podoynitsyna, H. van der Bij and J.I. Halman (2008), 'Success factors in new ventures: A meta-analysis', *Journal of Product Innovation Management*, **25**(1), 7–27.

Teece, D.J. (2010), 'Business models, business strategy and innovation', *Long Range Planning*, **43**(2–3), 172–94.

Teece, D.J., G. Pisano and A. Shuen (1997), 'Dynamic capabilities and strategic management', *Strategic Management Journal*, **18**(7), 509–33.

Tidd, J. and J. Bessant (2013), *Managing Innovation. Integrating Technological, Market and Organizational Change*, 5th edition, Chichester, UK: Wiley.

Van de Ven, A.H. and K. Sun (2011), 'Breakdowns in implementing models of organization change', *Academy of Management Perspectives*, **25**(3), 58–74.

Von Stamm, B. (2008), *Managing Innovation, Design and Creativity*, 2nd edition, Chichester, UK: Wiley.

Walker, R. (2005), 'Innovation and organizational performances. A critical review of the evidence and a research agenda', *Academy of Management Proceedings*, Supplement, B1–B6.

Yin, R.K. (1994), *Case Study Research: Design and Methods*, Thousand Oaks, CA: Sage.

Zahra, S.A. (2008), 'The virtuous cycle of discovery and creation of entrepreneurial opportunities', *Strategic Entrepreneurship Journal*, **2**(3), 243–57.

Zott, C. and R. Amit (2007), 'Business model design and the performance of entrepreneurial firms', *Organization Science*, **18**(2), 181–99.

Zott, C. and R. Amit (2008), 'The fit between product market strategy and business model: Implications for firm performance', *Strategic Management Journal*, **29**(1), 1–26.

Zott, C., R. Amit and L. Massa (2011), 'The business model: Recent developments and future research', *Journal of Management*, **37**(4), 1019–42.

18. Beyond creativity: implementing innovative ideas through human resource management

**Helen Shipton, Karin Sanders,
Tim Bednall, Veronica (Cai-Hui) Lin and
Naiara Escribá-Carda**

INTRODUCTION

There is growing interest in fostering innovation through harnessing the latent motivations and capabilities of employees across levels of the business (for example, Shipton et al., 2006; Collins and Smith, 2006; Zhou et al., 2013; Anderson et al., 2014). People who have in-depth knowledge and experience of performing a job – regardless of their position within the organizational hierarchy – have the potential to yield new insights that might be of value to the organization in dealing with the uncertainties and turbulence of the wider environment. This way of viewing innovation stands in stark contrast to perspectives that have traditionally viewed innovation as on the agenda of technical experts and research and development specialists. It suggests that recognizing, leveraging, and releasing the innovative behaviors of employees across levels of the business is a major source of competitive advantage.

Despite suggestive hints, it remains unclear *what* role (if any) human resource management (HRM) might play in achieving organizational innovation, *why* this might be so, and what this means for the various stakeholders involved, especially line managers, who are responsible for interpreting and enacting HRM practices to employees on the receiving end. Questions surround first identifying which HRM practices are most sought after for innovation. For example, what is the mechanism by which HRM practices release employee innovative behaviors? What HRM practices promote external interface as opposed to those facilitating internal collaboration and knowledge sharing? A second group of questions surrounds the *process* whereby certain HRM practices, implemented effectively, achieve the desired effect. Do HRM practices that convey a strong and unequivocal message reinforced by relevant stakeholders suppress or enhance employees' innovative behaviors? And, what is the role of line managers in communicating HRM policy and practice devised at strategic level to employees?

Following Collins and Smith (2006) we suggest that high-commitment HRM prompts innovation by creating a social climate that supports, guides, and facilitates knowledge exchange and combination. In building the social climate that gives rise to knowledge exchange and combination, HRM practices signal the importance of cooperation, offer opportunities for employees to develop shared codes and language and manifest trust in one another (Collins and Smith, 2006). A strong HRM system (that is, one prioritizing knowledge exchange and combination) is distinctive, consistent, and consensual (Bowen and Ostroff, 2004). It 'stands out' to employees, clearly signaling what actions are required to achieve strategic goals. Through consistency, high-commitment HRM is internally aligned; through consensus, all key stakeholders convey the same message to employees.

In what follows, we define creativity, innovation, and innovative behaviors to set the stage for our conceptualization of HRM practices and processes. Building on the Collins and Smith (2006) framework (cooperation, shared codes, and language, trust etc.) we extend the discussion on the HRM practices that are apposite for innovative behaviors by reference to knowledge sharing. Based on Lohman (2005), our view of knowledge sharing is that employees acquire knowledge and skills (such as those required for innovative behaviors) through interaction with others. Our interpretation is that interaction may extend to parties outside the organization; hence, we consider practices that facilitate engagement with the external context (via networking, exploratory learning and customer engagement). Turning to HRM process literatures, we consider the key challenges surrounding HRM implementation and how HRM practices in conjunction with HRM processes can elicit or constrain the knowledge sharing conducive to employee innovative behaviors.

INNOVATIVE BEHAVIORS AND ORGANIZATIONAL INNOVATION

Innovation represents the application of an idea that is both novel and valuable within the context where it is operationalized (West and Farr, 1990). Viewed as a two-stage process, innovation requires creativity followed by innovation implementation (Anderson et al., 2014; Škerlavaj et al., 2014).

Based on Piaget (1970) creativity entails extending and broadening existing cognitive repertoires in order to visualize new options. This process of accommodation can be contrasted with the assimilation phase, where connections are made with what is already known in order to effect change. Thus, creativity pushes out the boundaries of knowledge and makes *potential* new insights available to organizations. Innovation implementation by contrast involves making appropriate connections across employee groups and building joint understanding so that new ideas are incorporated into organizational functioning.

Recent work has suggested that the distinction between the two phases may not be clear-cut. Employees operate within a context where rationality and applicability (implementation considerations) are inevitably weighted alongside originality as new ideas are put forward (Fay et al., 2015). Furthermore, implementing ideas may require creativity. A new technology for ascertaining customer feedback, for example, will not add value to an organization unless it is implemented imaginatively, taking into account likely customer reactions. Given these considerations, our focus in this chapter is employee innovative behaviors (Scott and Bruce, 1994). Employees' innovative behavior refers to the process of initiation and the intentional introduction of new problem-solving ideas, thereby enhancing a product, service or process. It encompasses both idea generation (creativity) and the application of the new ideas within a group or organization (Amabile, 1988).

HRM AND INNOVATION

Generally, it has been argued that HRM bundles rather than HRM practices *per se* impact on performance outcomes, such as innovation (Combs et al., 2006). The combined effect of inter-related practices more than any specific variable achieves the desired effect (Huselid et al., 1997; Bae and Lawler, 2000). The evidence on this point is, however, far from clear. Although the prevailing picture is positive, several recent studies have reported insignificant relationships when assessing the effect of aggregation indices (that is, combined HRM practices) on performance outcomes (for example, Cappelli and Neumark, 2001; Chadwick, 2010). Several reasons have been put forward. First, depending on what the business is attempting to achieve some HRM practices are more important than others are. Schuler and Jackson (1987), for example, have proposed differential sets of HRM practices depending upon whether an organization's strategic goal is to achieve cost reduction, quality enhancement or innovation. Practices conducive to innovation are, it is argued, those that promote team work, knowledge-sharing, investment in employee skills and competencies, sophisticated selection, as well as mechanisms that embrace risk-taking and experimentation (Schuler and Jackson, 1987; Shipton et al., 2006). Despite insights from these various literatures, it remains uncertain whether certain components of the HRM bundle are more or less important for different performance outcomes (Chadwick, 2010) – in particular, for employee innovative behaviors.

A second reason why HRM practices may not have the desired effect on performance outcomes, including innovation, could be to do with their enactment in the workplace. An emerging body of research focuses on the 'HRM process': the way in which HRM bundles are communicated and enacted by various stakeholders in order to influence employee attitudes and behaviors in the direction of strategically important goals (Bowen and Ostroff, 2004; Sanders et al., 2014). An effective HRM *process* requires the enactment of HRM *practices*, such that clear, consistent signals are conveyed about what the practice is intended to deliver. Drawing on the covariation principle of the attribution theory (Kelley, 1973), Bowen and Ostroff (2004) have argued in favor of three components: *distinctiveness*, *consistency* and *consensus*. These components together explain whether an HRM system is strong – that is, that people understand what actions are needed to achieve strategic goals – or weak, in that there is ambiguity about what is expected and why. An interesting and important question concerns the role of the HRM process – based on attribution theory – in shaping the propensity of employees to engage in innovative behaviors.

HRM PRACTICES AND INNOVATIVE BEHAVIORS

While employee innovative behavior is desirable for organizations and provides a useful means of fostering adaptability, there are several barriers that may discourage employees from engaging in it (see Bednall et al., 2014). This kind of behavior requires time away from an employee's formal duties, which may reduce short-term productivity. As a result, management may be ambivalent about supporting this kind of behavior. Moreover, employees may be discouraged from showing innovative behavior because it contains *risk*. Risk refers to the possibility that something unpleasant will happen, for instance reputation damage, loss of time and other resources if the innovation fails, resistance from peers, and even losing their job. Employees can be discouraged from showing innovative behavior if they fear that they will be harshly criticized (ibid.). Similarly, if employees share their creative ideas with their colleagues, they may expose their methods to criticism and risk losing their unique value or 'expert power'. As change is often met with substantial resistance from the rest of the organization and potentially increases their workload, employees may be discouraged from engaging in innovative behavior.

In addition, *proactivity* is an important characteristic of innovative behaviors (Hayton, 2005; De Jong et al., 2013). Proactivity represents an opportunity-seeking, forward-looking perspective characterized by high awareness of external trends and events, and acting in anticipation thereof. Proactivity is associated with pioneering behavior, initiative taking to pursue new opportunities, and attempts to lead rather than to follow. Since employees' innovative behavior is typically not limited to one brilliant mind, and is related to searching for new information (exploration) and exploitation of existing knowledge (Lohman, 2005), it is vital to examine this relationship from a knowledge-sharing perspective. Knowledge sharing involves interaction with others, asking for feedback, sharing ideas, and being open to the suggestions for improvement of others (for example, Lohman, 2005).

Shipton et al. (2005) showed in a longitudinal study of 30 manufacturing organizations that a combination of sophisticated HRM practices predicted organizational innovation to the extent that they influenced each stage of the organizational learning cycle, defined as the creation, sharing, and implementation of knowledge. Laursen and Foss (2003) concluded that organizations should adopt 'high-performance' HRM practices, arguing that practices designed to elicit decentralization facilitate problem-solving at local level, thereby enabling organizations to draw upon the latent 'tacit' knowledge of those closest to the task in hand. They further suggested that knowledge dissemination is enhanced where organizations implement team-based working and where they are committed to practices such as job rotation and project work. According to Collins and Smith (2006) these practices also support shared codes and language among employees, by exposing them to the narratives and perspectives that are important across discrete areas of the firm.

One HRM practice that has received limited attention as a precursor for knowledge sharing is exploratory learning. Exploratory learning entails conscious efforts by the organization to prompt employee engagement with perspectives that are outside the day-to-day perspectives of employees. Project work, secondments, customer and supplier liaison, job rotation, and benchmarking practices outside the organization open cognitive channels to new and different ways of operating (Shipton et al., 2006). This helps people to appreciate the importance of new ideas and increases the likelihood that they will support new ideas through to implementation. Training that brings individuals into contact with novel ideas and individuals from outside their day-to-day frame of reference have a similar effect.

In sum, broadening and deepening connections with those stakeholders who have alternative perspectives – customers, for example, or suppliers – might cause individuals to review the novel ideas that others put forward in a more open and considered manner, thereby enriching knowledge sharing and fostering innovative behaviors.

Networking – connecting with others across boundaries both within and outside the organization – is also important for knowledge sharing. First, networking helps employees to visualize the opportunities for applying knowledge. A wide base of contacts increases the chances that individuals are primed about where potential problems exist and how new ideas might resolve the problem at hand. This is important for the positioning of a creative idea. Second, because networking entails making connections across vertical and hierarchical boundaries (Jolink and Dankbaar, 2010), it increases collaboration and cooperation, which in turn makes it more likely that feasibility and practicality implications are fully taken into account. Third, through networking, individuals are primed about where expert capability resides. In this way, less evident knowledge (for example, that derived from capable and informed junior employees) can be accessed and utilized.

We argue that knowledge sharing is further enriched and enhanced where HRM practices promote customer engagement (see also Lin et al., 2015). Through working closely with customers, employees initiate and maintain relationships that provide a vibrant source of knowledge for the organization. Even employees who do not directly interface with customers but who are open to customer needs strengthen the social climate that is conducive to knowledge sharing. Such employees, being aware of customer tastes and preferences, can 'augment' products and processes by improving the design with characteristics appealing to the customers, and implement ideas reliably (Liao and Subramony, 2008).

HRM PROCESS AND INNOVATIVE BEHAVIORS

In addition to HR practices, after the theoretical article of Bowen and Ostroff in 2004 more researchers have started to examine the implementation of HRM, and studied the effect of employees' perceptions of HRM (Sanders et al., 2014). In the HRM process-based approach, attention is moved to employees' perceptions, their satisfaction with practices and their understanding of HRM (Bowen and Ostroff, 2004; see also Sanders et al., 2014). This HRM process-based approach emphasizes the importance of the processes through which employees attach meaning to HRM in explaining the relationship between HRM and performance (Bowen and Ostroff, 2004). When focusing on employees' satisfaction with HR practices, and taking into account that many HR tasks are transferred to line managers, the role of the direct supervisor cannot be underestimated. Therefore Sanders et al. (2010) examined the relationship between leader–member exchange (LMX), employees' satisfaction with some individual HR practices (employee influence, flow, primary and secondary rewards, and work content) and employees' innovative behavior. Using data from four Dutch and German technical organizations (n = 272) the results showed that both LMX and satisfaction with HR practices (flow, primary rewards and, most important, work content) were positively related to innovative behavior. In addition, they found that satisfaction with HR practices mediates the relationship between LMX and innovative behavior, meaning that the relationship with the direct supervisor is seen as antecedents of employees' satisfaction with HR practices that lead to employees' innovative behavior.

Attribution theory is concerned with the attributions people make to understand their own and others' behavior. People use internal (dispositional) and external (environmental) attributions when answering the question why they and others behave the way they do. According to attribution theory, people use these causal explanations (*attributions*) to make sense of their surroundings, improve their ability to predict future events, and attempt to (re)establish control over their lives (Kelley, 1973). In addition, the attributions people make systematically influence their subsequent behaviors, motivations, cognitions and affect.

Only a few studies thus far have related employees' perceptions to the attribution process (for example, Li et al., 2011; Katou et al., 2014). Within this approach scholars highlight the importance of the psychological process through which employees attach meaning to HRM in explaining the relationship between HRM and employee outcomes. Moving from perceptions of HRM to attribution of HRM, Sanders and Yang (2015) examined whether high-commitment HRM (HC-HRM) is more effective on employees' innovative behavior when employees can make sense of HRM (attribute HRM to management). Results from a cross-level field study (n = 639 employees within 42 organizations) confirmed this hypothesis: the results showed that the relationship between HC-HRM and employees' innovative behavior was stronger when employees perceive HRM as distinctive, consistent, and consensual and could understand HRM as was intended by management.

HRM PRACTICES AND PROCESSES: A COMBINED EFFECT

As content- and process-based HRM can both be considered as important drivers of employees' innovative behavior, a next step for strategic HRM research is to further unravel the joint effect of the content (high-performance work systems) and process (employees' perception of HRM) on innovative behavior. Some progress has already been made. Bednall and colleagues examined the effect of performance appraisal (Bednall et al., 2014) and formal training (Bednall and Sanders, 2014) on innovative behavior, among other employee outcomes. Moreover, drawing on Bowen and Ostroff's (2004) theoretical framework, these studies investigate whether employee perceptions of distinctiveness, consistency, and consensus of the HRM (HRM system strength) influence their response to these two HRM practices. Using longitudinal data of Dutch teachers from vocational educational training, Bednall et al. (2014) and Bednall and Sanders (2014) found that the specific practices of performance appraisal and training had positive effects on innovative behavior. Participation in innovative behavior was increased when HRM was perceived as distinctive, consistent, and consensual, contrary to their expectations.

Several points stand out in rationalizing why and how HRM *practices* in combination with HRM *processes* are conducive to employee innovative behaviors. First, where HRM practices and HRM processes are in alignment they present an unambiguous message about strategic requirements that leaves no room for doubt in employees' eyes. According to Collins and Smith (2006), for example, group-based incentives that promote interaction and communication are important for promoting cooperation, as are team-based work design and organization-oriented compensation and rewards. The HRM process perspective would suggest that even where senior members agree on these practices there is a potential gap in bringing the policy to life. Ajzen's (1985) theory of planned behavior proposes that social pressure exerted by influential parties determines an individual's propensity to engage in an action (such as innovative behaviors). Where key parties such as line managers, interacting with employees on a day-to-day basis, communicate and signal appropriately, employees can envisage what the strategy means for them. Thus, to foster cooperation, the line manager might set up team-based projects and discuss with members exactly how team achievements will be recognized and rewarded. Since internal promotion policies, job rotation, and team-based work design offer the chance for people to understand better what roles others perform (promoting trust), line managers and supervisors seeking to implement the policy can actively search for opportunities for people to experience different roles and activities and to move up the organizational hierarchy given that they fulfill defined criteria. Similarly, for HRM practices that facilitate an external orientation, line managers and other relevant parties can communicate through example and through creating opportunities for working with customers and other relevant groups that employees are expected to engage externally. Taken together, HRM practices and HRM processes convey a strong and unequivocal message to the employees that an external orientation, knowledge sharing and the ensuing innovative behaviors are important and valued.

A second way in which HRM practices and HRM processes in combination foster employee innovative behaviors is through offering an unequivocal message of support. The innovation process is often messy, reiterative, and may often involve two steps forward for one-step backwards (King, 1992). Where new ideas are novel and experimental, the initiator is likely to face hesitation and skepticism from influential parties. This point influences the design and implementation of HRM practices. HRM practices like performance appraisal, for example, even where developmentally oriented and non-judgmental, may not gain traction as intended. To make performance appraisal work, those closest to the employee have to operationalize the policy. Distinctive features of the appraisal – helping employees to develop skills, being non-judgmental – should stand out, and here again the line manager has a key role, highlighting these elements during performance appraisal meetings and through daily interactions. Consensus, that is, these qualities are agreed across the organizational hierarchy, is important to this end, as is consistency, in that other HR practices, such as reward and training, convey similar signals. The overriding message is that support is available for measured experimentation and risk-taking and that the organization will not take punitive action against those who fail to achieve desired outcomes. The HRM process reinforces that while expectations are clear, support is available where unintended consequences arise.

Third, linked with the above points, HRM practices and HRM processes in alignment have the potential to create a social environment, defined as 'the collective set of norms, values and beliefs that express employees' views of how they interact with one another' (Collins and Smith, 2006; p. 547) that is conducive to employee innovative behaviors. A social climate enabling knowledge sharing suggests that new ideas are welcomed and people are open to opportunities proposed by others to improve current ways of working. Recruitment and selection practices attract and induct those who are inclined to act as team members, rather than working separately from others. Reward systems – designed such that there are no penalties where employees' suggestions fail to gain traction – convey important signals to employees about the importance of seeking new ideas. Furthermore, such systems provide the necessary encouragement and motivation for individuals to continue with their efforts, even after the creative idea has been put forward. Workplace structures, such as team-based working, as well as developmental practices such as mentoring and coaching, have the potential to provide the insights that individuals need in order to devise and effectively implement new ideas. HRM practices eliciting motivation may be especially important. Zhao and Chadwick (2014) found that HRM practices such as performance appraisal and reward – associated with promoting motivation rather than building employee capability – were more important for achieving innovation than practices such as training and development and competency profiling (building employee capability).

According to Bowen and Ostroff (2004) an organization's social climate comes about to the extent that employees perceive a strong HRM system. This means that employees understand, and are satisfied with HRM practices as a whole, and attribute meaning based on their perceptions of what HRM is intended to deliver. As suggested, the HRM practices described above are more likely to engender a social climate conducive to knowledge sharing and innovative behaviors where they are distinctive, consistent, and consensual. Taken together, this suggests two points. First, that considerations relating to HRM process (and implementation) should receive equal weighting in comparison with time and attention devoted to determining HRM content. Second, this perspective brings the line manager center stage. The line manager acts as an intermediary between strategic HRM policy and practice on one hand and employees on the other, communicating through their daily interaction what aspects of HRM practice matter, and which are less pressing (Shipton et al., 2013). Employee attributions are shaped by line managers based on what is detected about formal requirements, as well as unspoken assumptions. The challenge for line managers is to convey information about the organization's behavioral intent that is apposite for the particular context within which the daily interactions occur (McDermott et al., 2013).

OPPORTUNITIES, GAPS AND FUTURE RESEARCH

As highlighted above, HRM practices have the potential to foster employees' innovative behaviors, on one hand through enabling knowledge exchange and combination (Collins and Smith, 2006); on the other through revitalizing an organization's knowledge base via engagement with the wider environment. When we consider the HRM *process* in the equation, a possible tension becomes apparent. An effective HRM process will communicate unambiguously management performance expectations, for example, around knowledge sharing and innovative behaviors. Thus, theory suggests, performance appraisal creates an explicit link between individual performance and the organization's strategic goals (DeNisi and Sonesh, 2010), including innovative behaviors. It could be that a strong HRM process leaves little space or opportunity for employees to try out new alternatives or challenge the existing way of working. Performance outcomes such as innovative behaviors – that require high levels of proactivity on behalf of employees – may be suppressed or even negated (Ehrnrooth and Björkman, 2012). The question of whether HRM process enhances or constrains employee behaviors with particular reference to innovation is one that deserves further research attention.

Another gap in extant knowledge surrounds the effect of HRM process on work intensification and employee well-being. Through communicating a strong, unambiguous message about performance expectations, it has been argued that HRM practices and processes in combination exert control that pushes employees to achieve above and beyond what might be deemed reasonable in terms of their best interests (ibid.). In effect, HRM practices and processes in alignment promote what has been described as 'aspirational control' (Alvesson and Kärreman, 2007, p. 713). This means that employees' self-confidence and self-esteem becomes inextricably bound with their performance and career progress. A strong HRM process can foster this tight linkage simply because as discussed above performance expectations are unambiguous. As Ehrnrooth and Björkman (2012) point out, 'The more employees are subjected to performance-based pay, evaluation, goal-setting and development opportunities, in general, the stronger the signals of desired behaviors and rewards are the more they are to identify with their work and compete for their continued employment and career progress' (p. 1118). Recent work in the consultancy industry has found that the HRM process is positively associated with workload and work intensification, especially for employee creativity (Ehrnrooth and Björkman, 2012). The question of work intensification and employee well-being arising from HRM practices especially given growing interest in HRM process is one that requires further investigation.

Another question surrounds a potential differential effect of HRM content and HRM process on creativity as opposed to innovation implementation. Although as stated at the start of this chapter, we have based our framework on innovative behaviors, capturing both employees' ability to devise new ideas as well as their capacity to work collaboratively with others to foster innovation implementation, it is possible that some HRM practices (such as exploratory learning or networking) are more conducive to creativity than to innovation implementation. Furthermore, it is possible that other practices – such as team-based reward – are more apposite for the implementation aspects of innovation. Linked with this, it could be that some elements of HRM process have a stronger effect on creativity while others influence innovation implementation. Consensus and consistency might be important for the latter, while distinctiveness, especially around practices that expose individuals to new and different experiences, might be more to the forefront for the former.

Finally, there is growing interest in employees' attributions of HRM given cultural difference and the relative weighting attached to consensus (in more collectively oriented cultures). It has been shown that HRM is more effective in terms of employees' commitment and innovative behavior when employees can make sense of HRM (attribute HRM to management). Since perceptions are influenced by employees' cultural background (Hofstede, 1984) and innovative behavior is related to risk (uncertainty avoidance) and informal knowledge sharing (low power distance) it is worth considering the effect of power distance and uncertainty avoidance of a country on the joint effect of HRM practices and employees' attribution of those practices on innovative behavior. Power distance is defined as the extent to which the less powerful members of organizations and institutions accept and expect that power is distributed unequally. The uncertainty avoidance dimension expresses the degree to which the members of a society feel uncomfortable with uncertainty and ambiguity (Hofstede, 1980, 1984). Countries exhibiting strong uncertainty avoidance maintain rigid codes of belief and behavior and are intolerant of unorthodox behavior and ideas. Countries with weak uncertainty avoidance maintain a more relaxed attitude in which practice counts more than principles. Examining the effect of a country's power distance and uncertainty avoidance on the joint effect of HRM content in conjunction with HRM process on innovative behavior is an important next step for this line of work.

In conclusion, we would add that the whole question of HRM's role in promoting innovative behaviors is at a nascent stage. Added to this, the HRM process perspective is only just starting to be recognized as an important and vibrant stream of research. Our analysis is necessarily tentative, but we believe this to be an important and timely moment to review and question existing conceptualizations of HRM and performance, and test through well-designed empirical studies whether or not they hold out where innovative behaviors, and innovation at the organizational level, are outcome variables of interest.

REFERENCES

Ajzen, I. (1985), *From Intentions to Actions: A Theory of Planned Behavior*, Berlin/ Heidelberg: Springer.

Alvesson, M. and D. Kärreman (2007), 'Unraveling HRM: Identity, ceremony, and control in a management consultancy firm', *Organization Science*, **18**(4), 711–23.

Amabile, T. (1988), 'A model of creativity and innovations in organizations', in B.M. Staw and L.L Cummings (eds), *Research in Organizational Behavior*, Greenwich, CT: JAI Press, pp. 187–209.

Anderson, N., K. Potocnik and J. Zhou (2014), 'Innovation and creativity in organizations: A state of the science review, prospective commentary and guiding framework', *Journal of Management* [online], doi: 10.1177/0149206314527128.

Bae, J. and J. Lawler (2000), 'Organizational and HRM strategies in Korea: Impact on firm performance in an emerging economy', *Academy of Management Journal*, **43**(3), 502–17.

Bednall, T. and K. Sanders (2014), 'Formal training stimulates follow-up participation in informal learning: A three wave study', paper presented at the Academy of Management annual meeting, Philadelphia, PA, 1–5 August.

Bednall, T., K. Sanders and P. Runhaar (2014), 'Stimulating informal learning activities through perceptions of performance appraisal quality and HRM system strength: A two-wave study', *Academy of Management Learning and Education*, **13**(1), 45–61.

Bowen, D.E. and C. Ostroff (2004), 'Understanding HRM–firm performance linkages: The role of "strength" of the HRM system', *Academy of Management Review*, **29**(2), 203–21.

Cappelli, P. and D. Neumark (2001), 'Do "high performance" work practices improve establishment level outcomes?' *Industrial and Labor Relations Review*, **54**(4), 737–76.

Chadwick, C. (2010), 'Theoretic insights on the nature of performance synergies in human resource systems: Toward greater precision', *Human Resource Management Review*, **20**(2), 85–101.

Collins, C. and K. Smith (2006), 'Knowledge exchange and combination: The role of human resource practices in the performance of high-technology firms', *Academy of Management Journal*, **49**(3), 544–60.

Combs, A., Y. Liu, A. Hall and D. Ketchen (2006), 'How much do high-performance work practices matter? A meta-analysis of their effects on organization performance', *Personnel Psychology*, **59**(3), 501–28.

De Jong, J.P.J., S.K. Parker, S. Wennekers and C.-H. Wu (2013), 'Entrepreneurial behavior in organizations: Does job design matter?' *Entrepreneurship Theory and Practice*, **39**(4), 981–5.

DeNisi, A.S. and S. Sonesh (2010), 'The appraisal and management of performance at work', in S. Zedeck (ed.), *APA Handbook of Industrial and Organizational Psychology: Selecting and Developing Members for the Organization*, Vol. 2, Washington, DC: American Psychological Association, pp. 255–79.

Ehrnrooth, M. and I. Björkman (2012), 'An integrative HRM process theorization: Beyond signaling effects and mutual gains', *Journal of Management Studies*, **49**(6), 1109–35.

Fay, D., H. Shipton, M. West and M. Patterson (2015), 'Teamwork and organizational innovation: The moderating role of the HRM context', *Creativity and Innovation Management*, **24**(2), 261–77.

Hayton, J. (2005), 'Promoting corporate entrepreneurship through human resource practices: A review of empirical research', *Human Resource Management Review*, **15**(1), 21–41.

Hofstede, G. (1980), *Culture's Consequences: International Differences in Work-related Values*, Beverly Hills, CA: Sage Publications.

Hofstede, G. (1984), 'The cultural relativity of the quality of life concept', *Academy of Management Review*, **9**(3), 389–98.

Huselid, M.A., S.E. Jackson and R.S. Schuler (1997), 'Human resource management effectiveness as determinants of firm performance', *Academy of Management Journal*, **40**(1), 171–88.

Jolink, M. and B. Dankbaar (2010), 'Creating a climate for inter-organizational networking through people management', *The International Journal of Human Resource Management*, **21**(9), 1436–53.

Katou, A.P., Budhwar and C. Patel (2014), 'Content versus process in the HRM–performance relationship: An empirical examination', *Human Resource Management*, **53**(4), 527–44.

Kelley, H.H. (1973), 'The process of causal attributions', *American Psychologist*, **28**(2), 107–28.

King, N. (1992), 'Modeling the innovation process: An empirical comparison of approaches', *Journal of Occupational and Organizational Psychology*, **65**(2), 89–100.

Laursen, K. and N.J. Foss (2003), 'New human resource management practices, complementarities and the impact on innovation performance', *Cambridge Journal of Economics*, **27**(2), 243–63.

Li, X., S. Frenkel and K. Sanders (2011), 'How do perceptions of the HRM system affect employee attitudes? A multi-level study of Chinese employees', *International Journal of HRM*, **22**(8), 1823–40.

Liao, H. and M. Subramony (2008), 'Employee customer orientation in manufacturing organizations: Joint influences of customer proximity and the senior leadership team', *Journal of Applied Psychology*, **93**(2), 317–28.

Lin, C.H.V., K. Sanders, H. Shipton, J. Sun and E. Mooi (2015), 'Opening the black-box between HRM and firm innovation: The moderating effect of national power distance' (under review), Nottingham, UK: Nottingham Trent University.

Lohman, M.C. (2005), 'A survey of factors influencing the participation of two professional groups in informal workplace learning activities', *Human Resource Development Quarterly*, **16**(4), 501–27.

McDermott, A., E. Conway, D. Rousseau and P. Flood (2013), 'Promoting effective psychological contracts through leadership: The missing link between HR strategy and performance', *Human Resource Management*, **52**(2), 289–310.

Piaget, J. (1970), 'Science of education and the psychology of the child', trans. D. Coltman, New York: Orion.

Sanders, K. and H. Yang (2015), 'The HRM process approach: The influence of employees' attribution to explain the HRM–performance relationship', *Human Resource Management*, [online], doi: 10.1002/hrm.21661.

Sanders, K., H. Shipton and J. Gomes (2014), 'Is the HRM process important? Past, current, and future challenges', *Human Resource Management*, **53**(4), 489–503.

Sanders, K., M. Moorkamp, N. Torka, S. Groeneveld and C. Groeneveld (2010), 'How to support innovative behaviour? The role of LMX and satisfaction with HR practices', *Technology and Investment*, **1**(1), 59–68.

Schuler, R. and S. Jackson (1987), 'Linking competitive strategies with human resource management practices', *The Academy of Management Executive*, **1**(3), 207–19.

Scott, S. and R. Bruce (1994), 'Determinants of innovative behavior: A path model of individual innovation in the workplace', *Academy of Management Journal*, **37**(3), 580–607.

Shipton, H., K. Sanders, C. Atkinson and S. Frenkel (2013), 'The other side of the mirror: Signaling HRM in health-care', paper presented at the Improving People Performance in Healthcare Seminar, DCU Business School, Dublin, Ireland, 6 September.

Shipton, H., D. Fay, M.A. West, M. Patterson and K. Birdi (2005), 'Managing people to promote innovation', *Creativity and Innovation Management*, **14**(2), 118–28.

Shipton, H., M. West, J. Dawson, M. Patterson and K. Birdi (2006), 'Human resource management as a predictor of innovation', *Human Resource Management Journal*, **16**(1), 3–27.

Škerlavaj, M., M. Černe and A. Dysvik (2014), 'I get by with a little help from my supervisor: Creative-idea generation, idea implementation, and perceived supervisor support', *Leadership Quarterly*, **25**(5), 987–1000.

West, M. and J. Farr (1990), 'Innovation at work', in M.A. West and J.L. Farr (eds), *Innovation and Creativity at Work*, Chichester, UK: Wiley, p. 9.

Zhao, Z.J. and C. Chadwick (2014), 'What we will do versus what we can do: The relative effects of unit-level NPD motivation and capability', *Strategic Management Journal*, **35**(12), 1867–80.

Zhou, Y., Y. Hong and J. Liu (2013), 'Internal commitment or external collaboration? The impact of human resource management systems on firm innovation and performance', *Human Resource Management*, **52**(2), 263–88.

19. Organizing for co-creation and multi-polar learning communities

Maja Lotz and Peer Hull Kristensen

INTRODUCTION

Multinational firms (MNCs) are faced with increasing pressure to capitalize on creativity emerging from collaboration in and among various units and teams located within different contexts. Recent research suggests that, in contrast to traditional hierarchical models of multinational organization (for example, Egelhoff, 1991), MNCs' competitive advantage increasingly derives from their potential to co-create and innovate in lateral collaborative communities by transferring, sharing, and recombining practices and knowledge previously compartmentalized around the world (Ghoshal et al., 1994; Nobel and Birkinshaw, 1998; Doz et al., 2003; Singh, 2005; Herrigel et al., 2012).

Capitalizing on creativity has always been a challenge for organizations. Taylor's (1911) theory of scientific management can be read as an attempt to let the organization and the larger society, rather than individual workers and their collective, benefit from creativity that occurs on the factory floor. But the effects of creativity under Taylorism were often manipulated by workers, for example through time measuring, so that in the end it led to factory settings that differed highly in terms of how much workers had capitalized on and privatized gains from creativity (Crozier and Friedberg, 1980; Kristensen, 1986). The turn to high-performance work organizations and mutually performance-competitive teams partly overcame this problem by making the team the capitalizing unit. However, it also created the problem of how teams could benefit from the creativity of other teams. Thus, organizing cross-teams for the exchange of ideas became a necessary collaborative device that could complement the competitive rivalry among teams (Kristensen and Lotz, 2011). The challenge of capitalizing on collaborative creativity within a factory on a broader scale is, in principle, parallel to the challenge of capitalizing across subsidiaries of an MNC by organizing multi-polar learning communities.

Such multi-polar learning communities are crucial for harnessing the innovative capabilities of firms because they magnify the ability to accumulate knowledge and co-create new organizational innovations through knowledge-sharing and interactive learning across different domains and poles (Prahalad and Krishnan, 2008; Crossan and Apaydin, 2010). We define a multi-polar learning community as a community that is able to make inquiries and share knowledge effectively in groups that work towards a common object, but that are distributed across multiple and (often) polarized organizational divides. While multi-polar learning communities, empirically, have become an important competitive asset, little is known about how they are organized and managed. Drawing on empirical evidence from a case study in a Danish MNC that has experimented with the development of multi-polar learning relationships across production sites, this chapter addresses this research gap by asking: What are the organizational architectures of multi-polar learning communities? How are they governed? How do they facilitate co-creative interaction?

This chapter also empirically analyzes how multi-polar learning communities are organized in order to foster micro-practices of co-creation in global work arrangements. To gain a more nuanced and micro-level understanding of how multi-polar learning communities develop and change, we explore how organizational forms and governance arrangements are shaped and reshaped from below through everyday interactions between organization members (Orlikowski, 2002; Hargadon and Bechky, 2006). Learning in multi-polar communities is not simply about diffusing and implementing creative ideas from one team or subsidiary to the larger organization, it also involves the enabling of co-creation as these communities offer temporary spaces for encounters in which different perspectives can be voiced and shared, engage in joint inquiry, solve problems, and come up with new solutions in ways that no one working alone could have done. As we shall see, implementation itself becomes a part of the creative process.

RESEARCH SETTINGS AND METHODS

Our field is a Danish pharmaceutical MNC with subsidiaries in numerous countries. In the past, this MNC decentralized competencies to operative levels and benefitted from continuous improvements in team-based work practices and employee involvement, only to discover that it was at risk of developing very diverse local practices across production sites. Being unable to capitalize on best practices across sites was highly inefficient, and also very risky, because a failure in one subsidiary's production procedures could harm the reputation of the entire company. Consequently, the challenge was to institutionalize a system so that potential problems in production could be diagnosed, best practices could be identified and shared between sites, and a new level of codified practices could be monitored across subsidiary sites.

Given this challenge, the company has gradually built up experience with facilitating learning, and co-creation across its geographically distributed sites. One example is its standardization process. In 2008, the company began standardizing its work operations in all production areas. It planned to build its standards on existing best operational practices and to develop one global approach for integrating and standardizing best practices across its plants. The company began in one operational area and then rolled out the same approach to other areas. As part of this process, the company developed an organizational architecture they called 'global communities of practice' (GCPs), involving people from different sites jointly working on a standardization project within a particular area, sharing and learning from local experiences and practices across sites, and co-creating systems and feedback mechanisms to ensure the integration and continuous improvement of best practices.

A global community of practice typically consists of a mix of between 15 and 20 engineers, operators, technicians, and specialists working within a specific area of expertise/operations. Best practices are stored in a 'cookbook' that ensures a common approach to both ongoing and future standardization projects, and a set of governance procedures supports the continuous improvement of standards. During fieldwork, we observed how the introduction of three organizational components: (1) an organizational form of global communities of practice, (2) a cookbook representing a common set of guidelines, and (3) a set of explicit governance procedures gave rise to multi-polar learning dynamics. These organizational components allowed members to engage in collective inquiry and knowledge sharing across multiple polarized organizational boundaries, and thus to co-create effectively between their divergent practices.

Informed by this empirical landscape, the chapter illustrates how organization members experimented with new organizational forms and governance procedures to facilitate learning and co-creation across localities. The case study was conducted from 2011 through 2014, to help us understand how organizational members collaborate, connect (and disconnect), share knowledge, manage, and co-create through their everyday interactions in the MNC (Van Maanen, 1988). To achieve this, the study triangulated between three different data sources: talk, observations, and documents (Stake, 1998), including four-to-seven-day site visits to four of the company's plants; participation in numerous meetings among members of different GCPs; longitudinal shadowing and participant observation of meetings, workshops, and social activities focused on the development of global training standards; formal and informal interviewing of community members in the training group as well as of other stakeholders; observation and shadowing of HR managers and other staff involved in global training; and perusal of company documents and other secondary data (Spradley, 1979; Fetterman, 1989).

THEORETICAL FRAMEWORK

The last few decades' rapid increase in computer-mediated communication and global knowledge production have given rise to new forms of distributed work arrangements and collaborations between a multitude of different and often physically distanced actors, which entails knowledge-sharing practices that reach beyond face-to-face interaction and co-location. Though theoretical debates about organizational learning see proximity as a precondition for learning and knowledge collaboration (Knorr Cetina, 1981; Wenger, 1997), numerous members of MNCs today are tapped into networks of global collaborative work teams (for example, IBM and LEGO), where face-to-face encounters often go hand in hand with computer-mediated forms of interaction that transgress organizational boundaries. These virtual environments may be organized as hotspots for knowledge creation and implementation of shared practices (Grabher and Ibert, 2014), and call for new views regarding how knowledge is created, shared, and implemented.

We introduce the concept of multi-polar learning as an expression of the circularity of creation and implementation of new ideas and how they flow in geographically distributed communities that are socially distant and heterogeneous in character. Drawing on a pragmatist understanding, we conceptualize learning as a social process based on mutual engagement and participation in activities triggered by problematic situations and doubt (Peirce, 1877; Dewey [1938] 1997; Brandi and Elkjær, 2011). Within this view, learning is seen as a transformative and reflective experience that always takes place in a participatory context/situation, not only in the individual mind (Elkjær, 2000; Wenger, 2000). This concept seeks to overcome three 'blind spots' in social learning theory – particularly related to the concept of communities of practice (Lave and Wenger, 1991; Wenger, 1997, 2000) – that are biased in favor of socialization, harmony, and proximity. Taking the three blind spots into account, the concept of multi-polar learning offers a more differentiated view of knowledge creation and implementation in global work arrangements by appreciating inquiry, conflict, and distance as 'ingredients' of epistemological relevance equal to learning theory's traditional emphasis on socialization, harmony, and proximity. Such a take is able to analyze how organizational members may engage in participatory and reflective inquiries in their practices triggered by problematic situations, and how they learn through both harmonious and conflicting relationships across local contexts in multi-polar communities. Guided by this framework, we explore multi-polar learning communities both as 'hot spots' for multi-directional learning relations across boundaries and as arenas for co-creation.

The term co-creation is used as a metaphor to describe the interactions by which actors create and implement what none of them could have achieved alone (for example, ideas, material products, scripts, routines, practices). Co-creative interactions may appear, for example, when a project team works on a common task to shorten the ramp up time on a line; when operators co-create products and processes in collaboration with construction, customers, and other subsidiaries of the MNC; and when a group of engineers from different subsidiaries bring technologies from many sources together on a common platform. These co-creative situations emerge, or, in Heckscher and Adler's (2007, p. 21) words, materialize, 'when a collectivity engages cooperative, interdependent activity towards a common object'. This definition implies an understanding of co-creation as something that unfolds through interactions between people, not only in the individual mind. Creation is not separated from implementation; both happen in a recursive process. Co-creation happens by making inquiries into the situation at hand, to identify and solve problems and reuse old knowledge and experiences in new ways. Much discussion of post-bureaucratic organizational forms points to the growing significance of such collaborative orders of co-creation and how they entail recursive learning relations within an architecture of experimental governance (Sabel, 1996; Stark, 2009; Sabel and Zeitlin, 2012). Yet, empirical accounts of the organizational architectures and modes of governance nourishing multi-polar co-creation in MNCs have been limited (for an exception, see Herrigel, 2015; see also Herrigel et al., 2012).

The next section explores how a multi-polar learning community engaged in the development of global training standards across production sites is organized and governed, as well as how it triggers practices of co-creation.

CASE ANALYSIS

Analysis of our field data identifies three organizational components that play a role in triggering recursive learning and co-creation across diverse teams in the company under study. The first component involves organizing an architecture of 'global communities of practice' across the company's organizational structure. The second is the assembly of a 'cookbook' providing a common language and guidelines for coordinating work in the communities. The third is the formation of a set of governance procedures to support the continuous improvement of the projects in progress. One example of such a multi-polar recursive process evolves around the company's operational training practices. In 2010, the company organized a global community of practice to standardize training practices and enhance standardization across sites. The global training partner describes the project's intention in the following way:

> To drive flow and stability in production as well as productivity improvements in accordance with the strategy, we need to build organizational preparedness. This means that we must be able to rapidly ramp up competencies by delivering training effectively in the right place, quality, time and amount – whether due to new-hires, technology changes, new product introduction, or ramp-up of completely new facilities.

The training community is formed of members from all sites and represents a variety of organizational levels and areas of expertise within operations. It is managed by one project director, one global training partner, five local site training partners, 12 shop floor trainers of trainers, 30 shop floor trainers, and various other support staff who help to drive the process (for example, operators, technicians, specialists, human resource [HR] staff, etc.). The community is responsible for developing standardized training practices and training materials, identifying problems and differences across sites, sharing knowledge about best practices, aligning local training procedures, and searching for joint solutions to improve training effectiveness. It is also responsible for updating training standards when standard operation processes are changed or when new training needs or best training practices are identified locally and agreed upon globally (in other words, by the project director). The training partners constitute the core of the community. Working in five different locations, they have bi-weekly webcam meetings in order to collaborate in workshops.

When the community was first formed, there was no alignment of local training methods or use of standard training plans and most of the members did not know each other. Hence, the first task was to get to know each other, identify a common objective, decide on a pilot project, and develop training material to guide the process. During the first year of meetings and workshops, a pilot training project was developed in one operational area covered in all sites. As with standardization of work operations, this project is now being rolled out and developed to cover other areas to ensure flow and stability in production as well as productivity improvements. Through this process, the global training community has developed procedures by which stakeholders from the different sites meet on a regular basis to learn from each other's experiences, align methods, and co-create training materials and activities. All training modules and methods have been developed based on dialogue and collective reflection in the community. To guide training activities at local sites, a 'cookbook' was created. By taking stock of the work in the training community and identifying and integrating the most useful training practices across production sites, the cookbook describes how training of operational work tasks shall be handled concerning (1) identification of training needs; (2) development of training; (3) training of trainers; (4) training of employees; and (5) continuous updates of training practices according to changes in standard operating procedures (SOPs) and/or local procedural modifications of the training standards. The cookbook provides supporting guidelines, templates, and methods needed to ensure training effectiveness locally and serves as a forum for documenting the continuous improvements of training standards discovered and developed by the training community. A set of governance procedures have been introduced to support the standardization process and install a feedback mechanism to ensure continuous improvements. They consist of a six-step cycle, named 'the improvement wheel' (Figure 19.1).

First, the 'wheel' integrates creativity and implementation through training in a recursive process of continuous improvement. Second, training activities themselves are driven and governed by the six-step cycle. Working according to these procedures, the global training community never becomes fixed and determined by one central apex. Instead, the system is continuously developed, revised, and refined through joint problem-solving and diagnostic dialogue among members from different local areas, domains of expertise, organizational levels, and so on. In this way, the global training community constitutes the organizational architecture for a multi-polar learning system by bringing together three components: (1) an organizational platform; (2) common guidelines stored in a 'living document' of best practices; and (3) a set of governance procedures to ensure recursive continuous improvements.

Working in the global community creates unexpected opportunities for members to meet and engage in collective inquiry, as well as to identify problems and solutions by recombining knowledge in order to come up with ideas and solutions on improved training effectiveness that no one could have generated working on their own. Analysis of the field data identifies three particularly recurrent temporary spaces that provide the possibility for this: workshops, virtual webcam meetings, and onsite visits.

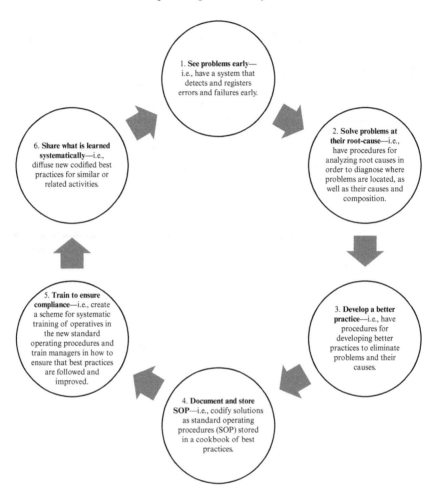

Figure 19.1   'The improvement wheel'

Below follows a sample of empirical vignettes providing insights into such multi-polar learning encounters.

Training material workshop – Denmark, August 2011
The training partners are organizing a five-day workshop in the GCP focused on the development of training materials that can be used as standard documents to guide training in local production areas. Thirty-three operators, technicians, and trainers are gathered from different sites to co-create job training plans (JTPs) for a filling line. A JTP is used by trainers to train new operators in a specific task on the line. The template describes

the training, and registers both successful completion of and the content of the training. On the third day of the workshop, people are split into five groups, each working on the development of a JTP for a particular area on the filling line (for example, the assembly offload station, closing station, outlet wheels, and piston station). In the group working on the piston station, two operators, two technicians, and two certified trainers are discussing what exact information is necessary in order to train new operators to be able to perform the tasks at the station. Trainers ask questions while one operator demonstrates how to perform the tasks: 'How do you know to do exactly this? What do you have to be careful with here? How would you know this if you had not been trained in this task?' Often the operators and technicians engage in discussions comparing and contrasting how they run the piston station in their respective localities as they work out a common training procedure. Such collective inquiry is a typical start. During the rest of the day they develop the JTP by articulating, recombining, and documenting their local experiences and tacit knowledge about work. First, they observe the trained operators performing the task several times. Second, they split the process into small steps and write a description of how the training should be conducted at each work step. Third, they adjust the training guideline and discuss the wording of the description. Fourth, one operator and a trainer test the JTP to see if anything is missing. Fifth, they ask a trainer and an operator from one of the other groups to test the JTP and comment on it.

Virtual webcam meeting between training partners from local sites –
Denmark, February 2012
The global training partner begins the meeting, giving an update on her recent meeting with the group of HR directors, who have discussed how to better link training work to the local managers and to other ongoing projects such as the lean project. She says:

> It is crucial that we involve people from the lean project and HR from the beginning. . . we have to share and learn from each other. If we want to have the 'improvement wheel' go around, we need to collaborate. The 'wheel' will not be a wheel if we don't work together across projects. Trainers need to know about the lean project and vice versa. The more others are involved the easier the training system will be to roll out. How have you handled this so far at your sites and how can we do it smarter in the future?

Her question triggers the training partners to discuss their local experiences and ideas, showing quite different ways to tackle this issue and noting that they do not agree on one best way. The Chinese training partner has had several meetings with the local HR unit and people from the lean project. Consequently, HR has invited one of the lean managers to become involved in the local training team. The training partners agree to integrate this practice at the other sites. The global training partner concludes by promising to support this idea at the level of HR directors.

Site visit: implementation and assessment of a training maturity model – USA, April 2012

The global community has developed training standards and modules, which have been implemented locally. The next step is to develop assessment tools to ensure alignment and continuous improvement of training. As a training partner explains: 'We need to create measurements that show the impact, and thus the value, of our training system'. Building on the lean project, the training group has developed a maturity model and set of indicators to measure the level of standardization. Local-site people, having invested a lot of resources in the training activities, are anxious that the assessment might rank them lower than other sites. Who should do the assessment? How can transparency and reliability be ensured? How can good qualitative indicators be developed? How can a root cause analysis that explains the assessment results be enabled? These are typical concerns. To answer them, the global training partner visits each site to both inform about and gather ideas for the assessment. Visiting the US site, she tells the local training team:

> My role is to bring in experiences from the other sites – your role is to find a way to drive the process that works best for you. We have created an overall frame together that is not final. Within this frame, you should decide how you would like to measure and manage the training at your site going forward.

The team then gathers material (for example, interview guides, PowerPoint presentations, etc.) and experiences from the other sites and uses this to co-create their own approach to the assessment and make it useful for mapping future training needs. The outcome of this work is documented and shared with the other sites at later meetings and workshops.

Global training partner workshop – alignment and preparation of the assessment of training at local sites – Denmark, March 2013

Each site has done a pilot project mapping its training system using a maturity model as the common assessment standard. Because training activities have been organized and implemented at different sites, the particular operating area being assessed should be decided locally. Although not directly comparable, the announcement of assessment scores created serious tensions across sites, but also led to a much stronger managerial awareness and focus on the importance of cultivating an effective training system locally. This pilot phase was finalized by a training partner's workshop aimed at sharing 'best and worse experiences' in order to improve future assessments. Each training partner presented posters and talked about what has and has not worked well in implementing the maturity model as an assessment tool; knowledge was shared, and a joint search for better solutions characterized the workshop. By comparing assessment approaches used at different sites, participants recombined and reframed previous experiences, co-creating new ideas for how best to handle and align the assessment process.

DISCUSSION AND CONCLUDING REMARKS

The empirical examples illustrate how micro-practices of co-creation are facilitated when members of the global community come together and share temporary spaces of multi-polar learning. Through such interactive forums, they engage in joint inquiry, making use of divergent local practices and perspectives, solving problems, and coming up with new approaches to developing an effective global training system that none of them would have been able to accomplish, working alone. The vignettes also reveal that mere participation in social contexts is not enough to generate learning in multi-polar communities. Inquiry triggered by a problematic situation, and doubt regarding how to handle that situation, appear to be a crucial part of learning dynamics among the training group. The stories indicate that members engage in both collaborative and conflictual relationships and that the global community is helped, not hindered, by its comparative differences in identifying and diagnosing problems, and searching for causes and solutions. Furthermore, the collective output in the form of SOP cookbooks and training templates constitute a framework that makes it possible for individuals within the global organization to direct their creativity toward a generalized process of continuous improvement, and given that suggested changes in SOP and training methods must be centrally codified, this creativity is institutionally connected to a far reaching process of implementation.

REFERENCES

Brandi, U. and B. Elkjær (2011), 'Organizational learning viewed from a social learning perspective', in M. Easterby-Smith and M.A. Lyles (eds), *Handbook of Organizational Learning and Knowledge Management*, Chichester, UK: Wiley.

Crossan, M.M. and M. Apaydin (2010), 'A multi-dimensional framework of organizational innovation: A systematic review of the literature', *Journal of Management Studies*, **47**(6), 1154–91.

Crozier, M. and E. Friedberg (1980), *Actors and Systems. The Politics of Collective Action*, Chicago, IL: University of Chicago Press.

Dewey, J. ([1938] 1997), *Experience and Education*, New York: Touchstone.

Doz, Y., J. Santos and P. Williamson (2003), 'The metanational: The next step in the evolution of the multinational enterprise', in J. Birkinshaw, S. Ghoshal, C.C. Markides, J. Stopford and G. Yip (eds), *The Future of the Multinational Company*, Chichester, UK: Wiley.

Egelhoff, W.G. (1991), 'Information processing theory and the multinational enterprise', *Journal of International Business Studies*, **22**(3), 341–68.

Elkjær, B. (2000), 'Learning and getting to know: The case of knowledge workers', *Human Resource Development International*, **3**(3), 343–59.

Fetterman, D.M. (1989), *Ethnography: Step by Step*, Thousand Oaks, CA: Sage.

Ghoshal, S., H. Korine and G. Szulanski (1994), 'Interunit communication in multinational corporations', *Management Science*, **40**(1), 96–110.

Grabher, G. and O. Ibert (2014), 'Distance as asset? Knowledge collaboration in hybrid virtual communities', *Journal of Economic Geography*, **14**(1), 97–123.

Hargadon, A.B. and B.A. Bechky (2006), 'When collections of creatives become creative collectives: A field study of problem solving at work', *Organization Science*, **17**(4), 484–500.

Heckscher, C. and P.S. Adler (eds) (2007), *The Firm as a Collaborative Community*, Oxford, UK: Oxford University Press.

Herrigel, G. (2015), 'Globalization and the German industrial production model', *Journal for Labour Market Research*, **48**(2), 133–49.

Herrigel, G., V. Wittke and U. Voskamp (2012), 'The process of Chinese manufacturing upgrading: Transitioning from unilateral to recursive mutual learning relations', *Global Strategy Journal*, **3**(1), 109–25.

Knorr Cetina, K. (1981), *The Manufacture of Knowledge*, Oxford: Pergamon.

Kristensen, P.H. (1986), *Teknologiske Projekter og Organisatoriske Processer* [Technological and Organizational Processes], Roskilde: Forlaget for Samfundsøkonomi og Planlægning.

Kristensen, P.H. and M. Lotz (2011), 'Taking teams seriously in the co-creation of firms and economic agency', *Organization Studies*, **32**(11), 1465–85.

Lave, J. and E. Wenger (1991), *Situated Learning: Legitimate Peripheral Participation*, Cambridge, UK: Cambridge University Press.

Nobel, R. and J. Birkinshaw (1998), 'Innovation in multinational corporations: Control and communication patterns in international R&D operations', *Strategic Management Journal*, **19**(5), 479–96.

Orlikowski, W.J. (2002), 'Knowing in practice: Enacting a collective capability in distributed organizing', *Organization Science*, **13**(2), 249–73.

Peirce, C.S. (1877), 'The fixation of belief', *Popular Science Monthly*, **12**, 1–15.

Prahalad, C.K. and M.S. Krishnan (2008), *The New Age of Innovation: Driving Co-created Value Through Global Networks*, New York: McGraw-Hill.

Sabel, C.F. (1996), 'Learning by monitoring: The dilemmas of regional economic policy in Europe', in OECD (ed.), *Networks of Enterprises and Local Development*, Paris: OECD Territorial Development, pp. 23–51.

Sabel, C.F and J. Zeitlin (2012), 'Experimentalist governance', in D. Levi-Faur (ed.), *Oxford Handbook of Governance*, Oxford, UK: Oxford University Press.

Singh, J. (2005), 'Collaborative networks as determinants of knowledge diffusion patterns', *Management Science*, **51**(5), 756–70.

Spradley, J.P. (1979), *The Ethnographic Interview*, Michigan, IL: Wadsworth Group.

Stake, R.E. (1998), 'Case studies', in N.K. Denzin and Y. Lincoln (eds), *Strategies of Qualitative Inquiry*, London: Sage.

Stark, D. (2009), *The Sense of Dissonance: Accounts of Worth in Economic Life*, Princeton, NJ: Princeton University Press.

Taylor, F.W. (1911), *Principles of Scientific Management*, New York: HarperCollins.

Van Maanen, J. (1988), *Tales of the Field*, Chicago, IL: University of Chicago Press.

Wenger, E. (1997), *Communities of Practice*, Oxford, UK: Oxford University Press.

Wenger, E. (2000), 'Communities of practice and social learning systems', *Organization*, **7**(2), 225–46.

20. Making innovations work locally: the role of creativity

Antonella La Rocca, Adeline Hvidsten and Thomas Hoholm

INTRODUCTION

In large organizational systems, new ideas are often understood to be developed into large-scale innovations following a classical view of innovation and diffusion processes comprising a series of discrete and rational steps (Dopson, 2005). However, previous studies have shown that when innovations are embedded in practice (May, 2013), they follow different pathways in their translation into local contexts and established local practices (Nicolini, 2010a), impacting the development of the innovation itself (for example, Engesmo and Tjora, 2006; Mørk et al., 2006; Jensen and Aanestad, 2007). As a consequence, scholars have stressed the importance of involving end users in the innovation process (Oudshoorn and Pinch, 2003) to align it better with the needs of local users and to make it flexible, enabling adaptation to local use. In this chapter innovation refers to the interrelated set of practices that are changed, or in more radical endeavors, replace the old practices. The 'core' of an innovation may be recognized as tangible (product, technology, etc.) or non-tangible (service, business model, organizing process, etc.). In practice, however, the introduction of new ideas to workplaces always involves both social and material elements in the process of changing, replacing, and relating several interrelated practices. In line with Chapter 12 of this volume, 'Creativity that works: implementing discovery' by Arne Carlsen and Liisa Välikangas, we believe that creativity and working with new ideas are ongoing processes that should not be seen as limited to the initial phases of innovation processes. In this chapter, we explore the local and creative work of mutually adapting innovation and related work practices during the introduction of electronic exchange of patient information among healthcare professionals. We argue that creativity is a condition for the introduction of innovations, particularly in achieving the local adaptations necessary to ensure the actual use of the innovations in practice.

SCOPE FOR CREATIVITY IN INNOVATION PROCESSES

Creativity, commonly associated with *novel* ideas that are both *useful* and *appropriate* (Amabile, 1996; Ekvall, 1996; Oldham and Cummings, 1996; Martins and Terblanche, 2003; Paulus and Nijstad, 2003; Young and Moultrie, 2009), is regarded as the fuel for innovation and it is generally accepted that there is no innovation without creativity (McLean, 2005). Regarding creativity as fuel might give the impression that it is needed throughout the innovation journey, but still the most common perspective is that creativity is fuzzy front-end work, manifesting itself in the idea generation stage of an innovation process. True to this, in a recent literature review on the topic, the link between creativity and innovation has been explained in these terms: '[creativity] refers to idea generation and innovation refers to the subsequent stages of implementing ideas' (Anderson et al., 2014, p. 1298).

The context in which creativity happens is regarded as important for understanding the dynamics of creativity in organizations (Woodman et al., 1993). Approaches focusing on the context of creativity have tried to explain the link between different organizational factors that enhance creativity in individuals (Amabile, 1996; Andriopoulos, 2001), creative organizational cultures (Martins and Terblanche, 2003) and climates (Ekvall, 1996), as well as the interplay between the individual, groups, and the organization (Woodman et al., 1993).

Complementing these approaches, Csikszentmihalyi and Sawyer (1995) argue that innovation and creativity should be seen as 'traits of the whole organization'. Furthermore, Hargadon and Bechky (2006) found that creative individuals often acknowledge that their accomplishments are collective. The notion of collective creativity moves beyond the individual level of analysis and is based on the notion that creativity is inherently social, although individual contributions are not ignored (ibid.). Such an approach holds that creativity is a process of solving problems, in which no single individual can be credited for coming up with the solution all by themselves.

Paulus (2002) views creativity as a cyclical and recursive process of idea generation and implementation and argues that without an idea, there will be no innovation to implement. Several scholars have argued that innovation is not a linear process (for example, Van de Ven et al., 2000); rather, it follows multiple paths, proliferates in many ideas and, as a result of contrasting forces, is continuously mutating (Hoholm and Olsen, 2012). Hartley et al. (2012) argue that creating meaning, as well as shaping users' preferences relating to innovation, are important creative activities, not restricted to the early phases of idea development. This resonates well with practice-based studies (for example, Nicolini, 2010b) proposing that creativity and change are needed throughout the innovation process and that innovation tends to change the way people act and think.

In this chapter we use some examples to illustrate how creativity may be observed throughout the innovation process; indeed, creative ideas and actions are needed to realize a new solution and introduce it, as well as to overcome resistance and to mutually adapt the innovation and the involved set of practices.

METHOD

This study is part of a larger longitudinal research project investigating change within and across healthcare organizations when introducing new electronic messaging and mobile solutions. Empirically, the investigation relies mainly on qualitative fieldwork methods, in particular, ethnography. The data used in this chapter originate from three full days of observation at a unit providing home nursing services in a district of Oslo, as well as 19 interviews with different healthcare actors. We interviewed four nurses/ heads of divisions working at different wards at Hospital H (which was the first in Norway to adopt the new ICT-based messaging system). We also interviewed four nurses in four related municipalities working at the so-called 'ordering office', which is the unit that has the authority to decide what care services a patient will need when discharged from hospital. At the home-care unit, we participated in the unit's meetings, observing workers' daily routines before and in-between their visits to patients. We also observed the work of the unit's coordinator office and interviewed eight employees about the use of various tools in the workplace – personal digital assistants (PDAs), work lists, planning software, electronic messages – and their translation into practice. In addition, we interviewed three electronic medical records system consultants employed in the IT service unit of Oslo Municipality at a training meeting they held in the home-care unit. The interviews, all lasting between 40 and 60 minutes, have been recorded and transcribed. The collected data were analyzed without the use of any specific software in order to identify instances of creativity in which users deploy different technological innovations – with their possible shortcomings – in their daily working activities.

INSTANCES OF CREATIVITY

While there are national standards for ICT-based coordination in health-care in Norway, wards at the hospital as well as staff in the different municipalities face the complex task of implementing new ICT solutions into different local contexts and practices. In our case examples, various healthcare professionals have to cope with the lack of alignment between standardized technologies and local practices, which must be adapted in different ways. In some cases, practitioners even have to use old and new solutions in parallel, requiring them to creatively manage adaptations in their respective practices. In order to overcome these challenges we observed three different types of 'creative coping'.

Coping with Mismatch in User Needs (Sharing of Functional and Medical Information)

Electronic health and care messages are sent between hospitals and munici-palities during a patient's hospital stay to provide updated information so that the municipality can plan and decide what municipal healthcare services to offer a patient on discharge. Seven types of messages are sent from and received by a module integrated in each actor's electronic patient journal (EPJ). This system implies a largely different way of communicating among various units and actors than the previous combined solution of fax and telephone, when messages were sent anonymously via fax and health profes-sionals had to call recipients to identify patients. After the formal and rela-tively successful, introduction of these messages between our case hospital and its related municipalities, several problems remained in terms of content/ information contained in the messages circulating between the parties and how well the actors involved understood each other's information needs.

This problem has been addressed in one of the wards in our studied hos-pital, where a local solution was developed in a cross-departmental project related to the patient pathway for a serious pulmonary disease. The ward was not satisfied with the format of the standardized electronic messages. One nurse pointed out that she understands the messages have to be stand-ardized, but they do not fit the way the departmental staff work – they are too complex in some aspects and lacking in others. In her experience, they had to use a 'dialogue function' to request more information – up to ten dialogue messages for each health information message. However, this means information is stored only in a dialogue string attached to the message and not in the message itself. In the next instance, then, it takes more time to communicate than before and to browse through all the previous dialogues looking for information.

The nurse participated in the pulmonary disease project, in which participants from the municipal service offices, patients and nurses from different divisions specified what kind of information they wished to receive from each other in the messages. Through this collaborative project the two 'levels' of care, specialist and primary care, established mutual respect for their information needs, which elsewhere in the sector is often a challenge. In the municipal healthcare units, the staff need specific information about the functionality of the patients in their daily lives. Such information is important in deciding where the patient should live and what kind of services and equipment should be provided after release from the hospital. The hospital treats the patient for a limited time and is more concerned with the medical/diagnostic information that will make their job of healing the patient possible. Because of the different needs, broadly speaking, the two levels of care speak two different languages: functional and medical.

To bridge this gap, the nurse created a 'messaging guide' to be used in the department, with the aim of filling out more of the required information in the electronic message so that less dialogue messages would be sent. The messaging guide is a little laminated card, just big enough to fit in the hospital nurses' pockets when they are walking around the division. It includes all the information the municipal actors in the project said they would need in a case where the patient suffered a certain pulmonary disease.

The card was implemented relatively quickly, as it could be produced and reproduced in the ward. As such, the electronic messaging solution was supported by a simple, cheap, flexible, and analog paper-based tool (paradoxically the messages were implemented for the sector to become 'paperless'). The laminated paper card has proved effective, shifting the focus towards the quality of the content in messages and resulting in fewer requests for additional information.

Creating New, Unintended Use (Negotiating Service Offer)

A government reform to enhance coordination between healthcare providers shifted resources, particularly by moving significant amounts (NOK5 billion) from hospital funding to the municipalities, thus giving more power to the municipalities, in principle. A hospital is a specialized healthcare service and 'expert power' comes with this distinction. As the sector is still suffering from silo organizing and power hierarchies, the redistribution of resources resulting from the reform has upset the balance of power.

As part of the Coordination Reform the new rules require the municipality to pay a fine of NOK4500 for every 24 hours a patient stays at the hospital after he or she has been declared 'ready for discharge'. Defining the patient as ready for discharge is done through the hospital sending the municipality a 'Notice of patient ready for discharge' electronic message. This message can be withdrawn by the hospital later, in case the patient's condition changes, using the 'Withdrawal of patient ready for discharge' message.

The moment the patient is ready for discharge and the municipality has been notified, the 'ownership' of the patient shifts from the hospital to the municipality. While the municipality is responsible for paying if it cannot offer a local healthcare service, it is also solely its decision what service should be offered to the patient.

Nurses working at the ordering office in the municipality have to decide what services patients in their municipality should be offered by different municipal service providers (in other words, short-term placement at nursing homes or home-care services). This is done upon communication with the hospital and visits to patients who are admitted in order to evaluate their functional status (technically called activities of daily living – ADL). These decisions, however, are often preceded by a sharp negotiation going on, partially in the dialogue strings of messages between the municipality and the hospital, partially by phone and partially during joint meetings at the hospital's ward where the patient is hospitalized. As the municipality holds the formal legal power to make decisions, this was somewhat unexpected.

The most prominent example we observed involved a patient who was in the hospital while we visited one of the municipal ordering offices. The patient was ready to be discharged, but was still in hospital. In the dialogue messages, the hospital had argued that the patient was to receive short-term placement in a nursing home, as she was not fit to stay at home alone. The nurse we interviewed was quite irritated. She had gone to the hospital to make an evaluation and was adamant this patient had no problem living alone – which was the patient's own wish as well. The hospital had sent the electronic message 'ready for discharge' on Friday, but upon asking the nurse what service they would offer (in a dialogue string) and getting this response, they immediately sent the withdrawal message. They then performed their own functional tests for a couple of days, before sending the results that supported their argument. The nurse was frustrated, 'I know this test, I saw this patient and she would not have failed'. But since the hospital had withdrawn the discharge message and performed their test, she could no longer argue with them.

Combined Use (Coordinating Service Provision Locally)

As part of our study we observed a home-care unit in one of Oslo's city districts, to see the responses of the staff to the introduction of a new technological innovation. In particular, we aimed to observe how users coped in their daily work with the (mis)match between old and new artifacts/practices and with the possible shortcomings of the new technologies in place. The unit has 17 permanent workers as well as several part-time and ad hoc workers, catering to approximately 200 patients. The workers in the unit are nurses, nursing assistants, and unskilled workers. The unit has a unit leader and a coordinator, who are responsible for administrative and logistics work and have no direct contact with patients. The setting is characterized by strict budgets and very tight time frames for the workers' visits to the patients' homes. Local information exchange and coordination of service provision are major concerns to perform the job with the necessary efficiency while ensuring the ongoing well-being of the patients. It is very important that information is exchanged among workers as they do not visit the same patient each time and if healthcare information is not updated in the EPJ and shared collectively it could, in the worst-case scenario, be fatal.

The unit's routine is to meet three times a day in the meeting room. Every day the coordinator creates an individual schedule for each worker for the following day in the EPJ. The schedule includes instructions on which patients a worker should visit and when and how many minutes each visit should take. These lists are then printed out and given to the workers. Each worker visits approximately 20 patients every day and each visit must be documented in the EPJ.

The work lists were supposed to be a temporary solution as the unit was one of the first in the district to get personal digital assistants (PDAs). However, the PDAs often fail and are unreliable. Therefore, the unit has not adopted them and is now waiting for new smartphones to finally replace the paper work lists (at least this is the ambition). The idea of the PDA was to provide communication with the next of kin or GP while at the patients' home, to access updated lists of medicine and the EPJ, as well as making notes to be directly stored in the EPJ. Currently, notes are taken on the paper work lists, which must be transferred to the EPJ on the computer. The paper work lists do not offer all the features of a PDA. Under this condition, workers in the unit have to be creative in their coordination efforts. Each morning each worker is given a personal list and attends the morning report meeting where information is shared. We experienced some problems with the distribution of patients: workers did not have the right competencies; they had too many visits for the time allocated to them and not enough cars. Hence, patients had to be redistributed among the workers. The solution is to manually move a patient's name from one list to another by cutting, pasting, ripping, taping, and clipping anything that is at hand.

During the lunch meeting, we observed that many workers have questions about their patients and need to consult others before documenting it in the EPJ. This problem has been solved through a display screen, where the unit can access the EPJ collectively. When uncertain about the condition of a patient just visited, the workers tend to share the information with colleagues and the coordinator in order to reach a joint decision. If there is a change in the level of the type of care a patient needs, this is documented in the EPJ while the others round the table check the screen, giving suggestions on everything from spelling to medical information.

MODES OF CREATIVITY FOR MAKING INNOVATIONS WORK: EXPANDING, REINTERPRETING AND ORCHESTRATING

Our examples illustrate how creativity serves the function of adapting an innovation to local practices and needs and vice versa and is not related only to the idea generation part of an innovation process. From the three examples illustrated above, we can identify three different modes of creativity for making innovations work locally. We have labeled these as: 'expanding', 'reinterpreting', and 'orchestrating'.

In the first example, we saw that a standardized electronic messaging solution was unable to cater for the specific local needs of various practitioners. In this example, the main purpose of the innovation – the sharing of functional and medical information among healthcare practitioners – could not be achieved in a satisfactory way just by using the solution according to the given instructions (intended use). The standard gave a format, but not a mutual understanding of information needs or a language for sharing functional information the municipalities needed. Hospital users found the solution too time consuming, especially when the introduction of the 'dialogue function' increased the number of inquiries from the municipalities. For municipal users the solution did not contain the kind of information they really needed, namely non-medical descriptions of how the patient would be able to cope in her or his daily life and hence what level of service had to be provided. The creative response to this by the pulmonary division was to *expand* the innovation to accommodate other functions. The result was a low-tech solution that helps to fulfill information needs in a practical way, constructed through involving the perspectives of various stakeholders from both the hospital and municipality. The use of low-tech artifacts to offset the shortcomings of more high-tech solutions is also a powerful way to understand what should be elaborated upon in future updates of the electronic messaging system (Wears et al., 2007). Without taking the long and uncertain route through the bureaucracy to change the national standard, local practitioners were able to exploit and adjust the standardized solution to fit local user needs, as well as to create better awareness and understanding of the needs of others and to adjust local practices to improve the quality of information accordingly. Hence, 'expanding' may be a potential creative response when the need for mutual adaptation of innovations and practices is encountered.

In the second example, we see how a specific function of the new communication system – 'the dialogue' – has been perceived and used by health professionals as a room for negotiation in relation to what service should be provided to the individual patient, thereby giving to the actors *a novel* and *factual* space for handling power relation dynamics. The coordination reform clearly aimed to discharge patients earlier compared to the past and reduce unnecessary admissions. Hospital beds are assumed to be more expensive than municipal service offerings and patients are assumed to be better off with more services closer to – or inside – their homes. Similar to other studies emphasizing the link between change of practices and power relations (for example, Nicolini, 2006), this movement of roles, responsibilities, and resources towards the municipalities by the government implies a strengthening of the municipal agencies' formal authority, while potentially undermining the expert power of the hospitals. In this context, the new dialogue function in the electronic messaging solution were *reinterpreted* and made an arena for negotiating the authority and power relations over singular patients' service offerings. On the one hand, the municipalities were frustrated when the hospital personnel gave rather insistent advice and manipulated patients' discharge dates to enforce their suggestions of service offerings. On the other hand, the hospitals did not seem to like the loss of influence, because they regard themselves as the experts to be trusted regarding the actual care needs of their patients. While this use is unintended and clearly problematic in terms of having such discussions documented in patient journals, it also reflects a real need to discuss the 'right' service to be offered among the different practitioners. In our experience, at least some of the practitioners at the hospitals found a way to manipulate the power relationship and to influence service decisions. Thus, 'reinterpreting' (a feature of) an innovation – the result of a sensemaking process (cf. Rauth and Nabergoj, Chapter 16 this volume) – can be identified as an important response when translating innovation locally. In our case, users in the municipalities have seen the new communication technology as the occasion/means to attempt transcending traditional primary–secondary care relationships, in which the hospital has always been the prevailing actor, while users at the hospital try to defend their privileged position.

In the third example, we have seen in action the 'frontline' of the service providers who have the least 'voice' in ICT-related innovation processes. We saw how they, without much influence on the technical solutions provided, had to cope with the coordination of their daily work practices with whatever means they had at their disposal. Equipped with a number of tools that were less than ideal, in an extremely stressful work situation, these home-care practitioners had developed a rather sophisticated and highly localized assemblage of artifacts and practices to *orchestrate* the necessary exchange of information and coordination of activities. The many potential shortcomings of electronic exchange of information were fully visible here. Indeed, paper lists resulted in more flexible and practical tools compared to PCs and PDAs. Still, the paper-based information had to be re-inscribed into the electronic patient journal back at the office and compensating technologies such as a big computer screen on the wall were employed to enhance the formal and informal exchange of information during lunchtimes and meetings.

This way of coping with the introduction of innovations by orchestrating an assemblage of artifacts and activities/practices shows how innovations often may require changes and adjustments; not only change of the innovation itself but also of a number of inter-related practices, locally and in the wider networks of practice as discussed in Chapter 21 'From breakthroughs in knowledge to integration in medical practices' (Mørk and Hoholm). In this particular setting, the electronic tools cannot easily be evaluated as 'successful' innovations in the sense of providing value to the users. As shown in other studies (Xiao et al., 2001; Bardram and Bossen, 2005) digitalization does not necessarily replace 'low-tech' solutions; rather, one may see 'layers' of old and new technologies in use complementing each other. The creative response of local users in the care unit was partial use alongside the *orchestration* of a set of additional tools and activities to enable the coordination of their work practice.

CONCLUDING REMARKS

Acknowledging that large-scale innovations will always be experienced as incomplete in meeting all local needs, we have sought to reinforce and develop the argument (Paulus, 2002; Oudshoorn and Pinch, 2003) that the successful implementation of ideas – in its performative sense as discussed in Chapter 1 'Capitalizing on creativity: on enablers and barriers' (Černe et al.) – is always conditioned by ongoing creative efforts by involved users. Moreover, the creative interplay between numerous user groups is likely to have a significant impact on the 'final' shape of the innovation, as it implies mutual shaping of innovations and practices, not just in the early developmental stage, but also throughout the process of introducing an innovation across multiple user groups and organizations.

REFERENCES

Amabile, T. (1996), *Creativity in Context: Update to the Social Psychology of Creativity*, Boulder, CO: Westview Press.

Anderson, N., K. Potočnik and J. Zhou (2014), 'Innovation and creativity in organizations: A state-of-the-science review, Prospective commentary and guiding framework', *Journal of Management*, **40**(5), 1297–333.

Andriopoulos, C. (2001), 'Determinants of organisational creativity: A literature review', *Management Decision*, **39**(10), 834–41.

Bardram, J.E. and C. Bossen (2005), 'A web of coordinative artifacts: Collaborative work at a hospital ward', in *Proceedings of the 2005 International Conference on Supporting Group Work*, New York: ACM Press.

Csikszentmihalyi, M. and K. Sawyer (1995), 'Shifting the focus from individual to organizational creativity', in C.M. Ford and D.A. Gioia (eds), *Creative Action in Organizations: Ivory Tower Visions and Real World Voices*, Thousand Oaks, CA: Sage, pp. 167–73.

Dopson, S. (2005), 'The diffusion of medical innovations: Can figurational sociology contribute?' *Organization Studies*, **26**(8), 1125–44.

Ekvall, G. (1996), 'Organizational climate for creativity and innovation', *European Journal of Work and Organizational Psychology*, **5**(1), 105–23.

Engesmo, J. and A.H. Tjora (2006), 'Documenting for whom? A symbolic interactionist analysis of technologically induced changes of nursing handovers', *New Technology, Work and Employment*, **21**(2), 176–89.

Hargadon, A.B. and B.A. Bechky (2006), 'When collections of creatives become creative collectives: A field study of problem solving at work', *Organization Science*, **17**(4), 484–500.

Hartley, J., J. Potts, T. Flew, S. Cunningham, M. Keane and J. Banks (2012), *Key Concepts in Creative Industries*, London: Sage.

Hoholm, T. and P.I. Olsen (2012), 'The contrary forces of innovation', *Industrial Marketing Management*, **41**(2), 344–56.

Jensen, T.B. and M. Aanestad (2007), 'Hospitality and hostility in hospitals: A case study of an EPR adoption among surgeons', *European Journal of Information Systems*, **16**(6), 672–80.

Martins, E. and F. Terblanche (2003), 'Building organisational culture that stimulates creativity and innovation', *European Journal of Innovation Management*, **6**(1), 64–74.

May, C. (2013), 'Agency and implementation: Understanding the embedding of healthcare innovations in practice', *Social Science and Medicine*, **78**, 26–33.

McLean, L.D. (2005), 'Organizational culture's influence on creativity and innovation: A review of the literature and implications for human resource development', *Advances in Developing Human Resources*, **7**(2), 226–46.

Mørk, B.E., T. Hoholm and M. Aanestad (2006), 'Constructing, enacting and packaging innovations', *European Journal of Innovation Management*, **9**(4), 444–65.

Nicolini, D. (2006), 'The work to make telemedicine work: A social and articulative view', *Social Science and Medicine*, **62**(11), 2754–67.

Nicolini, D. (2010a), 'Medical innovation as a process of translation: A case from the field of telemedicine', *British Journal of Management*, **21**(4), 1011–26.

Nicolini, D. (2010b), 'Zooming in and out: Studying practices by switching theoretical lenses and trailing connections', *Organization Studies*, **30**(12), 1391–418.

Oldham, G.R. and A. Cummings (1996), 'Employee creativity: Personal and contextual factors at work', *The Academy of Management Journal*, **39**(3), 607–34.

Oudshoorn, N.E.J. and T.J. Pinch (2003), *How Users Matter: The Co-construction of Users and Technology*, Cambridge, MA: The MIT Press.

Paulus, P.B. (2002), 'Different ponds for different fish: A contrasting perspective on team innovation', *Applied Psychology*, **51**(3), 394–9.

Paulus, P.B. and B.A. Nijstad (2003), *Group Creativity: Innovation through Collaboration*, New York: Oxford University Press.

Van de Ven, A.H., H.L. Angle and M.S. Poole (2000), *Research on the Management of Innovation: The Minnesota Studies*, Oxford, UK: Oxford University Press.

Wears, R., S.J. Perry, S. Wilson, J. Galliers and J. Fone (2007), 'Emergency department status boards: User-evolved artefacts for inter- and intra-group coordination', *Cognition, Technology and Work*, **9**(3), 163–70.

Woodman, R.W., J.E. Sawyer and R.W. Griffin (1993), 'Toward a theory of organizational creativity', *The Academy of Management Review*, **18**(2), 293–321.

Xiao, Y., J.M. Lasome, C.F. Mackenzie and S. Faraj (2001), 'Cognitive properties of a whiteboard: A case study in a trauma centre', in *Proceedings of the Seventh European Conference on Computer-Supported Cooperative Work*, Bonn.

Young, A. and J. Moultrie (2009), 'Exploratory study of organizational creativity in creative organizations', *Creativity and Innovation Management*, **18**(4), 299–314.

21. From breakthroughs in knowledge to integration in medical practices

Bjørn Erik Mørk and Thomas Hoholm

INTRODUCTION

This chapter is about how novel ideas and new practices in healthcare are created and implemented. Progress in medicine depends on highly specialized professionals who contribute to further developments in their fields of expertise. Even though around 80 percent of all treatments offered in 2010 were developed between 2005 and 2010, 70 percent of the employees' competence was acquired before 2005 (Hansen, 2004 in Grund, 2006). As March (1991) underscores, being able to effectively exploit established knowledge while also finding room for exploring novel ideas is not trivial. The increasing use of advanced technology changes professional work towards more cross-disciplinary collaboration (Fenwick et al., 2012). Important breakthroughs in knowledge fail to become translated into use because they lack alignment with established practices, challenge disciplinary boundaries or threaten established power relations (Swan et al., 2002; Newell et al., 2006; Mørk et al., 2010). Due to their training and culture, medical experts are often convinced that their specialty is the most capable of solving problems. Hence, whenever someone attempts to meddle in their practices with new ideas or by trying to implement changes this will meet opposition (Seeman, 1999, p. 113). This chapter will therefore address the following research question: Which practices are important for putting new knowledge into use in healthcare institutions?

Theoretically, we position our study within practice-based studies (PBS) (Nicolini et al., 2003; Gherardi, 2006; Nicolini, 2011, 2012) and we will apply the following three insights from PBS: that (1) practices are situated, (2) practices are socio-material, and (3) changing practices is political. Each of these three insights will be presented in more detail in the review.

Empirically, this chapter will utilize two longitudinal case studies from a medical R&D department at Oslo University Hospital. This department was established to develop new practices, compare them with established practices, and study the organizational, economic and social consequences of implementing changes. Through combining the expertise of different disciplines, novel ideas and new practices are explored.

RELATED RESEARCH

PBS is not a single unified theory, but several streams of research sharing certain assumptions about the relationship between practicing, knowing, and innovating. PBS takes practice as the unit of analysis, not individuals, groups, organizations, fields or populations. Even though practices can be discussed in isolation, they are always *connected* to other practices (Nicolini, 2012). We will now look closer at three main insights from PBS:

- *Practices are situated socially, culturally, and historically.* In contrast to literature seeing knowledge as a context-free and abstract substance, PBS talks about how 'knowing in practice' is a practical accomplishment (Orlikowski, 2002). As Nicolini (2011) underscores, knowing is sustained in practice. Knowing how to skillfully perform a practice means that practitioners understand how they are accountable to a community of practice (Brown and Duguid, 1991; Lave and Wenger, 1991). Whereas sharing practices and making incremental improvements of existing practices within communities or within 'networks of practices' (Brown and Duguid, 2001) works well, collaborating and negotiating with other communities is more demanding. Yet, when competencies and practices are exposed to other fields of expertise, novel ideas are developed and potentially implemented (Wenger, 2000). These challenges are demanding, as Mørk et al. (2008) found, partly because different communities belong to different 'epistemic cultures' (Knorr Cetina, 1999).
- *Practices are socio-material.* While previous organizational research has often just focused on the social issues, PBS has emphasized how social and material aspects play an important role in organizations (Dopson, 2005; Orlikowski, 2007; Nicolini, 2010). This is particularly evident within two streams of PBS, namely sociology of translation, which underscores how both human and non-human actors are important, and activity theory with its focus on objects (Nicolini, 2012). Expertise is not only carried through humans, but also through artifacts that have their own history and that to different degrees establish a relationship between groups (Mørk et al., 2015). PBS therefore underscores that change is what characterizes organizations rather than stability, and innovation processes are therefore highly contingent and complex (Nicolini et al., 2003).

- *Changing practices is political.* As Nicolini (2007) underscores, whenever practices are changing, this empowers some actors while disempowering others. This important insight has been downplayed in many studies of communities of practice (Mørk et al., 2010; Contu, 2014). The process of moving a novel idea into implementation depends on the relations between all the involved actors. It is very likely that such processes are fraught with conflicts, and the outcome of any such controversy throughout the process implies a greater or lesser chance of succeeding. New practices in healthcare can be 'competence destroying' (Christensen et al., 2000), and some actors may lose both prestige and economic resources. Consequently, professionals involved in innovations are normally well aware of the risks involved if changes are implemented (Swan et al., 2002).

METHODOLOGY

This chapter draws upon our research from 2000 to 2015 on innovation processes at the Intervention Centre (IVC), a medical R&D department at Oslo University Hospital. The IVC was established in 1996 to be a 'common toolbox on neutral ground' for different disciplines working within the areas of minimally invasive and image-guided surgery. The IVC also compares new practices with the established ones before considering implementation elsewhere. Over 80 people from 18 nationalities are affiliated with the IVC. From 1996 to 2013, over 12 000 patients were treated, over 20 new procedures were developed, 35 PhDs and 50 Master's theses were produced, around 350 peer-reviewed publications were written, 20 patents were developed and so forth (Mørk et al., 2012).

We will present here two innovation projects. The first case is a minimally invasive treatment of prostate cancer, while the second case is a catheter-based technique for treating patients with valvular diseases (transcatheter aortic valve implantation – TAVI). We chose these two for this chapter because (1) they represent important knowledge breakthroughs; (2) they require close inter-professional collaboration; and (3) implementing them is demanding since they have economic consequences and they challenge established power relations between disciplines.

To construct our data, we used extensive observations (including over 200 procedures), interviews and document analysis. From August 2000 to January 2007, the first author did an ethnographic study at the Centre and was there full-time. After that time, we participated in procedures, meetings and seminars. In total, more than 60 interviews, lasting on average 60 minutes each (all fully transcribed), were conducted. The topics discussed include (but are not limited to) roles of the informants, collaboration, the way innovation projects are organized, how the ideas underpinning the innovations came about, how the technologies and practices change over time, collaboration with other sites and so forth. In addition, video and document analyses of protocols, presentations, minutes and publications were done.

The analysis process has been iterative throughout the whole study. We have detailed field notes and several hundred pages of transcriptions from the interviews. The material has been coded in several rounds on the basis of topics that came up as particularly interesting[1] for understanding collaboration, learning, and innovation. We also discussed our interpretations with other researchers and our informants.

FINDINGS

This section presents findings from the two cases. Table 21.1 provides a summary of the two cases, while Table 21.2 specifically links the two cases to four different practices and types of knowing.

Prostatectomy Project (1999–2000)

This project aimed at developing a new minimally invasive laparoscopic technique[2] for treating prostate cancer. In 1999, some Norwegian surgeons got this idea while participating in a laparoscopy course in France. Traditionally, urologists are responsible for treatment of the prostate. In this case, the team also consisted of urologists and gastro-surgeons skilled in laparoscopy. Some days after returning to Norway, they performed the first procedure on patients (Mørk et al., 2010, p. 581).

After four to five procedures, the research group was able to drastically reduce the operation time by several hours by drawing upon the expertise of the different actors. The project was organized with a cross-disciplinary team that included a surgeon from the IVC, a surgeon from another hospital, two urologists from Rikshospitalet, an engineer, surgical nurses, and anesthesiology nurses. Since the medical domain was within urology, the project leader emphasized that he was a laparoscopist who could help the urologists. He thereby indicated that he was an expert in one field, but that the urologists were experts in another. The project was conducted at the Centre to give them a more flexible operation program and access to high-tech equipment, and because they had done many laparoscopic procedures earlier. By organizing the project with experts from different fields and

Capitalizing on creativity at work

Table 21.1   Summary of the two cases

Key Elements	Case 1: Prostatectomy Case	Case 2: TAVI Case
Time	1999–2000	2009–ongoing
Domain	Keyhole surgery for treating patients with prostate cancer. If untreated, these patients have a high risk of having cancer cells spread (metastasis) to other parts of the body, thereby increasing chances of passing away	Catheter-based technique for treating patients with a severe valvular disease. If untreated there is a 50% chance that the patients will die within two years
Number of patients	Ten	260 from when it started to 31 Dec. 2014 Plan to perform 160 procedures in 2015
Site for doing the procedures	IVC as a high-tech site with an operation room (often referred to as the 'laparoscopy room') well suited for laparoscopic surgery (i.e., keyhole surgery in the abdomen) on 'neutral ground'. The latter means that it is not owned by one particular medical discipline	IVC as a high-tech site with an advanced hybrid room (surgical operation room with advanced imaging equipment on 'neutral ground' not owned by one particular medical discipline). The hybrid room's higher safety and sterility standards enable them to quickly change from a catheter-based procedure to regular heart valve surgery if something unexpected occurs
Main internal and external actors involved	Cross-disciplinary team with a surgeon from the IVC, a surgeon from another hospital, two urologists from Rikshospitalet, an anesthesiologist, an engineer, surgical nurses, and anesthesiology nurses	Initially, cross-disciplinary team with cardiac surgeons, cardiologists, anesthesiologists, radiologist (internally and from another hospital), nurses (operation and anesthesia)

Table 21.1   (continued)

Key Elements	Case 1: Prostatectomy Case	Case 2: TAVI Case
Main internal and external actors involved	Later, no actors from Rikshospitalet were involved, while the urologists from the other hospital were trained by a highly skilled group of actors doing the procedure in France	Later, no radiologists were involved, and new cardiologists and support personnel enrolled Four technology providers, as well as other hospitals where doctors from the IVC have either been in the role of learners or in the role as experts teaching how to do TAVI
Accomplishments due to important breakthroughs in knowledge	Offering minimally invasive treatment to new patient groups and dramatically reduced operation time through practicing together; patients could go home several days earlier than with regular surgery and with less pain. IVC surgeon became proctor (an expert teaching at other sites) on this procedure	Over 260 inoperable patients have been treated. The team has gained lots of experience with how to skillfully perform TAVI from different access points and with different technologies. Several improvements in the procedure have also been made. Several actors from the team have worked as proctors at other sites in the USA and in Europe
Implementation challenges	Access to patients, lack of communication, collaboration across specialties and sites	Knowing when to use the different technologies, negotiating how to work together as a team, receiving sufficient funding, getting access to the postoperative unit and having enough resources (in particular anesthesiology) to scale up the activities from doing two to three TAVI procedures per day

Table 21.1   (continued)

Key Elements	Case 1: Prostatectomy Case	Case 2: TAVI Case
Outcome	The initial knowledge breakthroughs about treating patients with prostate cancer with keyhole surgery have successfully been translated into use on another site. The enrolled hospital was able to learn the new procedure through another constellation, while the IVC was not included in bringing the innovation forward when the other hospital withdrew from the project. Several Norwegian patients were treated in France	The initial knowledge breakthroughs gained elsewhere in treating patients with valvular disease with the catheter-based technique have successfully been translated into use at Oslo University Hospital. They plan to operate on 160 patients in 2015, and the procedure has been implemented at the hospital through a series of important breakthroughs in knowledge, enabling them to do the procedure faster and more safely

departments, the Centre also sought to create a better grounding for later implementing the procedure elsewhere (ibid., p. 528).

Meanwhile the project group also understood that they needed access to more patients and decided to enroll another hospital. According to our informants, the newly enrolled hospital interpreted the location of the project at the Centre as a potential threat, even though it was always intended that the procedure was to be moved away from the Centre as soon as it had been developed. The aim of this new hospital was to become a National Centre of Expertise in this field, and, according to some of our informants, they therefore wanted to be in charge of developing the procedure. After just a few joint procedures, they withdrew from the project without informing the other partners of the rationale for their decision. As they were in control of the 'patient flow' they thereby ended the project (ibid., p. 583).

If we look closer at how the experts in this project dealt with reproducing established practices while simultaneously working creatively in new fields, we observe some interesting differences. The project leader is an internationally well-known expert within laparoscopy and emphasized that his role was to reproduce these practices, this time in the field of urology

Table 21.2 Overview of practices, types of knowing and empirical illustrations

Practices	Knowing in Practice	Empirical Illustrations – Prostatectomy	Empirical Illustrations – TAVI
1. Enacting expertise in well-established fields	Knowing how to perform advanced procedures within your own discipline	Surgeon doing laparoscopic surgery, urologists doing procedures within their domain 'The urologists were familiar with treating the prostate, whereas I had lots of experience with doing laparoscopic surgery'	Cardiac surgeons doing valve surgery, cardiologists doing catheter-based procedures, radiographers assisting during image-guided procedures and so forth 'In order to perform TAVI we depend on the expertise of cardiologists who know how to handle catheters, surgeons who know how to do valvular surgery, anesthesiologists who can keep the patient stable and nurses that can assist us'
2. Exploring novel practices (advanced procedures) in new fields	Knowing how to recombine the competencies from different disciplines: collaboration and experimentation	Urologists, surgeons, and anesthesiologist jointly doing the first procedures together and learning from the other disciplines. Hence, in some ways all of the involved actors became novices again rather than having their well-established roles as masters. Downplaying the role of one's own expertise to improve collaboration and as an attempt to avoid turf battles, is illustrated with the following quote: 'None of the other participants had much experience	The TAVI team conducting the TAVI procedures together (under close supervision of proctors representing the technology providers) 'I am not an expert. I am just a practitioner who has gained lot of experience through performing over 200 TAVIs'

Table 21.2 (continued)

Practices	Knowing in Practice	Empirical Illustrations – Prostatectomy	Empirical Illustrations – TAVI
		with laparoscopy, but we solved the problem in the way that I operated on the patient, and then we had several urologists present. They stood by and observed, and we discussed the way it should be done'	
3. Improving the practices (procedures) in new fields	Knowing which aspects of a procedure could potentially be improved (balance simultaneous experimentation and improvement work)	Through observing what the other team members did, discussing the results and making changes in the different steps of the procedure they were over time able to drastically reduce the operation time, and provide better pain-killing regime for the patient 'We were able to reduce the operation time drastically from spending a full day with the first patient towards completing the procedure in four to five hours with excellent results'	Through defining a 50/50 division in access points, both of the main groups are able to continuously get training to improve the procedure through having main responsibilities in some of the procedures, and through observing when others are in charge By using different technologies, the TAVI team members can learn new ways of doing the procedure. More recently, they have started exploring doing the procedure in the catheter lab (but for various reasons they soon decided to continue doing the procedure at the Centre), giving local anesthesia rather than general anesthesia, and several other changes have been made 'With more experience, we are more capable of choosing which patients should undergo TAVI, the right valve size, which access point to use and so forth'

| 4. Relating novel practices to wider networks of practice | Knowing how to weave together local expertise to the broader landscape of practice | Surgeon from the IVC was proctoring at other sites, and presented findings from the project at conferences (also within urology) and won a prize for his achievements. The newly enrolled hospital, on the other hand, became part of another network of practice where experts from France played a key role and which taught them how to perform the procedure. Hence, both the community initially starting the procedure and the later enrolled community could do the procedure, but in other constellations

'I went to Denmark, Russia and England to solve urological problems. I always underscored that I was there to help, and that they could watch on the screen every move I made. They were not afraid of my expertise' | Any site that is about to start doing TAVIs has to send their team to undergo training at the main site of the vendors. Thereafter, they have proctors (experts) from the vendors present during the first procedures. Later, actors from the IVC have also become proctors and supervised other sites doing TAVIs. One of the informants at the IVC also learned TAVI through an extended period at another Scandinavian hospital. Team members have also visited several other sites doing TAVI, have regular visits from technology providers to get updates about new breakthroughs in knowledge and also organize events where different sites can meet to exchange experiences

'Since we are familiar with how other sites are doing TAVI, we understand which changes could be relevant to explore locally. Examples of changes we have made due to this include using local anesthesia rather than general anesthesia, and avoiding surgical cutdown (an operation technique used by surgeons) because we can do it with an alternative technique closer to the one we use in cardiology' |

Source: Inspired by Orlikowski's (2002, p. 257) table on repertoire of practice in the Kappa case study.

together with the urologists. Interestingly enough, the project leader was later seen as an expert when he went to other countries to teach them how to do the procedure. He even won an award at a large urology conference (ibid.).

The actors involved from Rikshospitalet reproduced their urology practices, while also participating in exploring new ways of doing this procedure. The hospital that joined late in the project took a different approach to take charge of the procedure since they saw themselves as the experts. They decided to withdraw from the project due to several factors, such as professional boundaries, collaboration challenges, and national politics. The Ministry of Health had decided to establish a 'prostate bridge' to France, where Norwegian patients were to be treated there rather than in Norway. The urologists from the hospital that withdrew went to France to learn the procedure there, hence becoming national experts in a new field (ibid.).

Transcatheter Aortic Valve Implantation (TAVI) (2009–Present)

TAVI is a novel catheter-based technique for replacing the heart valve, as an alternative to open heart surgery. These patients are elderly and, if untreated, with a prognosis comparable to patients with aggressive cancer. The idea to perform TAVI at the Centre came some years before they started in 2009, but for various reasons it took time to start. In parallel, TAVI was becoming more popular internationally, and by 2014 more than 125 000 had undergone TAVI. The Centre has now treated approximately 260 patients.

Materiality plays a crucial role in TAVI procedures, with special valves, introducer systems and special operating rooms. The 'hybrid room' is a radiological examination theater for doing catheter-based procedures and a regular operation theater. Normally hospitals have two rooms belonging to different departments for this, which means that they must move the patient across sites in cases with complications.

TAVI is a complicated procedure that requires a much closer collaboration between different specializations than most other procedures, above all between cardiologists and cardiac surgeons, who both have much at stake in this area. Later, when the new procedure has been 'stabilized' as a practice, one of these groups may end up being in charge of the procedure. Surgeons lack experience with catheter-based techniques and with viewing screens throughout an entire procedure rather than looking down at the patient. Cardiologists, on the other hand, cannot do valvular surgery. Before, during, and after the procedure, different specialist nurses and radiographers have to collaborate and learn from others. The team is also large, initially often with 12–15 individuals in the room, but this has gradually been reduced to seven or eight. The TAVI procedure can be done in different ways, and whereas one approach is closer to cardiology, other approaches are more similar to surgery. In TAVI meetings where both the cardiologists and surgeons in the team attend, the TAVI team decides which approach is most suitable for each patient.

The TAVI project has been an interesting example of both partly reproducing well-known practices and development of new practices at the same time. On the one hand, all of the involved parties have experience with the parts of the procedures that resemble earlier practices. Yet, the novelty lies in combining the expertise of different specializations. It is interesting to see how TAVI illustrates well how practices are not only local, but also translocal. This is because to be allowed to start doing TAVIs, the different technology providers have developed advanced training programs that the whole TAVI team will have to undergo. They will go to the supplier's main center in Europe for some initial training, and some experts ('proctors') from the companies will be present during the first procedures. Hence the practices that they learn from the producers have to be reproduced locally, and they will then continuously seek to further improve their way of doing the procedure after these initial rounds. The TAVI team also visits other sites, and attends conferences. This enables them to learn how to do the procedure more effectively, when to use different types of valves from different producers with the best possible results and so forth (Mørk et al. 2015).

DISCUSSION

In our analysis of these two medical innovation case studies, we have identified four distinct 'innovation practices' that are central to the development and implementation of novel ideas, moving from knowledge breakthroughs to integration in practice: (1) enacting expertise in established fields; (2) exploring potential novel practices; (3) improving novel practices; and (4) relating novel practices to wider 'networks of practice' (Table 21.2). This is also linked to how, from PBS, we know that practices are situated, socio-material and political. The commonality of unexpected events during innovation means that these four practices may have to be performed in various orders, and with various degrees of overlap in time and space. Our argument is that each of these four practices is necessary to succeed with innovation in knowledge-intensive settings like medicine.

Practice 1: Enacting Expertise in Well-established Fields

Medicine has been subject to extreme specialization throughout the last decades, leading to organizing foremost based on which discipline practitioners belong to. This is useful for quality purposes and for enabling competent experimentation. However, disciplinary organizing may represent challenges to inter-disciplinary collaboration. Communities of practice (locally) and networks of practice (distributed/globally) within a field of expertise are important arenas for sharing practices and for incremental improvements (Lave and Wenger, 1991; Brown and Duguid, 1991, 2000; Wenger, 2000). While established practice is situated in a particular socio-material setting (Orlikowski, 2007), both our cases show how decisions about what counts as valid knowledge within a field is negotiated beyond the local setting.

To become a well-regarded expert within a highly specialized community of practice may take many years of dedicated training. Still, mastery of the established practice is necessary to have a position from which the exploration of novel solutions may be possible. First, at any point one must be able to return to established practice when the situation requires it. Second, the exploration of novel practices is partly about producing convincing arguments (Mørk et al., 2010), which may be difficult if lacking the ability of systematic comparison of old and new practice.

Practice 2: Exploring Advanced Procedures in New Fields

While expertise in a field is a necessary condition for creativity and innovation, it is clearly not enough. While having to maintain high expertise in their established practices, innovators also have to allocate time, energy, and resources into inter-disciplinary experimentation with novel solutions. To gain a legitimate position from which to engage with creativity and innovation in healthcare does not come easily. In many cases, this means that it is necessary for practitioners to be both expert practitioners in the established practice and expert innovators in collaborating and experimenting for coming up with novel solutions. These challenges mean that most experts prioritize incremental research and development work within their own specialized discipline, as this will be a faster and less risky path towards becoming recognized within the academic meritocracy of medicine. It is all the more demanding to maintain the expert role in the established practice (which itself is moving at a high pace) while at the same time investing heavily into the highly uncertain venture of more radical innovation. Sometimes this is solved through distributing tasks across the project team and through aligning with strategic stakeholders across units and organizations. As we recall, changing practices is indeed political (Nicolini, 2007).

Practice 3: Improving the Procedures in New Fields

Meanwhile, to develop and learn something radically new often requires significantly different processes and conditions than the continuous improvement of established practices one may find in well-established disciplines. The IVC provides a favorable socio-material setting for exploring new practices for several reasons: it gives access to advanced technology, it provides employees used to working cross-disciplinary and with exploring new practices, and it represents a 'neutral ground' where no discipline can make special claims. In general it can be difficult to mobilize support for making radical changes in healthcare due to lack of traditions, tough budgets, limited experience with cross-disciplinary collaboration and departmentalized organizing. The practice of improving the new practice includes the ability to identify areas for systematic incremental improvements, upgrading the novel solution, while simultaneously having to do more radical explorations in other areas of the same practice. Changing practices also often redefines the boundaries between communities (Mørk et al., 2010; Contu, 2014), and hence this requires continuous negotiations and that the participants need to be able to point at positive clinical outcomes to gain acceptance for the innovation in the wider community of practitioners. Since knowing in practice is a practical accomplishment that is situated socially, historically, and materially (Lave and Wenger, 1991; Nicolini, 2011) it comes as no surprise that implementing new practices is demanding (Orlikowski, 2002).

Practice 4: Relating Novel Practices to Wider Networks of Practice

This innovation practice is about the work of relating novel local practices to the wider, often global, networks of practice (Brown and Duguid, 2001), within which experts orient themselves. During innovation, we can expect processes of sharing, comparing, discussing, and adjusting practices within such wider networks. Hence, different development paths across different sites may lead to mutual exchange and learning.

In the first case, the crucial alliance was between experts in laparoscopy (for example, from the IVC, or later from the French hospital) and recognized urology departments. This is a political resource, as the latter were in control of patient flows and had the legitimate rights to perform urological procedures (Mørk et al., 2010). It was hard for both camps to admit being learners rather than experts in the cross-disciplinary project, hence evoking turf battles and (inter-)organizational politics.

In the second case, expertise from two highly different specializations was crucial to the project, as the practitioners could not know in advance how their expertise would be needed later. Through close collaboration and negotiations about how to proceed they have managed to figure out how to implement the TAVI procedure. Accordingly, the suppliers could develop effective organizing of training teams in the new procedures, organizing visits at other sites, and allowing some practitioners to work internationally, thereby also supporting professional networks. This is crucial since the expertise in doing TAVI is not solely held by a single practitioner, community or organization (Mørk et al., 2015).

To sum up, interaction across wider networks of practice is important for three purposes. First, it provides variation in learning when similar solutions are developed and tested under different conditions. Second, it is the arena for establishing 'standards'; that is, common descriptions of how to do the (new) procedure. Third, there is a need for adapting the innovation to fit (or be adaptable to) a wider and more varied set of interconnected practices (Newell et al., 2006).

CONCLUSION

Our study contributes to our understanding of challenges of moving from breakthroughs in knowledge to implementation. We have argued that PBS is a useful lens on this topic, since it emphasizes how practices are situated, are socio-material and that changing practices are political. From our analysis of these two case studies, we outlined a set of four interrelated innovation practices: enacting established practices, exploring novel practices, improving novel practices, and relating new practices to wider networks of practice. Following from our analysis, we would like to emphasize three implications for succeeding in implementing novel and creative ideas in practice.

First, if we view innovation fundamentally as a process of recombining knowing in practice, and of interaction between actors with diverse interests, we also see how and why innovation processes are so uncertain. While fully acknowledging the traditional expertise of our medical experts, they do not have the same kind of expertise related to the effects of recombination and interaction.

Second, innovating experts will often have to master both the current practice within their discipline and exploring the novel practices in new fields. Sometimes this has to be done simultaneously; other times practitioners have to move back to focusing on their traditional practices, and combine this with doing new sorts of procedures where they gradually become more knowledgeable. Hence, this combination of having to master the current practice, while also committing to exploring novel practices, displays the highly demanding challenge of innovation in expert work.

Third, we have seen how the work to develop and align practices locally has to be combined with the work to adjust and learn translocal practices, illustrated well with the case of TAVI. This is demanding because local alignment requires compromises and creative combining with whatever means is at hand. As a medical practitioner one also has to be accountable to the global networks of practice, and their views on what constitutes relevant knowing in practice. Interestingly, we have in this chapter seen how one can be considered as an expert in other settings globally, while not receiving the same recognition locally.

NOTES

1. For further descriptions of our methodology see Mørk et al. (2006, 2008, 2010, 2012).
2. Laparoscopy, or so-called keyhole surgery means that the surgical instruments and a laparoscope with a video camera and light are inserted into the abdomen of the patient through small incisions. This enables the surgeon to examine and perform surgery on the organs (Mørk et al., 2010).

REFERENCES

Brown, J.S. and P. Duguid (1991), 'Organisational learning and communities of practice: Toward a unified view of working, learning and innovation', *Organization Science*, **2**(1), 40–56.

Brown, J.S. and P. Duguid (2001), 'Knowledge and organization: A social-practice perspective', *Organization Science*, **12**(2), 198–213.

Christensen, C., R. Bohmer and K. Kenagy (2000), 'Will disruptive innovations cure health care?' *Harvard Business Review*, September–October, 102–12.

Contu, A. (2014), 'On boundaries and difference: Communities of practice and power relations in creative work', *Management Learning*, **45**(3), 289–316.

Dopson, S. (2005), 'The diffusion of medical innovations: Can figurational sociology contribute?' *Organization Studies*, **26**(8), 1125–44.

Fenwick, T., M. Nerland and K. Jensen (2012), 'Sociomaterial approaches to conceptualising professional learning and practice', *Journal of Education and Work*, **25**(1), 1–13.

Gherardi, S. (2006), *Organizational Knowledge*, Oxford, UK: Blackwell Publishing.

Grund, J. (2006), *Sykehusledelse og Helsepolitikk – Dilemmaenes Tyranni* [Hospital Management and Health Policy – The Tyranny Dilemma], Oslo: Universitetsforlaget.

Knorr Cetina, K.D. (1999), *Epistemic Cultures. How the Sciences Make Knowledge*, Cambridge, MA: Harvard University Press.

Lave, J. and E. Wenger (1991), *Situated Learning. Legitimate Peripheral Participation*, Cambridge, UK: Cambridge University Press.

March, J. (1991), 'Exploration and exploitation in organizational learning', *Organization Science*, **2**(1), 71–87.

Mørk, B.E., T. Hoholm and M. Aanestad (2006), 'Constructing, enacting and packaging innovations: A study of a medical technology project', *European Journal of Innovation Management*, **9**(4), 444–65.

Mørk, B.E., M. Aanestad, M. Grisot and O. Hanseth (2008), 'Conflicting epistemic cultures and obstacles for learning across communities of practice', *Process and Knowledge Management*, **15**(1), 12–23.

Mørk, B.E., T. Hoholm, E. Manninen-Olsson and M. Aanestad (2012), 'Changing practice through boundary organising: A case from medical R&D', *Human Relations*, **65**(2), 261–86.

Mørk, B.E., D. Nicolini, J. Masovic and O. Hanseth (2015), 'Expertise as practice. The case of TAVI', in *Proceedings of the 7th International Process Symposium*, 24–27 June.

Mørk, B.E., T. Hoholm, M. Aanestad, B. Edwin and G. Ellingsen (2010), 'Challenging expertise: On power relations within and across communities of practice in medical innovation', *Management Learning*, **41**(5), 575–92.

Newell, S., M. Robertson and J. Swan (2006), 'Interactive innovation processes and the problems of managing knowledge', in B. Renzl, K. Matzler and H. Hinterhuber (eds), *The Future of Knowledge Management*, Basingstoke, UK: Palgrave Macmillan, pp. 115–36.

Nicolini, D. (2007), 'Stretching out and expanding work practice in time and space: The case of telemedicine', *Human Relations*, **60**(6), 889–920.

Nicolini, D. (2010), 'Medical innovation as a process of translation: A case from the field of telemedicine', *British Journal of Management*, **21**(4), 1011–26.

Nicolini, D. (2011), 'Practice as the site of knowing: Insights from the field of telemedicine', *Organization Science*, **22**(3), 602–20.

Nicolini, D. (2012), *Practice Theory, Work and Organization: An Introduction*, Oxford, UK: Oxford University Press.

Nicolini, D., S. Gherardi and D. Yanow (2003), *Knowing in Organizations. A Practice-based Approach*, London: M.E. Sharpe.

Orlikowski, W.J. (2002), 'Knowing in practice: Enacting a collective capability in distributed organizing', *Organization Science*, **13**(3), 249–73.

Orlikowski, W. (2007), 'Sociomaterial practices: Exploring technology at work', *Organization Studies*, **28**(9), 1435–48.

Seeman, J. (1999), 'Netværk som forandringsstrategi og strategier i netværk' [Network as change strategy and strategies in networks], in E.Z. Bentsen, F. Borum, G. Erlingsdóttir and K. Sahlin-Andersson (eds), *Når styringsambitioner møder praksis. Den svære omstillingen af sygehus- og sundhedsvæsenet i Danmark og Sverige*, Copenhagen: Handelshøjskolens Forlag.

Swan, J., H. Scarbrough and M. Robertson (2002), 'The construction of "communities of practice" in the management of innovation', *Management Learning*, **33**(4), 479–96.

Wenger, E. (2000), 'Communities of practice and social learning systems', *Organization*, **7**(2), 225–46.

PART V

What can we do about it as innovation
policy-makers?

22. Adjusting national innovation policies to support open and networked innovation systems

Marko Jaklič and Aleš Pustovrh

INTRODUCTION

In this chapter, we will focus on specific policies and decisions that policy-makers can make to foster innovation. These policies are facing new challenges and have to adjust to a new, much more open and globalized world that was unimaginable as recently as 20 years ago (Wooldridge, 2010). They are based on two major shifts in the economic environment. First, expansion of innovation activities from large companies to other companies (the decline of the Fordist regime of innovation organization after the 1970s). The share of industry R&D conducted by enterprises with more than 10000 employees has decreased from 85 percent of total business enterprise R&D in the 1970s to approximately 50 percent now (Ebersberger et al., 2011). Second, geographical expansion of innovation activities (globalization).

These changes influence innovation activities of all stakeholders. In the twenty-first century, companies innovate in an environment in which competition is global, knowledge is spread more widely, R&D investments are increasing, and product life cycles are shortening (OECD, 2008). Policy-makers need to adjust to these changes with new policies as well. Many national innovation policy strategies and countless policy measures have been implemented recently with a different degree of success but policy-making has not sufficiently responded to new, societal challenges that influence the environment of innovation and creativity (OECD, 2011).

This chapter intends to cover this gap in our knowledge. We've focused on the many ways that different innovation policies can influence actors in national innovation systems and influence their solving of the complex organizational problems involved in the transformation towards more open modes of innovating. Contrary to intuition, new innovation concepts like 'open innovation' (Chesbrough, 2003) and 'user innovation' (Von Hippel,

2005) actually support public policy intervention by adding the systemic failure argument to the traditional market failure argument (Arrow, 1962). But if public policies remain essential for successful innovation, what kinds of policies yield the best results? We explore narrowly focused innovation policy measures and broader policies, institutions, and social systems influencing the general innovation and business environment.

GOVERNMENT INTERVENTION IN SUPPORT OF MORE OPEN INNOVATION: NATIONAL POLICY MIX BEST SUITED FOR INNOVATION SUCCESS

What can policy-makers do to help facilitate the transition into a new growth regime and improve the societal benefits that innovation can bring about? The open innovation paradigm (Chesbrough, 2003) strongly supports the development of innovation collaboration and cooperation, including market transactions in research and development (R&D) and their commercialization. That is why the open innovation concept strongly supports the rationale behind strong support for intellectual protection of R&D. However, new ways of conducting innovation do not mean that the markets for innovation function well without government intervention.

In fact, open innovation strongly supports government intervention in order to achieve better allocation of resources for innovation and to improve linkages between actors (Herstad et al., 2008). Innovation is based on a complex evolutionary process that is distributed in a system of multiple socio-economic agents whose behavior and interactions are governed not only by market forces but also to a greater extent by non-market institutions (Bleda and del Río, 2013). Linkages between actors serve as channels for knowledge diffusion and recombination. Lack of linkages and networking across organizational boundaries represents a system failure, as do lock-ins to specific collaboration partners, sources of ideas and information or excessive overall 'closure' of learning processes (Herstad et al., 2010). These failures need to be tackled in a similar manner to market failures – with policy intervention (Klein Woolthuis and Lankhuizen, 2005).

Based on the market and system failure argument supporting innovation policies, it seems clear that open innovation systems need elaborate innovation policies. However, the new way of thinking about openness and innovation does influence the changes in innovation policies (Herstad et al., 2008, 2010). Different policy measures are needed to facilitate open innovation activities than were needed to support innovation in the past.

Recently, several papers and studies have discussed the question of how national innovation policies can be reframed in a context of open innovation (Herstad et al., 2010; Ebersberger et al., 2011). OECD findings show that in the global supply of science and technology, large corporations are increasingly creating their own ecosystems (Moore, 1993) spreading across several countries. Global innovation networks have their own R&D capabilities as well as cooperation agreements with outside partners and suppliers. In these networks, companies are dependent on knowledge from partners (De Backer et al., 2008).

These ecosystems and innovation networks are creating international hubs that connect regional and national innovation systems. The location of these innovation hubs is determined by the attraction of local innovation policies. Often, even competing ecosystems source their R&D and innovation in the same innovation hub in order to benefit from local policies and economies of scope and scale. As a result, boundaries of national innovation policies are increasingly blurred. New innovation policies need to be put into an international context from the beginning (Saxenian and Sable, 2008). The challenge of innovation policies in the open innovation framework is how to support domestic embedding of industrial knowledge development and innovation processes (Herstad et al., 2010).

However, if open innovation is influencing the regional location of innovation hubs, forcing different national innovation policies to compete among them to attract the evolution of such hubs in their territory, what kind of policies facilitate that? Are they dependent only on specific, narrow innovation policies focused on spurring on the value creation and value appropriation aspects of the innovation activities? There are many examples of such policies aiming to increase public and private investments for R&D, protect intellectual property and other narrowly defined policies that target increased innovation and their social returns. Are there other factors influencing the location of innovation activities in a modern, open and global innovation system? Besides traditional, 'narrow' innovation policies, other 'broad' policies that do not target innovation activities directly but influence them unintentionally by making the innovation environment more attractive for positioning innovation activities could also influence the local embedding of industrial knowledge development and innovation processes.

One example could be that modern innovators and entrepreneurs are global and able to choose an environment where they start up their new ventures. It makes sense for them to consider not only an innovation system where their venture will be established but also other factors that influence the overall quality of life for them and their employees. Essentially, modern entrepreneurs are global and, similar to global capital flows, choose the most suitable environment for their positioning. And, as with global capital flows, global entrepreneurial flows do not depend solely on the specialized policies aimed at attracting them but are dependent on 'broad' policies.

By introducing other, broader aspects of economic policies that could influence the positioning of innovation activities, we can tap into the existing approach of varieties of capitalism (Hall and Soskice, 2001). This framework is useful for understanding the institutional similarities and differences among the developed economies that can be compared by reference to the way in which firms resolve coordination problems. Institutional arrangements influence firms towards particular kinds of corporate strategies and thus influence innovation and their capacities.

The 'varieties of capitalism' view on innovation explains the cross-national differences in innovation activity between industrialized democracies as a result of the variance in political institutions. Different institutional and broad economic frameworks can have implications on the local positioning of innovation activities and facilitating the location of innovation hubs. The more a polity allows the market to structure its economic relationships, the more it will direct its inventive activity toward industries typified by 'radical' technological change. Conversely, the more a polity chooses to coordinate economic relationships via non-market mechanisms, the more it will direct its inventive activity toward 'incremental' technological change (Taylor, 2004).

Other studies have shown that institutional differences between market economies lead to variations in innovation strategies and patterns of innovative performance (for example, Whitley, 2000). Their argument is based on the institutional theory's premise that organizations are embedded within broader social structures, consisting of different types of institutions that exert a significant influence on the company's decision-making (Ioannou and Serafeim, 2012). National-level institutional heterogeneity can lead to comparative institutional advantage for those firms that operate within different countries (Jackson and Apostolakou, 2010).

As the 'varieties-of-capitalism' theory and 'national business systems' theory suggest, innovation is in fact not only dependent on 'narrow' innovation policies, but also that other, 'broader' policies also influence innovation matters as well. Examples of such broader, structural policies include labor market, high-skilled labor force, capital markets, health and social security systems among others (for example, OECD, 2004).

EMPIRICAL RESEARCH OF INNOVATION POLICY MIXES

In order to empirically test our propositions we gathered a comprehensive dataset of indicators that measure broader policies and social systems – what the OECD calls 'framework conditions' (OECD, 2004) – as well as indicators covering narrow innovation policies. Public support for basic research in universities and public research institutions, ease of knowledge transfers, intellectual property protection and sharing, construction of a broad knowledge base and support of 'innovation culture' is crucial to successfully implementing open innovation policies (De Backer et al., 2008). This insight has been operationalized by OECD, which has been gathering data on five principal policies designed to ease perceived constraints on the incentive for private firms to innovate (Jaumotte and Pain, 2005):

- direct public fiscal policies to stimulate innovation – measured as the government-financed gross expenditure on R&D (GERD) as a percentage of national GDP;
- the funding of public research organizations and measures to improve linkages between universities and industry – measured as the share of higher education R&D expenditure financed by industry;
- the regulation of intellectual property – measured as triadic patent families per million population;
- the availability of private finance for innovation expenditures – measured as industry-financed GERD as a percentage of national GDP;
- the availability of human resources for science and technology – measured as the share of total researchers (combined R&D personnel) in the total labor force.

Broader innovation policy indicators are based on the theoretical foundation of the varieties of capitalism (VoC) framework that helps understand institutional similarities and differences between developed economies. The indicators that we chose roughly correspond to the five VoC spheres the firms must develop relationships with (Hall and Soskice, 2001):

- financial system and governance;
- internal structure of firms;
- industrial relations;
- education and training skills formation;
- inter-company relations.

Additional measures such as an openness to invest and a tax regime were added due to their potential impact on the local positioning of innovation activities and innovative companies (Herstad et al., 2010).

In our final dataset, we therefore included indicators of broader innovation policies that cover the success of national health systems, retirement systems, education systems, labor market, flexibility of tax regimes, and openness for investments:

- national health system – measured as the ranking of national health systems published by WHO;
- national retirement system – measured as the actual average retirement age;
- labor market flexibility – measured by the rigidity of employment index published by the World Bank in the *Doing Business* report;
- tax regime flexibility – measured as the time to pay taxes data published by the World Bank in the *Doing Business* report;
- openness for investments – measured as the combined share of foreign direct investments and outward investments in the national GDP; and
- education system success – measured by the Programme for International Student Investment (PISA) score published by the OECD.

The most important and difficult measure was the one measuring innovation success. After a thorough investigation of innovation success measures such as total factor productivity, selected individual R&D indicators (of both R&D inputs such as share of R&D investments in GDP and R&D outputs such as granted patents), we have decided to use the output measures based on the data compiled in the Innovation Union Scoreboard (IUS). An integral part of the Innovation Union strategy of the European Union, it provides a comparative assessment of the research and innovation performance of the EU27 member states and the relative strengths and weaknesses of their research and innovation systems. As a benchmark, it provides comparisons with some other, large non-European countries. It helps member states to assess areas in which they need to concentrate their efforts in order to boost their innovation performance (Hollanders and Es-Sadki, 2013). The calculation of the annual composite IUS Summary Innovation Index allows the preparation of country rankings and assures considerable publicity in the media and in the interested public. This is also likely one of the most important results of the IUS initiative that assures its continuation into its 14th year. While there is some considerable criticism of this approach (Schibany and Streicher, 2008; Pustovrh and Jaklič,

2014), the IUS Summary Innovation Index provides a relatively good foundation for aggregate innovation outcome for a relatively large number of countries.

To analyze the data, we have utilized a novel research method of quantitative comparison analysis (QCA) (Ragin, 2000) to analyze different configurations of innovation policies leading to successful innovation outcomes (Schneider and Wagemann, 2012). This method is uniquely appropriate for the task since it specifically allows testing for causal complexity such as necessity and sufficiency of conditions leading to the outcome.

The QCA examines how the membership of cases in the set of causal conditions is linked to membership in the outcome set (Allen and Aldred, 2011). As such, it is particularly useful when analyzing country comparisons as their numbers are inherently small, but at the same time too high for the usage of other qualitative methods like case studies.

RESULTS

The results of our analysis show that there is no single condition, neither remote nor proximate, that would be present in all solution terms. This means that no single condition is necessary for innovation success. However, there are a number of sufficient conditions for it. In fact, there are a number of different solution paths to innovation success, each representing at least one country that has actually had this configuration of remote and proximate factors to obtain the outcome. This means that all of these paths lead to innovation success. We also observe that none of the paths are comprised solely of remote conditions or from proximate conditions. All of the paths are combinations of both.

The results show that a single solution path will lead to innovation success even in a situation with no apparent (successful) government intervention. Another solution path has only minimal government intervention by way of focusing on two specific narrow innovation policies. Even though the results are limited to a single solution path, this is sufficient to state that countries can have good innovation systems without successful government intervention.

There are four solution paths that have high government intervention in both narrow and broad policy measures. This allows us to conclude that countries with more and better public policies – either broad or narrow – will have more successful innovation systems.

The remaining solution paths show that countries can also have successful innovation systems by having relatively unsuccessful narrow policies but high level of government intervention in broad policies or by having low government intervention in broad policies but high intervention in narrow policies.

The existence of solution paths that lead to innovation success with very different levels of government intervention in either narrow or broad innovation policies shows that no single policy is either necessary or sufficient for innovation success. Even so, the results also show that there are more solution paths leading to innovation success with government intervention. Of the 25 solution paths, 16 show the presence of four (out of five) narrow conditions, two show the presence of three conditions, four show the presence of two conditions and two show the presence of a single condition. The fact that innovation success is feasible without (successful) specific policies does not mean that this is the best bet for a developing economy aiming to develop a successful innovation system.

DISCUSSION

The results of our analysis show that while narrow innovation policies are neither necessary nor sufficient, government intervention is more often associated with innovation success. There is a single path represented by a single country (Ireland) that is counterfactual to the notion that narrow innovation policies lead to innovation success. These results also clearly show that countries striving to become successful innovators should develop specific innovation policies. They would face many different options to develop their policy mix while those that will not focus on developing narrow innovation policies will be left with the sole path – trying to replicate Ireland's success. Ireland's apparent innovation success without successful innovation policies is not necessarily the result of an intentional approach – Ireland has implemented an innovation strategy (Innovation Taskforce, 2010) in the past and an apparent lack of innovation policies could simply be a lack of success from policies that were implemented. These considerations only show that this solution path, as well as Ireland's innovation system, are interesting for further in-depth case study research (as analyzed by O'Malley et al., 2008). However, for policy-makers, it is a much safer bet to develop specific 'narrow' innovation policies if they seek innovation success.

The results also show that it might make sense to specialize and to focus narrow innovation policies on a few specific policies. Specialization in specific narrow innovation policies is certainly feasible when pursuing innovation success and could likely prove to save significant resources in emerging economies when trying to achieve innovation success (Lundvall and Borrás, 1997). In our matrix (Figure 22A.1 in the Appendix), there are no solution paths that show all well-developed innovation policies and most 'narrow' innovation policies leading to innovation success specialize in few specific policies. Most solution paths include successful results in narrow innovation policies focusing on linkages between universities and industry (measured as the share of higher education R&D expenditure financed by industry) as well as strong protection of intellectual property rights (measured as triadic patent families). Other studies also show the special importance of linkages (for example, Pustovrh and Jaklič, 2014) and they have a sound theoretical foundation in the open innovation paradigm. These two narrow innovation policies seem to be the most likely policies to support when specializing.

A second set of implications from our results show that narrow innovation policies are important, but 'broad' policies and the structure of national business systems also matter. Initially, we can observe that both tax system flexibility and general openness for investment (or lack thereof) were not conditions leading to innovation success. They were simply not relevant for innovation success. Other conditions are generally linked to the five VoC spheres that the firms must develop relationships with (Hall and Soskice, 2001). Of special importance are labor market flexibility and social systems in individual countries. This reinforces the 'varieties of capitalism' approach that countries with different types of economic and institutional structure can become successful innovators.

In reality, all varieties of capitalism have become mixed to a certain extent, but significant differences in coordination mechanisms remain. Especially interesting examples are the Nordic countries as they can be just as productive as the USA and even more so in distinct sectors, but without the great income inequalities that allegedly increase the entrepreneurial effort (Acemoglu et al., 2012). They point to the fact that there is rather strong evidence against the claim that a US incentive system is necessary in order to be at the technology frontier (Maliranta et al., 2012). Nordic countries might be better in mobilizing human resources as a larger share of the working age population is employed due to more inclusive educational, social, and employment policies. Our analysis confirms this view since it shows that there are possible solution paths to innovation success both within the more coordinated and the more liberal market economies. While paths in a more liberal market economy (with less government intervention in broad policies) are slightly more numerous, it is impossible to claim that innovation success is only their domain – successful innovative economies can also develop in the coordinated economy. The enabling welfare state of the Nordic countries is a potential conceptual reference for further research of such policies (Kristensen and Lilja, 2009). However, even these systems can be improved and adjusted.

SOCIETAL INNOVATIONS ARE NEEDED THAT INFLUENCE TRANSITION INTO OPEN MODES OF INNOVATION

Innovation policies that support open innovation will likely also have to develop new institutions or at least change the content of the existing institutions. Innovative changes to institutions, social systems and broad policies that also influence innovation will lead to a different institutional structure of capitalism than we are familiar with today. The fast pace of changes in innovation activities, positioning and policy-making will demand more flexible institutions and faster changes of policy-making – a sort of a lean policy-making approach.

The third, digital industrial revolution, globalization of innovation, new structure of global value chains, more open methods of coordination in global business ecosystems, international competition for global entrepreneurs as well as international cooperation fostering the growth of their ventures are just some of the trends that will require profound, even societal changes of national business systems. We've tried to anticipate some of these changes and their effects.

They will need to improve the synergies between industries and the government, leading to new forms of private–public partnerships. The development of new public institutions and policies (essentially reorganizing the public sector) and organization of new private–public partnerships represent a growing need for societal innovation that results from the expansion of open innovation. These areas seem to have the most potential for public societal innovation that can facilitate open mode innovation.

Another example of broad, even societal changes needed in support of open innovation is the growing importance of SMEs. The current phase of capitalism has shown several trends influencing the development of open innovation systems that could benefit SMEs. Globalization allowed distributed production and global value chains to develop where contributors all over the world can take part in the economic process. Due to the changes, novel organizational forms are emerging, such as network companies. Some of the challenges of the networked world cannot even be considered from a firm-level perspective, any more than a complex ecosystem can be understood by studying one of its actors, or a chemical reaction can be understood by studying a single reagent.

The rise of networks has fundamental implications for business strategy and competencies. If Michael Porter's five forces (Porter, 1985) model puts the firm at the center and other forces outside, the new reality puts the firm and the five forces in the network itself. Concepts such as barriers to entry have less meaning, and the idea of rivalry, buyers, and suppliers is transformed by an environment of 'co-opetition'. A challenge for large companies is to develop network-centric business models and strategies to harness the power of the broader network. However, the challenge for SMEs is different – how to become a member of such a network? Changing market conditions force smaller firms to adapt or reinvent their business through new technologies and business models. They must collaborate with external and network partners (large and small) to innovate successfully. Open innovation is the logical solution. This often forces them to adopt business model innovation as well. Business model innovation is a crucial part of the open innovation concept (Chesbrough, 2006).

Additionally, much more research is needed into the different policy mix for stimulating creativity and innovation. How to create a culture, even a society that is more collaborative, more creative and more competitive, with individuals and institutions that are active, enquiring, imaginative and full of ideas and curiosity? How can a society transform itself into one that supports and fosters creativity and innovation (Phelps, 2013)? A lot of policies and institutions are functions of values and intrinsic beliefs. As the world of innovation is changing, this is influencing the need for the institutional framework to adjust. But to do so, the values will have to adjust and modernize as well. The failure to do so could result in a significantly slower rate of innovation than we have become used to.

Case Study: The Success Story of Estonia

Since it reclaimed its independence after the collapse of the Soviet Union, Estonia has become the economic success story of Eastern Europe. However, it is perhaps the most renowned for its development of its tech industry. With a population of less than 1.3 million, it was able to produce tech giants such as Skype as well as numerous less publicized but no less successful tech companies like TransferWise or Pipedrive.

Estonia is known for its widespread, free Wi-Fi connections, its commitment to e-government, building its future IT skills base and other Internet-related services. So key is online infrastructure to Estonia that, in 2000, the country's parliament passed a law that declared Internet access a fundamental human right and started a massive program to bring web connections to previously ignored rural areas. In achieving this, it created a perfect testing ground for start-up companies (Aasmae, 2012).

In recent years, both the state and the private sector have been encouraging the growth of the local start-up scene. Estonia produces more start-ups per head of population than any other country in Europe. It is also among the most attractive places for venture capital investments. It seems that

Estonia was successful in implementing a virtuous cycle, creating a positive feedback loop:

1. Start-ups with global potential were created (in the case of Skype even imported).
2. Start-ups quickly grew globally with the help of local investments – 'smart money' and support programs in business incubators and accelerators.
3. After the transition into a certain phase, these companies were sold ('made an exit') – sometimes through an initial public offering (IPO) on a stock exchange, and more commonly to a strategic investor, often a multinational company, that turned the once start-up into an internal R&D or center of excellence.
4. This brought more smart money into the ecosystem, which was reinvested and represented a financing source for new start-ups.
5. The successful entrepreneurs from the initial start-ups eventually made a spinout from the R&D center – a new start-up. They had the knowledge, the funds, and the connections to global companies.
6. Foreign investment increased due to past successes and international recognition. They invest directly into start-ups or into VC funds.
7. The dynamic development of the ecosystem allowed more companies to develop in the long term, greatly increasing economic growth and employment in the country and region.

This feedback loop shows how money, knowledge, and market connections circulate within the market, which becomes self-accelerating in growth and development. The ecosystem is thus made more attractive for companies and entrepreneurs from other close environments also. They see the advantage in moving to an ecosystem that allows them to grow and develop faster. A successful ecosystem thus quickly outgrows its local bounds and becomes regional and closely related to global ecosystems. Estonia seems to be the perfect example of this development.

Case Study: Why Croatia Failed to Follow Estonia's Example Even with a Better Science Base?[1]

While Croatia gained independence at the same time as Estonia and with arguably better science base, it has failed to become as innovative, successful or recognized. While Estonia was able to become a vibrant place with clear political and business focus on the development of a successful and vibrant innovative tech industry, Croatia has failed to capitalize on its inherited science base. It could have been used as a starting point in the transition towards a knowledge economy, but has not made the shift from an obsolete socialist-style science policy to a modern innovation policy.

Covert socio-political growth factors shaped by the country-specific historical heritage of Croatia have prevented the recognition of the need for structural adjustment to the new technology regime, and have led to the belief that the (narrow) innovation policy is not only irrelevant but is also a relict of the state interventionism inherited from socialism. This was the most serious obstacle to policy reform. It resulted in a combination of re-traditionalization (the process of de-secularization and the so-called 'moral and social renewal' back to the ethical values of the nineteenth century), de-industrialization resulting from the unsuccessful privatization of previously state-owned industrial companies that resulted in their destruction and of de-scientization (the marginalization of science by both the political and business elites). Tech industry in Croatia has not emerged and its innovation system's performance is well below EU average.

Croatia's example shows that the transition from a market economy to a knowledge economy requires a serious re-design of development policy, the effectiveness of which depends on social change determined by the political recognition and social assimilation of the new technological regime. Only the transition of the social norms and values, social systems and reforms of the broad policies create the conditions in which the narrow innovation policies can be implemented and yield results.

NOTE

1. This whole case study is based on Švarc (2006).

REFERENCES

Aasmae, K. (2012), 'Is Estonia the best place to start your start-up?' *ZDnet.com*, 19 November, accessed 10 December 2015 at http://www.zdnet.com/article/is-estonia-the-best-place-to-start-your-start-up/.
Acemoglu, D., J.A. Robinson and T. Verdier (2012), 'Can't we all be more like Scandinavians? Asymmetric growth and institutions in an interdependent world', *NBER Working Paper Series*, Cambridge, MA: NBER.
Allen, M.M.C. and M.L. Aldred (2011), 'Varieties of capitalism, governance, and high-tech export performance: A fuzzy-set analysis of the new EU member states', *Employee Relations*, **33**(4), 334–55.
Arrow, K. (1962), 'Economic welfare and the allocation of resources for invention', in *The Rate and Direction of Inventive Activity: Economic and Social Factors*, Vol. I, Cambridge, MA: NBER, pp. 609–26.

Bleda, M. and P. del Río (2013), 'The market failure and the systemic failure rationales in technological innovation systems', *Research Policy*, **42**(5) 1039–52.

Chesbrough, H.W. (2003), *Open Innovation: The New Imperative for Creating and Profiting from Technology*, Boston, MA: Harvard Business School Press.

Chesbrough, H.W. (2006), *Open Business Models: How to Thrive in the New Innovation Landscape*, Boston, MA: Harvard Business School Press.

De Backer, K., V. López-Bassols and C. Martinez (2008), 'Open innovation in a global perspective: What do existing data tell us?' *OECD Science, Technology and Industry Working Papers*, Paris: OECD.

Ebersberger, B., S. Herstad, E.J. Iversen, E. Kirner and O. Som (2011), *Open Innovation in Europe: Effects, Determinants and Policy*, Brussels: European Commission.

Hall, P.A. and D. Soskice (2001), *Varieties of Capitalism: The Institutional Foundations of Comparative Advantage*, Oxford, UK: Oxford University Press.

Herstad, S., C. Bloch, B. Ebersberger and E. van de Velde (2008), *Open Innovation and Globalization: Theory, Evidence and Implications*, Helsinki: Vision Era Net.

Herstad, S., C. Bloch, B. Ebersberger and E. van de Velde (2010), 'National innovation policy and global open innovation: Exploring balances, tradeoffs and complementarities', *Science and Public Policy*, **37**(2), 113–24.

Hollanders, H. and N. Es-Sadki (2013), *Innovation Union Scoreboard 2013*, accessed 7 December 2015 at http://era.gv.at/object/document/365/attach/ius-2013_en.pdf.

Innovation Taskforce (2010), *Innovation Ireland – Report of the Innovation Taskforce*, Dublin: Department of the Taoiseach.

Ioannou, I. and G. Serafeim (2012), 'What drives corporate social performance? The role of nation-level institutions', *Journal of International Business*, **43**(9), 834–64.

Jackson, G. and A. Apostolakou (2010), 'Corporate social responsibility in Western Europe: An institutional mirror or substitute?' *Journal of Business Ethics*, **94**(3), 371–94.

Jaumotte, F. and N. Pain (2005), 'An overview of public policies to support innovation', *OECD Economics Working Paper*, Paris: OECD.

Klein Woolthuis, R. and M. Lankhuizen (2005), 'A system failure framework for innovation policy design', *Technovation*, **25**(6), 609–19.

Kristensen, P.H. and K. Lilja (2009), *New Modes of Globalizing: Experimentalist Forms of Economic Organization and Enabling Welfare Institutions – Lessons from Nordic Countries and Slovenia*, Helsinki: Helsinki School of Economics.

Lundvall, B.-Å. and S. Borrás (1997), *The Globalising Learning Economy: Implications for Innovation Policy*, Brussels: DG XII, Commission of the European Union.

Maliranta, M., N. Määttänen and V. Vihriälä (2012), 'Are the Nordic countries really less innovative than the US?' *VoxEU.org*, accessed 7 December 2015 at http://www.voxeu.org/article/nordic-innovation-cuddly-capitalism-really-less-innovative.

Moore, J.F. (1993), 'Predators and pray: A new ecology of competition', *Harvard Business Review*, **71**(3), 75–86.

OECD (2004), *Benchmarking Innovation Policy and Innovation Framework Conditions*, Paris: OECD.

OECD (2008), *Open Innovation in Global Networks*, Paris: OECD.

OECD (2011), *Fostering Innovation to Address Social Challenges*, Paris: OECD.

O'Malley, E., N. Hewitt-Dundas and S. Roper (2008), 'High growth and innovation with low R&D: Ireland', in C. Edquist and L. Hommen (eds), *Small Country Innovation Systems*, Cheltenham, UK and Northampton, MA, USA: Edward Elgar Publishing.

Phelps, E.S. (2013), *Mass Flourishings: How Grassroots Innovation Created Jobs, Challenge, and Change*, Princeton, NJ: Princeton University Press.

Porter, M. (1985), *Competitive Advantage: Creating and Sustaining Superior Performance*, New York: Free Press.

Pustovrh, A. and M. Jaklič (2014), 'National innovation policies in the EU: A fuzzy-set analysis', *Economic and Business Review*, **16**(1), 39–62.

Ragin, C.C. (2000), *Fuzzy-Set Social Science*, Chicago, IL: University of Chicago Press.

Saxenian, A. and C. Sable (2008), *A Fugitive Success – Finland's Economic Future*, Helsinki: Sitra.

Schibany, A. and G. Streicher (2008), 'The European Innovation Scoreboard: Drowning by numbers?' *Science and Public Policy*, **35**(10), 717–32.

Schneider, C.Q. and C. Wagemann (2012), *Set-Theoretic Methods for the Social Sciences*, Cambridge, UK: Cambridge University Press.

Švarc, J. (2006), 'Socio-political factors and the failure of innovation policy in Croatia as a country in transition', *Research Policy*, **35**(1), 144–59.

Taylor, M.Z. (2004), 'Empirical evidence against varieties of capitalism's theory of technological innovation', *International Organization*, **58**(3), 601–31.

Von Hippel, E. (2005), *Democratizing Innovation*, Cambridge, MA: MIT Press.

Whitley, R. (2000), 'The institutional structuring of innovation strategies: Business systems, firm types and patterns of technical change in different market economies', *Organization Studies*, **21**(5), 855–86.

Wooldridge, A. (2010), 'The world turned upside down – special report on innovation', *The Economist*, 17 April.

APPENDIX

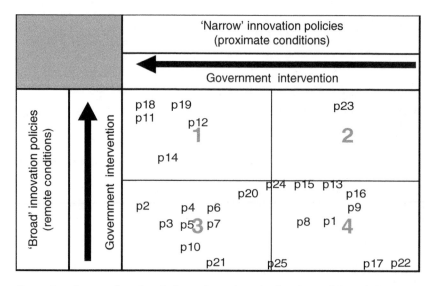

Note: In order to analyze the solution paths, we have developed a special matrix for presenting all solution paths – the innovation policy matrix. We start by organizing the solution paths in a result matrix that helps us to group solution paths based on the amount of government intervention that they require. We can see that a single path – p22 – will lead to innovation success even in a situation with no apparent (successful) government intervention, while another solution path – p17 – has only minimal government intervention by way of focusing on two specific narrow innovation policies. Even though the results are limited to a single solution path, this is sufficient to state that countries can have good innovation systems without successful government intervention. There are four solution paths that have high government intervention in both narrow and broad policy measures and can be classified into the first cell in our result matrix, allowing us to conclude that countries with more and better public policies – either broad or narrow – will have more successful innovation systems. The remaining solution paths show that countries can also have successful innovation systems by having relatively unsuccessful narrow policies but high level of government intervention in broad policies or by having low government intervention in broad policies but high intervention in narrow policies.

Figure 22A.1   Results matrix for all solution paths (with explanation)

23. Government ideation systems

Peter Parycek, Ralph Schoellhammer and Judith Schossböck

INTRODUCTION

It is believed that new governmental approaches and new modes of innovation in governance can increase transparency, support common interests, and support collaboration with citizens and communities. The idea of increasing participation in governance, reflected in concepts like 'open government' and participatory governance (Yishai, 2011), is the principal factor in open government data (OGD) and believed to help with the development of communication skills and citizen empowerment. Participation and collaboration in policy-making can foster innovation within the public sector, and more and more governments are realizing the potential of connecting to ideas of people and communities by means of information and communication technologies (ICTs).

This contribution addresses how governments can draw on the creative resources of a society by thinking about modes of innovation within governments. After a theoretical part dealing with the increased importance of innovation in governance structures, we focus on clarifying the relevant terms in the context of governance innovation modes from open government over open innovation to OGD, with a focus on the role of communities or crowds, networks, and the related hierarchies in that process. By presenting a case of OGD implementation and the success factors within the City of Vienna, we show how community innovation can be realized in the OGD context. Methodologically this is based on the evaluation of the OGD strategies in the City of Vienna by interviews, questionnaires (both internal and with external stakeholders) as well as internal documents.

Innovation in Governments

The question of innovation in governments is not one that immediately springs to mind if we think about tapping into the creative resources of society. While one would expect the state to ensure an environment in which innovative private organizations can prosper, the idea that innovation within government agencies could also be of importance is often overlooked. An efficient and innovative bureaucracy and public administration are cornerstones of a functioning state that would not be able to fulfill its core tasks without them. At the same time, however, the evolution of public administrations and the best way to manage them is a continuous challenge to policy-makers around the globe. As this chapter will show, there indeed is no one-size-fits-all approach to the establishment of state institutions. Progress in information technology has revolutionized the potential capabilities of public authorities, allowing them to either expand their democratic basis and include the population in decision-making, or use the same technology to build a suppressive surveillance state.

Yet there are additional reasons why the question of innovation within government structures will become increasingly important. While Western democracies had a comparative advantage when it came to managing their states in the past, this advantage is waning. The Office for National Statistics in Britain reported that private sector productivity increased by 14 percent between 1999 and 2013 – compared to a decline of 1 percent in the public sector between 1999 and 2010 (Micklethwait and Wooldridge, 2014, p. 19).

That innovation from outside and the inclusion of external experts in modernization of public administrations could be an important factor in reducing the influence of vested interests becomes clear if one looks at the following example from the United States: '94 percent of federal IT projects over the past ten years have failed – more than half were delayed or over budget and 41.4 percent failed completely' (ibid., p. 20). IT alone will not cure the problems that ail the system; what will be needed is the inclusion of outside expertise and the efficient use of autonomy within the public sector. The importance of this process cannot be overstated, for there is ample empirical evidence that the main driving force when it comes to innovation in the government sector is bureaucratic autonomy (Evans, 1995; Carpenter, 2001). An autonomous agency might be much less subjected to public scrutiny compared to other institutions, creating a sense of distrust within the population due to this lack of democratic accountability. Yet at the same time, inefficient democratization of government agencies can lead to an exploding number of potential veto players when it comes to decision-making (Fukuyama, 2013). This problem could be overcome by the new advances in technology and the ways they open up for participation. While originally the relationship between government and those it governed was strictly hierarchical, the future will most likely look more like a networked relationship between the state and its citizens (Ferguson, 2014). In some instances this is openly encouraged by state authorities that attempt to become more efficient and service oriented via technological solutions. In Denmark, for example, citizens can pay their taxes via SMS (Micklethwait and Wooldridge, 2014, p. 173). Such possibilities create a new pluralism in the flow and exchange of information that can be summarized under the expression 'open government'. As Micklethwait and Wooldridge point out: 'The desire to control everything is giving way to pluralism, uniformity to diversity, centralization to localism, opacity to transparency, and *immobilisme*, or the resistance to change, to experimentation' (ibid., p. 212).

CONTEXT AND MODE OF GOVERNMENTAL IDEATION: OPEN GOVERNMENT AND OPEN INNOVATION

Open Government

New governmental approaches like open government and the focus on participation and collaboration in policy-making are believed to increase transparency and to foster innovation within the public sector (Von Lucke, 2011). While non-governmental ideation systems and online platforms like Avaaz, Change.org or Care2 have become a popular way of bringing together the power of citizens and supporting people-powered politics by bottom-up means, governments are only just beginning to utilize new systems that are capable of bridging individual or community efforts with those of official institutions for the purpose of innovation or democratic ideations. Open government is a concept on the intersection of e-governance and e-democracy and refers to the process of opening up information and decision-making processes of governance work to a wider audience (Ringler et al., 2013). Open government is sometimes seen as theory of 'open statecraft' (Müller, 2010). By now, the concept has been integrated in public management theories and often in political theory. In the narrow sense, open government is about improving transparency and thereby accountability in all public affairs (Piotrowski, 2007).

Scholars have been promoting a social transformation toward an information society, with technological advancements having an effect on the flow of information that society relies on (Mayer-Schönberger and Lazer, 2007). Some argue that we do not face an information revolution, but a change in how information resourses are accessed and processed (Robins and Webster, 2004). However, the degree of transparency and openness of a state can depend on its information culture. The proactive publication of information and the right to access documents may vary between states because of cultural differences and divergent understanding of the role of public administrations (Parycek and Schossböck, 2014).

Open Innovation and Public Management

Concepts of open innovation generally deal with the opening of traditionally closed processes and aim at actively and strategically integrating outside knowledge into an organization. This is said to increase the potential for innovation and is defined as open innovation within public management theories (Chesbrough and Garman, 2009). Innovation can also mean to broaden a perspective or to distribute already existing knowledge (Parycek and Schossböck, 2014). According to Rogers, innovation is an idea, praxis or object that is experienced differently by an individual (Rogers, 2003). Businesses have established open innovation concepts for quite a while (for example, IBM, Gassmann, etc.). Gassmann and Enkel (2006) mention increased competitive pressure as well as shorter product cycles as driving forces for the importance to open up innovation processes. Methods like crowdsourcing itself can be seen as an attempt to use collective intelligence for economic goals (Parycek and Schossböck, 2014).

The following modes of innovation in the public and political sector by Pisano and Verganti (2008) describe different forms of participation used for collaborative innovation. Depending on open or hierarchical decision-making structures, there are different modes within the governance sector.

In 'open decision-making structures', innovation malls or innovation communities can be integrated in collaborative innovation. First, in an 'innovation mall', the organization defines the problem and chooses from the external, proposed solutions. Second, in an 'innovation community' or 'community of innovation', the community can overview the whole process from proposal of the problem to decision-making. The process can still be led by the administration, but the community also has an overview about the decision-making process. Often, such communities are called 'open innovation communities' (Fleming and Waguespack, 2007).

The models of open collaboration rely on a specific level of transparency. In a government with a flat organizational structure, processes of mass collaboration are supported. The concept of an innovation community appeals to those who like to look for solutions to a specific problem. If ideas are not integrated or implemented as useful solutions, a community can also leave again – a problem visible for instance in e-participation or open government dialogues.

In a rather 'hierarchical' decision-making structure the right to make decisions stays within the public administration or the decision-makers. The closed 'elite cycle' is a traditional, collaborative way of production that is mostly led by public institutions. Experts are asked for solutions to a specific problem, and most of the time external experts are pre-selected by the organization. By contrast, the 'consortium' is based on a flat governance structure and closed participation. An example in Austria would be the 'Verfassungskonvent' (Constitutional Convention). Additionally, 'communities of creation' have been proposed as a new governance mechanism for managing knowledge found in different companies for the purpose of innovation. Intellectual property rights are then owned by the community, although the community is governed by a central firm that acts as the sponsor. This model lies between the closed hierarchical model and an open market-based model (Sawhney et al., 2000). Whatever form of collaborative invention, collaboration in the governance sector will still need some form of management to 'deal with the complexity of such activities' (Edelmann et al., 2012).

Open Government Data (OGD)

OGD is a worldwide phenomenon with a worldwide movement, but also more local communities and crowd-based initiatives. OGD is defined as 'non-privacy-restricted and non-confidential data which is produced with public money and is made available without any restrictions on its usage and or distribution' (Janssen et al., 2012, p. 258). Governments and local authorities in countries such as the United States, Australia, New Zealand, the Netherlands, Sweden, Spain, Denmark, and Austria make their data accessible to the public by publishing it on the web (Sheridan and Tennison, 2010). The main reasons for implementing OGD are increasing democratic accountability, enhancing transparency, delivering citizen self-designed public services, and stimulating economic growth (Gurstein, 2011).

OGD changes not only the access to data and information but also the boundaries between the public and its governmental institutions (Janssen et al., 2012). In addition to the publication of data, it also includes users' feedback so as to improve governmental performance and mechanisms for monitoring. On this basis, new intermediate services for a wider audience are created. A crucial aspect of OGD is the provision of metadata and advanced descriptions of data acquisition processes. By now, OGD is repeatedly mentioned in European Commission and European Union agenda setting.

Open data has high aims and goals related to efforts of re-democratization; for example, transparency as a means to reduce corruption or as a catalyst for innovation, social innovation and economic growth (Millar, 2011; Ubaldi, 2013). Public value is created by 'enabling a richer and deeper understanding and dialog among policy-makers and others who are interested about what the data tells us about our lives' (Millar, 2011, p. 172). However, it should be noted that open data can also be used in an autocratic context – countries like China also have an interest in fighting corruption and the open data movement is starting to take off there as well. Scholars who are skeptical think that transparency or accountability is not ensured through OGD, and the relation to more participation is not proven yet and influenced by many different factors. However, we can assume that making information more open to the public can lead to better-informed decisions and form the basis for citizens' motivation to participate.

OGD in some aspects is very similar to the open source and open access movement (Braunschweig et al., 2012). Trends in open data also point to the optimization of big data in terms of 'infrastructure and skill sets', which can offer the opportunity for government agencies to improve their performance and service delivery.

Crowd- and Community-sourced Innovations

Looking at the structures that support participation and collaboration in collective actions, crowds and community-based systems play a huge role in the different recognition, reputation, and reward systems that groups relate to. This has implications for the design of governmental ideation systems and the related activities. Haythornthwaite (2009) makes a distinction between those two forms of peer production. The recognition, reputation, and reward systems that support these collectives affect who controls and contributes information (Raymond, 1999). Knowledge collectives can also add meaning to information (Haythornthwaite, 2011) – a process very relevant in OGD interpretation, which is relevant at a later stage of OGD implementation. The two extremes of crowds and communities are distinguished by a set of organizing principles, but most collectives are on a continuum (Haythornthwaite, 2009). An example would be Wikipedia, which is crowdsourced, yet also contains structural aspects of communities.

Crowdsourcing activities for the government may not always be the ideal solution, as the crowd may be reduced down to the lowest common denominator, and focus more on present issues rather than long-term issues. For a long-term strategy and concept, it is thus wiser to connect to communities and to offer reputational rewards. Another reason is that governments are often slow and often not yet experienced with network society principles (Schuler, 2011; Edelmann et al., 2012).

Looking closer at motivation and reputation as factors in collaborative innovation, reward systems play a major role in whether a community is willing to participate. When asking whether individuals or collectives will spend their time contributing to an effort or question, possibilities range from monetary awards to 'personal-but-shared everyday needs' (Benkler, 2006). A target group can have different benefits from the organizers, and there are usually different target groups in OGD activities with different expectations who see different potentials and benefits of OGD (for example, journalists, developers, politicians, companies etc.). Motivation to participate can start as orientation, but can be supplemented through internal mechanisms that support a heavyweight form of interaction (Haythornthwaite, 2011). Furthermore, reputation is built on visibility of contributions.

CASE STUDY: OGD IMPLEMENTATION WITHIN THE CITY OF VIENNA

Vienna has committed itself to an open and transparent system that makes governmental data available to the public. The city has reached out to a wide audience and different target groups, like citizens, businesses, the scientific community or journalists. We describe the case of OGD implementation within the city of Vienna with a view to the policy level within the city administration as well as the outside view of stakeholders and the OGD community. The data is based on data collected as part of the evaluation of OGD activities, in which those two goals were set (Parycek et al., 2013), to evaluate the value of the strategy for different target groups as well as from the internal organizational perspective.

Vienna is a quite decentralized administrative body, headed by the city directorate; regulations issued by the directorate are nonetheless very much dependent on the support by heads of departments. While a governing regulative document exists that effectively demands the cooperation of departments, departments retain control over what data they release and in what granularity. In the following, we emphasize the idea of OGD implementation as an outcome of an open innovation process within the City of Vienna and identify success factors for governmental ideation from an organizational point of view.

Methodological Approach

The description of this case is based on an evaluation of the OGD strategy of the City of Vienna conducted by the Centre for E-Governance in 2013 (Centre for E-Governance, 2012). The evaluation was conducted after the implementation of the Viennese OGD strategy. Apart from analysis of secondary literature to access the socio-political and organizational challenges, the evaluation built on document analysis including internal strategic documents of the City of Vienna, executive orders concerning procedures, cooperation within departments, as well as qualitative and quantitative data – qualitative interviews and online polls. We focused on the results on the internal level (employees and heads of department in the City of Vienna's administration departments) as well as the external level of the OGD community. We can learn from the example of the City of Vienna how to create the structural conditions to successfully implement open innovation and open collaboration principles in the OGD context and to draw on reputation systems within existing communities.

Success Factors: Organizational Structure, Community Integration and Reputation Systems

In the following, crucial success factors for open innovation via OGD implementation in the City of Vienna are summarized with a focus on the internal, organizational and the external, community-orientated perspective.

Success factors from an organizational perspective (internal view)

A major success factor can be seen in the technical solution of the implementation: the hub of Vienna's OGD is a Geo-server, an integrated information system that stores GIS data, ranging from historic data up to city planning level (Parycek et al., 2013). By using this server, departments can independently decide on the data to be released as OGD. The integration of the OGD platform into an existing content management system (CMS) helped to kickstart the process, as well as the homogeneity of the external-facing implementation. Departments with modern and integrated ICT systems have a higher willingness to publicize data as OGD. Thus, the implementation of modern, data-specific tools (for example, a cross-department information system via a common data bus) is a main success factor for OGD implementation.

Another success factor mentioned in the internal interviews was the definition of clear internal roles and responsibilities. A process model for OGD publication has been developed in close cooperation with the Centre for Administration Research (Krabina et al., 2012). That way, front-stage information input was balanced by back-stage discussions.

Different stakeholder communities were integrated in the OGD activities of the City of Vienna. Evaluation results showed that the perceived benefits of OGD differed throughout the target groups; however, a common political perspective (for example, regarding the view on increased transparency) and common goal helps to foster OGD implementation. The supporting political will in the City of Vienna (the government officially supported OGD activities) helped to embrace the cultural change related to such activities.

A major success factor was the integration of an external, already existing community, in this particular case the Austrian and local OGD community. Through the inclusion of an external community, the City of Vienna employed the concepts of the innovation mall and innovation community, drawing on the reputation systems of different target groups with dedicated measures. Through visibility and transparency of the process, traditional hierarchical roles have been softened and, due to the political will and support of the government, officially backed. While we still find classical hierarchical structures (the final decision-making always rested with the officials of public administration), different modes of participation were offered to the community, and the usage of ICTs or social media might have helped with that process. An example would be the model of the elite circle, with external experts being pre-selected by the organization. Such a model would apply to the judges of an OGD competition. However, with most OGD activities within the City of Vienna, the general openness of processes led to the integration of an innovation community – in theory, everyone could participate in OGD meetings of the City of Vienna. By integrating a kind of heavyweight community that also exists online, the City of Vienna drew on already existing structures of a community and their related goals; for example, the fight for more transparency and open publication. Front-stage information input (for example, in social media channels, where already existing OGD groups and platforms were addressed) was balanced by backstage discussions: the City of Vienna organized regular offline meetings that were open to the wider public and all members of a community. At a later stage, the City of Vienna drew on the innovation mode of an innovation mall by selecting experts for certain OGD challenges, for instance by establishing certain open data sub-working groups. Sub-working groups have been founded on topics like the 'Open Data Portal Austria' or 'Open Government Documents', and are usually led by an expert and formed by selected team members that are also part of the OGD community in Austria. The strong interconnections between the different sub-groups were another success factor for the provision of certain incentive systems. Further research would be needed to find out more about the systems' participation.

Success factor: community innovation – motivation and incentives (external view)

Compared to other stakeholder groups, the socio-political impact of OGD seen by developers is evaluated as comparatively low. The motivation of

developers to implement and design OGD applications seems to be independent from commercial success: this group is preliminarily interested in
the technical challenges. The main beneficiary of OGD for the citizens is
the administration itself with better reporting of mistakes and better internal processes. The group of journalists, in contrast, see themselves more as
a kind of socio-political voice.

Regarding the expectations and wishes of application developers, their
view is similar to those in science and research: economic parameters are
not the main motivator to engage in OGD activities. Respondents wish
for an integration in interest groups as well as in educational initiatives.
These results indicate that the community is very interested in taking
part in wider OGD networks and in good contact with governmental
and educational stakeholders. In interviews, the good communication
of the City of Vienna to the target groups was emphasized. Possibilities
for improvement were mentioned in the area of feedback channels to the
departments within the administration and to the providers of the OGD
portal. Furthermore, developers have shown great interest in linking OGD
to research projects or the integration of their knowledge in university
or other educational projects, which shows another motivational factor
relevant in open innovation in an OGD context.

A central result in this target group is that most of them have been
drawn to OGD due to technical interest, only occasionally a higher
income was expected. This reveals that reputation mechanisms in the
OGD developers' community cannot be measured in monetary means,
and offering monetary rewards to this group can help in creating awareness for OGD activities, but does not seem to be a central factor of
participation for developers. A surprising result was that apart from the
concentration on technical features, the whole OGD community does not
seem to play a crucial role for this user group – while the OGD community
outside the developer's view seems to focus on the socio-political benefits
of OGD, application developers are not likely to be reached by those
promises. OGD activities thus have to offer different reputation systems
for different target groups: a holistic strategy offering both monetary,
socio-political and technical incentives and reward systems is expected
to be most successful. One example of a successful, holistic reputation
incentive in the OGD context is an OGD competition. Such competitions
offer reputation for a community on many different levels (from visibility
within the wider OGD community, but also from a technological standpoint) and can foster reputation as a network effect (Haythornthwaite,
2011). In Austria, the Open Data Contest 'Apps for Austria' is an example
of a close cooperation of education, OGD initiatives ('Cooperation
Open Government Data Austria') and the 'Digital Austria' platform of

the Federal Chancellery). In a multi-level evaluation process by a jury consisting of experts of economy, science and public administration, the best applications based on data from the OGD platform data.gv.at were awarded a prize.

Apart from offering personal reputation systems and visibility to data developers, OGD contests also offer the possibility to demonstrate the benefits of opening data to a wider public. In the case of the Austrian OGD competition, recognition was still under the control of the authorities, but the process can be very motivating for an existing community. Assuming that members of the OGD movement consider it to be prestigious to be visible as part of an official project, further research could investigate to what extent which OGD target groups see themselves as a member of the OGD movement and to what extent such reputation mechanisms are crucial for participation in such processes.

As front-stage information input, application developers mentioned social media as an important feature of information to OGD: four of seven participants of the online survey stated that they receive information about OGD from social networks, and three of seven participants mentioned mails from the City of Vienna as their information source. Social media plays an important role in participation in groups: six of seven participants of the survey stated that they are members of a group with OGD focus in a social network. Stumbling over official OGD activities can also lead to an initial interest in joining an OGD community: an interviewee stated that he was only participating in the 'OGD scene' after the publication of the first data on the data portal of the city. Official OGD activities can thus foster community forming or enlargement, and mechanisms of mutual benefits between the external community and the internal goals have been created. In this case, motivation to participate started as orientation, but can lead to more heavyweight forms of interaction.

Another success factor regarding external groups was the inclusion of other external communities in the periphery of application developers, for example, the 'Metalab' group, a 230 m^2 hackerspace in Vienna next to Vienna City Hall. This space offers collaboration between technical-creative enthusiasts, hackers and founders, and is dedicated to providing infrastructure for projects and a physical space for interested people. The expenses of this lab are covered by membership fees, private and corporate sponsoring and so on, and also by subventions of the City of Vienna. This way, the City of Vienna drew on already existing networks and communities and officially supported them.

This evaluation revealed success factors of governmental ideation, through the clear definition of responsibilities, supporting political will, the relation to a clearly defined and visible OGD community, the implementation along a process model, and on the technical side the integration of the OGD platform into existing CMSs.

CONCLUSION AND OUTLOOK

The evaluation of OGD activities in the City of Vienna showed that incentives for the participation of communities as a precursor of open innovation are different according to different stakeholder communities. Whereas application developers are more focused on technical incentives, citizens are more focused on the socio-political outcome of such initiatives. The respective incentives for attracting members of the OGD developer group should thus follow an approach where technical achievements can be made visual and are honored, as done for instance in dedicated OGD application contests. Social-political factors should be part of the success criteria in the contest though, as they are important for advertising OGD solutions to the wider audience. OGD activities have to offer different reputation systems for different target groups: a holistic strategy offering monetary, socio-political and technical incentives will be most successful.

It has been shown how open innovation and the integration of open communities in public administration processes can form the structural conditions for an innovative government, allowing the development of autonomous structures in which innovation can happen. Financial crisis and more recent economic problems have led to the need to develop new ways of stimulating economic growth and innovation. A key mechanism has been ICT systems that contribute to new and innovative ways of delivering public services to citizens and businesses. With innovative structures that keep governments and its institutions dynamic, we can increase the capacity of such institutions to focus on the common good.

The challenges for governments is to find out which collaboration approach is suitable in which context, and to understand why individuals or groups will spend their time contributing and how they can be motivated to contribute in the long term. Governments can and should learn from existing examples and cases and draw on their implementation strategies and first experiences. Public administration has not yet completely found its new role in that environment but it is clear that closed, hierarchical governed systems will increasingly be untenable and open and collaborative production systems in governments and public administrations need to encourage stakeholders and citizens to participate in order to achieve and produce better solutions and outcomes (Edelmann et al., 2012), alongside a cultural change that is supported by ICTs and their ability to bring together new collectives and form a more collaborative relationship between the state and citizens.

REFERENCES

Benkler, Y. (2006), *The Wealth of Networks: How Social Production Transforms Markets and Freedom*, New Haven, CT: Yale University Press.

Braunschweig, K., J. Eberius, M. Thiele and W. Lehner (2012), 'The state of open data: Limits of current open data platforms', accessed 9 December 2015 at http://citeseerx.ist.psu.edu/viewdoc/summary?doi=10.1.1.309.8903.

Carpenter, D.P. (2001), *The Forging of Bureaucratic Autonomy: Reputations, Networks, and Policy Innovation in Executive Agencies, 1862–1928*, Princeton, NJ: Princeton University Press.

Centre for E-Governance, Donau-Universität Krems (2012), *Evaluation der Open Data Umsetzung der Stadt* [Evaluation of the Implementation of the Open Data City], Vienna: Krems.

Chesbrough, H.W. and A.R. Garman (2009), 'How open innovation can help you cope in lean times', *Harvard Business Review*, December, 68–80.

Edelmann, N., J. Höcht and M. Sachs (2012), 'Collaboration for open innovation processes in public administrations', in Y. Charalabidis and S. Koussouris (eds), *Empowering Open and Collaborative Governance*, London and New York: Springer, pp. 21–38.

Evans, P.B. (1995), *Embedded Autonomy: States and Industrial Transformation*, Princeton, NJ: Princeton University Press.

Ferguson, N. (2014), 'Networks and hierarchies', *The American Interest*, 9 June, accessed 15 July 2014 at http://www.the-american-interest.com/articles/2014/06/09/networks-and-hierarchies/.

Fleming, L. and D.M. Waguespack (2007), 'Brokerage, boundary spanning, and leadership in open innovation communities', *Organization Science*, **18**(2), 165–80.

Fukuyama, F. (2013), 'The decay of American political institutions', *The American Interest*, 8 December, accessed 14 July 2014 at http://www.the-american-interest.com/articles/2013/12/08/the-decay-of-american-political-institutions/.

Gassmann, O. and E. Enkel (2006), 'Open innovation: Die Öffnung des Innovationsprozesses erhöht das Innovationspotenzial [Open innovation. The opening up of the innovation process increases the potential for innovation]', *Zeitschrift Führung + Organisation*, **75**(3), 132–8.

Gurstein, M.B. (2011), 'Open data: Empowering the empowered or effective data use for everyone?', *First Monday*, **16**(2).

Haythornthwaite, C. (2009), 'Crowds and communities: Light and heavyweight models of peer production', in *Proceedings of the 42nd Hawaii International Conference of System Sciences*, Los Alamitos, CA: IEEE Computer Society.

Haythornthwaite, C. (2011), 'Democratic process in online crowds and communities', in P. Parycek, M.J. Kripp and N. Edelmann (eds), *CEDEM11. Proceedings of the International Conference for E-Democracy and Open Government*, Krems: Druckwerk Krems, accessed 20 February 2014 at http://www.donau-uni.ac.at/imperia/md/content/department/gpa/zeg/bilder/cedem/cedem11_proceedings_online.pdf.

Janssen, M., Y. Charalabidis and A. Zuiderwijk (2012), 'Benefits, adoption barriers and myths of open data and open government', *Information Systems Management*, **29**(4), 258–68.

Krabina, B., T. Prorok and B. Lutz (2012), *Open Government Vorgehensmodell* [Open Government Procedure Model], Vienna: KDZ, accessed 8 December 2015 at https://www.kdz.eu/de/file/11143.

Mayer-Schönberger, V. and D. Lazer (eds), *Governance and Information Technology*, Cambridge, MA and London: MIT Press.

Micklethwait, J. and A. Wooldridge (2014), *The Fourth Revolution: The Global Race to Reinvent the State*, New York: The Penguin Press.

Millar, L. (2011), 'Managing OGD', in P. Garvin (ed.), *Government Information Management in the 21st Century: International Perspectives*, Burlington, VT: Ashgate.

Müller, P. (2010), 'Offene Staatskunst' [Open statecraft], in P. Müller and M. Sengens (eds), *Offene Staatskunst – Bessere Politik durch 'open government'? Internet Gesellschaft Co:llaboratory*, 2nd edition.

Parycek, P. and J. Schossböck (2014), 'Adopting a new political culture: Potentials and obstacles of open government in Austria', in N. Götz and C. Marklund (eds), *The Paradox of Openness. Transparency and Participation in Nordic Cultures of Consensus*, Leiden: Brill, pp. 210–36.

Parycek, P., J. Höchtl and M. Ginner (2013), 'OGD implementation evaluation', *Journal of Theoretical and Applied Electronic Commerce Research*, **9**(2), 80–99 [online], accessed 8 December 2015 at http://www.scielo.cl/scielo.php?script=sci_arttext&pid=S0718-18762014000200007&lng=en&nrm=iso&tlng=en.

Piotrowski, S.J. and G.G. van Ryzin (2007), 'Citizen attitudes towards transparency in local government', *The American Review of Public Administration*, **37**(3), 306–23.

Pisano, G.P. and P. Verganti (2008), 'Which kind of collaboration is right for you?' *Harvard Business Review*, **86**(12), 78–86.

Raymond E.S. (1999), *The Cathedral & the Bazaar: Musings on Linux and Open Source by an Accidental Revolutionary*, Cambridge, MA: O'Reilly.

Ringler, P., P. Parycek and J. Schossböck et al. (2013), *Internet und Demokratie in Österreich* [Internet and Democracy in Austria], Vienna: SORA – Institut für Social Research and Consulting.

Robins, K. and F. Webster (2004), 'The long history of the information revolution', in F. Webster (ed.), *The Information Society Reader*, London: Routledge, pp. 62–80.

Rogers, E.V. (2003), *Diffusion of Innovation*, 4th edition, New York: The Free Press.

Sawhney, M. and E. Prandelli (2000), 'Communities of creation: Managing distributed innovation in turbulent markets', *California Management Review*, **42**(4), 24–54.

Schuler, D. (2011), 'Deliberation that matters', in P. Parycek, M.J. Kripp and N. Edelmann (eds), *CEDEM11. Proceedings of the International Conference for E-Democracy and Open Government*, Krems: Druckwerk Krems, pp. 17–22.

Sheridan, T. and J. Tennison (2010), 'Linking UK government data', in *Proceedings of the WWW Workshop on Linked Data on the Web*, Raleigh, NC.

Ubaldi, B. (2013), 'OGD: Towards empirical analysis of OGD initiatives', *OECD Working Papers on Public Governance, No. 22*, Paris: OECD.

Von Lucke, J. (2011), 'Innovationsschübe durch eine Öffnung von Staat und

Verwaltung, frei zugängliche Daten, Datenportale und Umsetzungswettbewerbe' [Innovative advances through an open state and administration, freely accessible data, data portals and implementation competitions], in W. Eixelsberger and J. Stember (eds), *E-Government – Zwischen Partizipation und Kooperation*, Vienna: Springer, pp. 213–26.

Yishai, Y. (2012), 'Participatory governance in public health: Choice, but no voice', in D. Levi-Faur (ed.), *The Oxford Handbook of Governance*, Oxford, UK: Oxford University Press.

24. Creation of a social media social venture

Benedicte Brøgger

INTRODUCTION

A business idea is a particular kind of idea. It proposes a new product or service and how to make money from it. A *social* business idea presents a new solution to a social problem as well as a way to make a living. Those who implement social business ideas are called social entrepreneurs, and their businesses social enterprises. The claim in the chapter is that to implement a social business idea, a social entrepreneur must engage in a triple-embedding process. Not only must they position their venture in the market, they also need to draw resources from state and voluntary sector sources simultaneously. Social enterprises may therefore expand the notion of what it means to capitalize on creativity.

The case discussed in the chapter is X.News, a media venture in a small community in Norway. The creative idea was to start a social media venture that would also be a media social venture. This needs some explanation: the entrepreneur, H2L, is an autist whose talent and consuming interest is news and who started a net-based local newspaper in 2000.[1] It started with a few 'printed' news items on the X.News domain, included feature articles in 2004, and some years later videos and streaming services. This is the *social media venture*. All the while, the company has only employed people from marginalized groups, including physically disabled and minority groups. This is the media *social venture*.

Below follows an introduction to social entrepreneurship research, the case and the research method. The main part of the chapter is the analysis of how X.News has managed the feat of staying true to its original creative idea while adhering to the tenets of the market, the state and the local community simultaneously.

THE SOCIAL TURN IN BUSINESS

There has been a 'social turn' in business as social and environmental impact are being included in core business strategies (Porter and Kramer, 2011). The turn is the result of the efforts of researchers, governments, foundations, fellowship organizations as well as social entrepreneurs (Nicholls, 2006, 2010). The field of social entrepreneurship research is fairly new and has mainly been concerned with conceptual and methodological problems in general (Peredo and McLean, 2006; Mair and Marti, 2006; Chell, 2007; Short et al., 2009). One key discussion is whether social entrepreneurship differs from commercial entrepreneurship in degree or in kind (Austin et al., 2006; Dees et al., 2010; Light, 2011). Another is how it differs from non-governmental organizations (NGOs) and government initiatives (DiMaggio and Anheier, 1990; Nicholls, 2006; Martin and Thompson, 2010) and from social work (Germak and Karun, 2010). A third line of inquiry is if social entrepreneurship is similar or different from other forms of societal entrepreneurship that have consequences for economic development (Barth, 1967, 1972; De Montoya, 2000; Kloosterman and Rath, 2003; Seelos and Mair, 2005; Peredo and Chrisman, 2006; Elkington and Hartigan, 2008; Dacin et al., 2010; Cimdina, 2014). Social entrepreneurship can be seen in all kinds of economic systems: capitalist, mixed, transitional and non-market economies (Dart, 2004; Kerlin, 2006; Bornstein, 2007; Bacq and Jansen, 2011).

This steadily growing body of research documents that there are legal as well as informal cultural rules that direct the flows of resources in different parts of society. Corporations may sell products to government institutions and get money in return, but cannot claim benefits. NGOs may receive financial support from private investors, but cannot pay dividends. Volunteers can contribute with their work, but cannot be paid and so on. Therefore there are considerable management challenges in managing a business that draws on resources from such disparate sources simultaneously. In order to achieve this the entrepreneur has to embed the venture in the fabric of the local society.

TRIPLE EMBEDDING

The challenges facing social entrepreneurs to some extent resemble those of immigrant entrepreneurs. Immigrant entrepreneurs are those who migrate to a new country and establish a business in their new homeland. These entrepreneurs operate according to two different systems, the economy of their new country and that of their ethnic community, in what has been identified

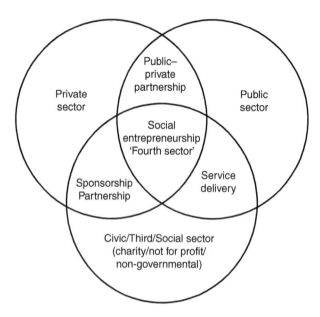

Source: Ellis (2010).

Figure 24.1   The fourth sector

as a double embedding process (Kloosterman and Rath, 2003). Most often immigrant entrepreneurs start by meeting the needs of the ethnic community. However, the enterprises that grow break out of the confines of the ethnic community and attract suppliers, distributors, and customers from the majority society (Krogstad, 2002). Immigrant entrepreneurs succeed when managing to attract resources from different institutional settings. Social entrepreneurs are engaged in even more complex institutional embedding processes (Desa, 2012). Social entrepreneurs must combine resources from three distinct sectors, the market, the state, and the local community, and by this constitutes a distinct 'fourth sector', as illustrated in Figure 24.1.

Resource theory is useful for investigating the specifics of the embedding processes that generates this fourth sector. The two original resource theories are resource-based theory and resource-dependency theory. Both define resources as financial assets, operational items (machinery, equipment, buildings) and human resources (work force, competence and relations). In resource-based theory a firm is defined as a 'bundle of resources', and requires both administrative and creative (entrepreneurial) resource management to grow (Penrose [1959] 2005). This theory is about the inner workings of firms. The resource-dependency theory brings management of external relations into the picture, and defines these relations as a specific kind of resource (Pfeffer and Salancik, 1977). The chapter makes use of what is implicit in both theories, that resources are not materially given, and combines this with a perspective that it is the uses to which resources are put that differentiate between them and that invest them with value (Zelizer, 1998). To an investor, 'human resources' may mean a number in an equation and to a manager the people he or she feels responsible for. In this perspective, resources are neither defined as universally valid theoretical concepts, nor as material objects with intrinsic qualities that can be objectively measured as if they were chemical substances. Rather, the perspective here is that the identity and nature of resources are determined by their uses. This does not mean that 'anything goes' in terms of the definition of resources. Human society is generally well organized, and resources gain their meaning from the organizational structure in which they are employed. The social entrepreneur must tease them loose from their established place and recombine them for the purpose of the business without breaking the formal and informal rules that shape their flows.

RESEARCH METHOD

The first time I heard of X.News was in a radio interview with H2L in 2012. The background for the interview was that X.News had published as news a story about a shopping cart abandoned at the side of a road. This was what caught my interest at first and made me turn up the sound on the radio. Here was a story about something that was not quite theft, after all a shopping cart is a kind of public item; it was not quite vandalism, as the cart was not destroyed; and it was about isolation, about a thing outside the context that gives it meaning. I found the story intriguing and enlightening in its quiet questioning of the taken-for-granted. The national media had a different understanding. H2L had been made fun of in a popular national Friday night show for the banality of the story. The radio interview was about this incident.

H2L said that he was an autist who loved news and had started the Internet newspaper in his teens. Later in the interview, he added that he only hired people with special needs. This piqued my interest even further. I was doing research with several social entrepreneurs at that time and his story resembled theirs. Furthermore, the day before I had received an email asking for nominations for a social entrepreneur of the year award. I thought he fitted the bill. Later that day I checked what he had said on the radio. First, I searched the registrar of companies and found that he ran a bona fide business. Next, I checked his newspaper and the other media sources and found that he indeed was a social entrepreneur. When I tried to nominate him, it turned out he had to nominate himself. I called him and explained the nomination and that he was a social entrepreneur. He was not familiar with the term, but agreed that he fitted the criteria. Also, since it came with a monetary reward he reflected that if he won it would benefit X.News. We spoke a couple of times after that, but he has not won any award, at least not yet.

His story had actualized a burning issue in my research: how do social entrepreneurs manage to operate across the boundaries of different institutional logics, which are strictly separated, by law as well as custom? This observation I had found difficult to relate to entrepreneurship theory, as do most other researchers in the field of social entrepreneurship. So, I dug deeper to find out how X.News had been started and operated. I used Excel to organize the data and interpreted them according to the Minnesota Innovation Research Program concept of an 'innovation journey'. Such a journey comprises of a number of situations in which people, ideas, transactions, adaptations, and outcomes make up a non-linear dynamic system that in the end determines whether an idea is successfully implemented or not (Van de Ven and Poole, 1990).

My interest was the social enterprise, so I limited the search about H2L to what was revealed about his social persona in electronic sources. I used a range of different sources all electronic, publicly available and free of charge. One was the published items of X.News itself. The archive of featured articles dates back ten years. The second kind of source was the electronic archives of local, regional and national media. In all, seven of these featured X.News and H2L at least once. Where three media features included the same picture, fact, date or figure I registered it in Excel. The third source was two reliable databases with company information: proff.no and purehelp.no. From here I got data on changes in corporate form, accounts and balance sheet information, name of managers, board members and their networks. Websites of local chambers of commerce and other voluntary associations corroborated information from other sources about projects financed as well as about networks and connections. Statistics Norway provided background information on a number of companies and their industries. Wikipedia and the websites of local towns and municipalities yielded background information for understanding the fabric of the X.News's local community more generally. The national press associations provide annual reports on the growth of e-media in Norway. The approach is hypothetical-deductive, and as outlined above, is based on assumptions from resource theory. Even from one or a few cases only more general conclusions can be drawn about critical conditions of specific situations (Evans and Handelman, 2006). The claim that triple embedding is a

Table 24.1   Development stages of X.News

Year	Main Stages	Enabling Conditions	Key Resources Acquired
2000	X.News – the creative idea	Digitalization of media Local community isolation Personal obsession Welfare system support Family relations	The personal resources of H2L Loan of school equipment Publicly funded personal assistant Gift of domain name from family
2010	Managing resource dependencies	Saleable products and services Diversified strategy Reliable and consistent service Brand name Ethnic community support	Steady cashflow from sales of ads Financial capital from NGO-funded projects TV/radio/digital equipment A pool of trained volunteers-cum-employees Goodwill
2014	Establishing a resource base	Local and regional business networks Corporate form	Hired, professional administration Organization structure and routines Financial capital from professional investors

condition for implementation of a social business idea was checked against social reality.

From this material I identified three stages of the journey as especially critical in the life of X.News and its resource mobilization – the start-up period in 2004, the present (2014), and 2010, in the aftermath of the financial crisis, when X.News was registered as a limited company for the first time. Table 24.1 sums up the main stages of the journey. Below it follows the discussion of the embedding process.

X.NEWS – THE CREATIVE IDEA

The business idea of X.News was to establish a web-based local newspaper for a small community of about 2000 people in X, a municipality in the hinterlands of Norway. The small towns in the fjords to the north (N) and south (S) of X have about 1000 and 1500 people each. In summer there is about an hour-and-a-half driving distance from N to S via X. In winter the roads often close. People make a living in a variety of ways, including employment in public services, tourism, a couple of manufacturers, retail and private services, all combined with subsistence fishing, farming and hunting.

In 2000 the idea of a web-based newspaper was a radical and creative idea on many accounts. First, the founder, H2L, was a social outsider. As he has explained in national media, he was severely harassed by his class-mates during his school years, and is diagnosed as an autist. Hence he is himself a special-needs person, and he received assistance from the educa-tion system and local health and social services. The school dropout rate is higher, the chance of getting regular employment is lower, and health and well-being indicators are lower for this group of citizens than other groups. In short, H2L had all the characteristics of a potential social client, entitled to financial and advisory support from the public welfare system. Instead he started a business.

Second, digitalization of the media industry had just begun. In the national and international media in 2005, electronic newspapers did not exist, and electronic publications were quite marginal (www.mediebedrift-ene.no, 2005). Social media were not invented (Facebook appeared in the USA in 2004) and mobile platforms were unknown. Norway is a country where digitalization was extensive early on and many people used comput-ers, especially companies and young people. H2L had the idea of utilizing the new technology and somehow capitalize on his own equipment and technological skills, as well as those of friends and supporters in the com-munity. Third, H2L loves news and could see the news value in events that for others were just trite everyday detail. The town where he lives was too small even for a little local newspaper. However, H2L moved around talking to people about what was going on anyway in his search for news, why not make use of the obsession? And he did. The first feature article appeared in the fall of 2004, and was about a local couple who visited the Norwegian king. Since then, X.News has continued to publish news four to five times a week. Fourth, local companies were interested in marketing themselves, and Internet marketing was a new channel. So H2L could sell ads to local companies. The ads were from day one prominently displayed on the first page of the newspaper and to either side of the news items. H2L had no intention of starting a social enterprise, or a business for that sake. X.News was created on the basis of an obsessive interest for news, competence with new technology, and sound local knowledge. He aimed to start a newspaper, and he did.

MANAGING RESOURCE DEPENDENCIES

H2L is adamant that his autism in an ability, not a disability. What is culturally defined as a social problem he redefines as an opportunity and social impact is part of the mission of the company. People with special needs are preferred employees, and he had added new services to support the minority groups in the local community. He identifies social aspects not as an externality, but as a strategic capability that can be positioned differently in the three sectors: government, local community and the market.

With regard to government, in Norway, the welfare state has full responsibility for education and health and social services (Grindheim and Selle, 1990; Selle and Øymyr, 1995). X.News has managed to benefit from this. H2L chose 'e-newspaper' as an elective subject at secondary school and got to use the school's technical equipment. Next, the school allowed him to continue to publish news on its home page in a win-win agreement. After school, H2L has continued to receive support for his project in the form of a personal assistant. This resource is human, and an entitlement. Hence, he has managed to draw on operational and human resources in the form of entitlements to realize his business idea.

Family and ethnic communities have also been important. At 16, when he was no longer a secondary school student, the family gave him the domain X.News for his birthday. They have continued to assist the business formally and informally, as members of the board and with mundane practical matters. Over the years X.News has also applied for and received grants from ethnic associations to publish in the local language and to participate in international activities. These resources come in the form of gifts, and are partly financial and partly operational. They are joined with the other resources and support a range of activities that all serve as means to implement his idea.

Regarding market, over the years, X.News has created a market for itself by offering a range of products that customers are willing to pay for. Companies and organizations pay for ads, private individuals pay to publicize news about their families, and municipalities and voluntary associations pay to have their meetings and seminars streamed, and pictures are sold to national and international media.

Between the community and the market are the people who work for X.News. As H2L stated, 'they just came by and stayed on'. For several years there were mainly H2L and his assistant, with the ad hoc aid of developers. At most 13 people were employed, but only two or three full-time, and on full pay. Many worked for little, out of interest or because of their belief in the social mission of the company.

ESTABLISHING THE RESOURCE BASE

Unlike social work or charity, which is based on giving, a business requires money in return for its services. A business is not an end in itself, but is set up in order to yield material results, a product, a service, a livelihood, a profit, preferably time and time again. Hence, business is about utility. That is why implementation becomes so important. Implementation and creativity are mutually dependent opposites. To capitalize on a creative idea some sort of routine must be established. It is about getting things done in the true and tested ways. Good administration is impersonal, efficient, transparent and predicable (Du Guy, 2000).

The administrative set-up of X.News took place gradually, and the details are somewhat vague, but the outline is as follows. The company in its first years was a classical example of a Mintzbergian 'muddling through' kind of company (Mintzberg, 1973). A few months after the first feature article had appeared on his domain, H2L established a sole proprietorship. In Norway this is a company form that requires little in the way of administrative structure. People came by, did a job and left. A grant for a project was obtained and the promised activity carried out and stopped. Things changed when in 2010 and 2011 two other companies were registered, one in the line of newspaper business, the other in design of web portals. Both were registered as NUFs (Norwegian Foreign Registered Companies). This company form became popular at that time because the requirements of the administrative structure were more lenient than those of a limited company, but limited risk in a manner that sole proprietorships did not. H2L is sole owner of both and was at first also managing director. This is when the sale of ads took off as well, and when it was decided to start web TV, a move that required some investment. However, the turnover has increased year by year, and the companies run with a profit. In 2012 a professional managing director was employed in a 70 percent position. He was a former mayor of a neighboring municipality and with business administration background. The two companies had the same board members, all business people, managing private equity funds, retail and real estate companies. Some are based in the local municipality, and some in other cities in the region. No one receives compensation for their work. The sole proprietorship was de-registered in 2012. In 2013 a limited company was registered, with H2L as sole shareholder and at first managing director, and with the same board members. This was the first time the company acquired debt, and with this became firmly embedded in the domain of the financial resources and relations. Later a new managing director was hired. That year the company laws required considerably lower share capital and no auditor for small companies. The company was restructured in 2013. Three employees had to find other jobs, while three were retained. When asked about the restructuring of the company, the chair of the board replied that the company did not have economic problems, and added 'at least not more than usual'.

X.News grew from the outside in. H2L worked with his network, his external relations. He was a known figure in the local community and from there established legitimacy as a dependable person, and from there gradually as a dependable business owner. H2L today titles himself 'advertising agent', 'owner' and 'editor'. The resource base from which to establish a steady cash flow and to reinvest came only gradually and with it, the need for administration of the different flows of resources, as Table 24.1 illustrates.

MAINTAINING EDITORIAL FREEDOM

What is unique with X.News is that the core of the business idea, to produce news, is kept separate from the flows of transactions and exchanges. That part of the activity is kept independent from the market, the community and the government domains. Literally in the main page of the newspaper, in the middle of video-streams, company marketing campaigns and family greetings – appears the very local news, which no one pays for. The newspaper does not have subscribers; the news is free and available for all. Even though some of the items have made a national laughing stock of the company as mentioned above, the majority of the features are about local events of only local interest, such as the opening of new garage, a fire, a dance at the pub. This is where the life in a local community appears, respectfully and systematically reported. The people who pay for the products and services are featured, but as the editor chooses, not as people and product placement. The one condition that makes X.News unique and that has fostered its continued existence is that it has managed to establish itself as a legitimate public sphere where the different domains are brought together. In Durkheimian terms, X.News has established a social basis for its contracts, a 'social contract' of its own. This is the key condition for its existence, and it cannot be bought and sold or be the objects of negotiation for favor or care.

CONCLUDING REMARKS

The creative force than fueled the start of X.News in 2000 has continued to spur the growth of the company although in the later years it has been directed at administrative issues. H2L took advantage of new technology to establish his newspaper, and then has managed to take advantage of legal changes to continue to operate the business. All the while he has utilized his local network to mobilize resources. The company started out with the support of 'friends, fools and family', as most new ventures do, but in addition could draw on financial and advisory resources from the government, and from the local community and voluntary associations. Today X.News has become part of the local business community. Also business professionals have been more systematically involved in the administration of the company in order to handle the challenges of drawing resources from disparate sources, but even so its social basis has not been eroded.

X.News has a clear commercial bent and narrow attention to local micro-events. However, unlike most local newspapers, it has managed to stay in business without changing its journalistic credo, its editor or its subscribers. The founder and the employees have managed a triple embedding process that has positioned the company within the different demands and opportunities in the business community, the public sector and the local community, while all the time staying true to the original creative idea. X.News document that social entrepreneurship is different in kind and not only in degree from both commercial entrepreneurship and other forms of societal entrepreneurship.

NOTE

1. X.News and H2L are not the real names of the company or the entrepreneur, but abbreviated and slightly altered versions of them to ensure anonymity.

REFERENCES

Austin, J., H. Stevenson and J. Wei-Skillern (2006), 'Social and commercial entrepreneurship. Same, different or both?' *Entrepreneurship Theory and Practice*, **30**(1), 1–22.
Bacq, S. and F. Janssen (2011), 'The multiple faces of social entrepreneurship: A review of definitional issues based on geographical and thematic criteria', *Entrepreneurship & Regional Development*, **23**(5–6), 373–403.
Barth, F. (1967), 'Economic spheres in Darfur', in R. Firth (ed.), *Themes in Economic Anthropology, ASA Monograph No. 6*, London: Tavistock, pp. 149–74.
Barth, F. (ed.) (1972), *The Role of the Entrepreneur in Social Change in Northern Norway*, Oslo: Universitetsforlaget.
Bornstein, D. (2007), *How to Change the World*, Oxford, UK: Oxford University Press.
Chell, E. (2007), 'Social enterprise and entrepreneurship towards a convergent

theory of the entrepreneurial process', *International Small Business Journal,* **25**(1), 5–26.

Cimdina, A. (2014), 'The unnoticed entrepreneurship and innovation in Latvia's rural economy', *Journal of Baltic Studies* **45**(1), 79–104.

Dacin, P.A., M.T. Dacin and M. Matear (2010), 'Social entrepreneurship. Why we don't need a new theory and how we move forward from here', *Academy of Management Perspective,* **24**(3), 37–57.

Dart, L. (2004), 'The legitimacy of social enterprise', *Nonprofit management,* **14**(4), 411–24.

Dees, J.G., J. Emerson and P. Economy (2010), *Strategic Tools for Social Entrepreneurs. Enhancing the Performance of Your Enterprising Nonprofit,* Chichester, UK: Wiley.

De Montoya, M. (2000), 'Entrepreneurship and culture. The case of Freddy the strawberry man', in R. Swedberg (ed.), *Entrepreneurship. The Social Science View,* Oxford, UK: Oxford University Press, pp. 332–55.

Desa, G. (2012), 'Resource mobilization in international social entrepreneurship: Bricolage as a mechanism of institutional transformation', *Entrepreneurship Theory and Practice,* **36**(4), 727–51.

DiMaggio, P.J. and H.K. Anheier (1990), 'The sociology of nonprofit organizations and sectors', *Annual Review of Sociology,* **16**(1), 137–59.

Du Guy, P. (2000), *In Praise of Bureaucracy. Weber. Organization. Ethics,* Thousand Oaks, CA: Sage.

Elkington, J. and P. Hartigan (2008), *The Power of Unreasonable People: How Social Entrepreneurs Create Markets that Change the World,* Boston MA: Harvard Business School Press.

Ellis, T. (2010), *The New Pioneers. Sustainable Business Through Social Entrepreneurship and Social Innovation,* Chichester, UK: Wiley.

Evans, T.M.S and D. Handelman (eds) (2006), *The Manchester School: Practice and Ethnographic Praxis in Anthropology,* Oxford, UK: Berghahn Books.

Germak, A.J. and K.S. Karun (2010), 'Social entrepreneurship: Changing the way social workers do business', *Administration in Social Work,* **34**(1), 79–95.

Grindheim, J.E. and P. Selle (1990), 'The role of social voluntary social welfare in Norway: A democratic alternative to a bureaucratic welfare state', *Voluntas,* **1**(1), 62–76.

Kerlin, J. (2006), 'Social enterprise in the United States and Europe. Understanding and learning from the differences', *Voluntas,* **17**(3), 267–73.

Kloosterman, R. and J. Rath (ed.) (2003), *Immigrant Entrepreneurs: Venturing Abroad in the Age of Globalization,* Oxford, UK and New York: Bloomsbury Academic.

Krogstad, A. (2002), *En stillferdig revolusjon i matveien. Etniske minoriteter og kulinarisk entreprenørskap* [A Subdued Food Revolution. Ethnic Minorities and Culinary Entrepreneurship], Oslo: Institutt for samfunnsforskning ISF-rapport 7 2002.

Light, P.C. (2011), *Driving Social Change,* Chichester, UK: Wiley.

Mair, J. and I. Marti (2006), 'Social entrepreneurship research. A source of explanation, prediction and delight', *Journal of World Business,* **41**(1), 36–44.

Martin, F. and M. Thompson (2010), *Social Enterprise. Developing Sustainable Business,* Basingstoke, UK: Palgrave Macmillan.

Mediebedriftene (2005), 'Historiske opplagstall avis' [Newspaper circulation history], accessed 9 December 2015 at http://www.mediebedriftene.no/Tall--Fakta1/Opplagstall/Historiske-opplagstall-avi.

Mintzberg, H. (1973), 'Strategy-making in three modes', *California Management Review*, **18**(2), 44–53.

Nicholls, A. (2006), 'Social entrepreneurship', in S. Carter and D. Jones-Evans (eds), *Enterprise and Small Business. Principles. Practice and Policy*, London: Prentice Hall.

Nicholls, A. (2010), 'The legitimacy of social entrepreneurship. Reflexive isomorphism in a pre-paradigmatic field', *Entrepreneurship Theory and Practice*, **34**(4), 611–33.

Penrose, E. ([1959] 2005), *The Theory of the Growth of the Firm*, New Brunswick, NJ: Transaction Publishers.

Peredo, A.M. and J.J. Chrisman (2006), 'Towards a theory of community based enterprise', *Academy of Management Review*, **31**(2), 309–28.

Peredo, A.M. and M. McLean (2006), 'Social entrepreneurship. A critical review of the concept', *Journal of World Business*, **41**(1), 56–65.

Pfeffer, J. and G.R. Salancik (1977), 'Who gets power – and how they hold on to it', *Organizational Dynamics*, **5**(3), 3–21.

Porter, M.E. and M.R. Kramer (2011), 'Creating shared value', *Harvard Business Review*, January–February, 62–77.

Seelos, C. and J. Mair (2005), 'Entrepreneurs in service of the poor. Models for business contribution for sustainable development', *Business Horizon*, **48**(3), 241–7.

Selle, P. and B. Øymyr (1995), *Frivillig organisering og demokrati. Det frivillige organisasjonssamfunnet endrar seg 1940–1990* [Voluntary Organizations and Democracy. Voluntary Organization Changes in Society 1940–1990], Oslo: Samlaget.

Short, J.C., T.W. Moss and G.T. Lumpkin (2009), 'Research in social entrepreneurship. Past contributions and future opportunities', *Strategic Entrepreneurship Journal*, **3**(2), 161–94.

Van de Ven, A.H. and M.S. Poole (1990), 'Methods for studying innovation development in the Minnesota Innovation Research Program', *Organization Science*, **1**(3), 313–35.

Zelizer, V.A. (1998), 'The proliferation of social currencies', in M. Callon (ed.), *The Laws of the Market*, Oxford, UK: Blackwell Publishers, pp. 58–68.

PART VI

What does it all mean?

25. Succeeding with capitalizing on creativity: an integrative framework

Miha Škerlavaj, Anders Dysvik, Matej Černe and Arne Carlsen

Looking across the chapters in this anthology one might recognize four recurring patterns deterministic of capitalizing on creative ideas at work. These four common threads are: (1) bottom-up micro-emergence; (2) top-down contextual influences; (3) leadership; and (4) cyclic and polar processes (see Table 25.1, and Table 25A.1 in the Appendix).

In terms of bottom-up emergence processes, we observe that contributions in the book predominantly address micro-level innovation processes (Chapters 2, 3 and 4), how ideas emerge and evolve from individuals up into the teams. However, there are also attempts (Chapters 5, 6 and 7) to utilize novel developments in multi-level theorizing and methodology to understand idea capitalization across levels of analysis (from the individual to the team level).

Top-down contextual influences are the second most strongly represented common thread. There are eight chapters across individual (Chapter 2), team (Chapter 8), organizational (Chapters 13, 15, 17, 18), and policy levels (Chapters 22 and 23) of analysis.

Leadership is the third topic that spans across three chapters (Chapters 9, 10 and 11) and all of them are at the individual level.

Fourth, a recurring and most strongly present approach to the topic of capitalizing on creativity is a process view on idea implementation. Here there are 11 contributions across individual (Chapters 2, 6 and 7), team (Chapter 6) and organizational level (Chapters 12, 15, 16, 17, 19, 20, 21 and 24).

WHAT HAVE WE LEARNT?

It comes as no surprise for such a complex topic as capitalizing on creativity to claim that there is no single, simple rule or guiding principle on how to do it. Effective implementation of creative ideas depends on a number of contingencies. As such, we cannot offer any simple and straightforward recipe. Instead, the reader should by now understand that this is a dish with many ingredients and spices.

This book was an attempt to bring together 42 innovation authors from 13 countries and four continents, in a variety of empirical settings (such as hospitals, manufacturing organizations, automotive industry, service firms, public sector, oil exploration, multinationals, R&D teams, science- and high-tech-based companies, IT companies, pharmaceutical, start-ups/ new ventures, cities and countries, small and medium enterprises [SMEs] and insurance). In order to study capitalizing on creativity as accurately as possible, contributors have used both qualitative and quantitative approaches across levels of analysis. Among quantitative contributions, authors applied multi-level methods, experiments, field surveys, and social network analysis. Qualitative methods most often used are case studies, narratives, secondary data, action research, longitudinal observations, grounded theory, and interviews.

Bottom-up Emergence

Take-aways from the bottom-up emergence common thread are mostly related to topics of idea emergence via job crafting, flow experience, cultural intelligence and diversity, idea championing, and intuition/curiosity vs cognition. Taken together, the six chapters (2, 3, 4, 5, 6 and 7) cover a diverse set of antecedents of both creativity and idea implementation: job design, motivation, personality and individual differences, and self-management of the creative process.

With regard to job design, a number of individual-level factors were identified in Chapter 2 as important not for the creative, but for the idea implementation process. However, only job crafting embodies the spirit of bottom-up emergence. It can be seen as going hand-in-hand with proactivity in terms of creating a context for enabling proactivity to flourish, but also a way to enhance autonomy in idea implementation and further increase curiosity pertaining not only about how to come up with something, but also how to make it useful and lead to its ultimate implementation (Chapter 7).

The question of curiosity is also closely related to the issue of whether to use intuition or rationality/cognition (Chapter 6), and how to alternate between the two in order to implement creative ideas, raising almost ambidextrous types of questions that will likely need more conceptual and empirical work. However, the key take-away can definitely be seen in light of the fact that the traditional view that pinpoints curiosity as good for creativity, and only rationality and cognition as beneficial for implementation, does not hold any more, with increasing expectations for the managers and knowledge workers to alternate or jump between the two in order to fulfill the frequently recursive process of innovation leading to idea implementation. While creativity stands at the start of any innovation, it also plays its part in transforming the idea into reality.

The remaining set of studies (Chapters 3 and 4) dealt with traditionally individual-level factors, but with important consequences for the innovation process and output at multiple levels. The factors of motivation and personality have long been regarded as important antecedents of both creativity and innovation, and their influence has now, by those two studies, been extended to predicting idea implementation as well. Flow with absorption and enjoyment of an innovative task thus serves as an important factor of individual-level idea implementation, and can have beneficial consequences for the (diversity, openness, and cultural intelligence when operating in a cross-cultural environment).

With regard to diversity, several studies opened separate avenues for investigating it in the context of idea implementation, looking, however, at the heterogeneity from two different angles. The two different aspects of diversity thus include a cultural view more emphasized in Chapter 4 as well as a job-related view tackled by Chapters 2 and 14. The job-related view narrows in on the formal or informal networks, and thus focuses on the organizational design issues, which are also manifested in task-related and social job characteristics of the narrower job design. A cultural view deals with diversity with regard to a trainable trait of cultural intelligence, which offers a complementary view on diversity, speaking also to the importance of heterogeneous teams pinpointed in Chapter 16. In this respect, the chapters offer a cross-cultural contribution with respect to estimating the most beneficial level of cultural diversity. It seems that some diversity with regard to either job characteristics or cultural background is beneficial for implementing creative ideas, but too much becomes difficult to manage. Job or organizational design can help in this regard.

The majority of studies thus remain at the individual level and have only touched upon the matter of generalizability, diffusion and meaning across levels. However, two chapters directly tackle the issue of bottom-up emergence, not only theoretically and conceptually, but also operationally and empirically (Chapters 5 and 6). As mentioned, this endeavor is limited to the emergence from the individual to the team level. This speaks to the main challenge (and vast opportunity at the same time) of a multi-level approach in management in general. The majority of studies actually deal not with a multi-level, but a levels approach, simultaneously accounting for only two levels in their conceptualizations and operationalizations.

Nevertheless, such a bottom-up approach is still novel and underdeveloped in the innovation research, and the two studies presented here build upon the multi-level theory to present interesting insights into the emergence of the predictors of idea implementation at the team level with regards to intuitive and cognitive elements of human psyche, or the actual team-level innovation process components (idea generation and championing) leading to team-level idea implementation. As such, they conceptualize the emergence pattern from the individual to the team level in a way that could be seen as a stark contrast to each other.

Chapter 6 models their emergence as an additive composition-based type by focusing on the average of team members' intuition and need for cognition. On the other hand, Chapter 5 delves deeper into the bottom-up emergence patterns by pinning different composition, compilation, and configurational models against each other and compares the effects of maximum, average, and dispersed idea generation and championing for team-level idea implementation. The result is a two-level estimation of the individual- and team-level innovation process leading to idea implementation, which can occur either for everyone to see, or under the radar (creative bootlegging, stealth innovation). Both approaches that were applied in these respective studies enabled the authors to achieve their conceptual and empirical results, and can be seen as model benchmarks for further studies on the bottom-up emergence of innovation antecedents or the actual innovation process leading towards the implementation of creative ideas.

Top-down, Contextual Influences

Chapters on top-down, contextual influences on creative idea implementation identify several contingencies that may accelerate or dampen effectiveness of capitalizing on creativity. These range from job design for innovative behavior (Chapter 2), motivational climates (Chapter 8), disruptiveness and performance gap of business models (Chapters 13 and 17), idea implementation social networks (Chapter 14), top management support, staffing, facilitation of innovation processes (Chapter 15), human resource practice mix (Chapter 18), as well as regional (Chapter 23) and national policy innovation mixes (Chapter 22).

The first set of studies, while applying a top-down logic, is still mostly micro-level based. These studies (Chapters 2, 8, 14, 15 and 18) mostly offer micro-level solutions in order to stimulate idea implementation, or those that relate to what the managers can do in everyday work in order to maximize innovation outcomes. In general, we could conclude that they relate to human resource (HR) solutions that are manifested in an appropriate practice mix, job design, or employee network design, and reveal the importance of HR managers in developing custom-made tools needed to develop job characteristics fit for their individual employees. These studies speak both to the importance of direct support of the managers, as well as about specific managerial and organizational practices that are applied in a top-down manner in order to stimulate idea implementation. Nevertheless, a key take-away seems to be that what matters is not the existence of practices and systems *per se*, but how they are interpreted and enacted by the managers, and how they are perceived by the employees.

The second set of studies ranges from the companies' business strategy and business model logic (Chapters 13 and 17) to an even broader view – regional and national policy innovation mixes (Chapters 22 and 23). While appearing to focus on two different aspects of innovation management, the cases presented in the four studies reveal some similarities: a key take-away for the top management is to set up the business strategy and companies' business models in a way that they are aligned or respond to the innovation systems. On the other hand, innovation (and broader) policy mixes should account for 'champions' in terms of the most innovative companies in their ecosystems, and set up the policies in a way that would enable the growth of these firms in order to maximize the innovation outcomes for the whole regions or economies.

Leadership

Three presented leadership chapters (Chapters 9, 10 and 11) address different facets of leadership behaviors and their influence on innovative behavior processes at the individual level.

Chapter 9 shows through experimental studies and illustrative cases how constructive leadership styles represented in the form of perceived supervisor support (PSS) help employees balance the process of idea generation and idea implementation thus enabling them to better deal with highly creative employee ideas.

Chapter 10 extends previous research on leader–member exchange (LMX) by introducing the concepts of social LMX (SLMX) and economic LMX (ELMX) within the realm of innovative behavior processes. They theorize that SLMX outcomes will align well with traditional high-quality LMX but note that ELMX is to be considered a separate leadership style where the supervisor takes on a more reserved, formal and distal role towards their employees. In their conceptual piece they caution against immediate supervisors that ground their exchanges with subordinates based on ELMX – that is, economic incentives, transactions, formal regulations and distal interpersonal style when dealing with creative ideas.

The last of the chapters on leadership, Chapter 11, raises a cautionary note against highly authentic leaders perceived as narcissistic. While previous research suggests that a range of beneficial outcomes emerge from authentic leaders, 'too much of a good thing' implies these leaders are seen as narcissists by their followers. In turn, this leads to diminished employee idea implementation levels among their followers, probably because of their dominant behaviors and that they are less willing or able to consider the contributions of others.

Taken together, the three chapters indicate that leadership approaches, styles and behaviors act as crucial contingencies for transforming creative ideas into implemented innovations. In line with the devolution-to-the-line perspective in management, through the role of immediate supervisors, leadership can directly influence the implementation processes, not only present a distal contextual contingency. Moreover, supervisors also shape the context of idea implementation with regard to the situation or general climate in the work units or groups that is either supportive or inhibitive to implementation, which is something future research should tackle in more detail.

Cyclic and Polar Processes

Finally, many of the chapters in this book testify to and expand on what has previously been described as the prevalence of paradoxes and tensions in innovation and creativity (Csikszentmihalyi, 1996; George, 2007; George and Zhou, 2007; Carlsen et al., 2012). What seems clear here is that processes for capitalization of creativity are cyclic and polar. This has two sets of assertions and implications. First, rather than linear processes with ideas travelling neatly from idea generation to selection to retention, or implementation, the research in this book speaks to the cyclic nature of innovation, with multiple iteration between idea generation, evaluation, testing, and new idea generation. Successful adaptation of a new IT system for electronic patient journals requires engaging the creativity of users (Chapter 20). Reaping the awards of breakthrough knowledge from R&D means more exploration of new solutions (Chapter 21). Creativity spurs curiosity that may boost early adoption (Chapter 7) and perhaps further spur creativity. The core mark of a great architectural design is that it is generous enough to stimulate creativity in other project members and in users (Chapter 12). Business models are not just 'implemented', but recursively and significantly reconstructed as entrepreneurs adapt to new contingencies and external demands (Chapter 17). Sensemaking is first of all iterative as new experiences are accommodated and debated (Chapter 16). Capitalizing on creativity means, quite paradoxically, more creativity. Or in other words: it involves more fully and broadly recognizing

Table 25.1   A conceptual matrix of the book by topics, levels and common threads

Key Threads:	Bottom-up	Top-down	Leadership	Process View
Levels Individual	Job crafting Proactivity Flow Diversity Cultural intelligence Championing Emergence Intuition and cognition	HR practice Job design Structural position: centrality, brokerage, clustering Key idea champions	Supervisor support Moderate levels of authentic leadership Social leader– member exchange	Non-linear capitalization Emergence Curiosity
Team	Championing	Mastery and performance climates		Intuition and cognition Emergence/ aggregation mechanisms Creative bootlegging, stealth innovation
Organizational	New high-tech ventures	Disruptive business model innovation Science-based entrepreneurship Social network Top-management support Trained facilitators for voicing and promoting ideas High-commitment, internally consistent HRM systems		Adequate and efficient business models – business model evolution, adaptation Ideation process, discovery, experimentation Design thinking and iterative sensemaking Multi-polar learning communities, co-creation Cross-disciplinary work
Policy-making	Collective action	Narrow and broad innovation policies Policy configuration Governmental ideation systems		

the inherent cyclic nature of all innovative work as an experiential learning process (Kolb, 1984; Kelley and Kelley, 2013).

Second, rather than explaining successful implementation of ideas as taking place through a set of unambiguously well-known and homogeneous practices where people act in singular modes, the chapters in this book speak to the multi-modal, conflictual, and paradoxical nature of innovation. There is balance between zooming in and out or balance between reflection and action in repeated bouts of prototyping (Chapter 12). Mastering existing practices is necessary to explore new ones, and local adaptation requires simultaneous trans-local alignment (Chapter 21). Social entrepreneurship means being able to simultaneously handle the sometimes conflicting demands in both private, public and civic sectors. Sensemaking of innovations thrives on conflicting views of stakeholders (Chapter 16). Learning communities that work well are multi-polar (Chapter 19).

We may see the first of these observations, the cyclic nature of successful implementation, as speaking to a dialectical model of change (Van de Ven and Poole, 1995), with alteration and iteration between different modes of acting as complementary. The second is more truly dialogical in the sense of being able to hold contradicting polarities in the process (Morin, 2008).

A LOOK AHEAD

Having a complete picture over ideas, topics, and findings from the authors of this book, we would like to think that much has been accomplished in understanding capitalization of creative ideas in this book. We also need to be humble enough to realize that much more remains to be done in future.

First, we recognize the need for emphasized research efforts in multi-level studies of idea implementation. If we assume a holistic perspective, we can observe that the book is multi-level in nature, but particular aspects of the multi-level approach should be tackled directly by specific standalone contributions in the field. For example, the bottom-up emergence processes of the implementation process and its antecedents. In addition, more research is needed that would estimate these processes with studies that would go across three or more levels simultaneously and account for all of them in their theorizing and operationalizations, true multi-level, beyond two-level or levels approach. Such an approach would allow us to truly understand the complexity of ideation processes and the way they unfold across levels in their contexts.

Second, even at the separate levels of analysis there is more to know and learn. At the individual level, very little was written about the influence of personality. While Chapter 2 and Chapter 15 did look into the enabling factors of proactivity at work, psychological traits such as proactive personality (Parker et al., 2006; Kopperud et al., 2014 – task and role flexibility: taking charge, promotive voice) and their role in the process of creative idea implementation should be elaborated further.

Third, the book was also unable to cover all aspects at particular levels of research to an extent it deserves. For example, we have made a humble attempt to touch upon the policy section, as the narrow and broad innovation policies and macroeconomic systems play an important role in the facilitation of idea implementation.

Fourth, from the leadership point of view, we see an absolute need for research and practice in designing leadership development programs in a direction that would empower leaders to be better equipped for their role as idea champions, hence supporting processes of idea capitalization beyond the idea generation phase alone. Voice literature and innovation has promise in this direction.

Fifth, at the conceptual and ontological level, understanding capitalization of creativity requires that we reorient our understanding of what we mean by the notion of ideas. The very term 'implementing ideas' carries assumptions of ideas as entities, things that stay more or less the same through time. We have shown that capitalizing on creativity means embracing more a process view on ideas, where they first of all exist in their making, in the work done to them. Beyond our own ignorance, the degree to which practitioners also come to hold such a process view is an interesting topic of further research. Does capitalizing on creativity mean that people accept the inevitably iterative, experimental, and messy nature of innovation? How then do they come to accept and grow into such an understanding?

Sixth, are all highly creative ideas also those that should be implemented? Naturally not. However, we do admit that an inattentive reader of our book might fall into such a mental trap. Research on ethical aspects of creativity, innovation and ideation for sustainable growth is warranted.

Last but not least, as educators, we have a task of moving beyond the fascination for creativity and playfulness of idea generation, towards harsh business realities of capitalizing on ideas under constraints. As educators, we have a role in facilitating students at various levels to better deal with ideation processes and their controversies, contradictions, and non-linearities.

Capitalizing on creative ideas is a complex process, a multi-player game, with numerous cyclic processes and even polarizing forces at multiple organizational and societal levels. Organizations and their members engage in a multitude of approaches ranging from bottom-up initiatives to push the idea through the organization to top-down structural attempts to create facilitating conditions. While context matters, leaders have a vital role in moving ideas into products, services, business models and other innovations of tangible benefit. It is our hope that this book has opened a Pandora's box of good ideas on how we can all benefit from good ideas.

REFERENCES

Carlsen, A., S. Clegg and R. Gjersvik (eds) (2012), *Idea Work. Lessons of the Extraordinary in Everyday Creativity*, Oslo: Cappelen Damm.

Csikszentmihalyi, M. (1996), *Creativity. Flow and the Psychology of Discovery and Innovation*, New York: HarperCollins.

George, J.M. (2007), 'Creativity in organizations', *The Academy of Management Annals*, **1**(1), 439–77.

George, J.M. and J. Zhou (2007), 'Dual tuning in a supportive context: Joint contributions of positive mood, negative mood, and supervisory behaviors to employee creativity', *Academy of Management Journal*, **50**(3), 605–22.

Kelley, T. and D. Kelley (2013), *Creative Confidence: Unleashing the Creative Potential Within Us All*, New York: Random House.

Kolb, D.A. (1984), *Experiential Learning: Experience as the Source of Learning and Development*, Vol. 1, Englewood Cliffs, NJ: Prentice-Hall.

Kopperud, K.H., Ø. Martinsen and S.I.W. Humborstad (2014), 'Engaging leaders in the eyes of the beholder on the relationship between transformational leadership, work engagement, service climate, and self–other agreement', *Journal of Leadership & Organizational Studies*, **21**(1), 29–42.

Morin, E. (2008), *On Complexity*, Cresskill, NJ: Hampton Press.

Parker, S.K., H.M. Williams and N. Turner (2006), 'Modeling the antecedents of proactive behavior at work', *Journal of Applied Psychology*, **91**(3), 636–52.

Van de Ven, A.H. and M.S. Poole (1995), 'Explaining development and change in organizations', *Academy of Management Review*, **20**(3), 510–40.

APPENDIX

Table 25A.1 Overview of the chapter findings along four common threads of capitalizing on creativity

Common Thread	Level	Chapter	Concepts Explored	Setting and Methodology	Key Findings
Bottom-up emergence of ideas	Individual	2	Job crafting	University professors Theoretical overview	Proactive approaches to job design drive employee innovative behaviors – ideas are not born, they are made
Bottom-up emergence of ideas	Individual	3	Flow experience	Start-up companies Interview and secondary data	Flow shortens time between intention to carry out an idea and implementation
Bottom-up emergence of ideas	Individual	4	Cultural intelligence Cultural diversity	Cross-culturally diverse environments	Cultural intelligence mitigates adverse effects of cultural diversity for idea implementation
Bottom-up emergence of ideas	Multi-level: individual and team	5	Idea championing	Two Slovenian and 12 Chinese SMEs; one study of an insurance company	Underlying emergence mechanisms of idea champions at micro- and team-level: best innovative performance if team has a person that stands out; special cases: early bird finishing last, creative bootlegging, stealth innovation

Table 25A.1 (continued)

Common Thread	Level	Chapter	Concepts Explored	Setting and Methodology	Key Findings
Contextual, top-down factors	Individual	2	Job design	University professors Theoretical overview	Traditional top-down job design as HR practice has a significant role for employee innovative behavior
Contextual, top-down factors	Team	8	Mastery and performance climates	Quantitative	Ideas are most frequently implemented in context with both high mastery and performance climate
Contextual, top-down factors	Organizational	13	Business model innovation	Three case studies	Business model innovation intended to gain competitive advantage; disruptive BMI has company- and industry-level impact, and established businesses less likely to innovate in business models
Contextual, top-down factors	Organizational	17	Business model innovation, science-based entrepreneurship	Innovative new ventures in Italy, science based and high-tech	Performance gap of new high-tech ventures is explained with both inadequacy and inefficiency of business models

Contextual, top-down factors	Organizational, individual, relational	14	Idea implementation social network, structural position – centrality, brokerage, clustering	Medium-sized knowledge-intensive IT company	Support for social and interactionist perspective to micro-innovation process: formal and social structures interact in idea implementation
Contextual, top-down factors	Organizational	15	Employee proactive behavior	Three automotive case studies	Factors that stimulate employee proactivity and idea implementation are top-management support, assigned personnel in charge of innovation, trained facilitators for voicing and promoting ideas
Contextual, top-down factors	Organizational	18	Human resource practices	Conceptual overview	High-commitment, internally consistent HRM systems prompt idea implementation
Contextual, top-down factors	Policy	22	National innovation policy mixes Narrow and broad innovation policies	Quantitative comparative method	No individual policy is sufficient or necessary condition for innovation success, innovation policy configurations matter
Contextual, top-down factors	Policy	23	Participation and collaboration in collective action	Governmental ideation systems, City of Vienna, case study	Citizens participate in governmental ideation systems if their ideas lead to action

Table 25A.1 (continued)

Common Thread	Level	Chapter	Concepts Explored	Setting and Methodology	Key Findings
Leadership	Individual	9	Perceived supervisor support	Experiments and illustrative case studies	Perceived supervisor support helps the implementation of highly creative ideas
Leadership	Individual	10	Economic and social leader–member exchange	Conceptual	SLMX is favorable and ELMX is non-favorable for implementation of creative ideas
Leadership	Individual	11	Authentic leadership Narcissism	Field study and experiment	High levels of perceived authentic leadership lead to perception of narcissism and damage employee idea implementation
Cycles and polarities	Individual	2	Job design	University professors Theoretical overview	Capitalizing on creativity is not linear
Cycles and polarities	Multi-level: individual and team	6	Intuition, cognition	R&D teams in four German and Slovenian companies	Intuition more strongly relates to team idea generation, while team need for cognition relates to team idea implementation

Cycles and polarities	Individual	7	Curiosity, discovery narratives, early adaptors	Short accounts from Apple, museums as 'curiosity cabinets' and Hollywood pitch meetings are used as reasoning devices	Curiosity as an outcome of creativity and a social resource that influences how people connect with, adapt to and disperse new creative products
Cycles and polarities	Organizational	12	Idea work; implementation through discovery that involves more creativity	Process and practice approach to creativity with four (Statoil, IKEA, Snøhetta, Pulse News) plus one (Valio) illustrative cases	Ideas are more or less always in flux and worked upon. Implementation means shuttling between action and reflection and zooming in and out in cycles of experimentation
Cycles and polarities	Organizational	15	Employee proactive behavior	Three automotive case studies	Idea implementation is daily activity and integrated into working processes
Cycles and polarities	Organizational	16	Design thinking and iterative sensemaking	Three projects in MNC	Design thinking workshops from a sensemaking perspective. Identified six practices (functionally and hierarchically diverse individuals, heterogeneous teams, iterative involvement,

Table 25A.1 (continued)

Common Thread	Level	Chapter	Concepts Explored	Setting and Methodology	Key Findings
					exposure to, engagement in and acting upon conflicting views) that facilitate idea implementation across organizational levels and functions
Cycles and polarities	Organizational	17	Business model innovation, science-based entrepreneurship	Innovative new ventures in Italy, science based and high-tech	Market potential of innovative start-ups is not rooted only in its initial business model, but requires adaptation and fine-tuning of the initial idea
Cycles and polarities	Organizational	19	Multi-polar learning communities Co-creation	Danish pharmaceutical MNC, case study	Temporary spaces and co-location of members from global teams contributes to idea implementation via joint inquiry, divergent local practices and perspectives, problem-solving and new synergistic approaches

					Mere participation is not enough, inquiry triggered by problematic situation and doubt regarding how to handle it is a crucial part of learning and co-creation dynamics
Cycles and polarities	Organizational	21	Innovations in cross-disciplinary settings	Longitudinal case study of capitalizing on R&D knowledge in two projects in a Norwegian medical institution, practice-based approach	Capitalization through four sets of practices that involves mastering existing practices while adopting new ones and aligning practices locally as well as translocally
Cycles and polarities	Policy	24	Social entrepreneurship	Case study of the founding and growth of a small social media venture	Capitalization through a triple embedded process that unfolds simultaneously in the private, public and civic sector
Cycles and polarities	Organizational	20	The role of creativity in the local adaptation of innovations	Case study of the adaptation of new IT system for patient journals, practice-based approach	Successful implementation means engaging the creativity of users who cope with the new systems in processes of expanding functionality, reinterpretation and orchestration of resources

Index